PowerScore

GRE

VERBAL REASONING BIBLE

A Comprehensive System for Attacking
GRE Verbal Reasoning Questions!

PowerScore®
TEST PREPARATION

Published by
PowerScore Publishing, a division of PowerScore Incorporated
57 Hasell Street
Charleston, SC 29401

Author: Victoria Wood

Special thanks to Terry Bray for editorial assistance.

Manufactured in Canada
06 11 20 20

ISBN: 978-0-9908934-3-1

Guess what?

We offer GRE Prep Courses & Private Tutoring too!

CONTENTS

CHAPTER ONE: INTRODUCTION TO THE GRE

CHAPTER TWO: THE BASICS OF GRE VERBAL REASONING

CHAPTER THREE: FILL-IN-THE-BLANK MASTERY SOLUTION STRATEGY BASICS

CHAPTER FOUR: FILL-IN-THE-BLANK MASTERY DECONSTRUCT THE QUESTION STEM

Chapter Five: Fill-in-the-Blank Mastery
Analyze the Answer Choices

Chapter Six: Fill-in-the-Blank Mastery
Decode the Vocabulary

Chapter Seven: Reading Comprehension Mastery
General Reading Strategies

CHAPTER EIGHT: READING COMPREHENSION MASTERY STRATEGIES FOR LONG PASSAGES

CHAPTER NINE: READING COMPREHENSION MASTERY STRATEGIES FOR SHORT PASSAGES

CHAPTER TEN: READING COMPREHENSION MASTERY ANALYZE THE ANSWER CHOICES

CHAPTER ELEVEN: READING COMPREHENSION MASTERY READ THE QUESTION

CHAPTER TWELVE: READING COMPREHENSION MASTERY VOCABULARY-IN-CONTEXT QUESTIONS

CHAPTER THIRTEEN: READING COMPREHENSION MASTERY LITERAL COMPREHENSION QUESTIONS

CHAPTER FOURTEEN: READING COMPREHENSION MASTERY EXTENDED REASONING QUESTIONS

CHAPTER FIFTEEN: READING COMPREHENSION MASTERY ARGUMENT PASSAGES

CHAPTER SIXTEEN: VERBAL REASONING MASTERY PROBLEM SETS

CHAPTER SEVENTEEN: TEST READINESS

APPENDICES: ROOTS AND AFFIXES DICTIONARY AND REPEAT OFFENDER VOCABULARY WORDS

INDEX

Acknowledgements

Full text of the passages and excerpts used in the *GRE Verbal Reasoning Bible* can be found in the original sources:

Page 179, 184, Passage 2: "The Federal Role in U.S. Education." eJournal USA: U.S. Society & Values. June 2000: 13. <http://www.ait.org.tw/infousa/enus/education/overview/docs/ijse0600.pdf>

Page 189, 199, Passage: Rosengarten, David. "We Are What We Eat: We are a Nation of Immigrants!," eJournal USA: Society & Values. July 2004: 8-9. December 2011. <http://www.ait.org.tw/infousa/zhtw/DOCS/ijse0704.pdf>

Page 205, Passage: "Pursuing Free Trade Agreements." eJournal USA: Economic Perspectives. January 2006 <http://www.ait.org.tw/infousa/enus/economy/trade/proscons.html>

Page 216, 218, Passage 2: MacKenzie Jr., Clyde L. "History of Oystering in the United States and Canada, Featuring the Eight Greatest Oyster Estuaries." Marine Fisheries Review, Volume 58(4). 1996. <http://spo.nmfs.noaa.gov/mfr584/mfr5841.pdf>

Page 236, Passage: Donaldson, Scott. "A Few Words about F. Scott Fitzgerald." The Public Domain Review. <http://publicdomainreview.org/2011/09/26/a-few-words-about-f-scott-fitzgerald/>

Page 252, Passage: Kosman, Joshua. "A New Music for a New Century," eJournal USA: Society and Values. June 1998: 22-23. December 2011. < http://www.4uth.gov.ua/usa/english/arts/ijse0698/kosman.htm>

Page 298, Passage: Carter, William C. "Lost in Translation: Proust and Scott Moncrieff." The Public Domain Review. <http://publicdomainreview.org/2013/11/13/lost-in-translation-proust-and-scott-moncrieff/>

Page 306, Passage 2: Hodas, Nathan O. and Kristina Lerman. "The Simple Rules of Social Contagion." U.S. National Institutes of Health's National Library of Medicine. <http://www.ncbi.nlm.nih.gov/pmc/articles/PMC3949249/>. This work is licensed under a Creative Commons Attribution 3.0 Unported License. To view a copy of this license, visit http://creativecommons.org/licenses/by/3.0/

Page 307, Passage 3: Glassie, John. "Athanasius, Underground." The Public Domain Review. <http://publicdomainreview.org/2012/11/01/athanasius-underground/>

Page 310, Passage: Somma, Angela. "The Environmental Consequences and Economic Costs of Depleting the Oceans," eJournal USA: Economic Perspectives. January 2003: 14-15. December 2006. <http://usinfo.state.gov/journals/ites/0103/ijee/somma.htm>

Page 381, Passage 2: Editor's Note. eJournal USA: Society & Values. August 1997. December 2011. <http://www.4uth.gov.ua/usa/english/society/ijse0897/ijse0897.htm>

Page 372, Passage: Polk, Noel. "Faulkner at 100." Humanities September/October 1997. Volume 18/Number 5. December 2011. <http://www.neh.gov/news/humanities/1997-09/polk.html>

Page 383, Passage 3: "How Does Climate Change Influence Alaska's Vegetation? Insights from the Fossil Record." U.S. Geological Survey, June 1997. FS-071-97. <http://pubs.usgs.gov/fs/fs-0071-97/>

Page 384, Passage 1: Sutton, Emma. "Simple Songs: Virginia Wolf and Music." The Public Domain Review. <http://publicdomainreview.org/2013/01/09/simple-songs-virginia-woolf-and-music/>

Page 384, Passage 2: Showalter, Dr. Mark. "New Pluto Moon Discovered." Hubble 2011: Science Year in Review. <http://hubblesite.org/hubble_discoveries/science_year_in_review/pdf/2011/new_pluto_moon_discovered.pdf>

Page 385, Passage 1: Adams, Max. "John Martin and the Theatre of Subversion." The Public Domain Review. <http://publicdomainreview.org/2012/07/12/john-martin-and-the-theatre-of-subversion/>

Page 385, Passage 2: Parrett, Aaron. "Lucian's Trips to the Moon." The Public Domain Review. <http://publicdomainreview.org/2013/06/26/lucians-trips-to-the-moon/>

Page 386, Passage: Reidy, Joseph P. "Black Men in Navy Blue During the Civil War," Prologue Magazine. Fall 2001, Volume 33, Number 3. December 2011. < http://www.archives.gov/publications/prologue/2001/fall/black-sailors-1.html>

Page 387, Passage: "Evaluating Online Learning: Challenges and Strategies for Success," U.S. Department of Education. July 2008. December 2011. < http://www2.ed.gov/admins/lead/academic/evalonline/report_pg6.html>

Page 388, Passage: Van Whye, John. "Was Charles Darwin an Atheist?" The Public Domain Review. <http://publicdomainreview.org/2011/06/28/was-charles-darwin-an-atheist/>

About PowerScore

PowerScore is one of the world's fastest growing test preparation companies. Headquartered in Charleston, South Carolina, PowerScore offers GRE, GMAT, LSAT, SAT, and ACT preparation courses in over 125 locations in the U.S. and abroad. For more information, please visit our website at powerscore.com.

About the Author

Victoria Wood is a test preparation expert, specializing in the GMAT, GRE, and SAT. With over 20 years experience in education and test preparation, she has assisted thousands of high school and college students in exceeding their standardized testing goals in reading, writing, and mathematics. She is the author and co-author of many acclaimed PowerScore publications, including the *GMAT Sentence Correction Bible*, the *GMAT Verbal Bible Workbook*, and the *SAT Essential Flash Cards*. Currently, Ms. Wood serves as a Senior Curriculum Developer at PowerScore Test Preparation.

Introduction to the GRE

Introduction to the GRE

Introduction

Welcome to the *PowerScore GRE Verbal Reasoning Bible*! The purpose of this book is to introduce you to the three types of reading questions and to teach you new strategies for approaching the Verbal section on the GRE. We are certain that you can increase your Verbal Reasoning score with close study and application of the PowerScore techniques.

Because access to accurate and up-to-date information is critical, we have devoted a section of our website to *GRE Verbal Reasoning Bible* students. This free online resource area offers supplements to the book material, suggests study plans, and provides updates as needed. There is also an official book evaluation form that we strongly encourage you to use. The exclusive *PowerScore GRE Verbal Reasoning Bible* online area can be accessed at:

powerscore.com/grevrbible

The concepts and techniques discussed in this book are drawn from our live GRE courses, which we feel are the most effective in the world. If you find that you need a more structured learning environment, or would just like to participate in a live classroom setting, please visit our website to learn about our course offerings.

If we can assist you in your GRE preparation in any way, or if you have any questions or comments, please do not hesitate to contact us via e-mail at:

gre@powerscore.com

We look forward to hearing from you!

The first two chapters of this book cover the format of the GRE and its Verbal Reasoning sections. While the reading may be heavy at times, we recommend you thoroughly cover these chapters first so that you understand the construction of the test. However, if you are anxious to begin studying for the GRE, you can skip to Chapter 3, provided you return to the first two chapters at a later date.

Please do not hesitate to write in this book! Take notes, underline important sentences, and complete the problems presented. Your GRE success depends on your understanding of the concepts presented here, and achievement will only come with study and application.

Format of the GRE

The Graduate
Record Exam
(GRE) was first
administered in
1949.

The GRE is a standardized test used for admissions to thousands of graduate programs in America. The test assesses a student's ability to reason critically in math, reading, and writing, and predicts his or her success at the graduate level. It is written by testing experts who work for the non-profit assessment organization, Educational Testing Services (ETS).

Computer-Based GRE

The majority of test takers, including all students taking the test in the United States, will take the GRE on a computer at a testing center. This GRE has six sections, given over approximately three hours and forty-five minutes:

Section 1 on every GRE is the Analytical Writing section. Sections 2 through 6 are randomly assigned Verbal Reasoning or Quantitative Reasoning sections, one of which may be an Unscored experimental section.

Section Type	No. of Questions	Question Types	Time Limit	Section No.
Analytical Writing	2	1 "Analyze an Issue" essay 1 "Analyze an Argument" essay	30 minutes per essay	1
Verbal Reasoning	20 (approximately)	Reading Comprehension questions Text Completion questions Sentence Equivalence questions	30 minutes	2-6
Verbal Reasoning	20 (approximately)	Reading Comprehension questions Text Completion questions Sentence Equivalence questions	30 minutes	2-6
Quantitative Reasoning	20 (approximately)	Quantitative Comparison questions Multiple Choice questions (1 correct answer) Multiple Choice questions (1+ correct answers) Numeric Entry questions	35 minutes	2-6
Quantitative Reasoning	20 (approximately)	Quantitative Comparison questions Multiple Choice questions (1 correct answer) Multiple Choice questions (1+ correct answers) Numeric Entry questions	35 minutes	2-6
Unscored	20 (approximately)	An *unidentified* unscored Verbal or Quantitative section	30 or 35 minutes	2-6
Research	Varies	An *identified* unscored section may be used in place of the Unscored section.	Varies	6

The computer-based GRE test contains:
- 2 essays
- 40 verbal questions
- 40 math questions
- 20 unscored questions

In all, there are approximately 40 Verbal Reasoning questions and 40 Quantitative Reasoning questions that count toward your score. Another 20 or so questions in the Unscored or Research section will not contribute to your score, but since you will likely not know which section is unscored, you must attack every question as if it matters.

Scratch paper and pencils are provided and an on-screen four-function calculator is available for your use during the test.

You may not
bring your own
calculator to the
computer-based
or paper-based
GRE!

Paper-Based GRE

Test takers who live in areas of the world where the computer based GRE is not available will take a paper-based test. The paper-based GRE has five sections, given over approximately three hours and thirty minutes:

Section Type	No. of Questions	Question Types	Time Limit	Section No.
Analytical Writing	2	1 "Analyze an Issue" essay 1 "Analyze an Argument" essay	30 minutes per essay	1
Verbal Reasoning	25 (approximately)	Reading Comprehension questions Text Completion questions Sentence Equivalence questions	35 minutes	2-5
Verbal Reasoning	25 (approximately)	Reading Comprehension questions Text Completion questions Sentence Equivalence questions	35 minutes	2–5
Quantitative Reasoning	25 (approximately)	Quantitative Comparison questions Multiple Choice questions (1 correct answer) Multiple Choice questions (1+ correct answers) Numeric Entry questions	40 minutes	2–5
Quantitative Reasoning	25 (approximately)	Quantitative Comparison questions Multiple Choice questions (1 correct answer) Multiple Choice questions (1+ correct answers) Numeric Entry questions	40 minutes	2–5

The paper-based GRE test contains:
- 2 essays
- 50 verbal questions
- 50 math questions

Basic four-function calculators are provided at the testing site.

To learn more about the format of the paper-based GRE and whether the computer-based test is available in your location, visit gre.org. The remainder of this book will focus mainly on the characteristics of the computer-based GRE, although the test content and question types are identical for both the computer-based and paper-based tests. This book will help students master the test no matter which format they ultimately encounter.

Testing Schedule and Registration

The computer-based GRE is offered year-round at official test centers. While it's possible to register for the test one day and take it the next, testing appointments do book up, so it's important to register and schedule your test several weeks in advance.

This book focuses on the computer-based format test, but will help you master the test even if it is paper-based.

You can register for the GRE online (gre.org), by phone (1-800-GRE-CALL), or by mail. To begin your registration, refer to the booklet *GRE Information and Registration Bulletin*, which you can download from the website or obtain by calling ETS.

GRE Scores

The GRE is composed of three distinct scored sections—the Quantitative Reasoning section, the Verbal Reasoning section, and the Analytical Writing section. The scaled scores for these three sections appear as follows:

The GRE has been scored out of 170 points since 2011. The prior scale was 200 to 800 for each section.

- Quantitative Reasoning: 130–170 score scale in 1-point increments

- Verbal Reasoning: 130–170 score scale in 1-point increments

- Analytical Writing: 0–6 score scale in ½-point increments

The average GRE score may vary from year to year, but it is typically around 151 for each subject area. The average Analytical Writing score is approximately 3.7.

A GRE score is the only tool in your admissions file that truly compares you to other applicants. Grade point averages and real-world experiences are important, but they are difficult for anyone to judge in comparison with another student from another background. For example, the amount of work it takes to achieve an A in Algebra at State University may only equate to a C+ in Algebra at City College. While admissions officers maintain files with information about college programs and course difficulty in order to try to more adequately compare students from different schools, this system still presents great difficulty and potential unfairness. Therefore, because the GRE is standardized and taken by all applicants, it is used to directly compare students in math, reading, and writing.

Section-Level Adaptivity

For computer-based tests, the difficulty of the second Verbal Reasoning and Quantitative Reasoning sections are selected based on your performance on the first sections of each. In other words, the first sections of Verbal and Quantitative will be medium difficulty sections. If you score well, the computer will supply a somewhat harder second section on the assumption that your score is somewhere above that level. The questions within that section will then be used to help determine your exact score.

The computer will adjust the difficulty level of your second Verbal Reasoning section based on your performance in the first section.

No Penalty for Guessing

There is no penalty for guessing on the GRE, so you should make an educated guess on every question you cannot solve.

ALWAYS make an educated guess on the GRE! You should never omit a question.

Official Results

Before you leave the test center, you will be presented with your unofficial Quantitative Reasoning and Verbal Reasoning scores at the conclusion of your computer-based GRE. You will receive the official results and your Analytical Writing results in 10 to 15 days following your test date.

Scores for paper-based GRE tests take up to 6 weeks to be returned.

Raw and Scaled Scores

Each Quantitative Reasoning and Verbal Reasoning question that you answer correctly earns you 1 point toward a raw score. You are not penalized for wrong answers. Once a raw score is calculated from the points earned, test makers use a conversion table to produce a scaled score for each section. These scaled scores take into account differences among each individual GRE, such as difficulty level, and grants ETS the ability to assign each test taker a percentile rank. These percentile ranks allow admissions officers to make fair comparisons between applicants.

Percentile Ranks

Each scaled GRE score places a student in a certain relative position compared to other test takers. These relative positions are represented through a percentile that correlates to each score; the percentile indicates where the test taker falls in the overall pool of test takers. For example, a score of 159 on the Verbal section represents the 80th percentile, meaning a person with a score of 159 scored better than 80% of other test takers in the last year. Only 20% of test takers scored better. The percentile is critical since it is a true indicator of your positioning relative to other test takers, and thus graduate applicants.

Percentile tables provided by ETS are available on the following page. First, though, consider a summary of some benchmark scores:

The average GRE score is around 151 in the Quantitative Reasoning and Verbal Reasoning sections. The average Analytical Writing Score is 3.7.

Say you scored a 159 on the Verbal Reasoning section, equating to the 80th percentile. But if you scored a 159 in Quantitative Reasoning, you earned a spot in the 77th percentile.

Verbal Reasoning Scores

1% of test takers score 169 or higher.
5% of test takers score 165 or higher.
17% of test takers score 160 or higher.
35% of test takers score 155 or higher.
56% of test takers score 150 or higher.
76% of test takers score 145 or higher.
90% of test takers score 140 or higher.

Quantitative Reasoning Scores

1% of test takers score 170.
8% of test takers score 165 or higher.
19% of test takers score 160 or higher.
36% of test takers score 155 or higher.
57% of test takers score 150 or higher.
77% of test takers score 145 or higher.
91% of test takers score 140 or higher.

Analytical Writing Scores

1% of test takers score 6.0.
27% of test takers score 4.5 or higher.
89% of test takers score 3.0 or higher.
99% of test takers score 1.5 or higher.

GRE Individual Section Percentile Tables

Scaled Score	Verbal Percentile	Quantitative Percentile
170	99	99
169	99	98
168	98	97
167	97	96
166	96	94
165	95	92
164	93	90
163	91	88
162	89	86
161	86	83
160	83	81
159	80	77
158	77	74
157	73	71
156	69	68
155	65	64
154	61	60
153	57	56
152	53	52
151	49	48
150	44	43
149	40	39
148	36	35
147	32	31
146	28	27
145	24	23
144	21	20
143	18	17
142	15	14
141	12	11
140	10	9
139	8	7
138	6	5
137	5	4
136	4	3
135	3	2
134	2	1
133	1	1
132	1	1
131	1	1
130	—-	—-
Average	**150.8**	**151.3**

Scaled Score	Analytical Writing
6.0	99
5.5	96
5.0	92
4.5	73
4.0	49
3.5	30
3.0	11
2.5	6
2.0	1
1.5	1
1.0	1
0.5	1
0.0	—-
Average	**3.7**

Composition of the GRE

Although the Verbal Reasoning section is the focus of this book, let's briefly review the other sections on the computer-based GRE.

THE QUANTITATIVE REASONING SECTION

The computer-based GRE Quantitative Reasoning score is determined by approximately 40 questions from two sections. There are three types of questions.

Multiple Choice Questions

The first type of Quantitative Reasoning question is the Multiple Choice Question, the majority of which resemble standard multiple choice questions: select one answer from five answer choices. Each answer choice is accompanied by an oval "bubble" for you to select. Consider an example:

If x is an integer and 2 is the remainder when $3x + 4$ is divided by 4, then which of the following could be a value of x?

- ⬭ 0
- ⬭ 3
- ⬭ 4
- ⬭ 5
- ⬭ 6

A few Multiple Choice questions, however, ask for more than one answer choice. These questions may have as few as three answer choices or as many as ten. Notice that for these questions, the selection "bubble" is a square box.

If x is an integer and 2 is the remainder when x is divided by 4, then which <u>two</u> of the following could be a value of x?

- ☐ 0
- ☐ 4
- ☐ 6
- ☐ 10

Numeric Entry Questions

Numeric entry questions do not have answer choices from which to select correct answers. Instead, test takers must produce their own answer and then transfer that answer to a box:

What is the units digit of $(13)^2 (12)^3 (11)^4$?

```
┌──────────┐
│          │
└──────────┘
```

There are three types of Quantitative Reasoning questions: Multiple Choice, Numeric Entry, and Quantitative Comparison.

In all sections of the GRE, oval bubbles indicate a single correct answer; square bubbles are used for questions with more than one possible answer.

Since there are no supplied answer choices to assist you in Numeric Entry questions, be sure to read the questions carefully.

Quantitative Comparison Questions

Quantitative Comparison questions ask you to make a comparison between the quantities provided in two columns, determining whether one quantity is greater, whether they are equal, or whether the relationship is impossible to determine:

Quantity A	Quantity B
$[(3 + 1) - 2] \times 4$	$(3 + 1) - 2 \times 4$

(A) Quantity A is greater.
(B) Quantity B is greater.
(C) The two quantities are equal.
(D) The relationship cannot be determined from the information given.

Quantitative Comparisons questions, or Quant Comps as they are sometimes called, are a bit more intimidating to novice test takers. Their very nature, however, opens them up to several tips and tricks to help you tackle these questions.

Don't let Quant Comps scare you! Their odd nature leaves them vulnerable to many tips and tricks.

The mathematical concepts tested on the GRE are selected from Operations, Algebra and Functions, Geometry and Measurement, and Data Analysis, Statistics, and Probability. For more information on these types of questions and secrets to solving them, check out PowerScore's *GRE Quantitative Reasoning Bible*.

THE ANALYTICAL WRITING SECTION

The Analytical Writing score is determined by two 30-minute essays.

Analyze the Issue

The purpose of this task is twofold: one, to evaluate your critical thinking skills, and two, to assess your writing skills when putting those thoughts to paper.

For this essay, you are presented with a statement, such as "It is sometimes necessary to lie," and then asked to write an essay in which you explain the extent to which you agree or disagree with the statement. The directions vary from test to test, but they are very specific about the topics you must discuss while explaining your viewpoint, so it is important to read them closely.

Analyze the Argument

The test makers use this essay to appraise your ability to understand and criticize an argument, as well as your capacity for expressing your criticism in writing.

Did you know that it is perfectly acceptable—and even expected—for students to use the word "I" in their essays?

This essay begins with a short passage in which the author makes a claim advocating a specific approach. For example, the author might contend that a local government should quash plans to raze a historic building. The argument is then supported by evidence, which you must evaluate for its logic and coherence. Again, the directions for each essay vary, so it is important that you pay close attention to how the test makers want you to develop your analysis.

THE UNSCORED SECTION

Most computer-based GREs administered by ETS have one unscored 30- or 35-minute section. Sometimes called the experimental, variable, or equating section, this Unscored section is used to collect data, such as difficulty level and validity, about specific questions that will be used on future GREs.

During the test, it is impossible to know which section is Unscored. Therefore, you should attack every section as if it were contributing to your score.

The Unscored section will occur in section 2, 3, 4, 5 or 6 as an additional Quantitative Reasoning or Verbal Reasoning section. It is never an additional Analytical Writing section, so it never occurs in section 1. Some students feel that the Unscored section is more challenging than the other sections, but it is impossible to determine which section is experimental while the test is occurring. You *must* attack all Quantitative Reasoning and Verbal Reasoning sections as if they were being used to calculate your score.

Tests that do not have an Unscored section will have a Research section. This section always occurs at the end of the test and will be identified as an experimental Research section. The number of questions and the time limit vary from test to test.

The Computer-Based GRE Interface

Some students report that they feel intimidated by the computer-based format of the GRE, which is why it is imperative to familiarize yourself with the appearance of the computer screen before you sit down for a real GRE. It's not enough to study the interface here; you must take the free PowerPrep practice tests available at gre.org in order to become comfortable with the format.

When the test begins, each Verbal Reasoning question is presented on a slide similar to the following:

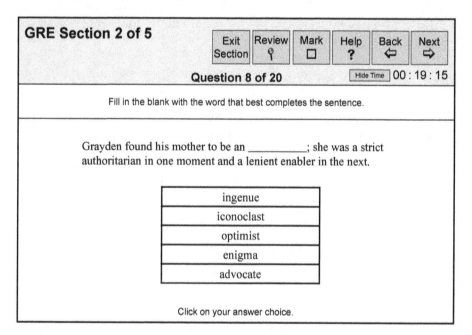

You navigate through the test by clicking on the buttons on the top right of the slide. Let's discuss each button briefly.

Exit Section

Selecting this button will end the section before time is up. Because we recommend that you never finish early (you should instead spend the remaining time reviewing your answers), you should never click this button! There is also a "Quit Test" button on some of the screens but you should not click this selection unless you want to cancel your scores.

Review

When you click on "Review," you will be taken to a screen that shows the status of each question in the section. It will indicate whether a question has been answered and whether you have marked the question for review. You can select a question from this screen and go directly to it without having to navigate the "Back" and "Next" buttons.

Be sure to download the free PowerPrep software at gre.org in order to practice with the computer-based testing format.

You should never finish early on the GRE! Spend extra time reviewing your previous questions.

Mark

If you omit a question or complete it but want to return if time permits, select "Mark." This will mark the question for review on the Review screen. Marked questions appear on the Review screen with a check mark next to them.

Help

A prepared test taker will never select the "Help" button! Study the directions before your actual GRE.

The "Help" button allows you to review the directions mid-test. You can find the question directions, section directions, and general directions here, but the clock will not stop. Reading this book will prepare you for the different types of questions, so you should never hit this button unless absolutely necessary.

Back

You can navigate to previous questions by selecting the "Back" button. This is a great option if you want to go back one or two questions, but if you need to return to a question at the beginning of the section, the "Review" button may get you there faster.

Next

Selecting "Next" will take you to the next question.

Hide Time

If the countdown clock intimidates you, select "Hide Time" to remove it from the screen. Once the clock disappears, you can click "Show Time" to bring it back. The most efficient test takers are always aware of the time spent on a question and the time left on the test, so we recommend that you practice *with* the clock.

For the ease of discussion and the conservation of paper, questions and examples throughout this book are presented in a paper-based format, rather than on the sample computer screen. We strongly recommend that you practice with the free PowerPrep software available from gre.org in order to become familiar with the computer interface.

About This Book

The PowerScore GRE Verbal Reasoning Bible is organized into three main sections. The first two chapters offer an introduction to the GRE and to the GRE Verbal Reasoning sections, highlighting basic information and the fundamentals of success on the test. The next four chapters discuss the content and strategy for succeeding on the Text Completion and Sentence Equivalence portions of the test. The following eight chapters cover the Reading Comprehension questions on the GRE. Finally, the appendices contain dictionaries of word roots and commonly tested vocabulary words. **We highly recommend that you begin studying the vocabulary words in Appendix B as soon as you start preparing for the GRE.**

Throughout the book, we use the margins to highlight important information. Some of these margin notes have specific topic names to help you organize your review of the book. The notes titled "Tips and Tricks" call attention to shortcuts and tricks designed to save time on the test. The notes called "Caution: GRE Trap" warn students about common wrong answer choices and mistakes made by previous test takers. Finally, the sidebars designated "Gratuitous Vocab" provide the definitions of vocabulary words used in the text. These words may not be in the Appendix, so be sure to note any new vocabulary.

Again, remember that the exclusive GRE Verbal Reasoning Bible online area can be found at:

powerscore.com/grevrbible

If we can assist you in your GRE preparation in any way, or if you have any questions or comments, please do not hesitate to contact one of our helpful instructors via email at:

gre@powerscore.com

Additional contact information is provided at the end of this book. We look forward to hearing from you!

<u>TIPS and TRICKS</u>
Look to Tips and Tricks for shortcuts and time-saving techniques.

CAUTION: GRE TRAP!
Don't fall into the traps set for you by the College Board. Learn to avoid these traps with these margin notes.

GRATUITOUS VOCAB
gratuitous (adj): free

The Basics of GRE Verbal Reasoning

The Basics of GRE Verbal Reasoning

The Basics of GRE Verbal Reasoning

There are two scored Verbal sections on the GRE. Each of these sections contains three types of questions: Text Completions questions, Sentence Equivalence questions, and Reading Comprehension questions.

All three of these question types test how well you understand written language. As you know, this skill is used more than any other in college and graduate school, so your GRE Verbal Reasoning score is considered an indicative sign of your readiness for further education. High verbal scores are also impressive because the skills required to score well are usually developed over a long period of time.

You have been practicing for the GRE Verbal Reasoning section since you learned to read in elementary school.

While Verbal Reasoning scores may be the most difficult to improve of the three sections on the GRE, it is certainly not impossible. With careful study of the strategies in this book, you can raise your score. You must also adjust your attitude toward the section and think positively about the sentences and passages you will read, no matter how difficult or dry they seem at first glance. To begin your analysis of the GRE Verbal Reasoning section, it is important to study the format and directions of the three question types.

Verbal Reasoning Fundamentals

It's essential to go into the GRE with a plan of attack, which must start with your basic knowledge of guessing and pacing on the test.

Guess When You Cannot Determine the Answer

There is no penalty for a wrong answer, so it makes sense to guess on every question that you do not know how to answer. If possible, make educated guesses; that is, eliminate wrong answers that may be extreme or illogical.

Know the Section Format

On each verbal section, there are approximately 6 Text Completion questions, 4 Sentence Equivalence questions, and 10 Reading Comprehension questions. Reading Comprehension questions come in two groups, one of which occurs at the beginning or end of a section and the second sandwiched between Text Completion and Sentence Equivalence questions. Consider two possible maps of the section order:

Section 1

Text Completion						Reading Comp.					Sent. Equivalence				Reading Comp.				
1	2	3	4	5	6	7	8	9	10	11	12	13	14	15	16	17	18	19	20

Section 2

Reading Comp.				Text Completion						Reading Comp.						Sent. Equivalence			
1	2	3	4	5	6	7	8	9	10	11	12	13	14	15	16	17	18	19	20

Remember that these maps are just *general* layouts. There may be 7 Text Completion questions and only 3 Sentence Equivalence questions, or the Reading Comprehension questions may be in groups of 6 and 4 instead of two groups of 5.

Manage Your Time Effectively

Because you can skip questions and return to them later, we encourage you to take three "passes" through each section. On your first journey through the section, answer the type or types of questions that you find easiest. For most test takers, these will be the Text Completion and Sentence Equivalence questions. So for example, in Section 1 mapped above, work through questions 1–6 (Text Completion) and then skip to questions 12–15 (Sentence Equivalence). Be sure to mark any question that you omit (including the Reading Comprehension questions) by selecting the "Mark" button so that you can easily return to those questions from the Review screen.

When you reach the end of the section, go back and complete the question type that you skipped. So if you omitted Reading Comprehension questions, use your second pass to attack questions 7–11 and questions 16–20. If you complete your second pass with sufficient time remaining, start again, working on any questions that you left unanswered or marked for review because of difficulty. You should complete your final pass through the section with approximately 20–30 seconds remaining so that you have time to guess on any questions that you have yet to answer.

This method will ensure that you gobble up all of the "sure thing" points in the quickest amount of time. It prevents you from spending too much time on one particular question, only to have time called without getting to one or more questions you would have gotten right.

Each Verbal Reasoning section is 35 minutes long and includes 20 questions. If you were to spend an equal amount of time on each question, you'd have 1 minute and 45 seconds per question. But consider the three types of questions: it doesn't make sense to spend the same amount of time on an easy Text Completion question as you do on a hard Reading Comprehension question, given that they are both worth the same amount of points. Plus, this doesn't allow any time to read the passages! In order to maximize your score on the GRE, you should follow the PowerScore pacing plan for each type of task on the test:

Since all of the questions are worth a single point, it makes sense to attack the easiest ones first.

1. **Text Completion Questions**

   Budget 45 seconds to 1½ minutes for each Text Completion question, depending on the number of blanks in the question. Obviously, one blank questions should be solved in 45 seconds, while you may need to take additional time for questions with three blanks.

2. **Sentence Equivalence Questions**

   These questions should be completed in 60 seconds or less.

3. **Reading Comprehension Passages**

   Aim to read the shortest passages in 45 seconds or less, and work on tackling the longest passages in under 2 minutes and 30 seconds. We will talk extensively about approaches to reading in later chapters, but you should not slow down your normal reading speed when covering GRE passages.

4. **Reading Comprehension Questions**

Obviously some might take longer than others, since there are many different types of comprehension questions, but on average, try to answer them in under 60 seconds.

Do not spend more than the allotted time on each question or you are robbing yourself of time on other, easier questions. If you find yourself working on a question longer than the suggested time limits, make a guess and move on, but mark the question in case you have time at the end of the section to return. It is important to make a guess after spending so much time on a question; you have likely eliminated at least one answer choice in that time, even if you are not consciously aware of it. If time is called before you can return to the question, at least you have a chance of earning a point if you have selected an answer.

To learn how to budget time for each question, practice taking the sections on the PowerPrep software using the clock on the screen. You can also take the paper-based test from *The Official Guide to the GRE* using a timer. You should soon learn how long 45 seconds and 60 seconds "feel," so that you can judge when it is time to make a guess and abandon a question.

Never Finish Early

TIPS and TRICKS
You should never finish early on the GRE! Spend any extra time reviewing each question.

You are never done on a GRE Verbal Reasoning section (or any section for that matter). If you finish your three passes before time is called and feel that you are finished answering questions, you should spend the remaining minutes looking for mistakes. Double check every problem, but spend the most time on those that you intentionally omitted because of difficulty on your first or second pass. Most of our students report that they find careless errors when they return to review their work.

For this reason, never select "Exit Section" from the menu of buttons at the top. You must review your test until time expires.

General Directions

At the start of the test, there are several screens of instructions. These screens are presented before the test begins, so you can spend time reading them without affecting your time on the test. However, should you need to revisit the directions during the test, the timer will not stop. For this reason we recommend that you become quite familiar with the directions before taking the real GRE.

The general directions for the entire test can be summarized as follows:

1. There is an optional 10-minute break after section 3. There will be optional 60-second breaks between each section.

2. If you have to leave your seat during the test, you must raise your hand. It is important to note, however, that testing will continue and the timer will not stop.

3. Anything written on scratch paper will not count toward your score, and scratch paper must be given to the test supervisor at the completion of the GRE.

4. You may skip and mark questions and return to them using either the Review screen or by clicking through the questions using the arrow buttons.

5. You must wait 30 days to take the GRE again, and you can only take it 5 times a year.

We highly recommend that you take the 10-minute break to give yourself a rest and prepare for the remaining sections.

At the start of each Verbal Reasoning section, ETS sets forth certain guidelines that apply to all questions in the section. Those guidelines are summarized below:

1. Selecting the "Help" button at the top of the screen will lead you to more detailed directions. *Note: By practicing with the PowerPrep software, you should be able to avoid clicking this button and wasting time going over directions.*

2. Multiple choice questions with ovals by the answer choices have one right answer. Multiple choice questions with square boxes by the answer choices have one or more right answers. The directions for each question will also indicate whether there is a single correct answer or multiple correct answers.

3. You may need to scroll to see the entire passage for Reading Comprehension questions.

TIPS and TRICKS
You should never take time to read the directions on the GRE; these directions should be studied before taking the actual test.

The specific directions for each question type are only provided once the test begins, so we urge you to become familiar with the question types and their general rules on the following pages to avoid wasting time on the actual test.

Fill-in-the-Blank Questions

Fill-in-the-Blank questions present a sentence or short paragraph with blanks in places of a word or phrase that has been removed. You are required to choose a word or words that complete the sentence when placed in the blanks. Thus, we call these "Fill-in-the-Blank" questions. There are two types of Fill-in-the-Blank questions: Text Completions and Sentence Equivalence questions.

Text Completion Questions

Text Completion questions require you to choose a word or words that, when inserted into the blanks in a sentence, best fit the meaning of that sentence. Each question has one to five sentences with one, two, or three blanks. Questions with one blank have five possible answer choices:

1. The battle between _____ and originality rages on in the technology sector, where some seek to advance through scientific breakthroughs and others seek to advance by riding the coattails of others.

innovation
imitation
prototypes
indigence
incongruity

Questions with two or three blanks have three possible answer choices for each blank:

2. The writer's description of the Revolutionary War battle was truly (i)_____, filled with bright imagery and clear description, making the scene easy to (ii)_____ for her readers.

Blank (i)	Blank (ii)
vapid	surmise
vivid	ponder
unique	envision

3. As soon as the judge (i)_____ that she had inadvertently allowed prejudicial evidence to be introduced during the trial, she (ii)_____ to the defendant and (iii)_____ herself.

Blank (i)	Blank (ii)	Blank (iii)
authorized	extended atonement	incriminated
ascertained	made repentance	recused
resolved	expressed remorse	exculpated

The format of the questions in this chapter most closely resemble the format used on the Computer Adaptive Test. Once we get into chapters about specific strategy, we will revert to paper-based question format (with answers labeled A, B, and so on) so that answer choices are more easily identified and discussed.

GRATUITOUS VOCAB

indigence (n): poverty

incongruity (n): state of being out of place

vapid (adj): boring

ascertained (vb): made certain

recused (vb): withdrew from a position

exculpated (vb): cleared from blame

There are many patterns and clues within these questions, from the use of certain words in the sentence to the types of wrong answer choices presented. We will examine them all starting in the next chapter.

The directions for these questions can be summarized as follows:

- Each passage has one, two, or three blanks in which a word or a set of words has been omitted.

- There are multiple answer choices that correspond to each blank.

- Choose the answer(s) with the word or set of words that best fits the meaning of the sentence.

Sentence Equivalence Questions

Sentence Equivalence questions are similar to Text Completion questions. You are presented with a single sentence containing a single blank. There are six answer choices, two of which complete the sentence correctly. You must select both answer choices.

1. In granting the controversial motion, the judge surprisingly characterized the complex issue as _____.

    ☐ plain
    ☐ intricate
    ☐ curious
    ☐ uncommon
    ☐ straightforward
    ☐ average

Sentence Equivalence Questions always have a single blank and two correct answers.

Like Text Completion questions, Sentence Equivalence questions have many patterns, clues, and answer traps. Learning these secrets can help you master these vocabulary reasoning questions.

The directions for these questions can be summarized as follows:

- Each sentence has one blank in which a word or a set of words has been omitted.

- There are six possible answer choices.

- Choose two answers with the words or sets of words that best fits the meaning of the sentence.

Reading Comprehension Questions

Reading Comprehension questions assess a test taker's comprehension of a segment of text. The majority of passages are a single paragraph, but you should expect two or three longer passages composed of several paragraphs.

The passage appears on the left side of the computer screen. If the passage is longer than the space provided, a scroll bar in the middle of the screen appears. The question is located on the right side of the screen.

In paper-based tests, the word and line reference will be provided in the question instead of highlighted in the passage.

GRE Section 2 of 5	Exit Section	Review	Mark	Help ?	Back	Next

Question 13 of 20   Hide Time 00 : 08 : 37

Questions 13 to 15 are based on the passage.

As a child, John Henry Holliday faced a life of adversity that was **tempered** by privilege. The sudden death of his infant sister was followed by the slow death of his mother, to whom the fifteen year old Holliday had a close attachment. These tragedies were compounded by his father's remarriage just three months after her passing, which John felt was a betrayal of his mother, thus leading to strained relations between father and son. Despite his disapprobation, Holliday used his father's wealth and influence to ease these and other burdens that less privileged teenagers may have faced in 1860s Georgia.

In context, the highlighted word "tempered" most nearly means

- ⚬ encompassed
- ⚬ angered
- ⚬ aggravated
- ⚬ mitigated
- ⚬ followed

Click on your answer choice.

The directions for these questions can be summarized as follows:

- The passages are followed by questions about their content.

- The answers are based on information that is <u>stated</u> or <u>implied</u> in the passage or in the italicized introduction.

Questions with ovals next to the answer choices have a single correct answer; questions with squares next to the answer choices have more than one right answer. There are three types of Reading Comprehension questions: Select One Answer Choice, Select One or More Answer Choices, and Select-in-Passage.

Select One Answer Choice

The overwhelming majority of Multiple Choice questions are Select One Answer Choice.

The questions that require only one answer resemble standard multiple choice questions. There are five answer choices, and each answer choice is accompanied by an oval "bubble" for you to click when selecting a single answer. The question above is an example of a Select One Answer Choice multiple choice question.

Select One or More Answer Choices

Questions with squares boxes next to the answer choices will have three possible answers. You must select all answers that are correct, whether it be one, two, or all three. There is no partial credit; if you select the first answer but the answer was both the first and second choices, you will receive no points toward your score.

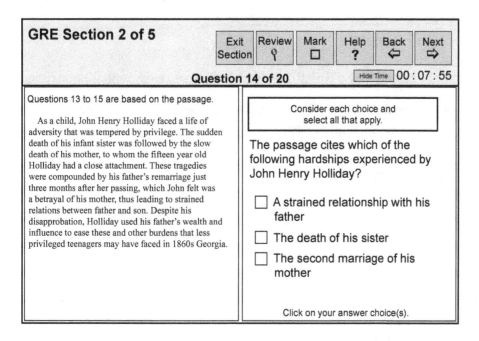

Select One or More Answer Choices will always have three possible choices; the correct answer may be one, two, or all three of them.

Select-in-Passage

To answer Select-in-Passage questions, you must select a sentence in the passage that satisfies the criteria of the question. You can click on any part of the sentence to highlight it.

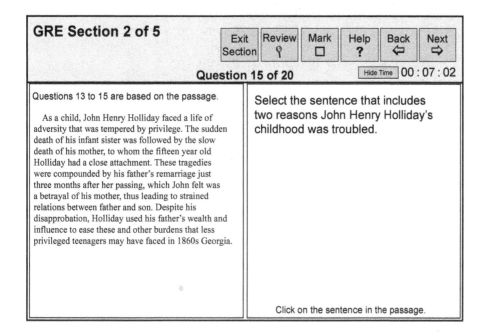

Clicking on any portion of a sentence will highlight the entire sentence.

Students who take the paper-based test will not have the Select-in-Passage questions. Instead, they will have a similar multiple choice question.

Chapter Summary

Guessing Strategy

- Guess when you cannot determine an answer.

- Eliminate obvious wrong answers.

Section Formats

- There are two Verbal Reasoning sections, each with 20 questions.

- Expect roughly 6 Text Completion questions, 4 Sentence Equivalence questions, and 10 Reading Comprehension questions.

Pacing and Time Management

- Determine whether the Fill-in-the-Blank or the Reading Comprehension questions are easier for you, and work on these questions first.

- Be sure to "Mark" any questions you skip so that you can easily come back to them.

- Spend 45 to 90 seconds on Text Completion questions, depending on the number of blanks the question has. Spend 60 seconds or less on Sentence Equivalence questions and Reading Comprehension questions.

- Aim to read short passages in 45 seconds or less; read long passages in under 2½ minutes.

- Complete one passage before moving onto the next.

- Never stop working before time is up.

Directions

- Understand the directions for each type of question before taking the GRE.

- Text Completion Questions are Fill-in-the-Blank questions. The passages are made up of one to five sentences and they have one to three blanks in the passage. Single blank questions have five answer choices to complete the blank; multiple blank questions have three answer choices per blank.

- Sentence Equivalence are the second type of Fill-in-the-Blank questions. The passage is a single sentence with a single blank. You must select two answer choices that complete the sentence.

- Reading Comprehension questions require you to read a passage and answer corresponding questions. There are two types of multiple-choice questions; Select One Answer Choice (represented by ovals) and Select One or More Answer Choices (represented by squares). You may also be asked to Select-in-Passage, meaning you click on a sentence that represents a specific description.

Fill-in-the-Blank Mastery: Solution Strategy Basics

Fill-in-the-Blank Mastery:
Solution Strategy Basics

Introduction

Both Text Completion and Sentence Equivalence questions have two parts: the question stem and the answer choices. The question stem is the sentence or sentences containing the blank or blanks, and the answer choices are the words or phrases following the question stem.

Text Completion

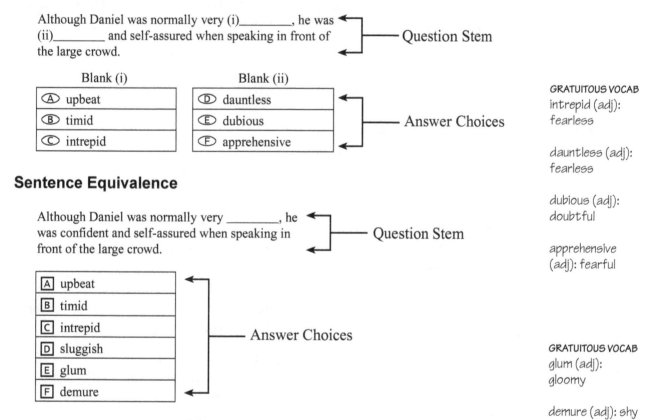

Sentence Equivalence

GRATUITOUS VOCAB
intrepid (adj): fearless

dauntless (adj): fearless

dubious (adj): doubtful

apprehensive (adj): fearful

GRATUITOUS VOCAB
glum (adj): gloomy

demure (adj): shy

Although there are two types of Fill-in-the-Blank questions on the GRE, their format is related and thus the strategies for mastering them are similar. But before we explore these processes, you must understand the format of the questions and the basic strategies for tackling them. For most test takers, it would be a good idea to review this chapter upon finishing the Fill-in-the-Blank Mastery chapters; it serves not only as a good introduction to these types of questions, but also as a revisited conclusion.

Question Format

Fill-in-the-Blank questions occur in one of four forms: single blank Text Completion, dual blank Text Completion, triple blank Text Completion, and single blank Sentence Equivalence. Single blank questions—whether Text Completion or Sentence Equivalence—make up a small majority on the GRE.

All of the answer choices in a Fill-in-the-Blank question will be the same part of speech. For example, in the question below, all of the answer choices are adjectives:

The possible answers for a particular blank will always be the same part of speech.

The dinner guest was _____, arguing with the other guests about everything from marriage to literature to cooking techniques.

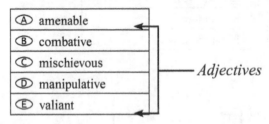

We will discuss the importance of this knowledge throughout the Fill-in-the-Blank chapters.

GRATUITOUS VOCAB
amenable (adj): agreeable

valiant (adj): brave

revamped (adj): redone, revised

duplicity (adj): deceitfulness

admonished (adj): scolded; warned

resolution (adj): determination

revered (adj): respected

In dual blank and triple blank questions, the words grouped for each blank are the same part of speech in all three choices.

The teacher was both admired and criticized for her (i)_____; such honesty about the school's poor performance was applauded by some administrators and (ii)_____ by others.

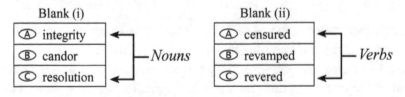

Many students fear the dual blank and triple blank questions because they feel that multiple missing words are harder to replace than one. However, these questions have two or three times as much information with which to work, so they are frequently easier than their single blank brothers. We will discuss strategies for attacking all formats throughout this chapter.

Context Clues

Every Fill-in-the-Blank question has clue words to help you find the word or phrase that best fits in the blank. Without these clues, the sentences, like the simplified example below, would be impossible to complete:

The man was excited to see his new _____.

Ⓐ	car
Ⓑ	bride
Ⓒ	office
Ⓓ	dog
Ⓔ	treadmill

All Fill-in-the-Blank questions have context clues in the sentence.

Any of the answers could correctly complete this question stem because the sentence does not contain any clues to help you fill in the blank. However, when we change just one word of the sentence, one of the answers seems more likely:

The runner was excited to see his new _____.

Ⓐ	car
Ⓑ	bride
Ⓒ	office
Ⓓ	dog
Ⓔ	treadmill

The word *runner* gives context, or meaning, to the sentence, and is thus considered a context clue. Of all the items in the answer choices, a treadmill is most likely to be used by a runner, so choice (E) is the best fit for the sentence. Look how the context changes with a new word:

The groom was excited to see his new _____.

Ⓐ	car
Ⓑ	bride
Ⓒ	office
Ⓓ	dog
Ⓔ	treadmill

Obviously, sentences on the GRE are much more complex than these examples. We often use simplified models in this book to help illustrate concepts and strategies.

With the word *groom*, the context of the sentence has changed. It does not make sense for a groom to be excited to see a *car*, an *office*, a *dog*, or a *treadmill*. The most logical answer choice is now (B), *bride*.

Be careful not to add extraneous information to a sentence. Some students might say "Well, the groom might be excited to see the limousine he rented for the wedding party, so (A) could work." If choice (A) had the word *limousine* instead of *car*, those students might have a valid point. But it is simply *car*, which does not fit into the context of a wedding. Plus, the possessive adjective *his* indicates ownership, and a rented limousine is not owned by the groom. Keep your background knowledge packed away when working in the Verbal Reasoning section of the GRE. If the sentence does not state or imply a relationship, do not create one.

Context clues are abundant in GRE Fill-in-the-Blank questions. These words help you understand what the question is looking for. Let's examine one of the previous examples from this chapter:

The dinner guest was _____, arguing with the other guests about everything from marriage to literature to cooking techniques.

Ⓐ	amenable
Ⓑ	combative
Ⓒ	mischievous
Ⓓ	manipulative
Ⓔ	valiant

The context for the blank is *arguing with the other guests about everything*. A person who constantly argues is *combative*, meaning *ready to fight*.

Can you find the context clues in this sentence?

The teacher was both admired and criticized for her (i)_____; such honesty about the school's poor performance was applauded by some administrators and (ii)_____ by others.

Blank (i)	Blank (ii)
Ⓐ integrity	Ⓓ censured
Ⓑ candor	Ⓔ revamped
Ⓒ resolution	Ⓕ revered

There are several context clues here. The first is *both admired and criticized*. It provides context for the second blank. The example for *admired* was *applauded*. The example for *criticized* will be a negative action, the opposite of *applauded*. Only *censured* has a meaning similar to *criticized*.

Another clue is *such honesty*. This gives context for the first blank. In fact, the first blank will be a synonym of *honesty*. The only answer choice that contains this synonym is (B), *candor*.

The PowerScore Four-Step Solution

Every Fill-in-the-Blank question can be solved in four steps:

1. Read the question stem.

2. Prephrase the answer(s).

3. Match the answer choice(s).

4. Backplug your selection(s).

Each of these steps, explained in more detail on the following pages, is crucial to your success on these questions. It is important to practice them with every Fill-in-the-Blank question you encounter.

1. Read the question stem.

Read each question stem one time. Do not read the sentence and try it with answer choice (A), reread the sentence and try it with answer choice (B), and proceed in this manner until you try all possible choices. This solution method can take up to five times longer than the PowerScore recommended method, and 90% of test takers do not have extra time to spare in the GRE Verbal Reasoning section.

TIPS and TRICKS
Read the question stem one time! Do not read it over and over with each answer choice.

For most sentences, one reading is sufficient for gathering meaning and understanding the context of the blank. Consider an example of a basic sentence:

1. The two books had plots that were so _____ they were virtually indistinguishable.

Most students can quickly read this sentence one time and have sufficient comprehension to proceed. Read the next two question stems and concentrate on finding the main idea in one reading:

2. Despite being instructed to conduct a thorough investigation on local water quality, the committee submitted a report that is _____. The board will likely determine that because of a lack of evidence and expert testimony, it cannot to support the committee's recommendations.

3. Although Trina dreamed of a (i)_____ wedding, she chose a simple ceremony at the courthouse and (ii)_____ reception in her parent's backyard.

You may find, though, that some sentences are substantially more demanding and require a second reading. Although a single reading is optimal, it is necessary to reread sentences if you do not understand them the first time through.

Some question stems, like the one below, are challenging because they contain vocabulary in the sentence itself.

4. Her husband insisted that the family's strict budget was the result of _____ fiscal policy rather than his penurious nature; that is, it was not so much stingy as wise.

Test takers may panic when they encounter the word *penurious* and either omit the question or make a hasty guess. However, this question is not as hard as it first appears. The second part of the sentence, *that is, it was not so much stingy as wise*, provides the definition of *penurious*: stingy. Similarly, the word that fits in the blank is synonymous with *wise*. Do not skip a question just because the sentence contains difficult vocabulary words. Read the entire sentence to see if synonyms or context clues are provided.

You may occasionally come across a question where your knowledge of the vocabulary in the sentence *is* required to fill in the blank. Consider the previous question with some changes:

5. Her husband insisted that the family's strict budget was the result of (i)_____ fiscal policy rather than his penurious nature; that is, it was not so much (ii)_____ as prudent.

Now it is more difficult to solve this question without knowing the meaning of *penurious* and *prudent*. In Chapter 6 we will present strategies for decoding vocabulary words, but if you employ these strategies and are still unable to understand what the blanks are looking for, we would advise you to guess and move on. Please note, however, that these situations are rare.

Other question stems are deemed difficult because of the sentence structure:

6. An institution judged by its reputation, such as a government department, is justified in monitoring the actions of its members, due to the fact that society is all too willing to _____ an entire body based on the behavior of a subset of that group's associates.

This sentence does not contain any usual words, but at 41 words long, it is bulky and awkward. It's likely that most students will not understand the sentence upon the first reading. There are four possible strategies you can employ for more difficult sentences like these that do not make immediate sense upon the first reading.

Strategy 1: Remove irrelevant words and phrases

Not every word in a Fill-in-the-Blank question is necessary for understanding the main idea of the question stem. Good test takers often drop irrelevant or unimportant words or phrases in order to simplify the sentence. Compare the original sentence to a paraphrased version:

Original:

"An institution judged by its reputation, such as a government department, is justified in monitoring the actions of its members due to the fact that society is all too willing to _____ an entire body based on the behavior of a subset of that group's associates."

"An institution judged by its reputation, ~~such as a government department~~, is justified in monitoring ~~the actions of~~ its members due to the fact that society is ~~all too~~ willing to _____ an entire body based on the behavior of ~~a subset of~~ that group's associates."

With irrelevant words and phrases removed:

An institution judged by its reputation is justified in monitoring its members due to the fact that society is willing to _____ an entire body based on the behavior of that group's associates.

By removing the unnecessary phrases, you should find the sentence easier to comprehend. Obviously you cannot physically delete words in a question on your test, but you can mentally omit them when reading a sentence.

This strategy becomes even more powerful when paired with the next one.

Strategy 2: Rephrase the sentence

Most successful Verbal Reasoning students will tell you that they paraphrase difficult question stems in both the Fill-in-the-Blank and Reading Comprehension sections. It is much easier to understand an idea when it is in your own words. Let's examine how a great test taker might rephrase the previous example:

Original:

"An institution judged by its reputation, such as a government department, is justified in monitoring the actions of its members due to the fact that society is all too willing to _____ an entire body based on the behavior of a subset of that group's associates."

Paraphrased:

An organization that is judged by its reputation, such as a government agency, is allowed to monitor its members' actions because society is willing to _____ the whole group based on the actions of a few members.

Paraphrased with irrelevant words and phrases removed:

An organization that is judged by its reputation is allowed to monitor its members because society will _____ the whole group based on the actions of a few.

Most students will agree that the paraphrased versions are much easier to comprehend.

Strategy 3: Read in chunks

The third strategy is to read a small chunk around the blank and work outward. For example, start with a phrase around the blank in the question above:

"society is all too willing to _____ an entire body"

The phrase *all too willing* is most often used in a negative context. For example, "My math teacher is all too willing to give extra homework" or "My boss is all too willing to criticize me." This is a valuable clue to the context of the word for which we are looking.

Working outward, add more phrases as you understand each small chunk:

"society is all too willing to _____ an entire body based on the behavior of a subset"

And then:

"due to the fact that society is all too willing to _____ an entire body based on the behavior of a subset of that group's associates"

The goal is to eventually understand the entire sentence by piecing together several small parts at a time.

TIPS and TRICKS
Put difficult phrases and clauses into your own words.

TIPS and TRICKS
If you have difficulty understanding a sentence, read in small chunks, starting around the blank.

Strategy 4: Relate the sentence to your own life

The final strategy for understanding complicated sentences is to try to put them into a context that fits your own life. We understand that which we can relate to much more than we understand the strange and unfamiliar. Think about when your friends come to you for advice; if you have similar past experiences, it is much easier for you to understand their feelings and relate. The same is true of GRE Fill-in-the-Blank questions.

Let's look at how one test taker might relate to the current question stem we have been studying:

> "An institution judged by its reputation, such as a government department, is justified in monitoring the actions of its members due to the fact that society is all too willing to _____ an entire body based on the behavior of a subset of that group's associates."

"An institution judged by its reputation...." *Huh. That's like a college. A college is judged by its reputation.*

"...is justified in monitoring the actions of its members...." *Well, a college should be allowed to monitor professors' and students' actions so that the college doesn't look bad.*

"...due to the fact that society is all too willing to _____ an entire body based on the behavior of a subset of that group's associates." *Yes, the public will judge the entire college based on one person's bad behavior. Just like when a few students were caught rioting after the football game last year. People across the country believed that everyone at our college was a trouble-making delinquent.*

This complicated sentence suddenly becomes much easier to understand when you can relate your own personal experience.

The best test takers use all four of these strategies, often in combination with one another. When you encounter difficult sentences throughout this book and in the *Official Guide to the GRE*, be sure to practice these strategies in order to become proficient at using them on test day.

Remember, the most efficient students will read each Fill-in-the-Blank question only once before moving to Step 2. However, if the question stem is among the more difficult questions, it may require a second, more deliberate reading for sufficient understanding.

Step 1 from solving Fill-in-the-Blank questions was *Read the Question Stem*. Now let's examine Step 2.

TIPS and TRICKS
If you can find a parallel between a difficult sentence and your own life, the sentence will likely be easier to understand.

We take several pages to explain these strategies, but with practice, they should take mere seconds to employ.

2. Prephrase the answer(s).

After you read the question stem, predict an answer <u>before</u> looking at the answer choices. PowerScore calls this powerful technique *prephrasing*. Consider one of the previous examples:

> The two books had plots that were so _____ they were virtually indistinguishable.

What word, when placed in the blank, completes the sentence? Most students would prephrase *alike* or *similar* for this question, but there are many that would fit. The word you choose should be simple and it must fit the meaning of the sentence.

Some prephrases might actually repeat a word that is already used in a sentence:

> The committee's report on local water quality is _____, lacking evidence and expert testimony to support its recommendations.

While some students might prephrase *incomplete, deficient,* or *insufficient,* it is perfectly acceptable to use *lacking*. Obviously the test makers are not going to use *lacking* as an actual answer choice (because good writers do not use the same descriptive word twice in a sentence), but the repeated term provides a synonym to help you find the right answer.

You may sometimes find that your prephrase is an actual phrase rather than a single word:

> Although Trina dreamed of an extravagant wedding, she _____ a simple ceremony at the courthouse and an understated reception in her parent's backyard.

The phrases *opted for* and *ended up with* would be adequate prephrases for the blank in this sentence. Although they are not single word answers, they will still lead you to the right single word answer.

For questions with more than one blank, prephrase answers for each blank:

> Her husband insisted that the family's strict budget was the result of (i)_____ fiscal policy rather than his stingy nature; that is, it was not so much (ii)_____ as wise.

Good prephrases for the first blank include *sound, smart,* and *wise,* while the second blank is best filled by *stingy* or *greedy.*

Nearly all GRE Fill-in-the-Blank questions can be solved using prephrasing. However, on rare occasion, you may encounter a question—especially those with more than one blank—in which it is impossible to predict words that complete the blank. Let's look at an example:

> Most of the students thought the new teacher would have a more (i)_____ classroom because he was less (ii)_____ than the previous instructor.

Many pairs of words fit this question stem:

> Most of the students thought the new teacher would have a more *disciplined* classroom because he was less *tolerant* than the previous instructor.

> Most of the students thought the new teacher would have a more *relaxed* classroom because he was less *structured* than the previous instructor.

> Most of the students thought the new teacher would have a more *boring* classroom because he was less *creative* than the previous instructor.

> Most of the students thought the new teacher would have a more *cluttered* classroom because he was less *tidy* than the previous instructor.

These are just a sampling of the dozens of opposite word pairs that can fit into the sentence and make sense.

If you come across a question like this, you will quickly realize that you cannot accurately prephrase an answer. Instead, test each answer in the blanks and find the two that express the appropriate relationship. These questions usually have answers with similar or contrasting meanings.

If you cannot prephrase a dual blank question, test each answer choice in the blanks.

Prephrasing Mini-Drill

Prephrase a word or phrase for each of the blanks and write your answer on the line provided. Suggested answers are on page 51.

1. Because Raquel hired an excellent tutor and studied diligently for the GRE, she received a _____ score.

2. Jack's boss praised him for his (i)_____ work, noting that Jack's report was completed faster and with fewer (ii)_____ than the reports of all other employees.

3. Although Kacey was an (i)_____ baby-sitter who had cared for infants for several years, she felt (ii)_____ when dealing with the fussy Smith twins.

4. The book was criticized for its _____; the topic was too broad to be covered in so few pages.

5. Aaron did his best to avoid listening to the pessimistic comments, preferring to remain _____.

6. Even those constituents who (i)_____ the senator admit that his environmental policy is (ii)_____; they cannot deny that he has failed to protect the state's rivers from factory run-off.

7. Many social studies educators, especially those who are saddled with teaching multiple subject areas, have begun to see the benefits of interdisciplinary instruction and thus are _____ math, language arts, and science into their history and geography curriculum.

8. Conservative (i)_____, the self-appointed authorities on party values, once (ii)_____ the governor as the embodiment of their conventional ideals but have now (iii)_____ him upon the discovery of his deceit regarding involvement in the disgraceful scandal.

GRATUITOUS VOCAB
diligently (adv):
in an attentive
manner

constituents (n):
voters

interdisciplinary
(adj): involving
multiple fields of
study

curriculum (n):
the plan of study

embodiment (n):
living example

3. Match the answer choice(s).

Once you select a prephrase, turn to the answer choices and read through all of them. Which one most closely matches your prephrase? In the following example, our previous prephrase was *similar*. The answer that has the closest meaning to *similar* is *comparable*:

The two books had plots that were so _____ they were virtually indistinguishable.

Ⓐ	ignorant
Ⓑ	comparable
Ⓒ	animated
Ⓓ	contrary
Ⓔ	revered

For dual blank and triple blank questions, all of your prephrases must match an answer choice:

Her husband insisted that the family's strict budget was the result of (i)_____ fiscal policy rather than his stingy nature; that is, it was not so much (ii)_____ as wise.

Blank (i)		Blank (ii)	
Ⓐ	irrational	Ⓓ	foolish
Ⓑ	straightforward	Ⓔ	tightfisted
Ⓒ	sensible	Ⓕ	prudent

We previously prephrased *wise* and *stingy* for this question. For Blank (i), only choice (C) matches our prephrase *wise*, and for Blank (ii), choice (E) means *stingy*. Notice that Blank (ii) uses *prudent*, a word whose meaning matches our prephrase, *wise*, for Blank (i). You have to be extremely careful to keep your prephrases straight in dual and triple blank questions.

Sometimes your prephrase might actually be the right answer! One of our prephrases for the following question was *deficient*, which happens to be answer choice (A):

The committee's report on local water quality is _____, lacking evidence and expert testimony to support its recommendations.

Ⓐ	deficient
Ⓑ	illegible
Ⓒ	eloquent
Ⓓ	concise
Ⓔ	weighty

Prephrasing can make Fill-in-the-Blank questions incredibly easy!

3

Confidence Quotation
"The difference between the impossible and the possible lies in a man's determination."
Tommy Lasorda, Major League Baseball coach

GRATUITOUS VOCAB
revered (adj): respected
tightfisted (adj): stingy
frail (adj): weak
eloquent (adj): expressing oneself powerfully
concise (adj): expressing much in few words

4. Backplug your selection(s).

The last step is the easiest and should take the least amount of time. Once you select an answer choice, plug it back into the sentence and reread the sentence with the new inserted word.

The two books had plots that were so *comparable* they were virtually indistinguishable.

Ⓐ ignorant
Ⓑ comparable
Ⓒ animated
Ⓓ contrary
Ⓔ revered

Her husband insisted that the family's strict budget was the result of *sensible* fiscal policy rather than his stingy nature; that is, it was not so much *tightfisted* as wise.

Blank (i)	Blank (ii)
Ⓐ irrational	Ⓓ foolish
Ⓑ straightforward	Ⓔ tightfisted
Ⓒ sensible	Ⓕ prudent

The committee's report on local water quality is *deficient*, lacking evidence and expert testimony to support its recommendations.

Ⓐ deficient
Ⓑ illegible
Ⓒ eloquent
Ⓓ concise
Ⓔ weighty

If the sentence makes sense with the new word, quickly move onto the next question. On the off-chance that the word does not work in the sentence, eliminate it and choose another.

Sentence Equivalence Strategies

While the previous strategies and Four-Step Solution process apply to both Text Completion and Sentence Equivalence questions, the nature of Sentence Equivalence questions dictates a few more strategies that are exclusive to these types of questions.

Text Completion questions have a single word from the answer choices that correctly completes each blank, but Sentence Equivalence questions may have several answers that make sense when inserted in the blank. Consider an example:

> The small island nation had never been visited by such _____ figure, so the enthusiastic members of the government planned lavish ceremonies and splendid celebrations for the Queen's visit.

A	an eminent
B	a virtuous
C	a notorious
D	an illustrious
E	an influential
F	a royal

CAUTION: GRE TRAP! More than two answer choices can complete a Sentence Equivalence blank. The correct two choices will be synonyms of each other.

In this question, choices (A), (D), (E), and (F) all make sense in the blank! By definition, a queen is an *eminent, illustrious, influential,* and *royal* figure (and she may very well be *notorious* or *virtuous*, but there is no context in the sentence to indicate that these particular attributes are true).

So how do you find the two right answers? The directions for Sentence Equivalence questions state that the two correct answers create sentences that are alike in meaning. For this reason, if an answer choice does not have a synonym or closely-related word in the list, eliminate it. Choice (E), *influential*, is alone in its definition, as none of the other answers means *having the capacity of producing effects*. Similarly, *royal* in choice (F) is a loner. It means *pertaining to a king or queen*. But answer choices (A) and (D) (*eminent* and *illustrious*) both mean *distinguished*, and are thus the correct answers. They make sense in the blank and they produce sentences with similar meanings.

TIPS and TRICKS If an answer to a Sentence Equivalence question does not have a synonym or a word with a closely-related meaning, eliminate that answer choice!

Of course, if you do not know the definition of a word, you cannot eliminate it. Let's say that you know the meaning of *illustrious, influential,* and *royal*, but not of *eminent*. At this point you can figure out that *eminent* must be one of the answers, because the other three words are not synonyms of each other. You must guess which of the remaining three words is its synonym. We will look more closely at decoding vocabulary words in Chapter 6.

So now we have looked at how synonyms can help you narrow down the correct answer choices. Be warned, though: just because an answer choice has a synonym does not mean it's a correct answer.

CAUTION: GRE TRAP!
Be wary of
synonym pairs
that do not fit
the meaning of
the sentence!

The Victorian view of mental illness—illustrated in short stories like "The Yellow Wallpaper"—held that women were _____ and prone to neurosis while men were vigorous and immune to emotional disorders.

A	tenacious
B	feeble
C	fragile
D	nurturing
E	unyielding
F	illogical

Notice answer choices (A) and (E): *tenacious* and *unyielding*. Both mean *firm* and *inflexible*. An unprepared test taker may see this synonym pair, and erroneously select them as the answer. Remember, there are two rules for Sentence Equivalence questions: the words must have similar meaning *and* they must make sense in the sentence. *Tenacious* and *unyielding* do not fit the meaning of the sentence, but *feeble* and *fragile* satisfy both of the criteria set forth in the directions.

Because these sentences sometimes contain less context than Text Completion questions, prephrasing may not always be a viable strategy. In the question about the Queen, we could have predicted *important*, *regal*, *famous*, *respected*, and many more words associated with a woman in a royal position. Still, though, our prephrases point to a positive word to complete the blank and their general meaning is similar. In the question on this page, we can prephrase *weak*, *irrational*, and *ill*, all of which are words with negative connotations. Use your prephrase to eliminate wrong answers. Unless the sentence has strict context, though, be willing to abandon your prephrase in favor of a word with similar meaning that is accompanied by a synonym.

Chapter Summary

Question Format

- Fill-in-the-Blank questions may have a single blank, a dual blank, or a triple blank. Single blank questions may be Text Completion or Sentence Equivalence questions, while all multiple blank questions occur in the Text Completion section.

- Dual blank and triple blank questions have more information with which to complete the sentence.

Context Clues

- All Text Completion questions have specific context clues in the text so that only one answer choice can be correct.

- Context clues in Sentence Equivalence questions may point to more than two answer choices, but of the possible contenders only two of those answers will be synonyms of each other.

The PowerScore Four Step Solution Method

1. Read the question stem.

   For difficult question stems, use one or more of the following strategies:

   - Remove irrelevant words and phrases.

   - Rephrase the sentence.

   - Read in chunks.

   - Relate the sentence to your own life.

2. Prephrase the answer(s).

   - It is imperative that you prephrase an answer before looking at the answer choices.

   - If you are unable to prephrase, test each answer choice in the blank(s).

3. Match the answer choice(s).

4. Backplug your selection.

Sentence Equivalence Strategies

- Eliminate answer choices that do not have a synonym or a word with a closely-related meaning.

- Be wary of synonym pairs that do not fit the meaning of the sentence.

- Understand that your prephrase can lead you in the general direction of the correct answers, but it may not always be a perfect match.

Solution Strategy Basics Answer Key

Prephrasing Mini Drill—Page 44

There are a number of possible answers for each of the prephrases in this exercise. The possibilities listed here are not an inclusive list.

1. *excellent, top, high, great*

2. Blank 1: *excellent, top-notch, perfect, good, great*
   Blank 2: *mistakes, errors, problems*

3. Blank 1: *experienced, great, practiced, excellent*
   Blank 2: *overwhelmed, inexperienced*

4. *shortness, brevity, lack of coverage*

5. *positive, an optimist, upbeat, optimistic*

6. Blank 1: *supported, liked, voted for*
   Blank 2: *bad, an issue, lacking*

7. *adding, putting, integrating, incorporating*

8. Blank 1: *critics, pundits*
   Blank 2: *hailed, praised*
   Blank 3: *rejected, shunned, turned their backs on*

Fill-in-the-Blank Mastery: Deconstruct the Question Stem

Fill-in-the-Blank Mastery: Deconstruct the Question Stem

Introduction

As we mentioned in the previous chapter, there are two parts to a Fill-in-the-Blank question: the question stem and the answer choices.

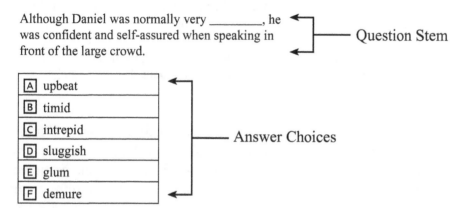

Although Daniel was normally very _____, he was confident and self-assured when speaking in front of the large crowd. — Question Stem

[A] upbeat
[B] timid
[C] intrepid
[D] sluggish
[E] glum
[F] demure

— Answer Choices

The question stem contains the sentence(s) with the blank or blanks, and is the focus of this chapter. We will discuss the answer choices in the next chapter.

Understanding the text or sentence in the question stem is an obvious necessity to your success on the GRE. But understanding the structure of the sentence that contains blanks is an overlooked strategy that can help you better comprehend the intention of the sentence and the context of the missing word.

All Sentence Equivalence questions and the majority of Text Completion questions have a single-sentence question stem. For this reason, and for the ease of discussion, we will look at the question stem as a lone sentence for most of this chapter, addressing multiple-sentence question stems at the end.

Nearly all Fill-in-the-Blank questions can be categorized as one of four types of question stems based on the type of context clues in the sentence:

1. Contrast Sentences

2. Similarity Sentences

3. Definition Sentences

4. Cause and Effect Sentences

Question stems come in four varieties on the GRE. Recognizing the type of question can help you determine the answer.

Learning to recognize these four sentence types not only helps you determine the meaning of a blank, but also makes the sentences more accessible and manageable. The best way to beat any test is to understand how the questions are written.

Contrast Question Stems

Some context clues provide direction; these words are like road signs that guide you in the direction of the answer. The most recognized direction clues are "U-Turn Words," those that indicate a sentence is about to travel in the opposite direction. Consider an example:

> *Rather than* agree to the terms of the new contract, the union members _____ to sign the document outlining their rights and responsibilities.

The phrase *rather than* indicates that the sentence will make a U-turn and contain a contrasting idea. The original direction is *agree to the terms of the new contract*. But with the use of *rather than*, the second portion of the sentence is going to show disagreement with the terms of the contract. Rather than agreeing, the union members will *refuse* to agree, or *refuse* to sign.

Let's examine another Contrast Question Stem:

> Violet originally intended to invite everyone she knew to the wedding; once her meager budget was set, however, she began _____ her list of guests to just close friends and family members.

The direction clue in this sentence is the word *however*. Working in conjunction with the context clues *originally*, *meager budget*, and *just*, *however* indicates that the original idea—inviting everyone she knew—has now changed and the opposite is true; she can only invite close friends and family members. Predicted answers for the blank include *trimming* or *cutting*.

Learning to spot U-Turn Words can help you quickly analyze a Contrast Sentence. The following words indicate that a sentence is heading in the opposite direction of the original idea:

TIPS and TRICKS
Recognizing "indicator words" can help you quickly pinpoint a question type.

4

	U-Turn Words	
but	although	while
however	though	whereas
not	even though	actually
yet	still	contradictory
paradoxically	despite	at odds
nonetheless	rather than	differ
regardless of	instead of	difference
in contrast	unlike	variation
conversely	in spite of	the reverse
otherwise	except for	even so
on the contrary	contrasting with	contrary
	on the other hand	

As we discussed at the beginning of this chapter, there are four types of question stems in the Fill-in-the-Blank sections. Each of these types can further be classified into structure types, and U-Turn Words often indicate the type of structure. For example, subordinating conjunctions are often the first word of a Contrast Sentence containing a dependent clause and independent clause:

> *Although* Doug had previously participated in CPR training, he froze and was unable to _____ chest compressions when faced with a real emergency.

> *Despite* his month-long slump, the baseball player was _____ the most valuable player trophy based on his performance earlier in the season.

> *Even though* the play has a serious theme, its comedy routines and musical numbers make it a _____ affair for audiences of all ages.

Subordinating conjunctions are words like *although, despite, regardless of, even though, rather than, whereas,* and *while,* that join a dependent clause (a clause that *cannot* stand alone as a sentence) to an independent clause (a clause that *can* stand alone as a sentence).

Contrast question stems may employ:
- a subordinating conjunction
- a coordinating conjunction
- a semicolon or a period

Subordinating conjunctions can appear at the beginning of the sentence or in the middle of the sentence as the beginning of a clause.

When a subordinating conjunction is the first word in a sentence, the question is probably a Contrast Question Stem and you should begin looking for an idea that contradicts the original statement.

Note that the subordinating conjunction does not necessarily have to be the first word in order to show contrast:

> Doug froze and was unable to _____ chest compressions when faced with a real emergency, *although* he had previously participated in CPR training.

> The baseball player was _____ the most valuable player trophy based on his performance earlier in the season *despite* his month-long slump.

> The play's comedy routines and musical numbers make it a _____ affair for audiences of all ages, *even though* it has a serious theme.

Another common Contrast Question Stem structure uses the coordinating conjunctions *but* and *yet* to link two independent clauses:

> Doug had previously participated in CPR training, *but* he froze and was unable to _____ chest compressions when faced with a real emergency.

> The play has a serious theme, *yet* its comedy routines and musical numbers make it a _____ affair for audiences of all ages.

Finally, some Contrast Question Stems use semicolons or periods, often with the conjunctive adverb *however*:

> The baseball player suffered through a month-long slump earlier this season; now, *however*, he is _____ the most valuable player trophy based on his performance after that period.

> The baseball player suffered through a month-long slump earlier this season. Now, *however*, he is _____ the most valuable player trophy based on his performance after that period.

Most Contrast Question Stems will follow one of these aforementioned structures. Some, however, do not follow any predictable pattern, but will still use a U-Turn Word:

Not all contrast question stems follow a pattern, but they all use U-Turn Words.

> The pastor's actions were *contradictory* to his sermons; he practiced violence when he preached _____.

Learning these sentence structures can help you quickly identify a Contrast Sentence and understand the meaning of the most difficult questions.

Contrast Question Stems often use antonyms, or words with opposite meanings, in the same sentence. Sometimes both antonyms are provided, as in the following question:

> Unlike most students who *disliked* complex mathematical equations, Manuel *enjoyed* assignments that required _____ calculations and meticulous attention to detail.

In this sentence, the antonyms *disliked* and *enjoyed* are both given and can be used as context clues to solve the meaning of the word in the blank. Many Contrast Sentences, however, use a blank in place of one of the antonyms, making the question easy to solve:

> Unlike most students who _____ complex mathematical equations, Manuel *enjoyed* assignments that required complicated calculations and meticulous attention to detail.

> Unlike most students who *disliked* complex mathematical equations, Manuel _____ assignments that required complicated calculations and meticulous attention to detail.

TIPS and TRICKS
Look for antonyms in Contrast questions to help you determine your prephrase.

Once you identify the contrasting idea in these sentences, you simply need to look for an answer choice that is an antonym to the word in the sentence.

Sometimes both antonyms will be removed, and the solution is the only pair of antonyms listed that make sense:

> Unlike most students who (i)_____ complex mathematical equations, Manuel (ii)_____ assignments that required complicated calculations and meticulous attention to detail.

Blank (i)	Blank (ii)
Ⓐ celebrated	Ⓐ traded
Ⓑ solved	Ⓑ enjoyed
Ⓒ disliked	Ⓒ avoided

Choice (C) in Blank (i) and choice (B) in Blank (ii) provide two antonyms that make sense in the blanks. Note that when both antonyms are removed from the sentence, prephrasing becomes difficult if not impossible.

Prephrasing becomes quite difficult if both antonyms are removed.

Contrast Question Stems Problem Set

Each of the sentences or paragraphs below has a word or set of words that has been omitted. From the answer choices, choose the word or set of words that best completes the meaning of the sentence. Answers begin on page 85.

1. Rather than judge a person on her _____ appearance, this pageant awards scholarships to women who possess qualities that constitute inner beauty, such as compassion and intelligence.

Ⓐ elegant
Ⓑ physical
Ⓒ familiar
Ⓓ unconscious
Ⓔ brilliant

2. Unlike many professors who put tremendous effort into their research but (i)_____ their teaching duties, Alice was (ii)_____ about imparting knowledge to her students.

Blank (i)	Blank (ii)
Ⓐ neglect	Ⓓ passionate
Ⓑ deplore	Ⓔ ambivalent
Ⓒ endorse	Ⓕ antagonistic

3. The financial speaker told (i)_____ tales about his days on Wall Street when the stock market soared, but much of the business-based audience suffered from (ii)_____ when he droned on for an hour about the taxes involved with owning a farm.

Blank (i)	Blank (ii)
Ⓐ captivating	Ⓓ trepidation
Ⓑ emphatic	Ⓔ indolence
Ⓒ strenuous	Ⓕ ennui

4. Although most of the current demand for oil emanates from developed countries, the vast majority of the world's oil supply is controlled by _____ economies.

Ⓐ defunct
Ⓑ emerging
Ⓒ preeminent
Ⓓ bureaucratic
Ⓔ prolific

5. Paradoxically, during Prohibition, the illegalization of alcohol that was meant to (i)_____ crime actually led to an increase in the number of people who (ii)_____ criminal activity.

Blank (i)	Blank (ii)
Ⓐ amplify	Ⓓ engaged in
Ⓑ curb	Ⓔ refrained from
Ⓒ sever	Ⓕ confessed to

6. In the wake of the scandal, the police chief opted for (i)_____ instead of secrecy; he believed that the more information he (ii)_____ the public at the start, the less backlash the department would receive if the truth was hidden and eventually leaked later on. Yet the media was quick to criticize him for such (iii)_____ transmissions.

Blank (i)	Blank (ii)	Blank (iii)
Ⓐ disclosure	Ⓓ shared with	Ⓖ clandestine
Ⓑ decorum	Ⓔ concealed from	Ⓗ overt
Ⓒ suppression	Ⓕ approved through	Ⓘ audacious

7. The lawyers are at odds with one another concerning their beliefs; while one regards capital punishment as (i)_____, the other deems it (ii)_____.

Blank (i)	Blank (ii)
Ⓐ prudent	Ⓓ archaic
Ⓑ illicit	Ⓔ unscrupulous
Ⓒ conscionable	Ⓕ boorish

8. In spite of the recession and the failing housing market, the realtor sold many homes and made _____ amount of money this year.

Ⓐ a paltry
Ⓑ a rigorous
Ⓒ an obsolete
Ⓓ a boundless
Ⓔ an exorbitant
Ⓕ a resilient

9. Calinda had long eschewed risky investments, but something about the Silverwater deal intrigued her; she invested in the high-risk stock despite her aversion to _____ financial ventures.

Ⓐ convoluted
Ⓑ precarious
Ⓒ callous
Ⓓ fastidious
Ⓔ impervious
Ⓕ speculative

10. The professor was usually _____ instructor, fussing over grammatical structure and diction, but upon recovering from her grave illness she no longer focused on rules or attended to minute details.

Ⓐ a punctilious
Ⓑ a banal
Ⓒ a pedantic
Ⓓ an ebullient
Ⓔ a petulant
Ⓕ an enigmatic

Similarity Question Stems

"One Way Words" are another type of Fill-in-the-Blank road sign. These context clue words indicate that an idea is traveling in the same direction as a previous idea; the word or phrase in the blank is similar to a word or idea that already exists in the sentence. Let's study an example:

> Organic food is more costly to grow as well as more _____ to purchase than conventionally grown produce, mainly due to the price of labor and management used in place of chemicals.

The phrase *as well as* indicates that the sentence is continuing with a word that is similar in meaning to *costly*. The context clue *to purchase* also points to the meaning of the required word. The best prephrase is *expensive*.

Consider another Similarity Question Stem:

> The media reported that the defendant was upset—even _____ by some accounts—over the news that she was not going to be allowed bail.

The direction clue—the word *even*—indicates that the word in the blank is similar to the word *upset*. In fact, *even* reveals that the word in the blank is of a higher degree of agitation than just being upset. Accurate prephrases include *hysterical* or *distraught*.

Like contrast sentences, Similarity Question Stems may use direction words:

ONE WAY →	*One Way Words*	ONE WAY →
	equally	
and	similar	even
also	similarly	eventually
akin	moreover	almost
as well as	together with	corresponds to
in addition to	in like fashion	correspondingly
related	in like manner	parallel
coupled with	analogous to	just as
identically	comparable	same as
alike	comparatively	not only...but also
like	by the same token	both...and
likewise		not just...but

The most widely used One Way Words are conjunctions, such as *and*, *as well as*, *not only...but also*, and *moreover*:

> The investigation led police to three of the city's most prominent lawyers, who were _____ *and* suspended by the state bar association for participating in the dangerous scheme.

Notice that it is impossible to perfectly prephrase this blank, but that you can make many educated guesses: *fined*, *reprimanded*, *punished*, and *arrested* are just a few. Combined with our own logic, the One Way Word *and* lets us know that the blank has a negative context, similar to *suspended*.

Not all Similarity Question Stems can be prephrased perfectly, but the One Way Words should give you enough context to make a general and reliable prediction for the word or phrase that completes the blank.

Punctuation context clues are also prevalent in Similarity Question Stems. An adjective followed by a comma and an adjective blank (i.e. adj. *happy*, _____) always indicates that the missing adjective is similar in meaning to the prior adjective. We can verify that the blank requires an adjective by looking at the answer choices. Study an example:

> Even the defense had to admit—albeit grudgingly—that the prosecution presented an intelligent, _____ argument that created reasonable doubt for the jury.

A	artistic
B	faulty
C	sound
D	impartial
E	logical
F	deceptive

4

One Way clues may appear as:
- a conjunction
- an adjective followed by a comma
- a colon or semicolon
- a synonym

Since all of the answer choices are adjectives, we know that the blank requires an adjective. It also follows the adjective *intelligent* and is separated by a comma (*intelligent*, _____). Therefore, the word in the blank will be similar in meaning to *intelligent*. The synonym pair that is closest in meaning to intelligent is (C) *sound* and (E) *logical*.

Note that the first adjective can also be the missing word:

> Even the defense had to admit—albeit grudgingly—that the prosecution presented an _____, logical argument that created reasonable doubt for the jury.

When faced with two adjectives separated by a comma, know that the adjectives are always similar in meaning.

Colons and semicolons are the most commonly used road signs to signal similarity. These symbols join two closely related independent clauses; the clauses are so closely related in Fill-in-the-Blank questions that the second clause often paraphrases or summarizes the first clause. Let's look at a basic question:

> The veterinarian treats a _____ of animals: pet owners of a diverse array of species seek her medical expertise.

Synonyms are often the best context clues in Similarity Question Stems and this question is a great example. The blank is a synonym for *diverse array*. In cases like this one, you do not need to create a new prephrase, but can simply insert the synonym in the blank:

> The veterinarian treats a *diverse array* of animals: pet owners of a diverse array of species seek her medical expertise.

Consider another question, this one with a semicolon and the blank in the second independent clause:

> Charles was an accomplished traveler; he had _____ over 60 countries and documented his travels in his blog.

The blank is synonymous with *traveled to*, a clue we garnered from *traveler*. While colons and semicolons may indicate a Similarity Question Stem, they are not exclusive to this type of question. You may see these punctuation marks in all sentence types.

Synonym clues can appear in any sentence and are not necessarily bound to sentences with colons or semicolons:

> The veterinarian treats a _____ of animals, which is why pet owners of a diverse array of species seek her medical expertise.

> An accomplished traveler, Charles had _____ over 60 countries and documented his travels in his blog.

> Olivia was frightened by her recent hospital visit, a reaction that surprised her since she had never been _____ of medical procedures before.

Like the second example in this chapter, some Similarity Question Stems involve the word *even* to indicate a greater degree of intensity among adjectives. Consider an example:

> Most reporters find the actress disagreeable, even _____; in a recent interview the woman actually antagonized a journalist by calling his questions dull and repetitive.

4

TIPS and TRICKS
The use of the word "even" before a blank indicates the answer will have a greater degree of intensity than the previous adjective or adverb.

The context clue *even* reveals that the word in the blank will be of more extreme degree than the previous adjective, *disagreeable*. The simplest prephrase is *very disagreeable*, but others include *mean*, *nasty*, or *hateful*, because they demonstrate a greater degree of disagreeableness.

Note that the blank might take the place of the first, lesser adjective instead:

> Most reporters find the actress _____, even hostile; in a recent interview the woman actually antagonized a journalist by calling his questions dull and repetitive.

The correct answer in this case must have a lesser degree of hostility.

In this case, the word in the blank will be less negative than *hostile*, as indicated by the presence of *even*. Good prephrases include *unfriendly*, *disagreeable*, and *unkind*.

Just as dual blank Contrast Question Stems can be impossible to prephrase, dual blank Similarity Question Stems may leave you stumped when trying to predict an answer. Consider an example:

> The amateur poker player (i)_____ so often that he was labeled a (ii)_____ by all of the casino managers in town.

There are many verbs that can satisfy the first blank and an equal number of nouns to complete the second blank (*won/winner*, *lost/loser*, *bet/gambler*, etc.). For questions like these, review each answer choice and try to find the pair of words that has a similar relationship:

> The amateur poker player (i)_____ so often that he was labeled a (ii)_____ by all of the casino managers in town.

Blank (i)	Blank (ii)
Ⓐ wagered	Ⓓ swindler
Ⓑ disappeared	Ⓔ traitor
Ⓒ cheated	Ⓕ nuisance

Dual blank Similarity Questions are often difficult to prephrase when the two blanks are synonyms for one another.

The choices in (C) and (D), *cheated* and *swindler*, are related in meaning, and thus the best answer for this question.

Similarity Question Stems are closely related to Definition Question Stems, which we will cover in the next section, and are often used in combination with other types of sentences.

Similarity Question Stems Problem Set

Each of the sentences or paragraphs below has a word or set of words that has been omitted. From the answer choices, choose the word or set of words that best completes the meaning of the sentence. Answers begin on page 88.

1. The artist presented several of her pieces, explaining her inspiration for each of the lifelike, _____ paintings that seemed more like photographs than painted images.

Ⓐ arid
Ⓑ apt
Ⓒ petty
Ⓓ vivid
Ⓔ tactful

2. Most of Dr. Trice's scientific peers found her research on (i)_____ creatures (ii)_____, even ludicrous; few biologists believed in werewolves, vampires, or demons.

Blank (i)	Blank (ii)
Ⓐ preternatural	Ⓓ methodical
Ⓑ indigenous	Ⓔ laughable
Ⓒ endangered	Ⓕ redundant

3. In the 1950s, (i) _____ believed that the inhabitants of the uncharted, (ii)_____ island were best left alone; repeated contact with the outside world would only (iii) _____ the island's culture and regime.

Blank (i)	Blank (ii)	Blank (iii)
Ⓐ anthropologists	Ⓓ indigenous	Ⓖ damage
Ⓑ historians	Ⓔ insular	Ⓗ advance
Ⓒ philanthropists	Ⓕ traversed	Ⓘ alarm

4. The school board members were (i)_____ about the district's declining enrollment but the loss of federal funding was equally (ii)_____.

Blank (i)	Blank (ii)
Ⓐ nonchalant	Ⓓ worrisome
Ⓑ aloof	Ⓔ treacherous
Ⓒ disconcerted	Ⓕ culpable

5. Mrs. Vandercook was known for her _____; her exquisite dinner parties were the epitome of grace and _____.

Blank (i)	Blank (ii)
Ⓐ eloquence	Ⓓ refinement
Ⓑ cultivation	Ⓔ whimsy
Ⓒ judgment	Ⓕ audacity

6. The article in the local newspaper painted Dominic as (i)_____ financial manager, causing (ii)_____ to build among his clientele. He worked relentlessly to reverse the damage caused by report, but nothing could save the business; as quickly as he rose to affluence he fell to (iii)_____.

Blank (i)	Blank (ii)	Blank (iii)
Ⓐ an astute	Ⓓ distrust	Ⓖ insolvency
Ⓑ a cunning	Ⓔ assurance	Ⓗ opulence
Ⓒ a candid	Ⓕ dejection	Ⓘ despondency

7. While my family has been described as _____ , most of us are not greedy enough to truly fit the definition of the word.

Ⓐ obsolete
Ⓑ lugubrious
Ⓒ avaricious
Ⓓ disingenuous
Ⓔ mundane

8. Many of the musician's songs express feelings of loss and sorrow that reflect the _____ life he led.

A naive
B consecrated
C sustained
D pristine
E grievous
F mournful

9. The morning of graduation dawned bright and sunny, and despite the melancholy mood the previous evening, Will's disposition corresponded with the new day; he was _____ in anticipation of the afternoon's festivities.

A enervated
B listless
C lighthearted
D sanguine
E pensive
F somber

10. Citing the _____ of support for the proposal, the mayor asserted that he could not entertain its suggestions with such a dearth of the community's vote.

A abundance
B paucity
C scarcity
D plethora
E veracity
F inquiry

Definition Question Stems

Definition Question Stems live up to their name; the question stem provides a definition for a word or for a blank in the sentence. There are two key parts to these sentences: the word being defined and the definition of the word. Let's familiarize ourselves with a sample question before continuing our discussion:

> The museum curator explained that when the computer replaced the typewriter, the predecessor became _____, outdated and no longer in use.

The word in the blank is defined by *outdated and no longer in use*. Definition Question Stems are easy to prephrase because you can use part or all of the definition as your actual prediction:

> The museum curator explained that when the computer replaced the typewriter, the predecessor became *outdated and no longer in use....*

Definition Question Stems do not typically use direction words. Instead they use a limited number of sentence structures to indicate their solution method.

By far the most common sentence structure is illustrated in the example we just studied. The sentence contains a defined word near or at the end of an independent clause followed by a comma and a definition of the word. The blank is frequently used in place of the word being defined:

> Alicia's coworkers thought her husband was a _____, someone who is ill-mannered and rude.

The blank is defined by *someone who is ill-mannered and rude*, which occurs in the dependent clause after the blank and a comma. Try another:

> The new psychology textbook was highly recommended by the department because it was _____, both brief and comprehensive.

The word that completes the blank is defined by *both brief and comprehensive*, again in a phrase after the blank and a comma. Consider one more:

> The disgraced candidate _____ his face, covering it with his hands to avoid media scrutiny.

The blank here is defined by *covering*, which occurs in a dependent clause after an independent clause.

Definition questions require you to name a word based on a definition or provide part of that definition given the word.

Definition question stems do not use direction words.

Most Definition Question Stems that use this structure require a noun or adjective to complete the blank, but notice the last example is missing a verb. It is quite possible that the blank could also require an adverb. Knowing the part of speech that completes the blank is not essential, but you should definitely understand the structure of these sentences:

> *Definition Question Stem Structures:*
> Independent clause ending in _____, definition of blank
> Independent clause with _____ near end, definition of blank

In the previous examples, the blank represented the word being defined. A similar structure might be used, but this time the blank is part of the definition of the word that occurs at or near the end of the independent clause:

> Alicia's coworkers thought her boyfriend was a boor, someone who is _____ and rude.

The defined word is *boor*, and the definition, *someone who is _____ and rude*, contains the blank. Look at the second one:

> The new psychology textbook was highly recommended by the department because it was concise, both brief and _____.

In this example, part of the definition of *concise* is missing. Now examine the last one:

> The disgraced candidate shrouded his face, _____ it with his hands to avoid media scrutiny.

The word *shrouded* is being defined by the dependent clause, part of which has been replaced by a blank.

The structure for these sentences looks the same as the sentences on the previous page, but the blank is used in the definition:

> *Definition Question Stem Structure:*
> Independent clause with defined word, definition contains _____
> Independent clause with defined word near end, definition contains _____

Another common Definition Question Stem structure involves colons or semicolons. In some sentences with a colon, the structure is nearly identical to the examples on the previous page, but a colon is used in place of a comma:

> The new psychology textbook was highly recommended by the department because it was _____: both brief and comprehensive.

The blank of a Definition question can be in place of the word being defined or in place of a word from the definition.

Confidence Quotation
"Whatever the mind can conceive it can achieve."
W. Clement Stone, author & businessman

Colons and semicolons can be used with two independent clauses, where the second clause defines a word in the first clause. Consider a sentence with a semicolon:

> Alicia's coworkers thought her boyfriend was a _____; he was ill-mannered and rude.

The second independent clause, *he was ill-mannered and rude*, defines the blank in the first independent clause. The same structure can be used with a colon:

> The new psychology textbook was highly recommended by the department because it was _____: it is both brief and comprehensive.

The second independent clause defines the blank in the first.

As with the structures using commas, the blank can be either the defined word, as we saw above, or part of the definition:

> Alicia's coworkers thought her boyfriend was a boor; he is _____ and rude.

> The new psychology textbook was highly recommended by the department because it was concise: it is both brief and _____.

These structures are easy to identify:

> *Definition Question Stem Structures:*
> Independent clause ending in _____: definition of blank
> Independent clause with _____; independent clause with definition
> Independent clause with _____: independent clause with definition
> Independent clause with defined word; ind. clause with _____ in definition
> Independent clause with defined word: ind. clause with _____ in definition

An overwhelming majority of Definition Question Stems are single blank questions, but you may run into a dual-blank Definition question that uses these same sentence and punctuation structures:

> The mayor's speech was _____ and _____; it was powerfully moving and advocated drastic changes.

The first blank is defined by *powerfully moving*; the second blank is defined by *advocated drastic changes*.

Just as with single blank questions, dual blanks may provide the defined words and remove parts of the definitions:

> The mayor's speech was eloquent and radical; it was powerfully _____ and _____ drastic changes.

Or they may provide only one of the defined words and remove part of its definition:

> The mayor's speech was eloquent and _____; it was powerfully _____ and advocated drastic changes.

Dual Blank questions can contain two definitions.

4

The final common pattern might be miscategorized as a Cause and Effect Question Stem (covered in the next section) given that the pattern uses the direction word *because*, but the definition format is the key to the sentence. Let's examine a sentence using this structure:

> The solider was often described as _____ because he was aggressively hostile to other members of the platoon.

The word that fits in the blank is defined by the clause after *because*, the conjunction: *he was aggressively hostile to other members of the platoon.* Look at another:

> The glass in the shower is considered _____ because it prevents light from passing through.

Again, the clause after *because* (*it prevents light from passing through*) defines the word in the blank.

Most of these sentences use a variety of verbs (*described as, considered, categorized as, defined as, labeled, called,* etc.) with the defined word, and most include *because* before the provided definition. You should also watch for *since*; both of these conjunctions function just like a semicolon in other Definition Question Stems.

These sentences may also remove part of the definition and provide the defined word:

> The solider was often described as belligerent because he was aggressively _____ to other members of the platoon.

> The glass in the shower is considered opaque because it _____ light from passing through.

Although rare, the second independent clause could be subordinated and used as an introductory clause:

> Because the soldier was aggressively hostile to other members of the platoon, he was often described as _____.

Nearly all Definition Question Stems fit one of these structures. A random sentence might not follow any of the patterns, but is still solved by providing the defined word or part of the definition:

> The security guard was always on the lookout for danger and this _____ paid off when he thwarted a robbery at the store.

In this example, the word that best fits in the blank is defined by *always on the lookout for danger*. Just as with the other sentences in this section, the defined word might be provided while the definition has a portion removed:

> The security guard was always on the lookout for _____ and this vigilance paid off when he thwarted a robbery at the store.

Definition question stems are often combined with other types of question stems, which we will investigate later in this chapter.

Definition Question Stems Problem Set

Each of the sentences or paragraphs below has a word or set of words that has been omitted. From the answer choices, choose the word or set of words that best completes the meaning of the sentence. Answers begin on page 91.

1. Mrs. Rogers cited the Mugwumps' belief that society should be governed by its richest and most educated members as an example of the party's _____ ideals.

   Ⓐ bourgeois
   Ⓑ liberal
   Ⓒ elitist
   Ⓓ orthodox
   Ⓔ progressive

2. It enraged the citizens that the king considered himself _____, having unlimited authority over their daily lives.

   Ⓐ omnipotent
   Ⓑ motley
   Ⓒ militant
   Ⓓ lionized
   Ⓔ infantile

3. Historical scholars found the biography (i)_____ and incomplete; it was brimming with mistakes and (ii)_____ in coverage of important events.

Blank (i)	Blank (ii)
Ⓐ insufficient	Ⓓ incoherent
Ⓑ erroneous	Ⓔ crude
Ⓒ imprudent	Ⓕ deficient

4. The headmaster characterized the disrespectful girl as _____ because she lacked the seriousness needed to succeed at Wattswood Prep.

   Ⓐ indignant
   Ⓑ decadent
   Ⓒ exploitative
   Ⓓ reverent
   Ⓔ flippant

5. The meetings in which the group plotted to overthrow the despot were _____, executed with secrecy and held in undisclosed locations.

   Ⓐ specious
   Ⓑ obstinate
   Ⓒ clandestine
   Ⓓ eclectic
   Ⓔ incongruous

6. The island country was now home to thousands of exiles, people who had been _____ from their native lands for political unrest. One might expect these _____ to express animosity or disloyalty for the country that expelled them, but they possessed a surprising _____ to their homeland.

Blank (i)	Blank (ii)	Blank (iii)
Ⓐ chartered	Ⓓ expatriates	Ⓖ allegiance
Ⓑ sanctioned	Ⓔ constituents	Ⓗ hostility
Ⓒ banished	Ⓕ bureaucrats	Ⓘ reverence

7. The divorce lawyer was known for being _____ and _____; he was intensely passionate but at times overly aggressive.

Blank (i)	Blank (ii)
Ⓐ vehement	Ⓓ abrasive
Ⓑ apathetic	Ⓔ lucrative
Ⓒ ingenious	Ⓕ decisive

8. The comical illustration of the senator was obviously a caricature: it was a ludicrous _____ meant to draw attention to the woman's most noticeable physical traits.

Ⓐ amplification
Ⓑ exaggeration
Ⓒ abbreviation
Ⓓ epitome
Ⓔ idiosyncrasy
Ⓕ understatement

9. The foreign exchange student was disappointed to find his host family _____; they were cold and unwelcoming, which was unexpected given the warm and friendly letters they had sent before the exchange began.

Ⓐ archaic
Ⓑ inhospitable
Ⓒ unamiable
Ⓓ affable
Ⓔ humble
Ⓕ gracious

10. When dealing with rude customers, the manager showed admirable _____: he sustained patience and self-control.

Ⓐ autonomy
Ⓑ discord
Ⓒ forbearance
Ⓓ reciprocity
Ⓔ rashness
Ⓕ temperance

Cause and Effect Question Stems

Cause and Effect Question Stems contain two ideas, one of which causes the other. Look at an example:

> The photographer's images were consistently so _____ that the newspaper was forced to terminate his employment.

The sentence contains two ideas:

Cause: the photographer's images were consistently so _____
Effect: the newspaper was forced to terminate his employment

Cause and Effect Question Stems usually require you to draw logical conclusions. In this case, because the photographer was fired, you can conclude that something was wrong with his images. You cannot perfectly prephrase this sentence, but you can predict that the answer means something negative, like blurry, off-center, or out-of-focus. Safe, general prephrases include *bad, terrible,* or *disappointing*.

Try another:

> Once the police began using tear gas and arresting members of the mob, the rioters quickly _____, much to the relief of the store owners on the street.

The sentence has two cause and effect relationships:

Cause: the police began using tear gas and arresting members of the mob
Effect: the rioters quickly _____

Cause: the rioters quickly _____
Effect: the store owners on the street were relieved

The logical conclusion in the first relationship is that the rioters quickly left or dispersed once tear gas was used and arrests were made. It would be absurd for them to stay in such hazardous conditions.

The second relationship confirms our conclusion; the store owners felt relief when the rioters left. Because rioting involves violence (per the definition of rioting), the store owners were relieved when that threat was removed.

4

Cause and Effect questions require you to draw a logical conclusion.

Cause and Effect Question Stems may use some direction words to indicate their causal relationship:

Although it can be used in Definition Question Stems, the word "because" usually signifies a Cause and Effect question stem.

Cause and Effect Words

	in order to	
as	when	therefore
as a result	so	thereupon
because	so much so that	resulting
cause	so then	since
consequently	for this reason	subsequently
as a consequence	for this purpose	accordingly
in consequence	hence	thus
due to	otherwise	once
leading to	when	after

These sentences are not as orderly and predictable as Contrast, Similarity, and Definition Question Stems. There are some sentence structures that can pinpoint Cause and Effect Question Stems, but they are not used as often or as rigidly as the others. The most common structure involves the use of *because* as a conjunction. It may be used in the middle of two clauses, as in the following:

> The _____ of the new pool was delayed several days because the equipment operator had trouble maneuvering the backhoe.

Or it can be placed at the beginning of the sentence as a subordinating conjunction:

> Because the equipment operator had trouble maneuvering the backhoe, the _____ of the new pool was delayed several days.

No matter where the conjunction occurs, the sentence has the same cause and effect relationship:

> *Cause*: the equipment operator had trouble maneuvering the backhoe
> *Effect*: the _____ of the new pool was delayed several days

What would a backhoe be doing at a new pool site? Digging it! A logical prephrase is *construction* or *excavation*.

Other subordinating conjunctions, such as *after*, *as*, *once*, *since*, and *when* can be used in a similar manner to create a cause and effect relationship. Note that the blank can occur in all parts of the relationship. You might find it in the cause:

The company was quick to hire Peter since he was one of the most
_____ graphic designers in the country.

Or in the effect:

The company was _____ to hire Peter since he was one of the most
successful graphic designers in the country.

Or in both parts of the sentence:

The company was _____ to hire Peter since he was one of the most
_____ graphic designers in the country.

Some Cause and Effect Question Stems do not use any of the direction
words and you must rely solely on logic to recognize and solve them:

Worried about her previously _____ GRE scores, Sabrina decided to
spend the summer studying for the exam before retaking it in October.

There are no clue words to indicate cause and effect, but the relationship
between the two ideas is still easy to identify:

Cause: Sabrina was worried about her previously _____ GRE
  scores
Effect: she decided to spend the summer studying for the exam before
  retaking it in October

If Sabrina was worried about her past scores and was studying to retake
the test, it is safe to prephrase *low*, *mediocre*, or *poor* for the blank.

When employed, Cause and Effect Question Stems are frequently used in
conjunction with another question stem type, combinations which we will
explore in the next section.

Cause and Effect
questions do not
always use Cause
and Effect
words.

Cause and Effect Question Stems Problem Set

> Each of the sentences or paragraphs below has a word or set of words that has been omitted. From the answer choices, choose the word or set of words that best completes the meaning of the sentence. Answers begin on page 94.

1. Because cell phone technology has existed for only a short time, scientists do not yet know the _____ effects of its radiation on our health.

   - Ⓐ vague
   - Ⓑ hopeful
   - Ⓒ fruitless
   - Ⓓ fleeting
   - Ⓔ enduring

2. Irritated by the constant _____ between the two news anchors, the program director enrolled them both in a course designed to build teamwork skills.

   - Ⓐ bickering
   - Ⓑ complaining
   - Ⓒ wavering
   - Ⓓ discussion
   - Ⓔ carping

3. An influx of television shows that _____ lawyers and their profession led to _____ of attorneys in the 1980s.

Blank (i)	Blank (ii)
Ⓐ accentuated	Ⓓ an indictment
Ⓑ extolled	Ⓔ a surfeit
Ⓒ berated	Ⓕ a mandate

4. When threatened with drowning, fire ants join together to form an air-tight raft, a behavior that likely evolved because their native habitats are prone to _____.

   - Ⓐ bombast
   - Ⓑ drought
   - Ⓒ temerity
   - Ⓓ deluge
   - Ⓔ circumlocution

5. Once the doctor was publicly _____ for his advancements in cancer research, he was _____ by several drug companies competing to add such an innovator to their staffs.

Blank (i)	Blank (ii)
Ⓐ admonished	Ⓓ denounced
Ⓑ commended	Ⓔ honored
Ⓒ satirized	Ⓕ courted

6. The children at the magic show were understandably _____ by the _____ magician's impressive sleight-of-hand and astounding illusions.

Blank (i)	Blank (ii)
Ⓐ enthralled	Ⓓ dapper
Ⓑ chagrined	Ⓔ adept
Ⓒ disillusioned	Ⓕ wieldy

7. Sugary soft-drinks can _____ new cases of diabetes; therefore, people who are at risk of developing the disease should _____ their consumption.

Blank (i)	Blank (ii)
Ⓐ precipitate	Ⓓ indulge in
Ⓑ exacerbate	Ⓔ partake in
Ⓒ bolster	Ⓕ abstain from

8. After the failure of the outrageously expensive *Cleopatra* in 1963, studio executives _____ epic dramas and instead sought low-budget independent films.

Ⓐ relished
Ⓑ rebuffed
Ⓒ spurned
Ⓓ augmented
Ⓔ endured
Ⓕ espoused

9. The defense lawyer found _____ in the prosecution's case—specifically that the accused could not be in two places at the same time—which resulted in an acquittal of defendant.

Ⓐ an accord
Ⓑ a contour
Ⓒ an exposition
Ⓓ a discrepancy
Ⓔ an incongruity
Ⓕ a perspective

10. In 1861, the United States had an overwhelming majority of its experienced soldiers stationed along the western frontier, and consequently had to rely on _____ at the Battle of Bull Run.

Ⓐ courtiers
Ⓑ mercenaries
Ⓒ patriarchs
Ⓓ prodigies
Ⓔ greenhorns
Ⓕ neophytes

Combination Question Stems

So far we have studied question stems with a single structure: Contrast, Similarity, Definition, or Cause and Effect. Many GRE sentences, however, contain a combination of two sentence structures, like the following:

Despite Kalia's efforts to (i)_____ with her sister, the two remained (ii)_____, no longer close or affectionate.

Blank (i)	Blank (ii)
Ⓐ comply	Ⓓ jaded
Ⓑ coincide	Ⓔ estranged
Ⓒ reconcile	Ⓕ bereaved

This sentence is a combination of Contrast and Definition structures.

Contrast: *Despite Kalia's efforts to _____ with her sister, the two remained _____*

Definition: *the two remained _____, no longer close or affectionate*

Combination question stems provide more context with which to work.

The first part of the sentence has two blanks that contradict each other. The dependent clause, *no longer close or affectionate*, defines the second blank. It is difficult to predict the two blanks without the dependent clause, so start with the definition of the second blank. It requires a word or phrase meaning *no longer close or affectionate*. Good prephrases for the second blank include *distant*, *at odds*, or *apart*. Once you choose this prephrase, you can predict the first blank with an opposite meaning, such as *make up*, *resolve issues*, or *fix things*.

Most Combination Question Stems have more than one blank, but an occasional stem may only have a single blank. These are easier questions, though, because you have two logical contexts to use for solving the question. Consider the previous question with the first blank removed:

Despite Kalia's efforts to reconcile with her sister, the two remained _____, no longer close or affectionate.

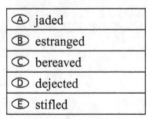

Ⓐ jaded
Ⓑ estranged
Ⓒ bereaved
Ⓓ dejected
Ⓔ stifled

Not only is the blank defined by *no longer close or affectionate*, it has a meaning opposite of *reconcile*. You have twice as much context with which to work when there is only a single blank so the difficulty level is lowered.

While Sentence Equivalence questions are always a single sentence, Text Completion questions can have one to five sentences. Question stems with multiple sentences usually contain a combination of Contrast, Similarity, Definition, and Cause and Effect clues. Let's look at an example:

Rossi gained fame for his paintings in the 1920s but was generally (i)_____ by his (ii)_____. They characterized him as an artist who lacked the imagination to create anything truly original and the self-awareness to perceive his own shortcomings. Modern critics, however, hail his (iii)_____ work for the attention it has garnered for the original masterpieces and artists.

Blank (i)	Blank (ii)	Blank (iii)
Ⓐ lauded	Ⓓ proponents	Ⓖ prolific
Ⓑ scorned	Ⓔ usurpers	Ⓗ whimsical
Ⓒ mimicked	Ⓕ contemporaries	Ⓘ derivative

In long passages, context clues are often found in surrounding sentences, rather than in the sentence that contains the blank.

The first blank has both a Contrast clue and a Definition clue. The conjunction *but* indicates that the blank has meaning somewhat opposite of *gained fame*, and it is defined by the characterization of Rossi by other artists. They believe he lacks imagination and self-awareness, so *scorned* is the best fit.

The second blank is difficult to prephrase until you reach the last sentence. The blank contrasts with *modern critics*, so *contemporaries* is the correct answer. Plus, the other two choices (*proponents* and *usurpers*) do not make sense in the blank.

The third blank is going to be similar to *lacked the imagination to create anything truly original*. This is confirmed by the cause and effect relationship in the last sentence: his unoriginal work caused attention for the originals. The best answer is *derivative*.

While some test takers fear longer question stems, you should welcome them on your GRE because they are often easier to solve. The text offers more information with which to work; in the question above, the first and third blanks had at least two clues to help you select the right answer choices. Keep in mind, too, that Text Completion questions with more than two sentences do not occur frequently. You will likely only have one or two to tackle on your test.

Combination Question Stems Problem Set

Each of the sentences or paragraphs below has a word or set of words that has been omitted. From the answer choices, choose the word or set of words that best completes the meaning of the sentence. Answers begin on page 97.

Answers begin on page 97.

1. Puzzle experts insist that a good riddle should intrigue and _____, rather than prove easy to solve.

Ⓐ dispel
Ⓑ query
Ⓒ lament
Ⓓ debilitate
Ⓔ confound

2. Because the cheetah is known for its (i)_____, the sports car company selected the swift animal as its (ii)_____, the symbol by which a business is known.

Blank (i)	Blank (ii)
Ⓐ habitat	Ⓓ motto
Ⓑ speed	Ⓔ crest
Ⓒ loyalty	Ⓕ trademark

3. Although the woman observed the suspects for several hours, the police were unable to (i)_____ them because her descriptions were (ii)_____.

Blank (i)	Blank (ii)
Ⓐ apprehend	Ⓓ vague
Ⓑ impede	Ⓔ dubious
Ⓒ sanction	Ⓕ hasty

4. Unlike most writers who (i)_____ their articles, this prize-winning author insists on publishing (ii)_____ pieces; her essays are in their original form, unaltered from her handwritten journal to the printed page.

Blank (i)	Blank (ii)
Ⓐ polish	Ⓓ flawless
Ⓑ translate	Ⓔ pristine
Ⓒ transcribe	Ⓕ refined

5. A (i)_____ between the two partners, caused by a disagreement about the future focus of the company, led to a (ii)_____ of the business.

Blank (i)	Blank (ii)
Ⓐ breach	Ⓓ consolidation
Ⓑ covenant	Ⓔ inquisition
Ⓒ rift	Ⓕ dissolution

6. Although the anti-wrinkle cream was (i)_____ by doctors, further research proved that it was actually ineffective and even (ii)_____ if used in excess.

Blank (i)	Blank (ii)
Ⓐ censured	Ⓓ curative
Ⓑ advertised	Ⓔ efficacious
Ⓒ endorsed	Ⓕ noxious

7. It is (i)_____ that many contemporary critics would describe Caterina van Hemessen as an especially talented painter, but most would agree that she was a (ii)_____ in self-portraiture. The Flemish Renaissance painter was the first to paint herself seated at an easel, a trend that was followed by Rembrant, Van Gogh, Chagall, and countless others. Although van Hemessen was quite a successful painter in the sixteenth century, her work now is described as plain and even (iii)_____. Critics acknowledge, however, that she was never able to fully develop her talent given that women were forbidden from studying the human form and forced to give up their craft upon marriage.

Blank (i)	Blank (ii)	Blank (iii)
Ⓐ common	Ⓓ pioneer	Ⓖ unemotional
Ⓑ unlikely	Ⓔ speculator	Ⓗ responsive
Ⓒ feasible	Ⓕ entrepreneur	Ⓘ intense

8. Obstetricians, in addition to the general populace, have become somewhat (i)_____ about twin pregnancies in large part because of the increased frequency of multiple gestation in today's society. They see no reason to initiate ancillary care for women who are carrying two babies. Doctors who treat twin pregnancies as high risk situations are therefore often considered (ii)_____ by peers and the public alike. Research suggests, however, that twin pregnancies are indeed worthy of (ii)_____ care; medical professionals who follow the professional standards' recommendations for vigilance in twin pregnancies report higher rates of live births and healthy infants, as well as lower rates of maternal and fetal complications, than those doctors who do not follow such strict protocol.

Blank (i)	Blank (ii)	Blank (iii)
Ⓐ blasé	Ⓓ overly cautious	Ⓖ less guarded
Ⓑ jaded	Ⓔ utterly rash	Ⓗ equally proficient
Ⓒ wearied	Ⓕ slightly unreliable	Ⓘ more diligent

Chapter Summary

There are four types of question stems in Fill-in-the-Blank questions.

Contrast Question Stems

- These use clues to indicate that the sentence is moving in the opposite direction of a previously stated idea.

- Contrast Questions usually employ U-Turn Words to show contrast.

- Contrast Questions may use a subordinating conjunction, a coordinating conjunction, or a semicolon.

Similarity Question Stems

- These use clues to indicate that the sentence is continuing in the same direction as a previously stated idea.

- Similarity Questions usually employ One Way Words to show continuation.

Definition Question Stems

- These questions require you to define a given word or provide the word given the definition.

- Definition Questions do not have a common vocabulary indicating the question type, but specific sentence structures can reveal their function.

Cause and Effect Question Stems

- These questions require you to complete a sentence by drawing a logical conclusion.

- Cause and Effect Questions usually employ Cause and Effect Words.

Combination Question Stems

- Some questions are a combination of two or more of the four different types of question stems.

- These questions are usually less difficult because they provide much more context than questions with a single question type.

Deconstruct the Question Stem Answer Key

Contrast Question Stems Problem Set—Page 60

1. B   Possible Prephrases: outer, outside, outward

   The U-Turn words *Rather than* indicate that the blank is an antonym of *inner*. Choice (B), *physical*, is the best answer.

   Vocabulary:
   elegant: graceful in appearance

2. (i) A   (ii) D   Possible Prephrases: (i) no effort into, not into, not   (ii) excited, happy

   The U-Turn word *but* reveals that the first blank has a meaning opposite of *put tremendous effort into*. Choice (A)–neglect–is the best fit.

   The second blank is solved using the U-Turn *Unlike*. Alice is unlike other professors who neglect their teaching duties. Only (D)–*passionate*–makes sense.

   Vocabulary:
   deplore: to strongly disapprove of   *ambivalent*: having mixed feelings

3. (i) A   (ii) F   Possible Prephrases: (i) exciting, fascinating, thrilling   (ii) boredom

   The word *but* is a U-Turn conjunction, showing that the audience felt one way for the first blank and the opposite way for the second blank. Logic dictates that a business-based audience would be interested in stock market tales but bored with stories about farm taxes. The context clue *droned* supports our prephrase for the second blank.

   Vocabulary:
   emphatic: with emphasis   *indolence*: laziness
   strenuous: vigorous   *ennui*: boredom
   trepidation: fear

4. B   Possible Prephrases: undeveloped, developing

   Although, a U-Turn word, indicates that the blank is the opposite of *developed*. Choice (B), *emerging*, is best.

   Vocabulary:
   defunct: no longer in use   *bureaucratic*: overly concerned with procedure
   emerging: newly formed   *prolific*: highly productive
   preeminent: superior

5. (i) B (ii) D Possible Prephrases: (i) stop, slow, decrease (ii) were involved in, took part in

The U-Turn words *Paradoxically* and *actually* indicate that the result has the opposite, rather than intended, effect. The intended effect of Prohibition was to stop crime, but Prohibition actually increased it. Choice (A) is best.

Vocabulary:
curb (vb.): control   *amplify*: to enlarge
sever: to separate

6. (i) A (ii) D (iii) H Possible Prephrases: (i) openness, honesty (ii) gave, provided, told (iii) open

The first blank contains a word that means the opposite of *secrecy*, as indicated by *instead of*. The second blank contains a word the shows the truth was exposed and not *hidden*. The final blank is similar to the first.

Vocabulary:
disclosure: exposure; revelation   *clandestine*: secret
decorum: proper behavior   *overt*: open
suppression: withholding information   *audacious*: extremely bold

7. (i) C (ii) E Possible Prephrases: Impossible to prephrase, but blanks have opposite meaning

It is impossible to accurately prephrase this sentence, but the two blanks have opposite meaning. There are just too many pairs of antonyms (fair/unfair, right/wrong, cruel/humane, etc) that fit the blanks. You can eliminate (A), (B), (D), and (F), though, because the words have no antonyms.

Vocabulary:
prudent: careful and sensible   *archaic*: old and outdated
illicit (vb.): illegal   *unscrupulous*: immoral
unconscionable: moral   *boorish*: rude

8. D and E   Possible Prephrases: a large, a huge, a tremendous, an excessive

The U-Turn words *in spite of* indicates that the expected outcome does not happen, but rather the opposite outcome results. We would expect a recession and failing housing market to decrease sales and profit. However, the opposite is true, so the realtor made a lot of money.

Vocabulary:
paltry: ridiculously small
rigorous: rigidly accurate; strict
obsolete: no longer in use

boundless: vast
exorbitant: highly excessive
resilient: easily recovering or rebounding

9. B and F   Possible Prephrases: risky, high-risk

The U-Turn word *despite* reveals that Calinda's actions went against her normal behavior. She invested in a high-risk stock despite her tendency to stay away from risky stocks.

Vocabulary:
aversion: a feeling of intense dislike
convoluted: complicated
precarious: risky; unstable transactions
callous: insensitive; emotionally hardened

fastidious: giving careful attention to detail
convoluted: complicated
speculative: relating to risky business

10. A and C   Possible Prephrases: picky, detailed, demanding

The U-Turn word *but* indicates that the professor is different than she used to be. Now she does not focus on rules or small details, but she did before. The word in the blank describes her previous behavior.

Vocabulary:
punctilious: extremely attentive to details
banal: repeated too often;overfamiliar
pedantic: overly focused on details while teaching

ebullient: extremely excited or enthusiastic
petulant: easily irritated over small issues
enigmatic: puzzling

1. D   Possible Prephrases: realistic, lifelike, clear

   The presence of an adjective (*lifelike*) followed by a comma and an adjective blank indicates the blank contains a word similar in meaning to lifelike. This is affirmed by the context clue *seemed more like photographs than painted images*. The best answer is *vivid*, (D).

   Vocabulary:
   arid: dry; lacking rainfall   *apt*: intelligent
   petty: of little importance; minor   *vivid*: realistic; full of life
   tactful: considerate in dealing with others and avoiding giving offense

2. A and E   Possible Prephrases: (i) magical, supernatural   (ii) silly, absurd, slightly ludicrous

   The presence of *even* indicates that the second blank is a word with a lesser degree of intensity than *ludicrous*; *laughable* is the only answer in the second column with similar meaning. The first blank is defined by *werewolves, vampires, or demons*. They are *preternatural* creatures.

   Vocabulary:
   preternatural: supernatural   *indigenous*: native to

3. A, E, and G   Possible Prephrases: (i) cultural scientists   (ii) uncharted, isolated   (iii) hurt

   This sentence has an adjective (*uncharted*) followed by a comma and an adjective blank. This indicates that the word in the second blank is similar to the adjective just before it. The context clue *alone* confirms our thesis. If the inhabitants were best left alone, then contact would cause problems for the island.

   Vocabulary:
   anthropologists: people who study human culture   *philanthropists*: appeal; attractiveness
   indigenous native to; natural   *insular*: isolated
   traversed: traveled

4. C and D   Possible Prephrases: (i) upset, worried   (ii) upsetting, worrisome

The context of the sentence (the district's declining enrollment and the loss of federal funding) indicate that the members will be upset or worried. Once you prephrase the first blank, you simply need the noun form of the same word for the second blank (*upset . . upsetting, worried . . worrisome,* etc.).

Vocabulary:
nonchalant: coolly casual and unconcerned
aloof: reserved or disinterested
disconcerted: worried

treacherous: deceptive or untrustworthy
culpable: worthy of blame

5. B and D   Possible Prephrases: (i) grace, loveliness, charm   (ii) grace, loveliness, charm

The context clue word is *grace*; the word that goes in both blanks will be similar to grace. Many test takers mistakenly believe the *eloquence* in (A) is the same as *elegance*.

Vocabulary:
eloquence: fluent in use of language
refinement: elegance
audacity: boldness or daring

cultivation: elegance
whimsy: light and fancy humor

6. B, D, and G   Possible Prephrases: (i) bad   (ii) worry, distrust   (iii) poverty, bankruptcy

Many pairs of words can fit into the first sentence (great . . confidence, poor . . worry, lazy . . anger, etc.) but the second sentence indicates that these words have a negative connotation. The first two blanks will have similar words; the second word being caused by the first word (this question is also a great example of Cause and Effect Sentences, which are discussed later in the chapter). The third blank is completed by a word that is the opposite of *affluence*, or wealth.

Vocabulary:
affluence: wealth
astute: intelligent and clever
cunning: deceptive and sly
candid: open and straightforward

dejection: depression
insolvency: bankruptcy
opulence: wealth
despondency: hopelessness

7. C   Possible Prephrase: extremely stingy

The word in the blank is an extreme degree of *stingy*. The narrator claims "We've been called extremely stingy, but we aren't that stingy."

Vocabulary:
obsolete: no longer in use
lugubrious excessively sad and gloomy
avaricious: extremely greedy

disingenuous: insincere
mundane: ordinary and somewhat boring

8. E and F   Possible Prephrases: sad, sorrowful

The word that completes the blank has a meaning similar to *loss* and *sorrow*.

Vocabulary:
naive: lacking experience or judgment
consecrated: sacred
sustained: supported

pristine: pure, clean, or unused
grievous: sorrowful
mournful: sorrowful

9. C and D   Possible Prephrases: bright, happy, pleasant, cheerful

The word corresponded tells us that Will's mood was *bright and sunny* like the new day. Choice (A) is a popular wrong answer. Students assume it means *energized*, but it actually means the opposite. This word claims many victims on the GRE.

Vocabulary:
enervated: lacking strength or vigor
sanguine: optimistic and cheerful
somber: gloomy and serious

listless: spiritless; showing no interest
pensive: thoughtful

10. B and C   Possible Prephrases: lack, absence

Since *dearth* means *lack,* the proposal is lacking support.

Vocabulary:
dearth: lack
paucity: an insufficient quantity
veracity: truth or truthfulness

scarcity: lack
plethora: overabundance
inquiry: a question

THE POWERSCORE GRE VERBAL REASONING BIBLE

1. C   Possible Prephrases: snobby, pompous, aristocratic

    The example, *society should be governed by its richest and most educated members*, provides the definition for the blank.

    Vocabulary:
    bourgeois: middle-class   *orthodox*: customary; traditional
    elitist: belief in rule by the most intelligent and educated members of society

2. A   Possible Prephrase: having unlimited authority

    The blank is defined by the phrase *having unlimited authority*.

    Vocabulary:
    omnipotent: having great or unlimited power   *lionized*: treated as a celebrity
    motley: diverse   *infantile*: childish
    militant: aggressive; fighting for a cause

3. B and F   Possible Prephrases: (i) brimming with mistakes   (ii) lacking, incomplete

    In the second independent clause, *it was brimming with mistakes* defines the first blank. The word *incomplete* is defined by *and _____ in coverage.*

    Vocabulary:
    erroneous: mistaken; containing error   *incoherent*: lacking meaning
    imprudent: unwise   *crude*: blunt; lacking polish

4. E   Possible Prephrases: disrespectful, lacking seriousness

    The blank is defined by the clause (*she lacked the seriousness needed*) after the conjunction *because*.

    Vocabulary:
    indignant: angry due to unfairness   *reverent*: respectful
    decadent: morally declining; decaying   *flippant*: disrespectful; lacking seriousness
    exploitative: using selfishly

5.   C   Possible Prephrases: secret, undisclosed

The blank is defined by the dependent clause (*executed in secrecy and held in undisclosed locations*).

Vocabulary:
specious: plausible but false   *eclectic*: diverse
obstinate: extremely stubborn   *incongruous*: out of place; inconsistent
clandestine: secret

6.   C, D, and G   Possible Prephrases: (i) exiled, removed   (ii) exiles   (iii) loyalty

For the first blank, the dependent clause following the comma is defining *exiles*. The second blank is a noun synonymous with *exiles*. The third blank is a Contrast blank with a meaning opposite of *animosity or disloyalty*.

Vocabulary:
chartered: authorized to start a new branch   *constituents*: citizens who are represented by
government
sanctioned: approved   *bureaucrats*: officials in a government
expatriates: people banished from their country *reverence*: great respect

7.   A and D   Possible Prephrases: (i) intensely passionate   (ii) overly aggressive

The first blank is defined by *intensely passionate*. The second blank is defined by *overly aggressive*.

Vocabulary:
vehement: intensely passionate   *abrasive*: overly aggressive
apathetic: lacking emotion or enthusiasm *lucrative*: profitable; making money
ingenious: clever and inventive   *decisive*: determined; definite

8.   A and B   Possible Prephrase: caricature

The independent clause following the colon is defining the word *caricature*.

Vocabulary:
epitome: a perfect example   *idiosyncrasy*: a characteristic that is peculiar

9. B and C   Possible Prephrases: cold and unwelcoming

The independent clause following the semicolon is defining the word in the blank, therefore the best prephrase is cold and unwelcoming.

Vocabulary:
archaic: old

inhospitable: unwelcoming

unamiable: cold in manner; unfriendly

affable: friendly

humble: not arrogant or prideful; modest

gracious: pleasantly kind

10. C and F   Possible Prephrases: patience and self-control

The blank is defined by the second independent clause (*he sustained patience and self-control*).

Vocabulary:
autonomy: independence

discord: disagreement

forbearance: patient endurance; self-control

reciprocity: mutual exchange

rashness: action without proper consideration

temperance: self-restraint

1. E   Possible Prephrases: long-term, long time

    Cause: cell phone technology has existed for only a short time
    Effect: scientists do not yet know the _____ effects of its radiation on our health

    Vocabulary:
    vague: not clear   *fruitless*: useless
    fleeting: passing quickly

2. A   Possible Prephrases: arguing, fighting, inability to work as a team

    Cause: Irritated by the constant _____ between the two news anchors
    Effect: the program director enrolled them both in a course designed to build teamwork skills

    The anchors are obviously not working as a team, so the blank contains an action that is in contrast to teamwork.

3. B and E   Possible Prephrases: (i) featured, highlighted   (ii) a lot, an influx, an abundance

    Cause: an influx of television shows that _____ lawyers and their profession
    Effect: led to _____ of attorneys

    Vocabulary:
    extolled: praised   *surfeit*: an abundance
    berated: scolded   *mandate*: an order or command
    indictment: an accusation of wrongdoing

4. D   Possible Prephrases: flooding, excess water

    Cause: [fire ants] native habitats are prone to _____.
    Effect: fire ants join together to form an air-tight raft

    Vocabulary:
    bombast: pompous or pretentious talk or   *temerity*: fearless daring
    writing   *deluge*: flooding
    drought: period of excessively dry weather *circumlocution*: an indirect way of
                                                 expressing something

5. B and F   Possible Prephrases: (i) praised, applauded   (ii) pursued, approached, hired

Cause: the doctor was publicly _____ for his advancements in cancer research
Effect: he was _____ by several drug companies competing to add such an innovator to their staffs

Vocabulary:
admonished: warned or scolded   *denounced*: openly spoke out against
commended: praised   *courted*: wooed; attempted to seek favor of
satirized: ridiculed

6. A and E   Possible Prephrases: (i) excited, fascinated, puzzled   (ii) skillful, good

Cause: the _____ magician's impressive slight-of-hand and astounding illusions
Effect: the children at the magic show were understandably _____

Vocabulary:
enthralled: captivated   *dapper*: neat and trim
chagrined: disappointed; annoyed   *adept*: highly skilled
disillusioned: freed from illusions   *wieldy*: easy to handle

7. A and F   Possible Prephrases: (i) bring on, increase   (ii) avoid, stop

Cause: Sugary soft-drinks can _____ new cases of diabetes
Effect: people who are at risk of developing the disease should _____ their consumption

Vocabulary:
precipitate: to bring about abruptly   *indulge*: to yield to a desire
exacerbate: to increase harshness or bitterness   *partake*: to participate
bolster: to support and strengthen   *abstain*: to hold oneself back

8. B and C   Possible Prephrases: rejected, ignored, turned down

Cause: the failure of the outrageously expensive *Cleopatra*
Effect: studio executives _____ epic dramas and instead sought low-budget independent films

Vocabulary:
relished: liked   *augmented*: enlarged or increased
rebuffed: turned away; rejected   *endured*: continued despite difficulty
spurned: rejected with intense dislike or scorn   *espoused*: adopted an idea

9. D and E   Possible Prephrases: a problem, an issue

Cause: The defense lawyer found _____ in the prosecution's case
Effect: an acquittal of defendant

Vocabulary:
acquittal: a 'not guilty' verdict; release

accord: agreement

contour: outline

exposition: display or explanation
incongruity: disagreement; quality of being inappropriate
discrepancy: inconsistency; difference
perspective: a visible scene

10. E and F   Possible Prephrases: exiled, removed, thrown out

Cause: the US had an overwhelming majority of its experienced soldiers stationed along the western frontier
Effect: [the US] had to rely on untrained _____ at the Battle of Bull Run

Vocabulary:
courtiers: members of a royal court; brownnosers
mercenaries: people hired to fight or kill
patriarchs: male heads of a family

prodigies: extraordinarily gifted people
greenhorns: untrained people
neophytes: beginners

1. E   Possible Prephrases: be difficult to solve, confuse, puzzle

    This is a combination of a Similarity structure and a Contrast structure. The meaning of the word in the blank is similar to *intrigue* and the opposite of *easy to solve*.

    Vocabulary:
    dispel: to drive away
    query: to ask
    lament: to express grief; to mourn

    debilitate: to make weak
    confound: to confuse

2. B and F   Possible Prephrases: (i) speed, quickness   (ii) logo, symbol, trademark

    This is a combination of Cause and Effect structure and a Definition structure:

    > *Cause*: the cheetah is known for its _____
    > *Effect*: the sports car company selected the swift animal as its _____

    The second blank is defined by *the symbol by which a business is known*, so you should start here with your first prephrase.

    Vocabulary:
    crest: a symbol of a family or office

3. A and D   Possible Prephrases: (i) catch, arrest, find   (ii) unclear, wrong, not good

    This is a combination of Contrast structure and a Cause and Effect structure:

    > *Cause*: the woman's descriptions were _____
    > *Effect*: the police were unable to _____ the suspects

    Given that the women observed the suspects for several hours, you would expect her descriptions to be *detailed* and *accurate*. The word in the second blank means the opposite, though, because the sentence uses the U-Turn Word *although*. And if the descriptions were unclear, then the police would be unable to catch them.

    Vocabulary:
    apprehend: arrest
    impede: to slow progress down
    sanction: approve

    vague: not clear
    dubious: doubtful; questionable
    hasty: quick

4. A and E   Possible Prephrases: (i) edit, revise   (ii) original, unedited

This is a combination of a Contrast structure and a Definition structure. The second blank is defined by *in their original form, unaltered* so you should start here with your first prephrase. The second blank has a meaning that is nearly opposite of the second blank.

Vocabulary:
transcribe: make a written copy   *refined*: having good taste
pristine: in original form

5. C and F   Possible Prephrases: (i) disagreement, argument   (ii) ruin, end, split

This is a combination of a Similarity structure and a Cause and Effect structure. The first blank is similar to *disagreement*. The second blank is the effect of that disagreement.

>   *Cause*: a _____ between the two partners
>   *Effect*: a _____ of the business

Vocabulary:
breach: break   *consolidation*: merge; combination
covenant: agreement   *inquisition*: investigation
rift: a break in friendly relations   *dissolution*: breaking up of an organization

6. C and F   Possible Prephrases: (i) recommended, prescribed   (ii) harmful, bad

This is a combination of a Contrast structure and a Similarity structure. The second blank is similar to *ineffective* and has a meaning that is even more negative. The first blank is filled by a word that indicates doctors were in favor of the anti-wrinkle cream.

Vocabulary:
censured: disapproved of   *efficacious*: effective
curative: tending to cure or restore to health   *noxious*: harmful to health

7. B, D, and G   Possible Prephrases: (i) not likely   (ii) leader, first   (iii) a word more negative than *plain*

The first blank may not seem clear until later in the paragraph. Her work is described as *plain and (something even more negative than plain).* So in this Cause and Effect stem, it's *unlikely* that critics would describer van Hemessen as talented. For the second blank, which is a Definition stem, van Hemessen was *the first to paint herself seated at an easel,* so she was a leader or *pioneer* in self-portraiture. The third blank is a Similarity blank, and the *even* means that the word is similar to *plain* but of a more negative value. The best choice from the list is *unemotional.*

Vocabulary:
speculator: a person who considers the future   *entrepreneur*: a person who organizes a business venture

8. A, D, and I   Possible Prephrases: (i) relaxed, unconcerned (ii) too careful (iii) increased; greater

The first blank is defined by the context of the entire paragraph, which basically says that women who are pregnant with twins need an increased level care than women who are pregnant with a single baby. So doctors who *see no reason to initiate ancillary care* have become too relaxed or *blasé*. The second blank, then, is a Cause and Effect stem; if most people think twin pregnancies deserve no extra care, they will deem doctors who provide extra care as *overly cautious*. The final blank is also a Cause and Effect stem; if increased care results in better outcomes, then twin pregnancies are indeed worthy of *more diligent* care.

Vocabulary:
blasé: indifferent due to overexposure   *wearied*: tired
jaded: having become dull or worn out

4

Fill-in-the-Blank Mastery: Analyze the Answer Choices

Fill-in-the-Blank Mastery:
Analyze the Answer Choices

Introduction

Once you have a firm understanding of the question stem, you must learn how to analytically evaluate the answer choices.

In a single blank Text Completion question, there are five answer choices, all of which are the same part of speech.

> That the commentator was dismissive of the radicals' education plan came as no surprise to viewers who had followed the conservative for years. What was unexpected, however, was his _____ reception of the environmental suggestions posed by the same liberal group.

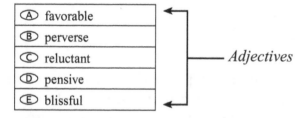

The answer choices for a particular blank are always the same part of speech.

5

Text Completion questions with two or three blanks provide three answer choices per blank. Each group of answers is made up of the same part of speech.

> Rather than feign ignorance, Miguel (i)_____ that he was aware of unethical behavior at the firm. The last thing he wanted was to be labeled a (ii)_____.

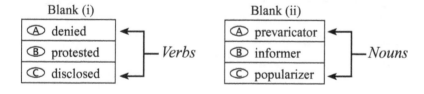

The answers will always correspond with the part of speech required in the blank. This is important to understand, as the knowledge can help you select the correct answer for some questions, which we will explain later in this chapter.

GRATUITOUS VOCAB

pensive (adj): thoughtful

disclosed (vb): revealed

prevaricator (n): liar

popularizer (n): one who makes a thing popular

For every Sentence Equivalence question there are six answer choices, two of which correctly complete the single blank. All six answer choices are always the same part of speech, as we saw with the Text Completion questions.

In spite of the economic _____ and the failing housing market, the realtor sold many homes and made an exorbitant amount of money this year.

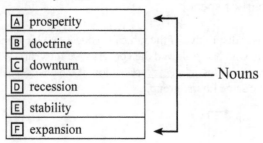

Most Text Completion and Sentence Equivalence questions will have missing adjectives, nouns, or verbs, but expect to see short phrases, too, such as a verb and preposition combination (i.e. *afraid of* or *mesmerized by*).

In spite of the economic recession and the failing housing market, the realtor sold many homes and made _____ amount of money this year.

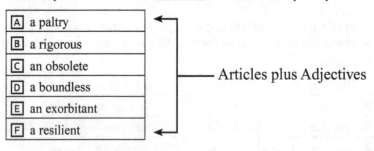

In this chapter we will study common answer trends and traps so that you are able to quickly eliminate wrong answers and identify right answers.

TIPS and TRICKS
Like your prephrase, answers can be a single word or a phrase.

GRATUITOUS VOCAB
doctrine (n): a taught principle

paltry (adj): small

boundless (adj): infinite

exorbitant (adj): excessive

5

Double Definition Answers

Many words have more than one definition. Some of these words, called homographs, sound the same for both meanings. The word *bark* is a homograph that can be used to refer to a dog's cry or a tree's covering. Other words, called heteronyms, may be pronounced differently for each meaning. Take the word *tear*: as a noun, a *tear* [teer] may be a drop of saline from your eye, but as a verb, to *tear* [tair] means to rip.

Most words with double definitions have two common meanings, like the examples above. Using the context of a sentence, students are easily able to differentiate between the two meanings when these words are used as answer choices. Test takers may get in trouble, however, when an answer choice has one common definition and another lesser-known meaning.

Double Definitions with Different Parts of Speech

Several times now we have mentioned that all of the answer choices are the same part of speech. We want you to remember this because you may come upon a question in which one of the words does not seem to fit; understanding the format of the question can help you choose the right answer:

> Although the commencement speaker had lived an interesting life, her speech was _____, boring the audience and graduates alike.

Ⓐ	compelling
Ⓑ	joyous
Ⓒ	disagreeable
Ⓓ	pleasant
Ⓔ	pedestrian

The first four answer choices are clearly adjectives, descriptive words that modify the word *speech*. But answer choice (E), *pedestrian*, appears to be a noun. After all, a pedestrian is a person who is walking. But how can that be? The *PowerScore GRE Verbal Reasoning Bible* harped again and again that all five answer choices must be the same part of speech!

Most students would prephrase *boring* or *dull*, but still choose (C), *disagreeable*, even though it does not match their prephrase or fit the meaning of the sentence.

Students who have read this book, however, would know that *pedestrian* has to be an adjective. ETS did not make a mistake and use a noun in a list of adjectives! In fact, students who really study this book would know that when a common word is used in an uncommon way, it is likely the correct answer.

CAUTION: GRE TRAP!
When an answer choice appears to be a different part of speech than the other answers, beware of a trap. All answer choices for a particular blank are the same part of speech!

TIPS and TRICKS
When a word commonly associated with one part of speech is used as another part of speech, it is likely the correct answer choice.

The word *pedestrian*, in this case, is an adjective. It means *dull* or *commonplace*.

Note that not all homographs and heteronyms are the right answers; some words have two very common meanings, like both *bark* and *tear*. Only use this tip when the word does not look like it belongs with the other answer choices, as this indicates that the word is being used in an unusual way.

Consider a list of words with both common and uncommon usages:

Word	Common Usage	Uncommon Usage
appropriate	(*adj.*) suitable	(*vb.*) to take
champion	(*n.*) winner	(*vb.*) to support or defend
compromised	(*vb.*) to settle by yielding	(*adj.*) vulnerable; endangered
concert	(*n.*) a musical show	(*vb.*) to plan together
consummate	(*vb.*) to complete	(*adj.*) perfect
converse	(*vb.*) to talk	(*n.*) the opposite
defile	(*vb.*) to make unclean	(*n.*) a narrow passage
discriminate	(*vb.*) to favor based on traits	(*adj.*) choosy or picky
dispatch	(*vb.*) to send	(*n.*) speed
evening	(*n.*) period before night	(*vb.*) to make smooth
exact	(*adj.*) strictly accurate	(*vb.*) to demand
fawn	(*n.*) young deer	(*vb.*) to seek favor by flattery
grave	(*n.*) burial place	(*adj.*) serious
incense	(*n.*) product burnt for odor	(*vb.*) to make angry
invalid	(*adj.*) not valid	(*n.*) a sickly person
lobby	(*n.*) entryway	(*vb.*) to influence
lower	(*adj.*) descended further	(*n.*) a threatening frown
minute	(*n.*) 60 seconds	(*adj.*) very small
pedestrian	(*n.*) a walking person	(*adj.*) dull or commonplace
preposition	(*n.*) part of speech	(*vb.*) to position before
refuse	(*vb.*) to decline or deny	(*n.*) garbage
row	(*vb.*) to propel a boat	(*n.*) an argument
supply	(*vb.*) to provide	(*adv.*) in a supple way; easily

Most of these words have been used on previous ETS tests in which the uncommon usage was required for solution to a reading question. The words *champion*, *consummate*, *discriminate*, *fawn*, and *pedestrian* are repeat offenders. It would be wise to study them and the others on the list for quick recognition should they appear on your test.

Familiarize yourself with the uncommon usage of these words so they cannot trick you on test day.

Double Definitions with the Same Part of Speech

Some words have two definitions that share the same part of speech. Consider the word *bat*; it can be a noun meaning *a winged mammal* or a noun meaning *a baseball club*. When words like this are used on the GRE, they are usually less obvious than those that function as different parts of speech. Let's study an example:

Despite the queen's public disapproval of imprisonment prior to conviction, she passed a law allowing the constable to _____ any person suspected of treason.

Ⓐ	intern
Ⓑ	liberate
Ⓒ	pardon
Ⓓ	accommodate
Ⓔ	shun

The U-Turn word *Despite* indicates that even though the queen disapproved of imprisonment prior to conviction, she allowed the constable to imprison people on suspicion alone. Most students will try all five words in the blank, finding none that match the prephrase *imprison*. To *intern* means *to work as an apprentice*; *liberate* and *pardon* both have meanings similar to *free*. And to *accommodate* means *to supply for*. Many of these students will go on to choose (E), *shun*, meaning *to avoid*, since it is the only word with a negative connotation.

If you eliminate all answer choices, do not select a word that you know does not fit in the blank. The word *shun* clearly does not mean the same thing as *imprison*. Instead, go back to each word and think about possible second meanings.

Have you ever seen the word *internment*? It means *imprisonment*. The correct answer is (A), *intern*, which means *to imprison*.

Understanding that words often have other meanings can prevent you from falling into answer choice traps. Remember, the correct answer is a perfect fit, and if your answer choice does not perfectly complete the question stem, return to the answer choices and consider alternate meanings.

TIPS and TRICKS
If you eliminate all answer choices, return to each word and consider alternate meanings.

Double Definitions with Science and Medicine Words

The GRE does, on occasion, assess your knowledge of scientific terms. Take the word *buoyant*. As most of us learned in elementary school, it means capable of floating. So if a Fill-in-the-Blank question needed a word describing a floating object, *buoyant* would fit perfectly.

More often than not, though, the GRE uses science and medicine words that have double definitions where the second definition can be applied to unscientific topics. Consider the word *buoyant* in a GRE sentence:

> Despite the many hardships she faced during World War II, Julia Child remained _____, inspiring others with her cheerfulness and resilience.
>
> | Ⓐ discouraged |
> |---|
> | Ⓑ secluded |
> | Ⓒ overbearing |
> | Ⓓ buoyant |
> | Ⓔ inventive |

In this case, *buoyant* means *cheerful and resilient*, and is thus the correct answer. It is not a difficult leap from the scientific to the unscientific definition; a buoyant item and a buoyant person are both light and difficult to keep down.

When you see a scientific word as an answer choice for an unscientific question stem, be suspicious of the test makers. It is likely the correct answer. Before selecting it, though, can you think of an alternative definition or find a way to apply its scientific meaning to people or situations? Let's try one more:

> The documentary showcased the famous football player's _____ rise from the lowly equipment manager to the star quarterback in just six short weeks.
>
> | Ⓐ gradual |
> |---|
> | Ⓑ spiteful |
> | Ⓒ meteoric |
> | Ⓓ youthful |
> | Ⓔ burdensome |

The science word in the answer choices is *meteoric*. A meteor is a fiery, fast-moving object that enters Earth's atmosphere. So when used to describe a person, *meteoric* means *like a meteor in brilliance or speed*. Do not dismiss a term from science or medicine because it does not seem to fit the context of the sentence; instead, suspect it is the correct answer and try to apply the common definition in an uncommon way.

Here is a list of common science and medicine words with unscientific definitions:

Again, learn the unscientific definitions of these words to prevent any stumbling on test day.

Word	Scientific Definition	Unscientific Definition
buoyant	capable of floating	cheerful and resilient
brackish	containing some salt	distasteful; unpleasant
bromide	a compound made of bromine	an overused saying
callus/callous	a hardened piece of skin	unfeeling; hardened
cerebral	of the cerebrum in the brain	involving intelligence
combustible	capable of catching fire	excitable
congeal	to go from a liquid to a solid	to make permanent
cultivate	to raise crops	to develop or improve
deciduous	shedding leaves yearly	not permanent
glacial	pertaining to a glacier	cold or hostile; very slow
gravity	force of attraction on Earth	seriousness
homogenize	to equally distribute fat in milk	to make similar
membranous	like a membrane	transparent
mercurial	of the metal mercury	lively and changeable
meteoric	pertaining to a meteor	quickly rising; brilliant
morass	a swamp	a troublesome situation
nebulous	of a nebula	hazy or confused
oscillate	to move like a pendulum	to go back and forth on beliefs
ossify	to harden like bone	to become inflexible in habits
polarize	to cause polarity to magnets	to divide into extreme groups
precipitate	to rain, snow, or sleet	to throw down headfirst or to bring about quickly
recessive	pertaining to a weaker gene	tending to go or slant back

Words that are most likely to appear on a GRE include *buoyant, callous, glacial, gravity, mercurial, meteoric, nebulous, oscillate,* and *precipitate.*

Double Definitions Problem Set

> Each of the sentences or paragraphs below has a word or set of words that has been omitted. From the answer choices, choose the word or set of words that best completes the meaning of the sentence. Answers begin on page 125.

1. Once the disease progressed to the final stages, my mother became an _____, bound to her bed and unable to care for herself.

   - Ⓐ understudy
   - Ⓑ emissary
   - Ⓒ autocrat
   - Ⓓ insinuator
   - Ⓔ invalid

2. The restaurant manager warned his waitstaff that he would _____ money from their paychecks to pay for any broken dishes.

   - Ⓐ revert
   - Ⓑ recycle
   - Ⓒ diffuse
   - Ⓓ squander
   - Ⓔ appropriate

3. Pundits were doubtful that the two parties would be able to set aside their differences in order to (i)_____ a feasible plan to stop government overspending. Surprisingly, (ii) _____ between the groups was reached mere hours after negotiations began.

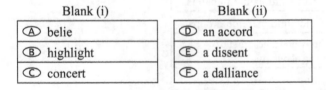

Blank (i)	Blank (ii)
Ⓐ belie	Ⓓ an accord
Ⓑ highlight	Ⓔ a dissent
Ⓒ concert	Ⓕ a dalliance

4. The safety of the soldiers and their covert mission was (i)_____ when a traitorous spy (ii)_____ their location to enemy combatants.

Blank (i)	Blank (ii)
Ⓐ ascertained	Ⓓ diverted
Ⓑ compromised	Ⓔ exposed
Ⓒ condemned	Ⓕ concealed

5. As one who was normally frivolous, Martika did not understand the _____ of her actions until she was sentenced to probation for six months.

A	severity
B	ambition
C	exhilaration
D	dullness
E	gravity
F	deceitfulness

6. The foreign exchange student found his host family both withdrawn and _____; they rarely spoke to him, and when they did, it was with bitter coldness.

A	amiable
B	frigid
C	revolting
D	glacial
E	heinous
F	invasive

7. As the cat fell, it demonstrated its well-known flexibility, _____ twisting in the air and successfully landing on its feet.

A	lithely
B	supply
C	warily
D	passively
E	feasibly
F	modestly

5

Opposite Answers

ETS knows how most test takers think, and they often use this knowledge against you. To see how, let's prephrase a question stem:

> After all of the sudden personal tragedies that had lately saddened Christie, people were surprised to find her in a _____ spirit at the memorial.

Christie was previously saddened by tragedies, so people would be surprised to find her *happy*. Can you match this prephrase—*happy*—with an answer choice?

> After all of the sudden personal tragedies that had lately saddened Christie, people were surprised to find her in a _____ spirt at the memorial.

Ⓐ	depressed
Ⓑ	blithe
Ⓒ	irate
Ⓓ	annoyed
Ⓔ	admirable

For most students, none of the answer choices immediately jump out as meaning *happy*. But there is one that means the opposite of *happy*—*depressed*. Sadly, many test takers select answer choice (A) and move on. Their reasoning goes something like this:

> *"Huh. <u>Depressed</u> is the opposite of <u>happy</u>. I don't know what <u>blithe</u> means. The last three—<u>irate</u>, <u>annoyed</u>, and <u>admirable</u>—just do not make sense in the blank. Maybe I misunderstood the question stem. I bet I missed something and I should have prephrased <u>sad</u>. Okay, answer (A) it is then."*

No! No! No! No! Never select an answer choice that has a meaning that is opposite of your original prephrase. The test makers know you will likely choose this answer if you cannot match your prephrase, so they often use Opposite Answers to trick you. If you are looking for *happy*, stay away from *sad*. If you prephrase *tall*, watch out for *short*. If you need *beautiful*, avoid *ugly* at all costs. Mentally cross out these Opposite Answers to prevent falling victim to a classic GRE trap.

The correct answer is *blithe*: it means *cheerful*.

CAUTION: GRE TRAP!
The test makers use Opposite Answers to make you doubt your reasoning process. Never select a word with the opposite meaning of your prephrase!

5

You will also likely find Opposite Answers in questions with multiple blanks:

Although the videotape of a supposed supernatural being from outer space visiting a child has been proven a (i)_____, belief in the encounter is still (ii)_____.

Blank (i)	Blank (ii)
Ⓐ phenomenon	Ⓓ valid
Ⓑ hoax	Ⓔ limited
Ⓒ certainty	Ⓕ widespread

While many will think the first blank can be prephrased *true* or *false*, the context clue *supposed* should make you lean toward *false*, as it indicates the author's skepticism. The word for the second blank, then, would show that the belief is still *widely held* or *common*.

Choice (B) is the correct answer for the first blank. *A hoax* is the closest match to our prephrase of *false*, but look at (C), *certainty*. It is the opposite of *a hoax*. Even (A), *a phenomenon*, could be construed as the opposite of *a hoax*.

Blank (ii) begins with *valid*, once again the opposite of *false*, even though it's a completely different blank! Our prephrase here was *widely held* or *common*, so the best answer is (F), *widespread*. The opposite, *limited*, is used in answer choice (E).

You can see how Opposite Answers can play havoc on your GRE score if you do not hold firm to your original prephrases! Remember to eliminate any answer choice that uses Opposite Answers.

Confidence Quotation

"Man is what he believes."
Anton Chekhov, Russian author and physician

Opposite Answers Problem Set

Each of the sentences or paragraphs below has a word or set of words that has been omitted. From the answer choices, choose the word or set of words that best completes the meaning of the sentence. Answers begin on page 127.

1. Because radio-frequency identification (RFID) tags are inexpensive and easy to manufacture, they are _____ technology found in everything from mobile phones to casino chips.

Ⓐ	an authentic
Ⓑ	a sinister
Ⓒ	a universal
Ⓓ	an antiquated
Ⓔ	a confined

2. Although Patricia smoked as a teenager in the 1960s, she could not (i)_____ such behavior in her grandchildren, now that she knew the (ii)_____ effects of cigarettes.

    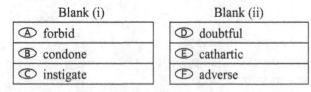

Blank (i)		Blank (ii)	
Ⓐ	forbid	Ⓓ	doubtful
Ⓑ	condone	Ⓔ	cathartic
Ⓒ	instigate	Ⓕ	adverse

3. Despite the popular belief that lawmakers only cut taxes in order to buy votes for the upcoming election, the reason was a lot less (i)_____ and instead more (ii)_____: without the tax cut, many workers would have fallen further into poverty.

    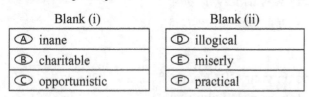

Blank (i)		Blank (ii)	
Ⓐ	inane	Ⓓ	illogical
Ⓑ	charitable	Ⓔ	miserly
Ⓒ	opportunistic	Ⓕ	practical

4. The new employee was neither expeditious nor _____; he took too long to complete reports that were ultimately filled with mistakes.

A	exact
B	tardy
C	erroneous
D	outrageous
E	accurate
F	corrupt

5. Even though the food industry has long been fighting legislation to ban bisphenol-A from disposable food containers, mounting evidence _____ the government's suspicion that bisphenol-A is a powerful carcinogen.

A	discards
B	negates
C	corroborates
D	substantiates
E	contradicts
F	hypothesizes

6. Having never openly spoken of the arrangement, their agreement was _____; Bradley knew that he would have to return the favor even though Jacob never specifically asked.

A	tacit
B	amoral
C	explicit
D	irrefutable
E	vast
F	implied

Related Answers

Humans are programmed to make logical connections, which is never more evident than in our classification of words. We group words by topic and meaning from an early age. For example, consider your early associations with the word *dog*. It is likely that as a small child just learning to talk, you learned other words associated with *dog*, like *bark*, *woof*, *tail*, *puppy*, and *spot*. This type of word grouping continues into adulthood, when you have a much more expansive vocabulary. If presented with the word *experiment*, you might associate it with *hypothesis*, *observation*, *science*, *control*, *conclusion*, and many more.

ETS takes advantage of this natural tendency by using wrong answer choices that are related to the topic in the sentence. Let's study a simple example:

> Because he often made ridiculous jokes in the courtroom, the judge was known as a _____ and most lawyers dreaded arguing a case in front of him.
>
> | | |
> |---|---|
> | Ⓐ | puppet |
> | Ⓑ | bailiff |
> | Ⓒ | buffoon |
> | Ⓓ | sage |
> | Ⓔ | patron |

CAUTION: GRE TRAP! If your prephrase is not associated with the topic of the sentence, beware of words that seem related to the topic. They are likely to be incorrect.

The question stem contains the law-related terms *courtroom*, *judge*, *lawyers*, and *case*. These words should not influence your prephrase, though; the context clue *ridiculous jokes* in the Cause and Effect Sentence should help you prephrase *joker* or *clown* for the blank. Some students, though, will get to the answer choices and immediately be attracted by *bailiff* because it is a word that they have heard associated with a courtroom. They will most definitely select this word if they do not know the definitions of the other four or if they cannot match their prephrase. But a bailiff is an officer who keeps order in the court, not someone who makes jokes, so it is definitely the wrong word for the blank.

If an answer choice uses a related word that is relatively common, you must understand the definition of the word before selecting it as an answer. It may likely be a trap.

That is not to say all related answers are wrong; some terms might actually be used with a question stem containing associated content. Let's look at another:

> The play almost closed when the lead actress was sidelined with a broken leg; luckily, the _____ was able to take over the role successfully.

Ⓐ	understudy
Ⓑ	toady
Ⓒ	missionary
Ⓓ	publicist
Ⓔ	stylist

5

The question stem contains the terms *play*, *lead actress*, and *role*, all of which are stage-related terms. And the best prephrase, *other actress*, is also associated with the stage. In this case, the best answer, *understudy*, is related to the content in the question stem.

So how do you know if related words are the right answer or the wrong answer? It all goes back to your prephrase. If your prephrase is not associated with the topic in the question stem (i.e. *joker* with law-related terms), then the answer will not be a related word. But if your prephrase is related to the question topic (i.e. *other actress* with stage-related terms), look for a related word to complete the blank. The more difficult the term, the more likely it will be associated with related words.

Related Answers Problem Set

Each of the sentences or paragraphs below has a word or set of words that has been omitted. From the answer choices, choose the word or set of words that best completes the meaning of the sentence. Answers begin on page 128.

1. In the battle between the two pirate ships, the large _____ was no match for the swift clipper, which could easily avoid attack and harass the sluggish ship with cannon fire.

   - Ⓐ catamaran
   - Ⓑ galleon
   - Ⓒ transporter
   - Ⓓ flatbed
   - Ⓔ excavator

2. The staff often sought the (i)_____ advice of Dr. Leaphart for difficult medical problems; she had a vast knowledge of diseases that helped diagnose the most (ii)_____ cases.

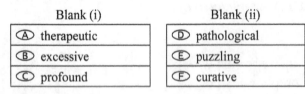

Blank (i)	Blank (ii)
Ⓐ therapeutic	Ⓓ pathological
Ⓑ excessive	Ⓔ puzzling
Ⓒ profound	Ⓕ curative

3. The author's poetry can be described as _____; closely packed with complex ideas, it is difficult to understand.

   - Ⓐ symbolic
   - Ⓑ slight
   - Ⓒ distant
   - Ⓓ obscure
   - Ⓔ figurative
   - Ⓕ dense

4. The computer company introduced a new program that can _____ e-mails by sender; communication from family, friends, colleagues, and companies can be delivered into four different accounts.

   - Ⓐ cull
   - Ⓑ scroll
   - Ⓒ winnow
   - Ⓓ dispel
   - Ⓔ browse
   - Ⓕ fragment

"Kind Of" Answers

You hear the phrase in discourse across America:

"I *kind of* understand the new health care plan."
"He *kind of* wants to see what she'll say."
"My neighbor is *kind of* crazy."

But the unfortunate fact is that the phrase *kind of* in place of *somewhat* is improper English. You should eliminate it from your vocabulary, just as you should eliminate any Fill-in-the-Blank answer choice that only *kind of* works.

"Kind of" in place of "somewhat" is improper English and it has no place on the GRE!

Fill-in-the-Blank answers are a perfect fit. The dictionary definition completely corresponds in style and meaning and there is no question about its correctness as the word for the blank. There is no room for words that somewhat fit, although ETS will be sure to choose some deliberate answer choices to make you hesitate. Take a look at the *kind of* answers in the following question:

Although Alice was given permission by her doctor to return to work after the disabling surgery, she still felt _____ on her first day back; in fact, she was too weak to lift any inventory.

| Ⓐ vigorous |
| Ⓑ queasy |
| Ⓒ bewildered |
| Ⓓ debilitated |
| Ⓔ depressed |

In this Contrast Sentence, the context clues *disabling* and *weak* indicate that Alice *still felt weak on her first day back*. But even armed with the prephrase *weak*, many test takers will contemplate answer choices (B) and (C) when they do not recognize a word meaning *weak* among the answer choices. Their reasoning might sound something like this:

"Well, I suppose Alice may feel sick to her stomach or nauseous after having anesthesia, so <u>queasy</u> kind of fits. I'll choose (B)." Or:

"Hmm. If Alice has been out of work for a long time because of her surgery, it makes sense that she might be confused when she returns, especially if anything has changed while she was gone. So <u>bewildered</u> kind of fits. I'm going with (C)."

This is GRE suicide! Never choose an answer that doesn't match your prephrase and never choose an answer that only *kind of* fits. You are better off selecting a word for which you do not know the definition.

Confidence Quotation
"The thing always happens that you really believe in; and the belief in a thing makes it happen."
Frank Lloyd Wright, architect

Let's analyze the first paragraph of faulty reasoning:

"Well, I suppose Alice may feel sick to her stomach or nauseous after having anesthesia, so <u>queasy</u> kind of fits. I'll choose (B)."

Does anything in the sentence reveal that Alice experienced nausea after her surgery? No. It does not even indicate that Alice had anesthesia! This test taker is overthinking the question stem and possibly transferring his own experiences to Alice, thus making unsafe assumptions that will ultimately cost him GRE points. If *queasy* were the correct answer choice, there would be context clues in the sentence indicating that Alice felt sick to her stomach, rather than clues pointing to her feeling weak and disabled. *Queasy* and *weak* are not synonyms.

The second line of reasoning is similarly faulty:

"Hmm. If Alice has been out of work for a long time because of her surgery, it makes sense that she might be confused when she returns, especially if anything has changed while she was gone. So <u>bewildered</u> kind of fits. I'm going with (C)."

The question stem does not reveal how long Alice was out of work; she could have returned the day after surgery or a year after surgery. It is unwise to assume she has been gone for a long time—or that anything has changed while she was gone. Plus, nowhere in the sentence does it demonstrate that Alice is confused. This test taker could just as easily, but foolishly, assume that Alice is the smartest woman alive working in the simplest job on Earth. Answer choice (C) just does not fit in the blank.

If you have to make a case for your selected answer choice, it is wrong. If you think to yourself, "This answer *kind of* works," you are most likely wrong about the answer choice and definitely wrong in your grammar. The correct answer is a perfect fit that needs no justification.

The correct answer for this question is answer choice (D), *debilitated*. It means *weak* or *feeble*. Note that choice (A) is an Opposite Answer.

"Kind Of" Answers Problem Set

> Each of the sentences or paragraphs below has a word or set of words that has been omitted. From the answer choices, choose the word or set of words that best completes the meaning of the sentence. Answers begin on page 129.

1. Although his teacher labeled him mentally confused, Thomas Edison was actually quite_____; his mother recognized this intellectual aptitude and chose to school him at home.

Ⓐ	enlightened
Ⓑ	qualified
Ⓒ	masterful
Ⓓ	determined
Ⓔ	intriguing

2. The designer created an office that was both _____ and practical; she used strikingly bold colors in a room that was conducive to everyday business.

Ⓐ	dismal
Ⓑ	repulsive
Ⓒ	flamboyant
Ⓓ	inspiring
Ⓔ	polished

Multiple Blank Answers

A common trap in Text Completion multiple blank questions occurs when the test makers use synonyms in the wrong columns. Let's examine a dual blank question that contains this trap:

The homeowners were impressed with the moving company whose employees worked (i)_____ but (ii)_____; the men packed the entire house in only six hours without breaking any furniture or valuables.

Blank (i)	Blank (ii)
(A) hastily	(D) fastidiously
(B) effortlessly	(E) promptly
(C) attentively	(F) crudely

5

Accurate prephrases are extremely helpful with dual blank questions because they help prevent you from becoming confused. The first blank is defined by *the men packed the entire house in only six hours*; the context clue *only* indicates that this packing was done *quickly*. The meaning of the second blank can be found in *without breaking any furniture or valuables*. The men worked *carefully*. Armed with a good prephrase (*quickly . . carefully*), you can begin analyzing the answer choices.

Notice that answer choices (A) and (E) both mean *quickly*, even though our prephrase *quickly* was for the first blank. And answers (C) and (D) both mean *carefully*, even though this was our prephrase for the second blank. A test taker who does not know the definition of *hastily* or *fastidiously* might be tricked into picking (C) and (E), but they would be wrong. Since our prephrase for the first blank was *quickly*, choice (A), *hastily*, is the answer. Our prephrase for the second blank was *carefully*, so *fastidiously* is the answer.

Watch for synonyms in dual blank and triple blank questions and be sure to avoid them if they are in the wrong columns.

Multiple Blank Answers Problem Set

Each of the sentences or paragraphs below has a word or set of words that has been omitted. From the answer choices, choose the word or set of words that best completes the meaning of the sentence. Answers begin on page 130.

1. When Thomas mended his relationship with his mother, he was both (i)_____ and (ii)_____ ; he was happy to be speaking with her again but worried she may not have changed.

Blank (i)	Blank (ii)
Ⓐ overwhelmed	Ⓓ relieved
Ⓑ mistrustful	Ⓔ apprehensive
Ⓒ pleased	Ⓕ ecstatic

2. Most neighbors avoided Mrs. Newsome because she was a (i)_____; she spread all rumors, regardless of whether they were factual or (ii)_____.

Blank (i)	Blank (ii)
Ⓐ gossipmonger	Ⓓ trivial
Ⓑ fabricator	Ⓔ scandalous
Ⓒ matriarch	Ⓕ concocted

3. Although Barbara demanded honesty from her friends and acquaintances, she was actually quite (i)_____ herself, which often resulted in (ii)_____ relationships. She was nearly sixty years old, but the longest lasting friendship she had ever maintained was her two-year relationship with her current hairdresser. Some might even argue that her stylist only (iii)_____ Barbara and her fables to preserve a professional relationship.

Blank (i)	Blank (ii)	Blank (iii)
Ⓐ obdurate	Ⓓ deceitful	Ⓖ patiently promoted
Ⓑ marred	Ⓔ severed	Ⓗ politely tolerated
Ⓒ mendacious	Ⓕ enduring	Ⓘ expressly denied

4. The editors must have followed the suggestion to (i)_____ the content of the textbook because the second edition was much less (ii)_____ than the first; the added material will benefit students and teachers alike.

Blank (i)	Blank (ii)
Ⓐ aggrandize	Ⓓ sparse
Ⓑ diminish	Ⓔ dense
Ⓒ ameliorate	Ⓕ reviewed

Chapter Summary

Beware of the different types of answer traps:

Double Definition Answers

- An answer choice that does not appear to match the other answer choices in part of speech is probably the correct answer.

- If you eliminate all answer choices, go back and consider alternative meanings.

- An answer choice that is scientific in nature accompanying a non-scientific question stem is likely the correct answer.

Opposite Answers

- The test makers use answers that have a meaning opposite of the right answer.

- Never select an answer choice with a meaning opposite of your prephrase.

Related Answers

- If your prephrase is a word that is unrelated to the topic of the question stem, be wary of answer choices that seem related to the topic.

- If your prephrase is a word that is related to the topic of the question stem, then look for answer choices that do seem related to the topic.

"Kind Of" Answers

- Never select an answer that only *kind of* fits in the blank.

- You should never have to work to justify the correct answer.

Multiple Blank Answers

- Watch for Multiple Blank answers to use several synonyms in the wrong columns.

Analyze the Answer Choices Answer Key

Double Definitions Problem Set—Page 110

1. E   Possible Prephrases: an extremely sick person, an invalid

    While the word *invalid* is often recognized as an adjective meaning *not valid*, in this case it is a noun, as indicated by the four other answer choices that are nouns. An invalid is a sickly person, unable to care for themselves.

    Vocabulary:
    understudy: a performer who learns another actor's role
    emissary: a person sent on a mission to represent the interests of someone else

    autocrat: a person who rules with complete power and authority
    insinuator: a person who gives hints or suggestions in a sly manner

2. E   Possible Prephrases: take, subtract

    The most common meaning of *appropriate* is *suitable*, in its adjective form. But based on the other four answer choices, it is clear that *appropriate* is being used as a verb in this sentence. As a verb, *appropriate* means *to take, often illegally or for one's own use*.

    Vocabulary:
    revert: to return to former conditions   *diffuse*: to spread
    squander: to waste

3. C and D   Possible Prephrases: (i) agree on, plan   (ii) an agreement, a compromise

    The most common definition of *concert* is the noun meaning *musical show*. But as a verb, it means to *plan together* or *to arrange by agreement*.

    Vocabulary:
    belie: to misrepresent   *dissent*: disagreement
    accord: agreement   *dalliance*: the deliberate act of delaying

4. B and E   Possible Prephrases: (i) jeopardized, in danger, risked   (ii) gave, told, revealed

    While *compromised* as a verb most often means *came to an agreement through concessions*, it can also mean *jeopardized* or *endangered*.

    Vocabulary:
    ascertained: made certain   *condemned*: to express strong disapproval of
    diverted: to turn from a course

5. **A and E**   Possible Prephrases: seriousness, consequences

Because this is a Contrast Question Stem, it helps to know the definition of *frivolous*, since the blank has the opposite meaning. *Frivolous* means *having a lack of seriousness*, so the blank means *seriousness*. While *gravity* is normally a science noun meaning *the force of attraction on Earth*, it can also be a noun meaning *seriousness*.

Vocabulary:
exhilaration: the feeling of liveliness and cheerfulness

6. **B and D**   Possible Prephrases: cold, unfriendly, icy

The context clue *bitter coldness* indicates that the meaning of the blank is *cold*. The word *glacial* typically refers to an actual glacier, but it also means *cold or hostile*, as does *frigid*.

Vocabulary:
amiable: friendly   *heinous*: hateful and atrocious
revolting: disgusting; repulsive   *invasive*: offensive; invading personal space or body

7. **A and B**   Possible Prephrases: flexibly, easily

Most students will see answer choice (B) as a noun or verb meaning *a quantity* or *to provide*. But *supply* is also an adverb meaning *in a flexible way*. The other four adverbs should make you realize that *supply* must also be an adverb, and is likely the answer. Choice (A) also means *in a flexible way*.

Vocabulary:
warily: in a watchful manner   *feasibly*: capable; likely
modestly: in a humble or unassuming way

1. C Possible Prephrases: a common, a widespread

   The context clue *found in everything* provides the meaning for the blank. Avoid answer choice (E), as *confined* means *limited*, the opposite meaning of the correct answer.

   Vocabulary:
   authentic: real; original   *antiquated*: old and outdated
   sinister: evil

2. B and F Possible Prephrases: (i) approve of, allow (ii) harmful, dangerous

   The best prephrase for the first blank is *allow*. Notice that (A), *forbid*, is the opposite of *allow*. The best prephrase for the second blank is *adverse*. Note that (E) can be construed as an Opposite Answer.

   Vocabulary:
   condone: to give approval of   *adverse*: unfavorable or harmful
   cathartic: purging for purification or healing

3. C and F Possible Prephrases: (i) selfish, evil (ii) kind, reasonable

   Answer (B) is opposite of the correct answer for the first blank, and choice (D) is opposite of the second prephrase.

   Vocabulary:
   inane: foolish   *miserly*: stingy
   opportunistic: taking advantage for personal gain

4. A and E   Possible Prephrases: correct, right

   The Contrast context clue *filled with mistakes* indicates that the meaning of the blank is *correct*. Avoid *erroneous* and *corrupt*, the opposites of the prephrase, and *tardy*, the opposite of *expeditious*.

   Vocabulary:
   expeditious: quick   *erroneous*: containing errors
   exact: correct

5. C and D   Possible Prephrases: supports, confirms

The evidence is either going to support or weaken the government's suspicion. Use the first clause, *Even though the food industry has long been fighting legislation to ban bisphenol-A from disposable food containers,* to see that the evidence *supports* the suspicion. Avoid answers (B) and (E), the Opposite Answers.

6. A and F   Possible Prephrases: unspoken

Answer choice (C), *explicit*, has the opposite meaning of the prephrase.

Vocabulary:
tacit: unspoken and implied   *irrefutable*: cannot be disproved
amoral: without morals   *vast*: immense; enormous
explicit: clearly expressed or demonstrated

Related Answers Problem Set—Page 118

1. B   Possible Prephrase: ship

Because the prephrase, *ship*, is related to the nautical-themed words (*pirate, clipper, ship, cannon fire*) in the question stem, the answer is likely a related word. A *galleon* is a large, sluggish warship used in the 15th to 17th centuries.

Vocabulary:
catamaran: a boat with two hulls   *excavator*: construction equipment that removes soil
flatbed: a type of truck with a flat bed

2. C and E   Possible Prephrases: 1. trusted, sound, knowledgeable   2. difficult, challenging

The prephrases are unrelated to medical terminology, so avoid answer choices with words that relate to medicine, such as *therapeutic* in (A), *pathological* in (D), and *curative* in (F).

Vocabulary:
profound: deep; complete   *pathological*: pertaining to disease

3. D and F   Possible Prephrases: closely packed, difficult to understand

The best prephrases are *closely packed* or *difficult to understand* so do not be swayed by the literary terms *symbolic* and *figurative*. Neither of them matches the prephrase.

Vocabulary:
obscure: not clearly understood or expressed

4. A and C   Possible Prephrases: sort, group

The prephrases, *sort* or *group*, are not commonly associated with the computer terms (*computer, program, emails, accounts*) in the question stem, so avoid a computer-related answer like *scroll, browse,* or *fragment*.

Vocabulary:
cull: to gather the choice items from   *dispel*: to drive away
winnow: to sort   *fragment*: to break

"Kind Of" Answers Problem Set—Page 121

1. A   Possible Prephrase: intelligent, clearheaded

The Contrast Sentence uses *Although* indicating that the word in the blank means the opposite of *mentally confused*. We also learn through the Similarity clause following the semicolon that the blank is similar in meaning to *intellectual aptitude*. *Intelligent* or *clearheaded* would be good prephrases. Only choice (A), *enlightened*, matches the prephrase. Choices (B) and (C) are "kind of" answers, but neither means *intelligent*, so they should be avoided.

2. C   Possible Prephrase: strikingly bold, flashy, showy

The word *practical* is defined by *conducive to everyday business*; the word in the blank is defined by *used strikingly bold colors*. *Flamboyant* means *strikingly bold or brilliant* and is the only perfect fit. Test takers may be tricked into thinking *inspiring* or *polished* "kind of" work given the topic of the sentence, but they should be avoided since they do not match the prephrase nor are defined by the sentence.

1.   C and E   Possible Prephrases: (i) happy   (ii) worried

Answer choice (B) is a synonym for worried, but it's in the wrong column. Similarly, choices (D) and (F) can fit in the first blank, but again, they are in the wrong column.

5

2.   A and F   Possible Prephrases: (i) gossiper   (ii) fictional, untrue, lies

In the first blank, choice (B), *fabricator*, is closely related to your prephrase for the second blank.

Vocabulary:
gossipmonger: one who likes and spreads rumors   *trivial*: unimportant
fabricator: liar   *concocted*: made up
matriarch: the female head of a family

3.   C, E, and H   Possible Prephrases: (i) dishonest   (ii) ruined, harmed   (iii) put up with

The prephrase for the first blank is *dishonest*; choice (D) in the second blank and choice (I) in the third blank are related to dishonesty. The prephrase for the second blank is *harmed*; choice (B) for the first blank is the synonym *marred*. Finally, choice (F) for the second blank matches our prephrase, *put up with*, for the third blank. Avoid these answers!

Vocabulary:
obdurate: stubborn   *severed*: broken
marred: damaged   *enduring*: tolerating or lasting
mendacious: dishonest

4.   A and D   Possible Prephrases: (i) add to, increase   (ii) thin, skimpy

The second prephrase is tricky but is key to solving this question. The first edition was thin, which is why there was a suggestion to add material. Therefore, the second edition is much less *thin*. Avoid (B), which is related to *thin* and (E), which is related to *aggrandize*.

Vocabulary:
aggrandize: to increase in scope   *sparse*: thin
ameliorate: to make better

Fill-in-the-Blank Mastery: Decode the Vocabulary

Fill-in-the-Blank Mastery: Decode the Vocabulary

Introduction

Debate has raged for years about whether the GRE is a vocabulary test. Proponents for intensive vocabulary study claim that it is; after all, with words like *bifurcate*, *lachrymose*, and *stentorian*, only students with an exceptional vocabulary and a penchant for words will know the definition of every word on the test. Others, who maintain that rote memorization of vocabulary lists is pointless, assert that the questions and the vocabulary are decipherable.

We believe that both parties have valid points. Few people will know the definition of every word on the test. High-scoring test takers do tend to have a more advanced vocabulary, but you can certainly achieve a perfect score without knowing the definition of every word.

For this reason, in this chapter we will discuss decoding strategies *and* studying the most commonly occurring GRE words. There are benefits to learning roots and affixes, word sense, and other vocabulary-decoding strategies, but there is also value in memorizing smaller lists of frequently used GRE words. We advise you to read this chapter now, but to return to its "Repeat Offender" appendix every day for vocabulary study.

The majority of examples and problems in this chapter are presented in single blank Text Completion and Sentence Equivalence questions. This is because we want to highlight vocabulary and vocabulary-decoding strategies; the five- and six-answer choice formats give us a simplified opportunity to study more words for each blank. These strategies, however, must be applied to all Fill-in-the-Blank questions, including dual and triple blank Text Completion questions.

GRATUITOUS VOCAB
bifurcate (adj):
to divide

lachrymose (adj):
mournful

stentorian (adj):
very loud

penchant (adj): a
strong liking

6

**Confidence
Quotation**
"Losing is not in
my vocabulary."
Ruud van
Nistelrooy.
soccer player

Vocabulary in the Question Stem

As we previously mentioned in Chapter 3, some Fill-in-the-Blank questions are made more difficult by employing challenging vocabulary in the question stem. Try not to panic when you encounter an extreme vocabulary word in the sentence; sometimes you do not even need to know the definition of the word to solve the question, as in the following example:

> Doctors recommend taking a zinc acetate lozenge at the first sign of an incipient cold in order to help (i)_____ the symptoms and (ii)_____ the duration of the illness.

Blank (i)	Blank (ii)
Ⓐ exacerbate	Ⓓ extend
Ⓑ alleviate	Ⓔ delay
Ⓒ augment	Ⓕ reduce

In this question stem, the word *incipient* is a difficult vocabulary word that few test takers know. The context of the sentence is not much help in deciphering the word, which could mean *debilitating*, *developing*, *severe*, and countless other things. Luckily, though, you do not need to know the meaning to complete the blanks. A cold is never a good thing, so doctors will help you *ease* symptoms and *shorten* its duration. Armed with these prephrases, you can confidently select answer choice (B) without ever defining *incipient*.

Even if you do need to define a vocabulary word in a question stem, many sentences will contain context clues or synonyms. Consider an example:

> While a zinc acetate lozenge may help reduce the duration of an incipient cold, the herbal remedy cannot alleviate a _____ illness; studies show that the lozenges are only effective if used at the first sign of symptoms.

Ⓐ	manageable
Ⓑ	progressed
Ⓒ	viral
Ⓓ	researched
Ⓔ	minor

The first independent clause contains a blank that is opposite in meaning of *incipient*. Some students might realize this and move on, afraid that they are unable to define the vocabulary word. But that would be a mistake; the context of the second independent clause defines *incipient*. Since the lozenges only work when used at the first sign of a cold, an incipient cold is one that is just starting to develop. The word in the blank will have an opposite meaning, such as *advanced* or *well-established*. The best answer is (B), *progressed*.

We would be remiss if we told you that you can always decode the vocabulary in the question stem. There may be times that you have to know the definition in order to solve the question. Consider the previous question again, this time with the last independent clause removed:

GRATUITOUS VOCAB
remiss (adj):
careless

> While a zinc acetate lozenge may help reduce the duration of an incipient cold, the herbal remedy cannot alleviate a _____ illness.

Ⓐ manageable

Ⓑ progressed

Ⓒ viral

Ⓓ researched

Ⓔ minor

Most students would quickly guess on this question and move on. But even if you cannot define *incipient*, you should still be able to eliminate one or two answer choices from this question, using only your common sense.

When would a remedy most likely work? It's more effective when a cold is weak, rather than strong. Or when a cold is basic rather than complex. Or when a cold is new and slight and only mildly bothersome instead of when it is old and rooted and ruining your daily life. Each of these examples uses a set of terms, one of which is less significant (*weak, basic, new, slight,* and *only mildly bothersome*) and one that is more serious (*strong, complex, old, rooted,* and *ruining your daily life*). The blank in the question stem needs to be completed by a more serious term, as this is when the lozenge will not work.

While we caution you from applying personal beliefs and from using reasoning with prior knowledge to find the right answer, you may be able to use common sense to eliminate the wrong answers.

Choice (A), *manageable* and choice (E), *minor*, are less significant terms. It makes more sense that the herbal remedy cannot alleviate an *unmanageable* or *major* illness. Eliminate these two choices.

Choice (D) does not make sense. When *researched* is used in the blank, the question stem states that illnesses that are researched cannot be helped by this remedy. Research will not affect how a cold will respond to a lozenge. You should be able to remove this answer choice from contention.

So you are left with two possible answers from which to choose: (B), *progressed*, and (C), *viral*. The term *progressed* fits our logical connection; compared to *new* or *developing*, it is a more serious term. Choice (C), *viral*, is a Related Answer. When faced with a question with difficult vocabulary, you would be wise to avoid related words. The correct choice is (B).

Never dismiss a Fill-in-the-Blank question just because it has vocabulary in the question stem. Even if you cannot decode the challenging words, you still may be able to eliminate one or more wrong answers before guessing.

Vocabulary in the Question Stem Problem Set

Each of the sentences or paragraphs below has a word or set of words that has been omitted. From the answer choices, choose the word or set of words that best completes the meaning of the sentence. Answers begin on page 155.

1. Despite her friends' attempts at light and cheerful conversation, Alaina remained morose; her (i)_____ could not be resolved by such (ii)_____.

Blank (i)	Blank (ii)
Ⓐ restraint	Ⓓ despondency
Ⓑ gratification	Ⓔ resolution
Ⓒ melancholy	Ⓕ merriment

2. The political commentator was known for his vitriolic criticism, so he surprised everyone when he responded to the governor's economic plan with less _____ analysis.

Ⓐ sulky
Ⓑ scathing
Ⓒ receptive
Ⓓ sympathetic
Ⓔ charming

3. Mr. Quinton was both foppish and _____; he was extremely elegant in dress and manner and felt superior to others whose sense of fashion did not resemble his own.

Ⓐ vain
Ⓑ disdainful
Ⓒ modest
Ⓓ humble
Ⓔ boastful
Ⓕ arrogant

6

Selecting an Unknown

So what happens when you do not know the definitions of two or more answer choices? For one thing, you cannot eliminate them. Test takers have a tendency to ignore or discount words they do not know, but this is counter intuitive to smart test taking. We have already discussed the absurdity of selecting an answer that you know does not perfectly fit in the blank, and it is equally absurd to eliminate a word that you cannot define.

ETS is aware of a student's inclination to avoid unknown words, so watch for an "All But One" question, where all but one of the answer choices are easy to define but clearly incorrect. The remaining answer choice is a more challenging word, but by process of elimination, is obviously the right answer. The test makers are not necessarily testing whether you know the challenging word, but whether you trust yourself to eliminate the four wrong answers and select a word you do not know. Consider an example:

> Studded with real diamonds and rubies, the _____ gown chosen by the princess was the subject of many conversations at the royal ball because of its extravagant cost.

Ⓐ	tasteful
Ⓑ	drab
Ⓒ	ostentatious
Ⓓ	smudged
Ⓔ	undersized

Good prephrases include words like *showy, luxurious,* and *expensive* because the dress had real jewels and an extravagant cost. But when reviewing the four answer choices that you likely know, none of them match your prephrase. Some might argue that (A), *tasteful,* "kind of" works because a dress with diamonds and rubies seems like it would be in good taste. There is nothing in the sentence to indicate that the dress was tasteful; it could have had so many gems on it that some people found it over-the-top and gaudy. Remember, *kind of* answers are wrong because the right answer is a perfect fit.

Similarly, other test takers might venture that (E), *undersized, kind of* works because a dress that is too small will definitely cause gossip and chatter. But the sentence states that ball-goers talked about the gown because of its high cost, not its small fit.

Choice (B), *drab,* does not fit; a dress with sparkly gemstones is not lacking brightness. And choice (D), *smudged,* does not make sense because the sentence does not indicate any dirt or smear being on the gown.

That leaves choice (C), *ostentatious*. The average test taker will not know its meaning (*designed to attract notice; showy*), but the practiced test taker will select it anyway. The other four choices have been eliminated, so *ostentatious* must be the correct answer. In "All But One" questions, you must trust your ability to eliminate answers and choose the one you do not know.

On most questions with difficult vocabulary, you will likely be able to eliminate several answer choices because you know the definitions of the words and they simply do not fit the blank. You may be left with more than one unknown word, so you will have to use other decoding skills to isolate the correct answer. Let's study an example:

The reporter was not being straightforward, asking _____ questions that were designed to trick the politician into admitting wrongdoing.

Ⓐ	lugubrious
Ⓑ	honorable
Ⓒ	evanescent
Ⓓ	incontrovertible
Ⓔ	sinuous

Because reasonable prephrases include *sneaky* or *tricky*, most test takers will eliminate *honorable*. But that leaves four unknowns, which may seem overwhelming.

The next two sections will delineate strategies for making educated guesses. For example, you can study root words and affixes. The root word of (D), *incontrovertible*, appears to be similar to *controversy* and the prefix, *in-*, means *not*, so *incontrovertible* might mean *no controversy*. This seems to have an opposite meaning of our prephrase, so it would be wise to eliminate this answer choice.

You can also use Word Sense, as described later in this chapter. The words *lugubrious* and *sinuous* sound negative, and since *sneaky* and *tricky* are negative prephrases, an educated test taker will select between these two answer choices. That leaves you a 50% chance of answering the question correctly!

You must not be afraid to select unknown words on the GRE, either when you know the answer is correct in "All But One" questions, or when you are unsure about the answer but making an educated guess.

GRATUITOUS VOCAB
lugubrious (adj):
gloomy

evanescent (adj):
vanishing

incontrovertible
(adj):
unquestionable;
impossible to
deny

sinuous (adj):
indirect; devious

Selecting an Unknown Problem Set

Each of the sentences or paragraphs below has a word or set of words that has been omitted. From the answer choices, choose the word or set of words that best completes the meaning of the sentence. Answers begin on page 156.

1. The paleontologist determined that the sharpened stone was _____ tool used by the first humans to inhabit Ethiopia over 3 million years ago.

Ⓐ	an academic
Ⓑ	a primeval
Ⓒ	a registered
Ⓓ	a redundant
Ⓔ	an irrelevant

2. Ms. West's _____ was contagious in the classroom; her students displayed an equal enthusiasm and joyfulness for learning.

Ⓐ	exuberance
Ⓑ	acrimony
Ⓒ	fatigue
Ⓓ	generosity
Ⓔ	moroseness

3. Cameron's parents were (i)_____ and (ii)_____; they catered to their son's every whim and failed to see his complete disregard of any rules.

Blank (i)		Blank (ii)	
Ⓐ	complaisant	Ⓓ	impercipient
Ⓑ	devastated	Ⓔ	exhaustive
Ⓒ	indulgent	Ⓕ	exalted

4. In the review of his show, the comedian was described as _____; he was playfully mischievous and good-humored.

A	dramatic
B	frolicsome
C	waggish
D	somber
E	striking
F	remote

Vocabulary Roots and Affixes

When faced with a Fill-in-the-Blank question that uses difficult vocabulary words in the answer choices, you may be forced to guess the answer. How you guess can greatly change your GRE score; educated guessing will earn you many more points than random selection, so it is important to learn how to make intelligent and logical guesses. Using your knowledge of root words, prefixes, suffixes, and related words is one strategy that can increase your accuracy when guessing on the GRE.

Roots and Affixes

"Affixes" is the collective term for prefixes and suffixes; a prefix is placed before a root word and a suffix is placed after the root word.

Most of us have a basic understanding of prefixes and suffixes from our reading lessons in elementary school. We know that when *un-* is attached to the beginning of a word it means *not*, as in *unimportant*, *unattached*, and *unstable*. And most test takers know that *-ist* added to a word creates a person who practices, believes in, or is involved with the root word; an *artist* practices art, a *scientist* practices science, and a *stylist* practices style.

See if you remember these most common prefixes:

Prefix	Meaning	Examples
anti-	against	antibiotics, antifreeze
de-	opposite	desegregate, detoxify
dis-	not; opposite of	disadvantage, disinfect
en-; em-	to make	encourage, empower
fore-	before	forecast, foreground
in-; im-	in, towards	insight, implant
in-; im-; il-; ir-	not	immature, irresponsible
inter-	between	intermingle, intertwine
mis-	wrongly	misspell, misfit, mislead
non-	not	nonfat, nonbeliever
pre-	before	preschool, precaution
re-	again	reload, retake, return
sub-	under	subpar, subcategory
trans-	across; over	transport, transplant
un-	not	uncooperative, unfit

The prefixes that indicate contradiction, including *anti-*, *de-*, *dis-*, *in-*, *im-*, *il-*, *ir-*, *mis-*, *non-*, and *un-*, are the most important to learn. Imagine being presented with the word *irrepressible*. If you decode the root word, *press*, you may correctly surmise that *repress* means to keep down. But if you ignore the prefix *ir-*, your ventured definition will be the opposite of the true meaning of the word. Because Fill-in-the-Blank questions use Opposite Answers, you can fall into a trap if you disregard a contradictory prefix.

Now consider the most common suffixes:

Suffix	Meaning	Examples
-able; *-ible*	capable of	forgettable, combustible
-al; *-ial*	like, characteristic of	comical, pictorial
-en	made of	weaken, wooden
-er	one who	faker, photographer
-ful	full of	fearful, joyful, wonderful
-ic	like, characteristic of	iconic, algebraic, symbolic
-ion; *-tion*; *-ation*	act, condition of	correction, attraction
-ity; *-ty*	state of	compatibility, maturity
-ive; *-ative*; *-itive*	having the nature of	informative, dismissive
-less	without	shameless, hopeless
-ly	like, characteristic of	briefly, happily, angrily
-ment	process, result	improvement, enjoyment
-ness	condition of	firmness, loudness
-ous; *-eous*; *-ious*	characteristic of	dangerous, courageous
-y	characterized by	happy, snobby, hairy

Similar to the prefixes that indicate contradiction, the most important suffix to watch for is *-less*. Most of the other suffixes help you determine the part of speech of a word or describe a condition of the root word. But *-less* reverses the meaning of the word; consider the difference between *power* and *powerless*.

If pressed for time, concentrate on the prefixes before studying the suffixes. Prefixes have more power to change word meanings, as we have demonstrated with all of the prefixes that indicate contradiction. While there is little difference in meaning between *inform* and *informative*, there is enormous difference between *inform* and *misinform*.

The affixes listed in these two tables are among the most common suffixes and prefixes used in everyday English. The first appendix of this book contains a dictionary of these and many more affixes for you to study prior to the GRE.

Confidence Quotation
"In fact, eloquence in English will inevitably make use of the Latin element in our vocabulary." Robert Fitzgerald, poet and translator

6

CAUTION: GRE TRAP! Pay close attention to contradictory prefixes and suffixes to avoid decoding an opposite meaning of a vocabulary word.

Appendix A contains a list of common affixes and root words.

Related Words

It is also important to know common root words, which is why they are included in the dictionary in the appendix. And while it is perfectly acceptable to memorize the meanings of roots, some students prefer to use their knowledge of related words to decode a root's definition.

Let's look at how this might help on the GRE:

> When the girls began to play the old, dusty instruments, a _____ of musical notes erupted; the neglected piano was jarringly out of tune and the broken French horn bleated a single shrill honk.

| Ⓐ lexicography |
| Ⓑ bounty |
| Ⓒ dearth |
| Ⓓ cacophony |
| Ⓔ subterfuge |

The clause after the semicolon indicates that the sound coming from the instruments was *jarringly out of tune* and *shrill*. So the word in the blank is going to illustrate this inharmonious sound.

Do any of the answer choices jump out right away as having to do with sound? Answer choice (A) includes the root *graph*. Typically this root is associated with writing or illustrating, as in *cartographer*, *paragraph*, and *graphic designer*. But examine choice (D), *cacophony*. The root in this word is *phon*. Can you think of related words that use *phon*? Try *phonics*, *symphony*, and *telephone*. The connection between all these words is *sound*, and since you are looking for a word about inharmonious sound, choice (D) is an excellent contender. Even if you do not know the meaning of the prefix *caco-*, you are still making a great guess. As it turns out, the meaning of the Greek root *caco-* is *harsh*. *Harsh sound* is an excellent prephrase and perfect fit for the blank.

When you know some prefixes and suffixes, your knowledge of root meanings or related words will open up even more challenging vocabulary terms. Consider some more:

infallibility
Prefix: *in-* (not)   Suffix: *-ibility* (the ability to)
Root Word: *fall*
Roots and Affixes definition: not able to fall
Actual definition: the quality of being incapable of making mistakes

TIPS and TRICKS
To determine the meaning of roots, consider other words with the same root.

GRATUITOUS VOCAB
lexicography (n): the act of writing dictionaries

dearth (n): a lack in supply

cacophony (n): harsh, jarring sound

subterfuge (n): something intended to deceive

6

recalcitrant
Prefix: *re-* (again) Suffix: *-ant* (characteristic of)
Root Word: *calci* (meaning *harden; to become bony*), calcium, calcify
Roots and Affixes definition: characteristic of being hardened again
Actual definition: hard to deal with

anthropocentrism
Prefix: *anthropo-* (meaning *human*) anthropology, philanthropy
Suffix: *-ism* (meaning *state of*)
Root Word: *centr* (meaning *center*) central, egocentric, centrifugal
Roots and Affixes definition: state of a human center
Actual definition: belief that humans are the center of the universe

Not all words are going to translate perfectly, but you may be able to get enough meaning from the roots and affixes to make a logical connection to your prephrase—or to eliminate a word that does not associate with your prephrase. For example, look at what happens when you decode the following word:

unequivocal
Prefix: *un-* (meaning *not*)
Suffix: *-voc* + *-al* (meaning *characteristic of*)
Root Word: *equi* (meaning *equal*) equidistant, equinox, equilibrium
Roots and Affixes definition: not equal
Actual definition: clear; having only one definition

While the two meanings do not at first appear related, think about a word that has only one definition. There is only one; it has no equal. If there were more than one definition, then it has equivalents and might be less clear.

Remember, you are still guessing when you decode words. You might not always guess correctly. But if you utilize the techniques presented here, you significantly increase your chances of guessing the right answer.

6

Decoding roots and affixes is still guessing, but it's educated guessing. The most gifted test takers employ this skill on every test.

Foreign Language Connections

Test takers who have learned languages derived from Greek and Latin, such as Spanish, French, and Italian, may have an edge on the GRE. Since these languages have many words with Greek and Latin roots, you may be able to apply translations to English word counterparts.

For example, take the English word *friend*. In French, it's *ami*. In Spanish, it's *amigo*. And in Italian, it's *amico*. Two common GRE words, *amiable* and *amicable*, share the root *ami* and both mean *friendly*.

Foreign words for *good* and *bad* can also help you decode GRE words:

English: *good*   Spanish: *bueno*   French: *bien*   Italian: *bene*
Related Words: *bene*volent (charitable), *bene*factor (a person who helps), *bene*diction (good wishes), *bene*ficial (helpful), *ben*ign (favorable)

English: *bad*   Spanish: *malo*   French: *mal*   Italian: *male*
Related Words: *male*volent (evil), *male*factor (a person who does harm), *male*diction (a curse), *male*ficent (evil), *mal*adroit (unskillful), *mal*ignant (harmful), *mal*feasance (harmful act), *mal*content (dissatisfaction), *mal*odorous (having a bad smell), *mal*nutrition (lack of nutrition), *mal*aise (illness)

These are just a sampling of the roots and affixes that translate from foreign languages to GRE roots.

It's important to remember that you are always taking a guess when selecting a word that you do not know, but by using your knowledge of roots, affixes, related words, and foreign translations, you are making an educated guess that is much more likely to earn you points on the GRE. Be sure to review the Roots and Affixes Dictionary in the appendix before your official test.

It's also essential to note that these connections should take you mere seconds to make. If you spend 15 seconds or more decoding a word, you are wasting too much time and will be unable to finish the section. While we take several pages to explain roots and affixes, it should only take you a moment to decipher a word once you understand the process. If you cannot decode a word, you cannot eliminate it, and you must leave it as a contender. But if you quickly decode its meaning, you can either eliminate it or select it as the correct answer.

6

Not all words translate, so there may be times this strategy leads you astray. For example, the English word malleable means moldable (the root comes instead from the Latin "malle," meaning "to hammer"), which is not necessarily bad. But you will earn more points using Latin roots than you will lose throughout your GRE preparation.

Root Word Imposters

There are some words in our language whose meanings do not match their apparent root words. Take the word *machinations*. Most students see the root word, *machin*, and automatically associate the word with *machine*, assuming the definition of *machinations* to be something like *products made by machines*. But the word *machinations* is an Imposter Answer; it means *crafty plots or schemes*, and has nothing to do with machines, other than one is a manufactured idea and the other manufactures products.

The GRE may try and trick you in one of two ways. The first occurs when the word is used like a Related Answer in a question with more difficult vocabulary:

> When the automaton broke down on the assembly line, the foreman worked feverishly to get it back into _____ so his employees could return to work.

> | | |
> |---|---|
> | Ⓐ | opulence |
> | Ⓑ | machination |
> | Ⓒ | paucity |
> | Ⓓ | refinement |
> | Ⓔ | kilter |

The best prephrases are *good shape* and *working order*. The question stem contains the word *automaton*, a robotic *machine*, so some students will be tricked into selecting choice (B), *machination*. But our prephrase has nothing to do with a machine! While question stems and answer choices may be related in easier questions, higher level difficult questions will never have such obvious associations. You should eliminate *machination* and any other wrong answer choice before making a guess.

The second way the GRE uses these imposters is also in more difficult questions. These Imposter Answers, however, will erroneously be eliminated if you are not careful. Consider an example:

> It was clear to everyone in the courtroom that the witness's testimony was _____; she dramatically threw herself onto the stand and produced exaggerated tears when providing her questionable alibi.

> | | |
> |---|---|
> | Ⓐ | histrionic |
> | Ⓑ | poignant |
> | Ⓒ | loquacious |
> | Ⓓ | legitimate |
> | Ⓔ | munificent |

6

GRATUITOUS VOCAB

opulence (n): wealth

machination (n): crafty schemes

paucity (n): scarcity

histrionic (adj): overly dramatic

poignant (adj): affecting the emotions

loquacious (adj): talkative

munificent (adj): generous

The best prephrase for this question is *overly dramatic* or *exaggerated*. Many test takers will be able to eliminate *legitimate* and *poignant*, so that we are left with three choices: *histrionic, loquacious,* and *munificent*.

Most students will study *histrionic* and choose to eliminate it because its root resembles the same root in *history*. But this would be a mistake, because histrionic is an Imposter Answer. If you look closely, the roots are actually different. In *histrionic*, the Latin *histrio* means actor. The word *history* comes from the Greek *histor*, meaning a learned man.

Histrionic means overly dramatic and is the correct answer. There are a handful of words with confusing roots or commonly misunderstood meanings that the GRE may use to try to trick you. We have gathered them here, so that you learn their true meanings now in the event you are faced with one on the GRE.

Word	Incorrect Association	Actual Meaning
autonomy	cars	independence
castigate	throwing	to criticize or punish
debunk	beds	to prove untrue
deleterious	deleting	harmful
dogmatic	dogs	opinionated about truths
gustatory	wind	relating to the sense of taste
histrionic	history	overly dramatic
intransigent	traveling	not permanent
officious	official	aggressive; forward
machination	machines	crafty schemes
parenthetical	parents	in parenthesis
temperate	temperature	moderate; not extreme

Vocabulary Roots and Affixes Problem Set

Each of the sentences or paragraphs below has a word or set of words that has been omitted. From the answer choices, choose the word or set of words that best completes the meaning of the sentence. Answers begin on page 157.

1. My grandmother preferred _____ devices to modern technology; she used a rotary telephone to make calls, a record player to listen to music, and a typewriter to compose letters.

Ⓐ	concurrent
Ⓑ	neoteric
Ⓒ	lustrous
Ⓓ	fragmentary
Ⓔ	antiquated

2. The supervisor was a _____ employee, taking great care to always arrive on time and paying extremely close attention to the details in his weekly reports.

Ⓐ	capricious
Ⓑ	conscientious
Ⓒ	remunerated
Ⓓ	supercilious
Ⓔ	officious

3. Carleton was the most _____ mechanic at the shop; he could complete an oil change in under sixty seconds and install new brake pads in just twenty minutes.

Ⓐ	catechized
Ⓑ	sophomoric
Ⓒ	apathetic
Ⓓ	fastidious
Ⓔ	expeditious

4. Despite the commercials touting the cough medicine as a wonder drug, it was _____ in suppressing Jackson's irritating cough.

Ⓐ	trenchant
Ⓑ	curative
Ⓒ	impervious
Ⓓ	inefficacious
Ⓔ	unvociferous

5. The movie was supposedly based on a true story but it lacked _____; the main character's bravery was exaggerated and he was not involved in an explosive car chase in real life.

Ⓐ	umbrage
Ⓑ	verisimilitude
Ⓒ	gaiety
Ⓓ	perturbation
Ⓔ	inexactitude

Word Sense

TIPS and TRICKS
When all other decoding strategies fail, use word sense to determine whether a word feels positive or negative.

GRATUITOUS VOCAB

amiable(adj): friendly

eloquent (adj): expressive

fidelity (n): loyalty

munificent (adj): generous

reverence (n): respect

furtive (adj): sneaky

ignominious (adj): disgraceful

malevolent (adj): evil

rancorous (adj): hateful

spurious (adj): fake

truculent (adj): brutally cruel

deleterious (adj): harmful

beneficent (adj): charitable

obstinate (adj): stubborn

There may be times that you are unable to eliminate or decode some answer choices. You know you should guess, but you are not sure how to make a good guess. Word Sense is a last-ditch effort, when roots and affixes fail.

Many words on the GRE have a positive or negative sense. Words like *plausible* and *adulation* just sound good, while terms like *extirpation* and *disingenuous* feel bad. Consider some others:

Positive (+) Sense	Negative (−) Sense
amiable	exasperation
eloquent	furtive
fidelity	ignominious
hilarity	malevolent
munificent	rancorous
reverence	spurious

Word Sense is used to make educated guesses when other strategies fail:

Alexandra may have been stingy with her family, but she was _____ to strangers; she volunteered in homeless shelters each week and donated thousands of dollars to charity.

Ⓐ truculent
Ⓑ deleterious
Ⓒ beneficent
Ⓓ reassuring
Ⓔ obstinate

Prephrases, such as *charitable* and *giving*, are clearly positive. You can likely eliminate (D), *reassuring*, since it does not make sense in the blank. That leaves you with four possible unknowns, to which you can assign positive and negative sense.

You can sometimes use your knowledge of prefixes and roots to determine word sense, as with choices (B) (*delete*) and (E) (*ob-* meaning against). These are negative affixes, and the resulting words likely have negative connotations. Most test takers agree that *truculent* in (A) sounds negative, thus leaving only one word with a positive sense, *beneficent*. This is the correct answer.

Not all GRE words have a positive or negative sense; some are neutral and therefore cannot be eliminated. Consider another example:

In the film, the villain offered to complete the heroine's accounting reports, a proposal she thought helpful; little did she know he had _____ plan to make it appear as if she were embezzling from the company.

Ⓐ	an equanimous
Ⓑ	an egalitarian
Ⓒ	an inoffensive
Ⓓ	an insidious
Ⓔ	a decorous

A good prephrase is *sneaky*, revealing that we are searching for a negative word. You likely can eliminate (C), *inoffensive*, as it does not match *sneaky*. Most test takers feel that (E), *decorous*, has a positive feeling, and thus eliminate it. That leaves (A), *equanimous,* and (B), *egalitarian*, two words that to many sound neutral, and (D), *insidious*, a negative-sounding word. You must make a guess between the three. Since your prephrase is negative, you should lean toward choice (D).

Again, you must recognize that this strategy is not fail-proof and that you are still guessing. A few GRE words do not follow Word Sense patterns. For example, consider the word *auspicious*. For most people, it sounds negative, like *suspicious*. But it actually means *favorable*. When you follow these strategies, you may make some mistakes, but they are worthwhile errors since you will likely gain more points than you will lose.

As with decoding words using roots and affixes, you should only spend mere seconds determining a word's positive or negative charge. These strategies can slow you down if you do not fully understand them or fail to practice using them quickly.

When faced with an unknown word, you should first consider a possible root word and any prefixes or suffixes in order to decode its meaning. If this strategy does not lead to a definition, determine the word's sense; does it sound positive or feel negative? After eliminating words using these two strategies, you should always make a guess on Fill-in-the-Blank questions.

6

Rarely, words do not match their sense. The best defense against mistakes is to boost your vocabulary by studying commonly-occurring words, which we discuss in the next section.

GRATUITOUS VOCAB
equanimous (adj): even-tempered

egalitarian (adj): believing in equality

insidious (adj): intended to harm

decorous (adj): proper and dignified

Word Sense Problem Set

Each of the sentences or paragraphs below has a word or set of words that has been omitted. From the answer choices, choose the word or set of words that best completes the meaning of the sentence. Answers begin on page 158.

1. Given that the author published a stunning 200 novels in only 20 years, it is easy to see the he is considered one of the most _____ fiction writers in history.

   - Ⓐ petulant
   - Ⓑ prolific
   - Ⓒ trite
   - Ⓓ tedious
   - Ⓔ jaded

2. The potential buyer was not swayed by the car salesman's _____; she could see through his oily charm and knew his flattery was quite insincere, aimed at coaxing her into a sale.

   - A fortitude
   - B serendipity
   - C sonorousness
   - D effervescence
   - E unctuousness
   - F sycophancy

Studying Vocabulary Words

The previous strategies are valuable skills for decoding words that you do not know. But it is no secret—the better your base vocabulary, the better you will do on the GRE. Not only will you know more definitions of words on the test, but you will have a broader word base to use when decoding related words, roots, and affixes.

A broad vocabulary translates into GRE success.

How you study vocabulary is very important. Trying to memorize 3000 words is pointless unless you are beginning your studies years before the GRE, and even then most educators doubt you will be able to retain those words long term. Memorizing short lists of frequently-occurring words, however, will definitely improve your score.

All students should learn the Repeat Offenders contained in the second appendix of this book. These words appear frequently on the GRE, so you are sure to encounter them again throughout your practice and official testing.

Do not study any words that you already know. Place a star next to these words and move on. You will also find many bonus vocabulary words throughout this book in the Gratuitous Vocab sidebars and in the Answer Keys of the Fill-in-the-Blank chapters of this book.

All of the Repeat Offenders are contained in Appendix B of this book.

Many students report that reading a classic novel or a challenging book prior to the GRE really helps them boost their vocabulary retention. There is a good reason for this. The first 1,000 words that we learn as toddlers are the most commonly used words by children and adults alike. Listening to normal conversation and watching television, we are exposed to very few new words outside of these first 1,000. But reading a challenging book reveals hundreds of unfamiliar words and provides them in a context that we can study and define. It is much easier to learn these words in context than it is to memorize them on isolated lists. If you choose to read a novel prior to the GRE, be sure to note any unrecognizable words as you read. Try to define them using the context of the sentence or paragraph, and then confirm your definition with a dictionary. You may choose to keep a list of these words on a paper bookmark for further study after you complete the book.

There are five vocabulary quizzes at the end of Appendix B to help you assess your progress.

Strategies for Studying Vocabulary Words

Everyone has unique learning styles and some methods may be more efficient for you than others. Select the strategy or strategies from this list that have been most successful for you in the past. The more ways you learn the words, the more likely you will retain the definitions.

1. **Write out the words and their meanings.**
   Transferring the words and their definitions to paper helps transfer the information into your long-term memory. Consider creating flash cards, either on paper or in a computer program like Quizlet.

2. **Write new sentences for each word.**
   Similarly, using the word in context helps cement its meaning.

3. **Draw a picture representing the word.**
   Pictures can create a connection to the definition, and test takers who are visual learners are sure to prefer this method of vocabulary study.

4. **Type the words and definitions.**
   Type each word list into a word processing document or spreadsheet. Then try to define them without looking at the definitions.

5. **Write a short story using 10 or 20 vocabulary words.**
   Trying to create a context for each word is sure to help you remember its definition on test day.

6. **Read the word aloud and say it in a sentence.**
   Some auditory learners find it easier to learn when they hear information. Record yourself for later playback.

7. **Analyze the roots, prefixes, and suffixes.**
   Can you find words that have the same suffix? If so, do they mean the same thing in both words? Learning to associate words with related words can help you solve even the toughest test questions.

8. **Group words by meaning.**
   Many GRE words have similar meanings. Organize your words so that you associate a meaning, such as "lacking money" or "friendliness" with all of the words in the group.

9. **Have someone quiz you.**
   Ask a friend or family member to quiz you.

10. **Write your own vocabulary quizzes.**
    Experts believe people learn best when they teach, so here is your chance! Write your own vocabulary quizzes, like the diagnostic on the following page, and then take the quizzes a week or two later.

Confidence Quotation

"One forgets words as one forgets names. One's vocabulary needs constant fertilizing or it will die."
Evelyn Waugh, English author

Vocabulary Diagnostic

Curious about how much vocabulary prep you need? Find out in the diagnostic below. Choose the word or phrase that is most synonymous in meaning with the vocabulary word and write its corresponding letter on the line; if you do not know the definition of a word, leave the question blank—do not guess! Recommendations for your preparation based on your results are included in the answer key on page 159.

Group A

1. ascertain _____
   A. to make sure
   B. to speed up
   C. to continue on
   D. to advertise

2. kindle _____
   A. to err
   B. to stick to
   C. to create
   D. to light up

3. tome _____
   A. a letter
   B. a burial place
   C. an approval
   D. a book

4. trite _____
   A. overused
   B. prized
   C. confused
   D. irritable

5. opaque _____
   A. selfish
   B. not clear
   C. unpredictable
   D. critical

6. affable _____
   A. funny
   B. friendly
   C. unlawful
   D. disrespectful

7. malice _____
   A. accusation of wrongdoing
   B. separation
   C. desire to harm
   D. subtle difference

Group B

8. plucky _____
   A. cheerful
   B. brave
   C. emotional
   D. rude

9. precocious _____
   A. mature
   B. valuable
   C. bitter
   D. cheap

10. paragon _____
    A. fictional writing technique
    B. a ten-sided figure
    C. last minute plan
    D. perfect example

11. alacrity _____
    A. danger
    B. strictness
    C. eagerness
    D. emphasis

12. clandestine _____
    A. historical
    B. lazy
    C. clever
    D. secret

13. enigmatic _____
    A. tidy
    B. puzzling
    C. greedy
    D. consistent

14. insolent _____
    A. rude
    B. depressed
    C. unsolvable
    D. bankrupt

Group C

15. malinger _____
    A. to wastefully spend money
    B. to cast out spirits
    C. to fake an illness
    D. to overstay a welcome

16. inexorable _____
    A. unnecessary
    B. unforgivable
    C. unyielding
    D. unintentional

17. soporific _____
    A. causing sleep
    B. immaturity
    C. excessively greedy
    D. creating harmony

18. truculence _____
    A. disturbance
    B. stubbornness
    C. hesitation
    D. cruelty

19. impugn _____
    A. to spread lies
    B. to exclude
    C. to attack as false
    D. to teach

20. charlatan _____
    A. a poet
    B. an imposter
    C. a wealthy person
    D. an expert

21. equanimity _____
    A. levelheadedness
    B. impulsiveness
    C. equality
    D. agreement

6

Chapter Summary

You may find vocabulary in the question stem or in the answer choices.

Confidence Quotation
"The soul never thinks without a picture."
Aristotle,
Greek philosopher

Vocabulary in the Question Stem

- The word is often irrelevant to the meaning of the word in the blank. Or the test makers might provide synonyms to help you decode the vocabulary word.

- If the definition of the vocabulary word is necessary to understand the meaning of the blank, try to selectively eliminate answer choices before guessing.

Vocabulary in the Answer Choices

★ Selecting an Unknown

- You cannot eliminate an answer choice if you cannot define it.

- When selecting a word for which you do not know the meaning, trust that you have eliminated the words you do know that do not fit in the blank.

★ Vocabulary Roots and Affixes

- Know some basic, common prefixes and suffixes.

- Consider Related Words, those with similar roots or affixes, when decoding words.

- Use your knowledge of foreign languages to help decode words.

- Know some common Imposter Answers so you can avoid GRE traps.

★ Word Sense

- As a last resort, make educated guesses based on a word's positive, negative, or neutral feeling.

The best defense against Fill-in-the-Blank questions is a broad vocabulary, and studying the most commonly-occurring words can help you efficiently prepare for the test. These words are listed in Appendix B.

Decode the Vocabulary Answer Key

Vocabulary in the Question Stem Problem Set—Page 136

1. C and F   Possible Prephrases: (i) sadness, depression   (ii) cheerfulness

   The word in the first blank is similar in meaning to *morose*. You can determine the meaning of *morose* using the context; if her friends were attempting light and cheerful conversation with her, she must have been sad or depressed. The second blank is the opposite of *morose* and is defined by *light and cheerful conversation*.

   Vocabulary:
   morose: gloomy   *despondency*: depression, sadness
   gratification: satisfaction   *resolution*: determination
   melancholy: gloominess; sadness

2. B   Possible Prephrases: bitter, caustic, harsh

   The blank has a meaning synonymous with *vitriolic*. If you do not know the meaning of this word, you must use common sense to eliminate answers. Criticism is often negative, bad, or harsh, so the commentator might have surprised people by being less negative, bad, or harsh. You can eliminate choices (C), (D), and (E) because they are not negative or bad. When guessing between (A) and (B), *scathing* is the most severe, meaning *bitterly harsh*. It is the correct answer.

3. B and F   Possible Prephrases: superior, arrogant

   The word *foppish* is defined by the first portion of the second clause: *extremely elegant in dress and manner*. It should not give you any hesitation when solving this question. The blank is defined by *felt superior to others*.

   Vocabulary:
   vain: excessively proud
   disdainful: finding others unworthy
   modest: displaying a moderate or ordinary opinion of one's own talents or abilities
   humble: not arrogant or prideful; modest

1. B   Possible Prephrases: an early, a primitive

    Most test takers should be able to eliminate (A), (C), (D), and (E), leaving only answer choice (B).

    Vocabulary:
    primeval: belonging to the first age, especially of the world

2. A   Possible Prephrase: enthusiasm and joyfulness

    Most test takers should eliminate (C) and (D). Did you guess correctly from the 3 remaining choices?

    Vocabulary:
    exuberance: abounding in joy and enthusiasm   *moroseness*: gloominess
    acrimony: bitterness

3. C and D   Possible Prephrases: (i) catering, giving   (ii) blind, oblivious

    You can eliminate (B) because *devastated* does not match your prephrase *catering*. The best answer for the first blank is *indulgent*. You can eliminate (E) because *exhaustive* does not match *blind*. Did you guess correctly from the remaining choices?

    Vocabulary:
    complaisant: inclined to please   *impercipient*: lacking perception
    indulgent: yielding; lenient; tolerant   *exalted*: raised in rank or honor

4. B and C   Possible Prephrase: playfully mischievous and good-humored

    Most test takers should be able to eliminate (A), (D), (E), and (F), leaving only answer choices (B) and (C).

    Vocabulary:
    frolicsome: merry and playful
    waggish: playfully mischievous; jocular and good-humored

1. E   Possible Prephrases: old, outdated

The root of *antiquated* is *antiqu-*, as in *antique*. It means *old* or *ancient*.

Vocabulary:
concurrent: existing at the same time   *fragmentary*: broken; in pieces
neoteric: new; modern   *antiquated*: old; outdated
lustrous: shiny

2. B   Possible Prephrases: attentive, careful, responsible

The root of *conscientious* is *conscien-*, as in *conscience*. Someone with a conscience is concerned about doing the right thing.

Vocabulary:
capricious: apt to change suddenly   *supercilious*: arrogantly disdainful
conscientious: taking extreme care and effort *officious*: aggressive
remunerated: paid; compensated

3. E   Possible Prephrase: speedy, fast

Avoid answer choice (D)! It would be too obvious a selection for a question with such difficult vocabulary.

Vocabulary:
catechized: educated   *fastidious*: giving careful attention to detail
sophomoric: immature   *expeditious*: quick, speedy
apathetic: lacking emotion or enthusiasm

4. D   Possible Prephrases: ineffective, not working

The root of *inefficacious* is *is efficac-*. Related words include *efficient* and *effective*.

Vocabulary:
trenchant: effective   *inefficacious*: ineffective
curative: serving to cure   *unvociferous*: quiet
impervious: not capable of being affected

5.   B   Possible Prephrase: truth

The root of *verisimilitude* is *simili-*, as in *similar*. The prefix, *veri-*, occurs in *verity*, *veritable*, and *veracity*, meaning *truth*. The roots and affixes definition is *similar to truth*.

Vocabulary:
umbrage: annoyance   *perturbation*: the state of being perturbed; agitation
verisimilitude: the semblance of truth   *inexactitude*: the state of being inaccurate
gaiety: happiness

Word Sense Problem Set—Page 150

1.   B   Possible Prephrases: productive

Most test takers find answer choices (A), (C), (D), and (E) negative and choice (B) positive.

Vocabulary:
petulant: easily irritated over small issues
prolific: highly productive
trite: repeated too often; overfamiliar through overuse
tedious: long, boring, and tiring
jaded: having become dull from overexposure

2.   E and F   Possible Prephrases: oily charm, false sincerity

Most test takers find answer choices (C), (E), and (F) negative and choices (A), (B), and (D) positive. You must guess among the three negative answers.

Vocabulary:
fortitude: strength   *effervescence*: enthusiasm and liveliness
serendipity: good fortune   *unctuousness*: oily charm; insincere earnestness
sonorousness: deep sound   *sycophancy*: self-serving flattery

Group A: These words are among the easiest in the Repeat Offenders list.

1. A   ascertain: to make sure
2. D   kindle: to light up
3. D   tome: a book
4. A   trite: overused
5. B   opaque: not clear
6. B   affable: friendly
7. C   malice: desire to harm

Number correct: _____   Number incorrect and omitted: _____

If you missed more than one or two in this group, we recommend intense vocabulary study, from memorizing the words in the Repeat Offenders list to keeping a notebook with all of the new words you encounter in books, magazines, and newspapers.

Group B: These words have a medium difficulty level in the Repeat Offenders list.

8.   B   plucky: brave
9.   A   precocious: mature
10. D   paragon: perfect example
11. C   alacrity: eagerness
12. D   clandestine: secret
13. B   enigmatic: puzzling
14. A   insolent: rude

Number correct: _____   Number incorrect and omitted: _____

If you correctly completed most of Group A but missed more than one or two in this group, you have an average GRE vocabulary. Be sure to study only words you do not know and keep track of new words that you come across in print.

Group C: These words are among the most challenging in the Repeat Offenders list.

15. C   malinger: to fake an illness
16. C   inexorable: unyielding
17. A   soporific: causing sleep
18. D   truculence: cruelty
19. C   impugn: to attack as false
20. B   charlatan: an imposter
21. A   equanimity: levelheadedness

Number correct: _____   Number incorrect and omitted: _____

If you correctly completed Group A and Group B but missed one or two here, you should be able to quickly identify the words in the Repeat Offenders that you do not know. While studying vocabulary benefits all students, you may be able to focus more closely on other areas of the test with limited time devoted to vocabulary.

6

Reading Comprehension Mastery: General Reading Strategies

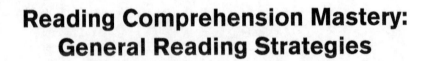

Reading Comprehension Mastery:
General Reading Strategies

Introduction

Reading is a skill that most students first learn in kindergarten or first grade. It is one that is continually honed through many years of practice, although the fundamentals of reading are rarely taught past elementary school or middle school, and almost never addressed in high school or college—at least not in a way that students understand they are reinforcing their reading proficiency. People who read for pleasure continue to polish many of these basic skills, often unconsciously, but those who only read when obligated by school or work almost never fully develop the skills needed to be a proficient reader.

This chapter is dedicated to correcting that oversight. By practicing the strategies here, test takers can improve their comprehension, retention, and reading speed, all of which are skills that are integral to your GRE success.

You should practice reading college-level texts every day from now until the GRE. Even spending 10 minutes a day familiarizing yourself with dry, difficult passages will translate into higher scores on test day. The GRE Verbal Reasoning Bible website (powerscore.com/greVRbible) has links to magazines and websites with articles written in styles similar to GRE passages. You can print portions of these works to use as your daily practice.

We will discuss strategies for attacking questions and answer choices in subsequent chapters, and we will address GRE-specific reading strategies in the following chapter. The information provided in this chapter, however, will simply address how to approach academic passages on the GRE.

NOTE: The information in Chapters 7-14 applies to both short and long passages. These passages are designed to assess your reading comprehension skills, and thus the following chapters address strategies for improving those skills. Argument passages, on the other hand, test your ability to identify and evaluate parts of an argument. They are extremely short paragraphs made up of two or three sentences, and we will discuss them separately in Chapter 15.

Confidence Quotation

"Resolve to edge in a little reading every day, if it is but a single sentence. If you gain fifteen minutes a day, it will make itself felt at the end of the year."
Horace Mann, reformer of American education

Adjust Your Attitude

Have you ever done well at anything you hated to do? Probably not. People who excel at a sport, skill, or art usually love what they do. Beethoven was a musical genius because he loved to play the piano. Shakespeare is the world's most famous playwright because he loved to tell tales. And Georgia O'Keeffe is one of the most celebrated artists in history because she loved to paint.

It's unlikely that your score will improve if you go into the test hating the reading passages. We admit that they are dry and boring. We know that they use prose that is difficult to read. But we insist that you love them just the same.

By pretending to love the passage you are reading, you will increase comprehension and retention.

You must attack each GRE reading passage as if it is an exciting novel you have been waiting to read for months. Enjoying a passage, and even pretending to enjoy a passage, can increase your comprehension and retention of the material you are reading. For example, what are you most likely to remember: an article in your favorite magazine or the reading assignment from a college humanities course? Plus, it is easier to read material in which we are interested. Even if the magazine article and humanities text are written for the same reading level, you are likely to breeze right through the article, but slow down, stumble, and lose focus in the humanities passage. Stimulating passages both hold our attention and increase our retention.

Confidence
Quotation
"Nothing great was ever achieved without enthusiasm." Ralph Waldo Emerson, American poet and essayist

So you must pretend that the GRE passage you are about to read is interesting. Tell yourself it is exciting. Act like it's a bestseller. Do whatever you have to do to expel those negative thoughts and beliefs, because they do nothing to improve your results. Lou Holtz, longtime Notre Dame football coach and sports commentator for ESPN, once said "Ability is what you're capable of doing. Motivation determines what you do. Attitude determines how well you do it." Change your attitude toward the GRE reading passages and you will improve your performance.

Practice Active Reading

You might remember "Active Reading" from your elementary school days, as it is commonly taught in early grades. There are five fundamental reading skills that help students engage in the text:

1. Predict

2. Question

3. Visualize

4. Relate

5. Rephrase

As basic as these skills might be, they are worth reviewing for the GRE. Good readers continue to practice active reading long after elementary school, but the average student leaves these skills behind with recess, coloring books, and show-and-tell.

1. Predict

Remember when your reading assignments had supplemental pictures? Your teacher would ask you to look at the pictures before you began reading and predict what you thought the story was going to be about.

Unfortunately, the GRE does not have pictures to go with the passages. But as you read the passage, you can make predictions about the author's beliefs or the outcome of a situation, especially if you encounter foreshadowing, those hints of what is to come. You might make conjectures between paragraphs when transitions suggest the next topic, or predict within paragraphs when a comparison leads to a contrast. Making predictions engages you in the text, which is the ultimate goal for increasing comprehension and retention.

2. Question

Good readers ask themselves many questions while reading GRE passages. The two most important questions are asked at the end of the first paragraph:

1. What is the main idea?

2. How does the author feel about the situation?

7

If the passage has more than one paragraph, stop briefly after each supporting paragraph and ask two more questions:

1. What is the topic of this paragraph?

2. How does this paragraph develop the main idea?

You should also ask questions about individual sentences and ideas throughout your reading. Some of your questions will be answered by subsequent text, others may go unanswered, and the rest you might answer yourself when drawing conclusions.

3. Visualize

The old adage says "A picture is worth a thousand words," and this is most certainly true on standardized tests. As you read a passage, visualize the setting. If the passage addresses an increase of genetic abnormalities in fish in Michigan, picture an angler on the banks of a Midwestern pond holding a fish with four eyes. Imagine scientists in their laboratory, collecting samples of abnormal fish. Any picture you conjure can help you connect to the passage and thus understand it and remember it more clearly. You can picture events taking place or reactions the author might have to certain situations. Even imagining the author delivering a reading of the text can help you pick up on emphasis, mood, and style.

4. Relate

As you read, ask yourself if there is anything in your background or experience that can help you relate to the people or the situations in the passage. For example, if the passage is about the preservation of a historical building, try to think of something you have tried to save or preserve or imagine a building in your town being threatened by demolition. If the author debates the benefits and risks of daily aspirin therapy, think about people in your life who may have experienced those advantages or those setbacks. How did they feel? What symptoms did they experience?

If you can find similarities between your own life and a dull, obscure GRE reading passage, the text will not only become easier to read, but also easier to remember. Comparing your feelings to those of an author helps you understand the tone and mood more effectively.

5. Rephrase

When good readers come to an important sentence that is complex or difficult to grasp, they rephrase the sentence using their own words. Which of the following is easier for you to understand and remember?

> *Original from passage:*
> An anthropological search that is indiscriminate will occasionally meet with promising, if not revolutionary results, but typically such developments are dependent on definitive, premeditated exploration.

> *Rephrased:*
> An anthropology search that is not well-planned may sometimes have good results but usually good results come from well-planned searches.

Remember, important sentences are main ideas, either of the entire passage or of individual paragraphs. There is no need to paraphrase a sentence that contains trivial details, but by rephrasing a topic sentence, you can quickly read the rest of the paragraph.

Active reading strategies may seem quite basic, but they are utilized by good readers of all ages and skill levels. Relearning these skills and applying them to GRE passages will ease your reading and boost your comprehension of important passages.

TIPS and TRICKS
Paraphrase important sentences of a passage by putting them into your own words.

7

Confidence Quotation
"The way a book is read—which is to say, the qualities a reader brings to a book—can have as much to do with its worth as anything the author puts in it."
Norman Cousins, journalist and author

Anticipate Passage Disciplines

The non-fiction passages used for both Short and Long Passages are generally taken from three disciplines: humanities, social sciences, and natural sciences. Identifying your weakness among these three subject areas can help you more effectively study for the GRE.

Humanities

Humanities passages cover topics with a cultural interest, such as philosophy, literature, music, and art.

> *Examples:*
> The architecture of Aldo Rossi
> The characters of Shakespeare's comedies
> Developments in jazz in the 1970s

In a majority of the humanities passages that we analyzed, the author viewed his subject positively, although the opinions of critics are often cited. Be careful not to confuse the author's viewpoint with the attitudes of others.

Social Sciences

These passages address current or past events with a focus on how those events affected society.

> *Examples:*
> The role of African American women in the Civil War
> The long term-effects of the New Deal
> The impact of 3-D televisions on buying trends

In social science passages, the author will likely provide her point of view of a particular event. She may cite an expert who agrees with her to bolster her main idea, or she may reference an expert who disagrees with her to refute his point of view. Either way, be sure to document any multiple viewpoints that may be provided.

The social science passage may be about an underrepresented group, and ETS uses passages that typically present minority groups in a positive light. If you come across a passage about Japanese immigrants, revolutionary era women, or Native American farmers, you can be sure that these groups are viewed favorably. If anyone is criticized, it is likely the group who has oppressed the underrepresented group. This knowledge can help you determine the author's attitude from the start of the passage.

<u>Confidence Quotation</u>
"Man, the molecule of society, is the subject of social science."
Henry Charles Carey,
19th century economist

Natural Sciences

Natural science passages involve scientific topics, from fields such as biology, geology, or astronomy. Many natural science passages address the effects of science on society.

Examples:
Wolf communication compared to human communication
The composition of lava
How images from the Hubble Telescope are used in school curriculum

Some test takers find the natural science passages easier than the humanities or social science passages, especially if the passage is more about science and less about humans. If the author does not inject his opinion that often, as is the case with some scientific passages, then you are mostly dealing with facts, which are easy to find and prove when you are answering questions.

Natural science passages may contain some unknown vocabulary, but this should not worry you, as it is always explained. The author might define the term in a surrounding sentence, as in this example with the word *cyclotron*:

> The cyclotron, built in 1963, is located in a laboratory on the campus of Michigan State University. A cyclotron is a machine used to accelerate charged particles making them useful for nuclear physics experiments.

TIPS and TRICKS
Separate facts from opinions as you read natural science passages.

Even though most natural science passages are stacked with facts, be on the lookout for the author's point of view. He likely has an opinion on the subject.

Identify the Passage MAPS

When reading both Short and Long Passages you should have four main goals, which you can remember by using the mnemonic device "MAPS." Each letter stands for an element of the passage you should identify:

M   Main Idea

A   Author's Attitude

P   Purpose

S   Structure

The two most important elements of a passage are the Main Idea and the Author's Attitude. Let's look at them, as well as Purpose and Structure, more closely.

Main Idea

Your primary goal on every passage is to determine the main idea. The main idea is the central idea of an entire passage. Sometimes this theme is a fact that the author explains throughout the piece, but more often it is an opinion that the author is trying to prove.

Do not wait until finishing the passage to determine the main idea. Understanding the main idea as soon as it is introduced will help you understand the rest of the passage. We will discuss in detail the location of the main idea and separating it from other viewpoints in the chapters on Short and Long Passages.

Author's Attitude

The author's attitude toward the subject about which he is writing is called the tone of the passage. Because test takers often confuse *tone* with *mood*, we think it is easier to remember the word *attitude* when interpreting the author's feelings.

The author's attitude will not change during a GRE passage.

The tone of a passage is constant; that is, it is maintained throughout the passage, and not just specific to one sentence or one paragraph. If the author starts out showing his respect for a sculptor's work, he will not suddenly become critical halfway through the passage. He may present the viewpoints of two people or two groups of people, such as one who respects the artist and one who is critical of the artist, but his personal opinion will not change.

Unlike the main idea, the tone cannot always be determined at the beginning of a passage or even in a single short passage. On the GRE, authors usually leave clue words to indicate their feelings toward the topic, and we will examine this later in this section.

Purpose

Some GRE questions will ask you to provide a reason that the author wrote a passage. Is she trying to stop the destruction of an endangered owl's natural habitat? Or hoping to gain support for the use of stem cell research? Maybe she is encouraging her readers to write in cursive instead of print.

There are many reasons that people write, and identifying the specific reason that a GRE author might be writing a passage can help you when you have to answer the questions. Like the author's attitude, you likely will need to finish the passage before you are able to name the purpose with certainty. For many GRE passages in Humanities and Social Sciences, the author is writing to persuade. She wants her readers to change their minds or take action against something about which she feels strongly. Many Natural Science passages are simply meant to inform the reader about a phenomenon. But these generalizations are simply that—generalizations. You might come across a passage on the architecture of Frank Lloyd Wright that simply explains his style or a passage on the three toed sloth that implores you to protect their habitat.

You should not spend more than a few seconds considering the purpose of a passage. Once you finish reading, and before moving on to the questions, review the main idea and identify the author's attitude. Then briefly consider why the author wrote the passage and move on to the final element of MAPS, the Structure.

Structure

The structure of the passage refers to its organization. How did the author arrange the information? Many passages open with the main idea and each subsequent sentence or paragraph contains an example or supporting evidence. In longer passages, some body paragraphs may also provide reasons for, consequences of, or solutions to a particular issue or event. Finally, you may also see a paragraph that compares a related idea or one that offers a contrast to the main idea.

Because longer passages offer more opportunity for an author to consider arrangement, you can expect most questions about the structure of a passage to come from passages with two or more paragraphs. But this is not to say that structure does not exist in single-paragraph passages; how an author organizes sentences within the paragraph can serve as question topics as well.

Many Humanities and Social Science passages are written to persuade.

7

Most GRE questions will send you back to the passage with a specific line reference or with a highlighted sentence, so you know exactly where to return to find the answer. But some questions ask about particular information without providing line references. Consider an example:

The author cites all of the following as components of a community EXCEPT

Ⓐ supportive relationships
Ⓑ membership drawn by a common interest
Ⓒ a location common to all members
Ⓓ a population with diverse backgrounds and interests
Ⓔ members who work towards a common goal

This question asks the reader to find four specific details in a passage without directing the reader to any specific locations. While it is not a direct question about the structure of the passage, test takers who keep track of the organization can quickly pinpoint the four examples in the text. Those who do not pay attention to the structure of a passage will waste time skimming the entire passage again.

Given that the GRE is taken on a computer, you obviously cannot physically notate the development of a passage on the screen; you can, however, mentally recognize the organization as you read. Additionally, when reading a Long Passage, you can create a simple outline on the scratch paper provided. This will save you time when faced with questions like the one above. We will discuss this technique more in the next chapter.

Recognize Patterns on the GRE

Learning to recognize specific patterns in passages can help you more easily identify the main idea and the author's viewpoint.

Pivotal Words

Once the main idea is stated, the remaining sentences of a Short Passage and the remaining paragraphs of a Long Passage will explain, support, or elaborate the main idea. This is most often done by providing examples that prove the thesis, but the author may also add details, compare a similar concept, or quote an authority on the subject. He can also cite opposing viewpoints in order to explain why those opinions are wrong.

Pivotal words are those that guide a reader through an author's ideas. Spotting these words throughout a passage can help you determine the author's attitude and opinion concerning the main idea, which will ultimately help you when faced with the questions at the end of the passage. Just knowing that the author favors childhood vaccines or that he disapproves of internet sales tax can help you eliminate wrong answer choices. The following lists contain the most important pivotal words for which to watch when reading a GRE passage.

Pivotal words include "however," "thus," and "in fact," and are those that indicate the direction that the passage is heading.

7

1. U-Turn Words

Just as Text Completion and Sentence Equivalence question stems use U-Turn Words to indicate contrast, the reading passages may use these same words to highlight opposing ideas. These are the most important pivotal words in a passage; if you miss one, you likely miss the author's point and believe the opposite idea to be true. Consider an example:

> Scholars long believed the painting was completed in 1678, but recent evidence indicates that it was not finished until the turn of the century.

In this sentence, the U-Turn Word *but* contradicts the first idea. Test takers who fail to notice the U-Turn Word might mistakenly believe that the painting was completed in 1678, when recent evidence indicates that it was completed in 1700 or later.

U-Turn Words may also be subordinating conjunctions at the beginning of a sentence:

> While an argument can be made that certain programs on television are harmful to children, not all shows have such negative consequences.

CAUTION: GRE TRAP! Missing a U-Turn Word can result in missing the author's main idea or attitude.

The U-Turn Word *while* foreshadows that the second part of the sentence is going to oppose the first part. The author believes that some television shows do not have negative consequences. However, if you do not pick up on *while*, you might erroneously determine that the main idea is that programs on television are harmful to children.

The U-Turn Words in reading passages are similar to those in the Fill-in-the-Blank question stems:

but	on the contrary	still
although	on the other hand	nonetheless
yet	instead of	in contrast
despite	conversely	rather than
while	even though	whereas
however	nevertheless	paradoxically
even so	in spite of	not

When U-Turn Words are used in a passage, the author's viewpoint most often lies in the contrasting idea, which is usually the second portion of the sentence.

2. One Way Words (Additional Information)

The reading passages also share One-Way Words with Fill-in-the-Blank questions. One Way Words that add information to a text are words and phrases that indicate that the author is continuing with or expanding the same idea:

and	besides	in addition
also	further	moreover
as well as	furthermore	too
not only ... but also	both ... and	

3. One Way Words (Comparable Information)

Another type of One Way Word indicates that the author is making a comparison or recognizing a similarity between two things. Words in this list include the following:

equally important	at the same time	similarly
in like fashion/manner	likewise	analogous to
akin to	comparable to	by the same token
just as	parallels	similar to

4. Cause and Effect Words

When the author is citing reasons that something has occurred, he will likely use Cause and Effect Words to get his point across:

because	since	so
due to	accordingly	thus
therefore	consequently	for this reason
hence	then	as a result
leading to	in order to	resulting in

Cause and Effect words are important question indicators because the test makers will likely ask you about either the cause or the effect described.

5. Example Words

A common GRE passage type presents a main idea which is followed by sentences or paragraphs containing examples. The author may introduce examples with the following words:

for example	for instance	as
such as	like	specifically
a case in point	namely	in particular
including	to illustrate	markedly

6. Opposing Viewpoint Words

If an author acknowledges that there are other viewpoints or beliefs on the topic besides her own, she may set them off with one of the following words or phrases:

granted that	yes	of course
admit	concede	accept

You should expect a U-Turn Word to introduce the author's opinion following a sentence that provides an opposing viewpoint:

Example: **Of course** some doctors argue that postponing treatment is dangerous, and with many types of cancers—especially aggressive cancers—they are correct. **Yet** in the case of this cancer and other slowly progressive maladies, they are simply wrong.

TIPS and TRICKS
If the author acknowledges an opposing viewpoint, expect him to attack it immediately after. The main idea or a restatement of the main idea is often contained in the attack. Plus, you can almost always expect a question corresponding to an opposing viewpoint.

7. Emphasis Words

The author can emphasize a point in two ways. He can repeat or rephrase a statement, using specific emphasis words to introduce the reiteration:

again	to repeat	in other words
that is	in essence	in fact

Emphasis Words often provide attitude clues to the author's feelings about the subject.

Or he can use emphasis words or phrases to show the importance of the original statement. These words may reveal the main idea or tone of a passage:

above all	indeed	more important
chiefly	especially	singularly
and even	undeniably	undoubtedly
obviously	clearly	certainly
surely	unquestionably	definitely

8. Conclusion Words

If the author offers a conclusion, pay close attention. She is likely summarizing the main idea. Watch for these words to set off a conclusion:

in conclusion	to sum up	in brief
for these reasons	after all	all things considered
in any event	on the whole	finally
in summary	to summarize	to conclude

Let's examine a long passage to see how these pivotal words introduce ideas.

Scientists have long hypothesized that the abundance of species in the Amazon river basin was the result of[1] climatic stability, based on their observations of life in—of all places—the deep sea.
Line 5 Because[2] the abyssal zone, that deepest part of the ocean that is consistently cold and dark, has such a high level of species diversity, scientists concluded that its constant climate and conditions attracted numerous species. Similarly,[3] they noted, the Amazon river basin
10 maintains a relatively unfluctuating tropical rainforest climate, as well as[4] supports a multitude of species.

Recent theories about the Amazon basin, however,[5] dispute this long-standing theory. Some biologists are now suggesting that the rainforest of the Amazon does
15 not, in fact,[6] have a stable climate, but[7] rather one that has seen significant variation over time.

To illustrate[8] their new theory, these biologists point to an oddity among bird species. Although[9] the rainforest is currently constant, with green forest
20 spread throughout, different species of birds inhabit different areas. Scientists studying species distribution wondered why certain parrots lived in specific areas and not elsewhere in the forest. If the conditions were constant, why wouldn't a species spread out? The same
25 mud-dwelling invertebrates can be found in the deepest parts of all the world's oceans, so why couldn't these parrots be found all over the Amazon rain forest?

These biologists proposed that the bird distribution was the result of climactic changes in the Amazon
30 basin during ice ages. They noted that different species of birds were found on low ground than on high ground, and suggested that each of the thirteen ice ages divided the basin in two: the low ground became dry plains, while[10] the high ground retained
35 moisture. This division also[11] separated the resident bird population by both[12] physical location and[12] genetic makeup, forcing each isolated group to adapt to the new climate. With each subsequent ice age, the once continuous population was further divided,
40 thus[13] increasing diversity of species and permanently altering the locality of the birds.

This new theory not only[14] questions the climactic stability of the Amazon River basin, but also[14] provides an alternative argument for the cause of such great
45 species diversity in the rainforest. Granted,[15] there is no conclusive evidence to substantiate this new theory, but[16] its very existence acknowledges that scientists recognize there might be other possible reasons for an abundance of species besides climactic stability.
50 It causes one to wonder if biologists may soon re-examine their beliefs about species diversity in the deep sea.

[1] Cause: climatic stability
Effect: species diversity

[2] Cause: species diversity
Effect: scientists concluded

[3] One-Way Word compares deep sea to river basin

[4] One-Way Word provides additional detail

[5, 7] U-Turn Words indicate contradiction of previous paragraph

[6] Provides emphasis of the main idea

[8] Introduction of an example

[9] U-Turn Word contrasts reality with expectations

[10] U-Turn Word contrasts two locations

[11] Indicates an additional consequence of division

[12] Gives two equal effects

[13] Cause: Further division
Effect: Increased species diversity and permanent change in locality

[14] Give two equal effects of theory

[15] Acknowledges weakness with theory

[16] U-Turn Word de-emphasizes the weakness and highlights consequences of theory

Did you identify the main idea? It occurs in the second sentence of the second paragraph.

Obviously you cannot notate or even read a passage this closely on the GRE. But learning to identify Pivotal Words while practicing can be internalized to help you quickly process them on test day.

7

Learning to spot these pivotal words in GRE passages can increase your comprehension and even your reading speed. Pay particular attention to U-Turn Words and Cause and Effect Words, as these most often signal important ideas, especially those that are asked about in the questions following the passage.

Attitude Clues

The tone of a passage is simply the author's attitude toward the subject about which she is writing. Some passages, especially natural science passages like the one on the previous page about the Amazon River basin, are matter-of-fact and impartial, but many GRE passages have a clear tone. On rare occasion—particularly on those in which the passage uses the first person pronoun "I"—an author might explicitly state how she feels about a topic:

> I am fascinated by ancient cathedrals. Their architecture is worthy of respect and imitation, which I have graciously practiced since I started designing buildings twenty years ago.

In this passage, the author clearly expresses her fascination and respect, which together constitute the tone or attitude of that paragraph.

Tone is not usually that obvious, though, and must be inferred instead. You can do this by identifying key words that hint at the author's feelings. Consider an example:

> The United States education system must be changed if our graduates are to compete for jobs with students from other countries. Our school calendars lack hours in a day and days in a year compared to European and Asian schedules, resulting in students who are academically behind. Part of the blame can be laid on American parents, who often value freedom and individuality more than discipline and education.

In this passage, the author uses the words *must be changed*, *lack*, and *blame*, which indicate her criticism. The tone of this passage is *critical*.

As you read, be on the lookout for words that reveal the author's true feelings. You may want to jot them down on scratch paper as you read in case you have a hard time determining the tone through the passage; you can review all of your words at the end of the passage to easily establish the author's attitude toward the subject.

Pivotal Words and Attitude Clues Mini-Drill

> In each passage below, circle any pivotal words or phrases and underline tone clues. At the end of the passage, note the main idea and the tone of the passage. Answers begin on page 184.

1:   Surprisingly, the argument that graffiti is legitimate art has many proponents in the art world. They point out that a graffiti artist must create an intricate plan before they begin, just as a painter plans on canvas. These artists use a standard medium—spray paint—just as a painter of canvas uses oils or watercolors. And graffiti communicates to its spectators, just as the *Mona Lisa* or *Water Lilies at Giverney* speaks to the beholders of such masterpieces. While these facts are seemingly true, there is one obvious difference between graffiti and other artistic forms that just may revoke graffiti's status as art: graffiti is illegal.

If creating a work of art is a crime, is it truly art? Advocates for graffiti say that the crime is immaterial, but would they then classify a burglar's ransacking of a home as interior design? Likely not. This example illustrates the fine line between creation and destruction, and gives credence to challengers of graffiti as art. The debate is a murky one, with strong support on each side, but it seems as if the legality of a craft should play a part in determining true art.

Main Idea:

_____

_____

_____

_____

_____

_____

Author's Attitude:

_____

_____

_____

7

2:   The federal government has always been a subordinate partner to states and localities in terms of the amount of education funding that comes directly from its level. The federal share of total revenues for elementary and secondary school education peaked in the late 1970s at less than 10 percent, and today is less than seven percent of the overall expenditures. States and local school districts have retained control over curriculum content and instructional methods; in fact, federal law prohibits U.S. Government interference in these areas.

Still, the federal government has influenced education to a degree that goes well beyond the small share of funding provided. In recent years, to achieve greater impact, federal dollars have been heavily concentrated on certain priorities, such as educating children from lower-income backgrounds, rather than on general school support. Presidents and other national leaders have used the prominence of their office to call attention to a problem and rally people around a national goal. When the rights of individuals are at stake, the federal government has required states and localities to take certain corrective actions.

Main Idea:

_____

_____

_____

_____

_____

Author's Attitude:

_____

_____

_____

Multiple Viewpoints

As if GRE reading passages are not difficult enough, the test makers like to select passages that contain multiple viewpoints. The more opinions a passage contains, the more likely test takers are going to misinterpret the author's viewpoint, which is often the main idea. Consider an example:

> Literary critics have praised author Toni Morrison for her deft handling of female character development in novels that typically feature powerful and troubling themes. While some have called the author a feminist, Morrison has never referred to herself as such, asserting that she seeks to craft viewpoints which embrace equality for all. But one of the strengths of her writing is the uniquely female point of view her characters bring to situations of intolerance and oppression. By their very nature, Morrison's dynamic portrayals assert that women deserve equal rights in any forum.

GRATUITOUS VOCAB
deft (adj): skillful

This passage contains the opinions of four different people or groups of people! Were you able to decipher the author's point of view?

> Literary critics have praised author Toni Morrison for her ----- Literary critics' view
> deft handling of female character development in novels
> that typically feature powerful and troubling themes. While
> some have called the author a feminist, Morrison has never ----- Some people's view
> referred to herself as such, asserting that she seeks to craft ----- Morrison's view
> viewpoints which embrace equality for all. But one of
> the strengths of her writing is the uniquely female point
> of view her characters bring to situations of intolerance ----- Author's view
> and oppression. By their very nature, Morrison's dynamic
> portrayals assert that women deserve equal rights in any
> forum.

CAUTION: GRE TRAP!
Multiple viewpoints are used to make passages more difficult. Avoid this trap by identifying each viewpoint as you read.

In Long Passages, multiple viewpoints may occur in different paragraphs, but beware just the same: they can still cause confusion when determining the author's main idea and attitude toward the subject. Remember, also, that U-Turn words can separate the viewpoints of two people in a single sentence:

> Some watchdog groups argue that television is harmful to children, **but** not all programs have negative effects.

This sentence presents the viewpoint of some watchdog groups (*television is harmful to children*) and the opinion of the author (*not all programs have negative effects*).

Double Negatives

Another strategy used by ETS is to present passages with double negative statements. Although you were likely taught never to use a double negative (such as "I do not have no homework"), there are exceptions to every rule. These expressions are grammatically correct when two negatives make a positive:

Double Negative	Actual Meaning
It is not unlike him to yell.	It is like him to yell.
It is not impossible to win.	It is possible to win.
He is not unfriendly.	He is friendly.

If you come across a double negative in a GRE passage, slow down and closely read the sentence to make sure you understand its meaning. You can even mentally cross out the double negative so that you do not stumble on the sentence if you have to return to that portion of the passage to answer a question:

> Although the monks from the northwest quadrant have no dietary restrictions, it is not uncommon to find members of the monastery who are practicing vegetarians.

> Although the monks from the northwest quadrant have no dietary restrictions, it is ~~not un~~common to find members of the monastery who are practicing vegetarians.

By eliminating *not un-*, you remove the double negative and can more clearly see that the meaning is *it is common*. While double negatives are not prevalent in every passage on the GRE, they are "not uncommon."

CAUTION: GRE TRAP!
Double negatives are used to add confusion to the passage. Avoid any issues by mentally removing the double negative.

7

Multiple Viewpoints and Double Negatives Mini-Drill

In each passage below, underline the multiple viewpoints and notate the owner of the viewpoint to the right of the passage. Then answer the question about the double negative statement. Answers begin on page 185.

1:   File sharing, the practice of allowing the electronic exchange of files over a network such as the Internet, has in recent years led to the emergence of a new and complex set of legal issues for intellectual property owners. Identifying offenders is not unfeasible, but the rapid and often undetectable movement of digital copies of copyrighted material makes identification particularly difficult. In addition, prosecuting such offenses is time-consuming and expensive.

Many owners of intellectual property have claimed that enforcement of these violations is necessary in order to send a signal to other possible offenders. For example, in 2000, members of the band *Metallica* filed suit against a music-sharing company to end the free distribution of their copyrighted material. "From a business standpoint, this is about piracy—a.k.a. taking something that doesn't belong to you and that is morally and legally wrong," said drummer Lars Ulrich. The file sharers, however, typically claim that they did not know they were sharing copyrighted material, and that regardless, the widespread use of file sharing networks renders the protection of copyrights impossible. And then there are some copyright holders, like 50 Cent and Moby, who encourage file sharing as a means to promote their music. "What is important for the music industry to understand is that this really doesn't hurt the artists," said Curtis Jackson, the rapper known as 50 Cent, in a 2007 interview. "A young fan may be just as devout and dedicated no matter if he bought it or stole it."

How does the author feel about identifying offenders in the highlighted portion of the text?

(A) It is possible.
(B) It is impossible.
(C) It is illegal.
(D) It is legal.

2:   Federal rules of evidence have long prohibited the presentation in court of many types of "hearsay," evidence that is recounted second-hand rather than reported directly by a witness. This decision is based on the notion that only the most readily verifiable evidence should be allowed consideration by any court in making its determinations. Much like in a childhood game of "Telephone," the words of the original speaker have a way of becoming altered and warped when passed from person to person. Dr. Kinsley has argued, however, that the rules of evidence as currently written are unacceptably overreaching, defining too many types of evidence as hearsay when the value of that evidence would far outweigh any associated detriment if allowed court admissibility. But modern hearsay rules are not unwarranted.

How does the author feel about modern hearsay rules in the highlighted portion of the text?

(A) They are overextended.
(B) They become distorted.
(C) They are needed.
(D) They are not needed.

Chapter Summary

There are several strategies you should employ when reading GRE passages:

1. Adjust Your Attitude

- Attack the passage as if you are excited to read it.

- Pretend that the topic is interesting.

2. Practice Active Reading

1. Predict: Make guesses about the outcome and author's reaction.

2. Question: Ask questions as you read.

3. Visualize: Picture the setting and the author reacting.

4. Relate: Connect to the passage by comparing it to your personal experience.

5. Paraphrase: Rephrase difficult text using your own words.

7

3. Identify the Passage MAPS

- Main Idea (the central theme of the passage)

- Author's Attitude (how the author feels about the subject)

- Purpose (the reason the author wrote the piece)

- Structure (how the passage is organized)

4. Recognize Patterns on the GRE

- Pivotal Words: Watch for words that indicate change, similarity, conclusion, emphasis, or other direction to help pinpoint opinions.

- Attitude Clues: In order to determine the tone, note words or phrases as you read that indicate an author's feelings towards his subject.

- Multiple Viewpoints: Be careful not to confuse the author's main idea with the opinions of critics or other people or groups mentioned in the passage.

- Double Negatives: Mentally eliminate double negatives (*Soccer is not unlike football*) in order to reveal a positive message (*Soccer is like football*).

General Reading Strategies Answer Key

Pivotal Words and Attitude Clues Mini Drill—Page 179

Circle pivotal words and underline tone clues:

Passage 1:

Surprisingly, the argument that graffiti is legitimate art has many proponents in the art world. They point out that a graffiti artist must create an intricate plan before they begin, just as a painter plans on canvas. These artists use a standard medium—spray paint—just as a painter of canvas uses oils or watercolors. And graffiti communicates to its spectators, just as the *Mona Lisa* or *Water Lilies at Giverney* speaks to the beholders of such masterpieces. While these facts are seemingly true, there is one obvious difference between graffiti and other artistic forms that just may revoke graffiti's status as art: graffiti is illegal.

If creating a work of art is a crime, is it truly art? Advocates for graffiti say that the crime is immaterial, but would they then classify a burglar's ransacking of a home as interior design? Likely not. This example illustrates the fine line between creation and destruction, and gives credence to challengers of graffiti as art. The debate is a murky one, with strong support on each side, but it seems as if the legality of a craft should play a part in determining true art.

Main Idea:

Graffiti as art is debatable, but the legality of the medium should be considered in determining whether it is art.

Author's Attitude:

Skeptical
Somewhat critical

Passage 2:

The federal government has always been a subordinate partner to states and localities in terms of the amount of education funding that comes directly from its level. The federal share of total revenues for elementary and secondary school education peaked in the late 1970s at less than 10 percent, and today is less than seven percent of the overall expenditures. States and local school districts have retained control over curriculum content and instructional methods; in fact, federal law prohibits U.S. Government interference in these areas.

Still, the federal government has influenced education to a degree that goes well beyond the small share of funding provided. In recent years, to achieve greater impact, federal dollars have been heavily concentrated on certain priorities, such as educating children from lower-income backgrounds, rather than on general school support. Presidents and other national leaders have used the prominence of their office to call attention to a problem and rally people around a national goal. When the rights of individuals are at stake, the federal government has required states and localities to take certain corrective actions.

Main Idea:

The federal government's role in education is limited but they still take an active, positive role when and where they can.

Author's Attitude:

Appreciative of federal government's efforts

Multiple Viewpoints and Double Negatives Mini Drill—Page 182

Passage 1:

File sharing, the practice of allowing the electronic exchange of files over a network such as the Internet, has in recent years led to the emergence of a new and complex set of legal issues for intellectual property owners. <mark>Identifying offenders is not unfeasible, but the rapid and often undetectable movement of digital copies of copyrighted material makes identification particularly difficult.</mark> In addition, prosecuting such offenses is time-consuming and expensive.

Viewpoint—Author

Many owners of intellectual property have claimed that <u>enforcement of these violations is necessary in order to send a signal to other possible offenders</u>. For example, in 2000, members of the band *Metallica* filed suit against a music-sharing company to end the free distribution of their copyrighted material. "<u>From a business standpoint, this is about piracy—a.k.a. taking something that doesn't belong to you and that is morally and legally wrong</u>," said drummer Lars Ulrich. The file sharers, however, typically claim that <u>they did not know they were sharing copyrighted material, and that regardless, the widespread use of file sharing networks renders the protection of copyrights impossible</u>. And then there are some copyright holders, like 50 Cent and Moby, who <u>encourage file sharing as a means to promote their music</u>. "What is important for the music industry to understand is that this really doesn't hurt the artists," said Curtis Jackson, the rapper known as 50 Cent, in a 2007 interview. "<u>A young fan may be just as devout and dedicated no matter if he bought it or stole it</u>."

VP—Many owners

VP—Lars Ulrich

VP—File sharers

VP—Some copyright holders

VP—50 Cent

How does the author feel about identifying offenders in line 5?

(A) It is possible.
(B) It is impossible.
(C) It is illegal.
(D) It is legal.

The correct answer is (A). The author states:

> "Identifying offenders is not unfeasible."

If you cross out the double negative, it becomes:

> "Identifying offenders is ~~not un~~feasible."

Or:

> "Identifying offenders is feasible."

The author believes it is feasible, or possible, to identify offenders.

Passage 2:

Federal rules of evidence have long prohibited the presentation in court of many types of "hearsay," evidence that is recounted second-hand rather than reported directly by a witness. This decision is based on the notion that only the most readily verifiable evidence should be allowed consideration by any court in making its determinations. Much like in a childhood game of "Telephone," the words of the original speaker have a way of becoming altered and warped when passed from person to person. Dr. Kinsley has argued, however, that <u>the rules of evidence as currently written are unacceptably overreaching</u>, defining too many types of evidence as hearsay when the value of that evidence would far outweigh any associated detriment if allowed court admissibility. <mark>But modern hearsay rules are not unwarranted.</mark>

VP—Kinsley

VP—Author

How does the author feel about modern hearsay rules in lines 14 and 15?

(A) They are overextended.
(B) They become distorted.
(C) They are needed.
(D) They are not needed.

The author states:

> "Modern hearsay rules are ~~not un~~warranted."

Or:

> "Modern hearsay rules are warranted."

The author believes that hearsay rules are warranted, or needed.

Reading Comprehension Mastery: Strategies for Long Passages

Reading Comprehension Mastery: Strategies for Long Passages

Introduction

The GRE features three types of passages: Long Passages, Short Passages, and Argument Passages. In general, the shorter the passage, the more difficult the accompanying questions, mainly because there is not as much text or information with which to work. For this reason, we are going to start with Long Passages, as many of the suggestions about them will also apply to Short Passages in the next chapter.

Expect one or two Long Passages on your GRE.

You should expect at least one—and possibly two—Long Passages on the GRE. Long Passages are usually 3 to 5 paragraphs in length, consisting of 400 to 500 words. As explained in Chapter 2, the passage is located on the left side of the computer screen. Because the Long Passages take up more space than the screen allows, a scroll bar is added to the right of the passage:

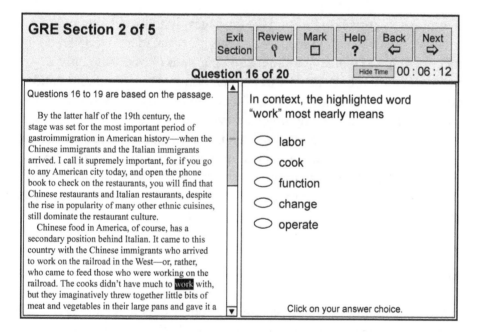

Long passages can have up to six questions associated with them, but in our experience, most of them have four accompanying questions.

Long Passages can be followed by as many as six questions, but most will be followed by four questions.

As mentioned in the last chapter, your goal for all passages—including Long Passages—is to identify the MAPS of the text. Understanding common passage structures can help you more easily pinpoint the main idea, author's attitude, and purpose.

8

Adjust Your Reading Speed

Good readers are like good drivers. The best drivers adjust their speed according to the design and conditions of the roadways. They slow down through curves and on wet roads, and they speed up on straightaways and in good weather. Similarly, the best readers adjust their speed according to the design and conditions of the material. They slow down for the main idea and obscure sentences, and they speed up for supporting paragraphs and easier text.

Most test takers mistakenly believe that they need to slow down their normal reading speed in order to fully understand a GRE passage. But research shows that there is little correlation between your reading rate and comprehension; how well you understand the passage depends on how well you pull information out of it, not on how slowly you work through it.

To improve your pacing through the passages, it helps to study the differences between good readers and inefficient readers. Good readers process groups of words at a time, allowing their eyes to stop only a few times on each line (usually at punctuation marks like commas and periods). Inefficient readers, on the other hand, study every word and their eyes slow or stop many times on every line of text. They may also move their lips while reading; this is a huge mistake because their very quick brains can suddenly move only as fast as their lagging lips. You do not have the luxury to process every single word of a long GRE passage. By learning to read groups of words, you can increase your speed exponentially.

Pacing Strategies

With longer, multi-paragraph passages, good readers take in the main idea and topic sentences slowly, usually more slowly than inefficient readers. Then those experienced readers process the supporting details quickly— much more quickly than their less successful counterparts. Begin these long passages at your normal reading rate because the main idea is almost always in the first paragraph. Slow down when you find it and read it carefully. You may also note any of the author's prevalent feelings toward the subject.

Once you locate the main idea, read the supporting paragraphs quickly. Good readers usually slow down for the first and last sentence of all supporting paragraphs, but read the details in between quite rapidly. The topic sentence of the supporting paragraph usually provides enough information to help you quickly process any other details in the paragraph. It's unlikely that you will understand all of the information in the supporting paragraphs, and that's okay, too. You might not be asked about that specific portion of the text, and if you are, the test will provide a line reference so that you can come back and study it more closely. By reading the less important details quickly, you are preserving time to carefully read the questions and answer choices, which is imperative for your success.

Although it is acceptable to skip difficult supporting details, you must ensure that you understand the main idea of the passage. If you finish the first paragraph and do not yet understand the main idea or the general meaning of the paragraph, do not continue reading. The remaining paragraphs are likely to confuse you even more, rather than help you make sense of the first paragraph. At this point you have two options:

1. Skip to the last two sentences of the passage to see if the author summarizes his argument in a more straightforward manner.

2. Reread the first paragraph more carefully.

Always try option 1 first. If you find that the last two sentences do indeed explain the main idea, you can go back and begin reading the second paragraph. If these final sentences do not clear up your confusion, you are forced to reread.

Suggested Time Limits

For most test takers, this suggestion of reading slowly for main ideas and quickly for supporting details will seem foreign or unnatural. That is why it is extremely important that you practice this technique, preferably with a timer or stopwatch. Aim to read Long Passages in 2½ minutes or less. If you find that you are taking longer than 3 minutes to read a Long Passage, you are reading too closely—and too slowly! Work on slowing down for the main ideas and reading more quickly through the details.

Confidence Quotation
"Books had instant replay long before televised sports."
Bern Williams, English philosopher

8

TIPS and TRICKS
Use a stopwatch or timer while you practice reading passages to help you get a feel for two and a half minutes.

Plan Your Attack for Long Passages

The previous chapter discussed general strategies to employ while reading. Those strategies are especially helpful on the GRE, but they can be applied to all of your reading, from school assignments to articles from your favorite magazine. In this chapter, however, we will continue our discussion of GRE-specific steps for reading a Long Passage.

Read the entire passage before looking at questions

You must read the entire passage on the GRE before moving to the questions. It does not matter what your English professor recommends or what your friend did on the GRE four years ago; while they may be experts in English or other fields, they are not GRE experts who have dedicated hours, weeks, months, and years of study strictly to standardized tests, and in particular, to the GRE. Students who consistently do well in the reading comprehension section of the test always read the entire passage. Our instructors who take the GRE and score in the 99th percentile or higher always read the entire passage. We emphatically advise this strategy because some of our students have bought into several myths about the GRE:

<u>Myth 1: You should skim the passage.</u>

Skimming works well when reading newspaper and magazine articles, as these sources are written for simplicity and entertainment. The GRE, on the other hand, is written to cause confusion and ennui. The test makers know that some students employ skimming, so they use text that is difficult to analyze with a cursory glance. The amount of time that you save by skimming will be lost, along with additional time, once you reach the questions.

<u>Myth 2: You should read the questions first.</u>

On an untimed test, this might be an advisable strategy because you have the luxury to go between the questions and the passage as often as you please. But on the GRE, you simply do not have time to read the questions, read the Long Passage, and then read the questions again. We have had our expert instructors practice this approach in the past and all of them reported running out or nearly running out of time before completing the section. If these 99th percentile scorers (several of whom were English majors in college) struggle with this strategy, we are quite sure it will not benefit the average test taker.

8

GRATUITOUS VOCAB
ennui (adj): boredom

Skimming the passage or only reading portions of it are ineffective strategies. Similarly, you do not have time to read the questions before reading a Long Passage.

Myth 3: You should only read the first and last sentence of each paragraph.

This strategy is based on the misconception that the main idea of the passage and of each paragraph is always in the introductory or concluding sentence of a paragraph. A student who uses this strategy would completely miss the main ideas of these passages!

Efficient and proficient readers read the entire passage before moving to the questions. They do not skim and they do not omit sentences. They know that the passages are designed to sabotage any strategies that involve reading shortcuts. Finally, they practice the general strategies for active reading that we highlighted in the previous chapter. It would be wise to reread that chapter or revisit its summary at the completion of this section.

Take notes as you read

The GRE is unique in that the passages and questions appear on a computer screen, rather than in a test booklet. Test takers who are used to taking notes directly on the passage may be uncomfortable with the CAT format at first. This is one reason why it is imperative that you practice with the PowerPrep software provided by ETS.

It is impossible to remember all of the details from a long GRE passage. Our short term memory is like a guard whose sole purpose is to allow only 5 or 6 facts into our brains at one time and deny entrance to any other new information. Most test takers read a GRE passage once and then have to reread each paragraph when they return to answer specific questions. Good readers, however, take measures to prevent time-consuming, redundant rereading by constructing a simple outline on the scratch paper provided. After questioning themselves about the main idea and topic of each paragraph, they write a short, 3 or 4 word summary for each long paragraph or each group of related paragraphs. The key word is *short*; writing full sentences is time consuming.

A short, simple outline invokes active reading skills and keeps your short term memory from becoming overcrowded and unreliable when you turn to the questions. It also reveals the structure of the passage, a key step in identifying the MAPS of the passage.

We will continue our discussion of note-taking in the next chapter, looking at specific strategies for creating the most effective notes.

8

TIPS and TRICKS
Taking notes on scratch paper as you read not only helps your remember the important ideas from the passage but also assists you in determining the passage structure.

Identify the Long Passage Structure

Expository essays, such as the Long Passages found on the GRE, have common text structures that writers employ to clearly and effectively make their arguments. Understanding these structures on the GRE can help you identify an author's point of view in passages that are filled with complicated vocabulary and jargon meant to confuse you. There are five main types of text arrangement in Long Passages.

Description

The most common form of a Long GRE Passage describes a theory, study, phenomenon, idea, or other topic. This description itself can come in a couple of styles:

1. Point and Example

In this text structure, the author typically states the main idea in the opening paragraph and then provides examples that support the main idea in subsequent paragraphs.

Example Outline:
I. Point: Shakespeare's appeal has endured because of his writing skills
II. Example: Characters are compelling
III. Example: Stories illuminate the human condition
IV. Example: Timeless phrases were coined

2. Theory and Critique

If a theory is being discussed, look for it to be introduced in the first paragraph. Near the end of the paragraph, the author will likely state either her agreement with or her objection to the theory. The supporting paragraphs will then present the strengths or weaknesses in the theory; if the author supports the theory, those paragraphs will provide justification for her support, but if she criticizes the theory, those paragraphs will point out the theory's flaws to justify her criticism.

Example Outline:
I. Theory: Dogs were domesticated 32,000 years ago in Europe
II. Support: DNA from fossils in Europe is similar to dogs' DNA today
III. Support: Cave paintings from time period in Europe include dogs

Example Outline:
I. Theory: Dogs were domesticated 32,000 years ago in Europe
II. Criticism: Researchers looked only at European species, ignoring Asia
III. Criticism: Researchers looked only at small portion of animals' DNA
IV. Alternate theory: Dogs were domesticated in Asia

Description passages, which explain a single theory or idea, are the most common Long Passage type on the GRE.

8

Most authors will use distinct transition words or signal words that indicate a specific passage structure. Skilled readers do not pause when encountering these words, but they do note them to help determine the type of essay and the most important points in the text.

Description Signal Words:

for example	for instance	such as	including
to illustrate	is like	characteristics	specifically

Comparison

Comparison essays are also fairly common Long Passages on the GRE. They, too, may come in a couple of forms:

1. Point and Counterpoint

Point and counterpoint essays compare two ideas or two theories. Each idea is usually described in its own paragraph with a neutral tone. A final paragraph may reveal which theory is preferred by the author, or in some cases, provide reasons why both theories are invalid.

Example Outline:
  I. Point: Dogs were domesticated 32,000 years ago in Europe
  II. Counterpoint: Dogs were domesticated 40,000 years ago in Asia
  III. Author's Belief: Asian domestication is best theory

2. Compare and Contrast

In this type of passage, the similarities and differences of two subjects are analyzed. The passage might present separate paragraphs for each subject (similar to a Point and Counterpoint Essay), group similarities and differences into separate paragraphs, or consider one aspect of both subjects in the same paragraph.

Example Outline:
  I. Point: A comparison of Neanderthal brains and human brains
  II. Similarities: How Neanderthal brains are similar to human brains
  III. Differences: How Neanderthal brains are different from human brains

Example Outline:
  I. Point: A comparison of Neanderthal brains and human brains
  II. Size and shape: The Neanderthal brain vs. the human brain
  III. Rate of development: The Neanderthal brain vs. the human brain
  IV. Mental capability: The Neanderthal brain vs. the human brain

Comparison essays are similar to Description passages, but they explain—and compare—two or more theories or ideas.

8

Comparison Signal Words:

however	even though	by contrast	yet
but	despite	still	on the contrary
otherwise	in comparison	on the other hand	similarly
as opposed to	nevertheless	although	different
alike	same as	in the same way	just like
just as	likewise	where as	while
rather	instead of	conversely	differ

Cause and Effect

Cause and Effect passages describe the relationship between a result and the cause of that result.

There are two common cause and effect essay formats: the first lists several causes of a single effect and the second gives a single cause for multiple effects.

Example Outline:
   I. Point: Several factors can contribute to heart disease
  II. Cause: Sleep deprivation
 III. Cause: Smoking
  IV. Cause: Diet
   V. Effect: Heart disease

Example Outline:
   I. Point: Sleep deprivation results in many health issues
  II. Cause: Lack of sleep
 III. Effect: Obesity
  IV. Effect: Depression
   V. Effect: Heart disease

Cause and Effect Signal Words:

because	for this reason	thus	since
therefore	in order to	as a result	consequently
due to	for this reason	on account of	reasons why
so that	hence	leading to	if...then
effect	affect	accordingly	so much that

8

Problem and Solution

Similar to cause and effect passages, these essays identify a current or past problem and propose a solution. The passage may simply offer a single solution, or discuss and dismiss several possible fixes before presenting the author's preferred solution method.

Problem and Solution passages present an issue and possible solutions to that issue.

Example Outline:
  I. Problem: Standardized testing in schools is detrimental to children
  II. Solution: Students should be evaluated using portfolios instead

Example Outline:
  I.   Problem: Standardized testing in schools is detrimental to children
  II. Insufficient Solution: The tests should assess core curriculum
  III. Insufficient Solution: School-wide results should be scrutinized, rather than individual results
  IV. Best Solution: Students should be evaluated using portfolios instead

Problem and Solution Signal Words:

| problem | dilemma | if...then | question/answer |
| puzzle | solution | because | cause |

Sequence

Passages that present a sequence of events in their order of occurrence are easy to spot, but they are a bit more rare than the other types of passages on the GRE. They may detail a process—such as the step-by-step guide to carbon dating—or they may describe the sequence of actions that contributed to a historical event—such as the causes of the American Revolution.

A sequence passage is easy to identify because it outlines the process or actions in the order they occur which lead to a result.

Example Outline:
  I.   Point: The process of carbon dating
  II. Step 1: Organic material is excavated and cleaned
  III. Step 2: A small sample is ground into small pieces, treated with hydrochloric acid, and freeze dried
  IV. Step 3: The sample is burned and the carbon is converted to CO_2
  V.   Step 4: The CO_2 is heated to produce benzene, which is tested for its rate of decay
  VI. Step 5: The data is analyzed to find the radiocarbon age of sample

Example Outline:
  I.   Point: The events that lead to the American Revolution
  II. Event 1: Proclamation of 1763
  III. Event 2: Series of tariffs from 1764–1767 (Sugar Act, Stamp Act, etc.)
  III. Event 3: Boston Massacre of 1770
  IV. Event 4: Tea Act and the Boston Tea Party of 1773
  V.   Event 5: Intolerable Acts of 1774

Sequence Signal Words:

first	then	before	now
second	next	after	previously
third	later	when	dates (ex. 1973)

Combinations of Structures

The previous list of passage structures—while common on the GRE—is not necessarily exhaustive. Authors may use a less common structure, or more often, a combination of passage structures.

Example of a Cause and Effect/Problem and Solution passage:
  I.   Cause: Sleep deprivation due to apnea
  II. Effect/Problem: Obesity
  III. Solution: Sleep study and CPAP sleeping device

Example of a Comparison/Sequence passage:
  I. Point: The events that lead to the American Revolution
      A. Proclamation of 1763
      B. Series of tariffs from 1764–1767 (Sugar Act, Stamp Act, etc)
      C. Unrest in Boston from 1770–1774
  II. Point: The events that lead to the Civil War
      A. New states resulting from war with Mexico in 1848
         —Compared to Proclamation of 1763
      B. The Fugitive Slave Act of 1850
         —Compared to the series of tariffs prior to the Revolution
      C. John Brown's raid of Harper's Ferry in 1859
         —Compared to the Boston Tea Party in 1773

To help identify the structure of a passage, start by identifying the purpose of each supporting paragraph. On your scratch paper outline, jot down each paragraph's purpose as you read. Does it have a positive purpose, such as to support, to illustrate, or to explain the main idea? Or does it have a negative purpose, such as to criticize, to contradict, or to undermine the thesis? These notes will help you determine passage structure and answer questions.

8

Combinations of passage structures are very common on the GRE. Understanding the parts of a particular passage type can help you comprehend the passage as a whole.

Identify the Long Passage Structure Mini-Drill

Read the following passage and identify the Main Idea, Author's Attitude, Purpose, and Structure. For the Structure, identify the type and outline each paragraph accordingly. Suggested answers begin on page 202.

PASSAGE 1

By the latter half of the 19th century, the stage was set for the most important period of gastroimmigration in American history—when the Chinese immigrants and the Italian immigrants arrived. I call it supremely important, for if you go to any American city today, and open the phone book to check on the restaurants, you will find that Chinese restaurants and Italian restaurants, despite the rise in popularity of many other ethnic cuisines, still dominate the restaurant culture.

Chinese food in America, of course, has a secondary position behind Italian. It came to this country with the Chinese immigrants who arrived to work on the railroad in the West—or, rather, who came to feed those who were working on the railroad. The cooks didn't have much to work with, but they imaginatively threw together little bits of meat and vegetables in their large pans and gave it a name: chop suey. As this type of cooking hit the big cities, and spread across the country, a whole new cuisine emerged: Chinese-American, replete with Egg Rolls, Wonton Soup, Fried Rice, Chicken Chow Mein, and Spare Ribs. It never had quite the reach of the Italian-American food that was spawned a little bit later—because, though most Americans ate this food, they didn't usually try to cook it at home. However, it did accomplish something extremely significant—it opened up the minds and palates of almost every 20th-century American to the exotic allure of Asian food, paving the way for the absorption of many Asian cuisines into our national eating habits.

A bit later came the big one: Italian-American food. Around 1880, the first wave began—immigrants from Naples, arriving at Ellis Island. Before long, they were living around Mulberry Street in Manhattan, where they desperately tried to reproduce the food of their homeland. They failed, because they could not obtain the ingredients that they used back in the old country. Through sheer ingenuity, however, they made do with what they had. So what if the new dishes used dried herbs instead of fresh, canned tomatoes instead of fresh, more sauce on the pasta than is traditional, and more meat in the diet? The Italian-American cuisine that they created was magnificent—though, if you were born after 1975, you'd never know it, because the best "Italian" chefs in America today eschew Italian-American cuisine, preferring to climb ever-higher mountains of radicchio, anointed with ever-older bottles of balsamic vinegar.

But the real triumph of the cuisine is in the American home—where pizza, lasagna, manicotti, meatballs, veal parmigiana, through frozen food, or delivery food, or home cookin', or routine items such as hot dogs and hamburgers play a tremendously vital role in the everyday fare of Americans. And, I daresay, what we learned from Italian-American food is extremely important—that food with origins in another country can not only become an interesting diversion here, but solidly part of our mainstream fare.

Main Idea: _____

_____

Author's Attitude: _____

Purpose: _____

Structure: _____

_____

_____

_____

_____

_____

Identify the Long Passage Structure Mini-Drill

PASSAGE 2

As the 150th anniversary of the battle of Gettysburg dawned, renewed debate arose among historians regarding their interpretations of warfare at one of the most important events of the American Civil War. The central issue of controversy concerned their perspectives on whether J.E.B. Stuart's late arrival to Gettysburg was to blame for the loss of the battle, which all agree to be the turning point of the war, and subsequently thus the loss of the war.

Critics of the major general assert that his absence left General Robert E. Lee without vital intelligence when Stuart misinterpreted or disregarded his orders to gather intelligence to the west and instead deemed it necessary to conduct a raid to the east (a failed raid, no less), removing him from contact with his commanding officer for eight days. Lee himself once remarked that Stuart "never brought me false information," and most historians will agree that Stuart was a master of reconnaissance; thus, Stuart's detractors contend that the lack of information—specifically the number of federal soldiers and where those soldiers were located—from Lee's most trusted surveyor affected the general's ability to make warfare decisions. Historical records indicate that Stuart's believed culpability is not a novel idea, either: Stuart's peers pointed to his "fatal blunder" as the cause of the loss of Gettysburg, as evidenced by statements of General Jubal Early, a proponent of the Lost Cause postbellum movement, and the less partisan General Thomas L. Rosser, who faithfully served under Stuart. Additionally, Stuart was passed over for the promotion to lieutenant general when he was appointed to the corps command; this was in contrast to every predecessor who received the same nomination and in spite of his subordinates advancing to the equivalent rank of major general, so many view the lack of promotion as implied censure.

Supporters of J.E.B. Stuart, however, defend his actions and lay the blame for Gettysburg on the head of the Confederate army. They assert that the major general indubitably followed Lee's orders, which although somewhat ambiguous concerning the direction Stuart should scout, gave him permission to conduct a raid of the Union railroad as it was the best use of his light cavalry. These same historians aver that Stuart was not Lee's only option for reconnaissance, and that Lee had many highly trained scouts at his disposal who could have gathered the intelligence he claimed was needed for the victory. Despite the fact that Lee took full responsibility for the loss at Gettysburg, disappointed Southerners refused to believe that the great Robert E. Lee was fallible, and thus sought out a scapegoat. A previous failure of Major General Stuart at the Battle of Brandy Station—the only blemish in an otherwise flawless military career—was recent enough in the minds of the media to translate into blame for Gettysburg as well.

It's likely that J.E.B. Stuart was partially responsible for the devastating loss at Gettysburg. He was a trusted member of Lee's army who was counted on for his ability to amass exceptional intelligence and he arrived after two-thirds of the battle had been waged. Yet the success or failure of a battle does not rest on one man alone. Lee's instructions were vague and a deadline was not specified. Additionally, he had other brigades to gather reconnaissance and his decision not to use them to negotiate enemy territory was calamitous, a judgment that cannot be blamed on Stuart.

Main Idea: _____

_____

Author's Attitude: _____

Purpose: _____

Structure: _____

_____

_____

_____

_____

8

Chapter Summary

There are several strategies you should employ when reading GRE passages:

Adjust your reading speed

- Read most of the passage at your normal reading speed.

- Slow down for main ideas and the first sentence of each paragraph.

Plan your attack for Long Passages

- Read the passage before looking at the questions.

- Take notes as you read.

Identify the Long Passage structure

1. Description

   - Point and Example

   - Theory and Critique

2. Comparison

   - Point and Counterpoint

   - Compare and Contrast

3. Cause and Effect

4. Problem and Solution

5. Sequence

6. Combinations of structures

8

Strategies for Long Passages Answer Key

Identify the Long Passage Structure Mini Drill—Page 199

PASSAGE 1
Main Idea:
Chinese and Italian immigrants brought their cuisine to America, where it became a staple in American cooking and eating.

Attitude:
The author could be described as *appreciative*, *admiring*, *enthusiastic*, and *respectful* of Chinese and Italian food. He reveals his feelings with the words *supremely important*, *imaginatively*, *accomplish something extremely significant*, *exotic allure*, *ingenuity*, *magnificent*, and *triumph*.

Purpose:
The author appears to be writing to celebrate Chinese and Italian immigration or to applaud Chinese and Italian cooking. A piece like this might appear as an introduction to an ethnic cookbook or as a sidebar in a textbook about the history of Chinese and Italian immigration.

Structure:
Point and Example
Point (Paragraph 1): Introduction and Main Idea
Example (Paragraph 2): Chinese immigration's effect on American cuisine.
Example (Paragraph 3): Italian immigration's effect on American cuisine.
Result/Summary (Paragraph 4): Italian cuisine became a staple in our diet.

PASSAGE 2
Main Idea:
Two theories exist about who is to blame for Confederate loss at Gettysburg, and both theories are partially true.

Attitude:
The author seems *neutral*, citing two points of view but remaining dispassionate about either one. He assigns blame to both parties.

Purpose:
The author is writing to qualify two existing theories.

Structure:
Point and Counterpoint
Introduction (Paragraph 1): Two theories exist about culpability for Confederate loss at Gettysburg.
Point (Paragraph 2): Jeb Stuart is to blame.
Counterpoint (Paragraph 3): Robert E. Lee is to blame
Author's Belief (Paragraph 4): Both are to blame.

Reading Comprehension Mastery: Strategies for Short Passages

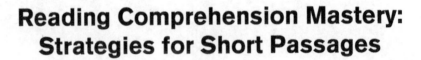

Reading Comprehension Mastery: Strategies for Short Passages

Introduction

There are two types of short passages on the GRE: basic Reading Comprehension Passages and Argument Passages. When we refer to Short Passages in this chapter, we will be discussing those that are assessed by basic reading comprehension questions. The Argument Passages will be covered later in this book.

The majority of passages on the GRE are Short Passages; you should expect to see seven or eight on your exam. An overwhelming majority of the Short Passages are composed of a single paragraph, made up of roughly three to eight sentences, but you may also see a Short Passage containing two paragraphs.

On the computer-based GRE, Short Passages are contained entirely in the reading window on the left side of the computer screen, so a scroll bar is not necessary.

There are seven to eight Short Passages on the GRE.

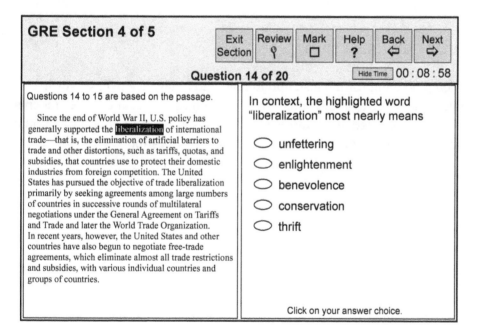

GRE Section 4 of 5

| Exit Section | Review ♀ | Mark ☐ | Help ? | Back ⇐ | Next ⇒ |

Question 14 of 20   Hide Time   00 : 08 : 58

Questions 14 to 15 are based on the passage.

Since the end of World War II, U.S. policy has generally supported the **liberalization** of international trade—that is, the elimination of artificial barriers to trade and other distortions, such as tariffs, quotas, and subsidies, that countries use to protect their domestic industries from foreign competition. The United States has pursued the objective of trade liberalization primarily by seeking agreements among large numbers of countries in successive rounds of multilateral negotiations under the General Agreement on Tariffs and Trade and later the World Trade Organization. In recent years, however, the United States and other countries have also begun to negotiate free-trade agreements, which eliminate almost all trade restrictions and subsidies, with various individual countries and groups of countries.

In context, the highlighted word "liberalization" most nearly means

○ unfettering

○ enlightenment

○ benevolence

○ conservation

○ thrift

Click on your answer choice.

Each passage is accompanied by one to four questions, although most Short Passages have two subsequent questions.

GRATUITOUS VOCAB
subsidies (n): financial aid

unfettering (n): freeing

benevolence (n): goodwill

9

Adjust Your Reading Speed

There is a general rule of difficulty for reading comprehension questions on standardized tests that says the shorter the passage, the more difficult the questions that follow. And there is a simple explanation for this: longer passages allow more opportunities for readers to gather the main idea. After all, the thesis is stated, summarized, and supported in multiple paragraphs. Shorter passages, however, tend to provide the main idea once. Without an abundance of details, readers may struggle to locate the main idea or pull inferences out of the passage.

While it's important to maintain your normal reading speed on GRE passages, you may need to slow down for difficult sentences in the shorter passages. Every sentence counts in a Short Passage, so if you encounter one that is difficult to comprehend at first, reread it with more deliberation. Remember, efficient readers will paraphrase a difficult sentence using their own words so that it is easier to understand and remember.

Suggested Time Limits

When practicing for the test, aim to read and notate Short Passages in a minute or less. Obviously, this is just a rough estimate, and some students may read a passage much more quickly. By setting your goal for a minute, you will allow yourself at least 45 seconds per question.

Read Short Passages more slowly than Long Passages because every sentence counts.

Aim to read Short Passages in 60 seconds or less.

9

Plan Your Attack for Short Passages

Short Passages present their own challenges, so you must have a plan of attack slightly different than for Long Passages.

Know where to start

As noted in the previous chapter, because of time constraints, you should never read the questions before reading a Long Passage. This rule is true for most Short Passages, too, but there is one exception: when the passage has a single accompanying question, read the question before reading the passage.

Above each passage, the computer screen alerts you to the number of questions that follow. For example, it may say "Questions 8 to 10 are based on this passage," indicating that the passage has three accompanying questions. In this case, read the passage before reading each question. But if the screen indicates that there is only a single question ("Question 11 is based on this passage"), then you should read the question first. Because there is only one question, you can focus on extracting that single answer as you read.

Take notes

Efficient readers don't just read—they take notes as they read. We've mentioned this several times in this book, but it bears repeating again (and again) because so few students follow through with this suggestion. Our brains are not designed to remember the entire content of a passage, so we must assist them by recording what we have learned.

Even the Short Passages need a few notes to help you digest the text. These passages are chosen for their difficulty—passive readers will undoubtedly forget important points or misunderstand the main idea, because ETS creates passages designed to trick you.

9

The computer-based test makes it impossible to take notes next to the passage, but you can still use your scratch paper to record important ideas as you read. Your notes should be in your own words; remember, paraphrasing is another component of active reading to help you retain main ideas. These passages are short, so your notes should be, too. Use abbreviations and your own shorthand to create simple memos about the most important sentences in a Short Passage. There are some conventional symbols to know to assist you with your shorthand:

w/	with	→	resulting in, leading to
w/o	without	←	caused by
#	number	ex	example
+	and, plus, also, in addition	cf	compare
b/c	because	∴	therefore, thus
>	greater than	=	is, equals
<	less than	≠	not equal, not the same
vs	versus, against	∨	decreasing
re	regarding, about	∧	increasing

Additionally, create an abbreviation system. The most common schemes eliminate the final letters of a word (ex. lang = language, atmos = atmosphere) or remove vowels, retaining only enough consonants to recognize the word (ex. gvt = government, cbn = carbon). Unlike the notes you took in college, where you returned to them hours or even days later, you are either immediately reviewing these or ignoring them altogether—after all, they are meant to help you internalize the passage. So aim for brevity.

While we recommend an outline format detailing the main idea for each paragraph of a Long Passage, your Short Passage notes may not fit into or warrant an outline. It's likely that you will record only two or three ideas, so a short list often suffices.

Let's look at how an efficient test taker might jot down some notes on a Short Passage:

> Recent commentary about biotechnology has relied on rhetorical intimidation to incite fear and panic among the general public. Critics of this important science draw parallels between catastrophic disasters resulting from chemical and nuclear pollution, going so far as calling genetically-modified foods "genetic pollution" and "Frankenfoods." These detractors manipulate the public's distrust of large corporations to further create alarm, citing financial gain as the root cause of a national health issue that has never truly been about money. While society has accepted much of this fiction as fact, it is time for scientific accuracy to take center stage. The populace must be presented with authentic evidence and analysis about the benefits of genetically modified foods.

GRATUITOUS VOCAB
rhetorical (adj): used for style or effect

detractors (n): critics

Reader's paraphrased thoughts:
Critics scare people concerning
    genetically-modified foods.
Examples of fear tactics include
    genetic pollution & Frankenfoods.
Blame large corporations for greed.
It's not true and time to correct this.
Need to present benefits of
    genetically-modified foods.

Reader's abbreviated notes:
Crit scare ppl re GMOs
    Ex. gen pollu & Franken

Wrong to blame lg corp

∴ show bnfts of GMOs

Confidence Quotation
"He listens well who takes notes." Dante, Italian poet

In an ideal world, the test would not be timed and we could create perfect paraphrased notes. But given the time limits, abbreviated notes like the ones above are easier to understand than the original passage, and they summarize it in a quick, convenient method that will ultimately help you comprehend and retain the main idea of the paragraph.

9

Identify the Short Passage Structure

Short Passages are condensed versions of Long Passages; where Long Passages make a detailed point through an entire paragraph, a Short Passage makes the same point in a sentence or two. Let's look again at the Long Passage example we studied in the Mini Drill at the end of Chapter 8:

GRATUITOUS VOCAB

culpability (n):
blame

novel (adj): new

partisan (adj):
partial to one
side

censure (n):
criticism

indubitably (adv):
unquestionably

ambiguous (adj):
unclear

fallible (adj):
capable of
mistakes

calamitous (adj):
disastrous

As the 150th anniversary of the battle of Gettysburg dawned, renewed debate arose among historians regarding their interpretations of warfare at one of the most important events of the American Civil War. The central issue of controversy concerned their perspectives on whether J.E.B. Stuart's late arrival to Gettysburg was to blame for the loss of the battle, which all agree to be the turning point of the war, and subsequently thus the loss of the war.

Critics of the major general assert that his absence left General Robert E. Lee without vital intelligence when Stuart misinterpreted or disregarded his orders to gather intelligence to the west and instead deemed it necessary to conduct a raid to the east (a failed raid, no less), removing him from contact with his commanding officer for eight days. Lee himself once remarked that Stuart "never brought me false information," and most historians will agree that Stuart was a master of reconnaissance; thus, Stuart's detractors contend that the lack of information—specifically the number of federal soldiers and where those soldiers were located—from Lee's most trusted surveyor affected the general's ability to make warfare decisions. Historical records indicate that Stuart's believed culpability is not a novel idea, either: Stuart's peers pointed to his "fatal blunder" as the cause of the loss of Gettysburg, as evidenced by statements of General Jubal Early, a proponent of the Lost Cause postbellum movement, and the less partisan General Thomas L. Rosser, who faithfully served under Stuart. Additionally, Stuart was passed over for the promotion to lieutenant general when he was appointed to the corps command; this was in contrast to every predecessor who received the same nomination and in spite of his subordinates advancing to the equivalent rank of major general, so many view the lack of promotion as implied censure.

Supporters of J.E.B. Stuart, however, defend his actions and lay the blame for Gettysburg on the head of the Confederate army. They assert that the major general indubitably followed Lee's orders, which although somewhat ambiguous concerning the direction Stuart should scout, gave him permission to conduct a raid of the Union railroad as it was the best use of his light cavalry. These same historians aver that Stuart was not Lee's only option for reconnaissance, and that Lee had many highly trained scouts at his disposal who could have gathered the intelligence he claimed was needed for the victory. Despite the fact that Lee took full responsibility for the loss at Gettysburg, disappointed Southerners refused to believe that the great Robert E. Lee was fallible, and thus sought out a scapegoat. A previous failure of Major General Stuart at the Battle of Brandy Station—the only blemish in an otherwise flawless military career—was recent enough in the minds of the media to translate into blame for Gettysburg as well.

It's likely that J.E.B. Stuart was partially responsible for the devastating loss at Gettysburg. He was a trusted member of Lee's army who was counted on for his ability to amass exceptional intelligence and he arrived after two-thirds of the battle had been waged. Yet the success or failure of a battle does not rest on one man alone. Lee's instructions were vague and a deadline was not specified. Additionally, he had other brigades to gather reconnaissance and his decision not to use them to negotiate enemy territory was calamitous, a judgment that cannot be blamed on Stuart.

9

This passage is a Point and Counterpoint essay, as explained in the previous chapter:

Outline:
    I. Introduction (Paragraph 1): Two theories exist about culpability for Confederate loss at Gettysburg.
    II. Point (Paragraph 2): Jeb Stuart is to blame.
    III. Counterpoint (Paragraph 3): Robert E. Lee is to blame.
    IV. Author's Belief (Paragraph 4): Both are to blame.

Now let's look at how these same ideas might be presented in a Short Passage:

As the 150th anniversary of the battle of Gettysburg dawned, renewed debate arose among historians regarding their interpretations of warfare at one of the most important events of the American Civil War. Critics of Major General J.E.B. Stuart assert that his absence left General Robert E. Lee without vital intelligence when Stuart misinterpreted or disregarded his orders to gather intelligence to the west and instead deemed it necessary to conduct a raid to the east (a failed raid, no less), removing him from contact with his commanding officer for eight days. Others, however, defend Stuart's actions and lay the blame for Gettysburg on the head of the Confederate army, Robert E. Lee, who gave Stuart permission to conduct the raid because there were many highly trained scouts at Lee's disposal who could have gathered the intelligence instead. It's likely that both men were responsible for the devastating loss at Gettysburg, because the success or failure of a battle does not rest on one man alone.

This passage conveys the same general ideas, but in a much shorter format:

Outline:
    I. Introduction (*Sentence* 1): Two theories exist about culpability for Confederate loss at Gettysburg.
    II. Point (*Sentence* 2): Jeb Stuart is to blame.
    III. Counterpoint (*Sentence* 3): Robert E. Lee is to blame.
    IV. Author's Belief (*Sentence* 4): Both are to blame.

Note that the Short Passage takes the first sentences from the first three paragraphs of the Long Passage and drops the Main Idea at the end.

In Chapter 8 we studied Description, Comparison, Cause and Effect, Problem and Solution, and Sequence texts. You should expect all of these passage structures to appear in condensed versions as Short Passages, too.

9

Confidence Quotation

"Outside of a dog, a book is man's best friend. Inside of a dog, it's too dark to read."
Groucho Marx, comedian and actor

Passage Structure and the Main Idea

Knowing where to find the main idea in Short Passages can give you an advantage on test day. There are four common placements for the main idea on the GRE.

1. The first or second sentence is the main idea.

While we like to think of the test makers as nefarious villains, our paranoia often causes us to overlook the benevolence of ETS. Their kindness in the Verbal section most often occurs in the first or second sentence of a reading passage, where they spoon-feed us the main idea. The rest of the paragraph then elaborates or explains the thesis. If the author cites an opposing viewpoint, expect her to reiterate her personal point of view—the main idea—in the final sentence or sentences of the paragraph. Consider an example:

GRATUITOUS VOCAB
Nefarious (adj): extremely wicked

Benevolence (adj): kindness

Writers know that it's never a good idea to leave their readers with the opposing viewpoint, so you can expect the main idea to follow contradictory ideas.

9

To devotees accustomed to the narrative style and moral rectitude of Alexandra Tharrington's nineteenth century novels, the newly discovered autobiographical text from the author will come as a great surprise. — **Main Idea**

While her fictional pieces use lyrical language to paint stories of honorable, courageous women, this biographical document exposes the character of an unprincipled, insecure woman in a style that is discordant and terse. These personal accounts from Tharrington herself—such as the anecdote in which she steals from her bed-ridden mother—reveal a much different temperament than previously thought by fans and critics alike. — **Main Idea Elaboration**

Some of these critics argue that this nonfiction text was written toward the end of her life when she was left destitute and alone, thus altering her outlook on morality and self-sufficiency. They contend that Tharrington was both scrupulous and intrepid, like her heroines, when she was publishing novels. — **Opposing Viewpoint**

However, they cannot dispute that this new biographical evidence will both astonish her fans and shake the foundation of her legacy. — **Restated Main Idea**

GRATUITOUS VOCAB
devotee (n): devoted follower

rectitude (n): virtue

discordant (adj): disagreeing

terse (adj): brief

destitute (adj): poor

scrupulous (adj): moral

intrepid (adj): fearless

This immediate placement of the main idea is most common in science passages but can appear in humanities and social science passages as well. Note that Long Passages often start with the main idea, too. Even though they are described as "Long," they are relatively short when compared to the scholarly articles from which they are drawn. The authors must state the main idea early and save the remaining paragraphs for supporting evidence.

2. The main idea follows an opposing viewpoint.

When a passage opens by citing the opinions of critics, researchers, scientists, experts, or the general public, expect the main idea to disagree with this conventional wisdom. The thesis will follow these opinions, often in the final sentence of the first paragraph or in the opening lines of the second paragraph. Consider an example of this type of passage opening:

TIPS and TRICKS
Knowing where the authors typically place the main idea can help you quickly find it and notate the structure as you read.

> For centuries, historians held that Christopher Columbus discovered the Americas when he landed in the Bahamas in 1492. His accomplishment was commemorated with a federal holiday, state capital, national capital, and even a country named in his honor. Millions of America's school children have been taught to revere the courageous explorer, despite a self-written journal that paints a portrait of a man who was heartless and inhumane toward the resident population. His character was not of importance; we were to idolize the man simply because he discovered our country and made European settlement possible.
>   Now, however, this theory is under investigation, as <u>new evidence suggests that the Phoenicians first visited the Americas in 1600 B.C.</u> Archaeologists believe that an ancient Phoenician coin depicts a map of the world, which includes two land masses that cannot be anything but North and South America.

Opposing Viewpoint

← Main Idea

Because of the difficulty presented when opposing viewpoints are introduced in a passage, ETS relies heavily on their usage in Short and Long Passages. If faced with this type of Point and Counterpoint passage, watch for words that show contrast, such as *however, conversely, despite, but,* and *though.* The author's point of view or main idea will follow words like these.

9

In fact, these contrast words frequently signal the approach of the main idea, even in passages that do not open with opposing conventional wisdom. Many of the passages in *The Official Guide to the GRE* have a main idea set off by contrast words.

Because of the complexity created when an author cites opposing viewpoints, expect to see them frequently on the GRE.

In the majority of both Long and Short Passages, you will find that the main idea is revealed in one of these first two types of passage structures; it's either the first sentence of the paragraph or a sentence in the first paragraph that opposes an accepted idea. But let's look at two more ways that the passage may be set up.

3. The main idea is the answer to a question.

If a passage opens with a question, expect the answer to that question to be the main idea. This answer may come immediately after the question, so that the rest of the paragraph elaborates or explains the thesis. Or the answer may not come until the last sentence of the paragraph or the first sentence of the second paragraph. If this is the case, the preceding information will hint at the answer, explain the answer slowly, or offer contrary opinions. Let's study an example:

> Why does the sight of a snake cause instant terror for ← Question
> most people? These reptiles get little credit for eliminating
> rodents, bugs, and other household pests that may also
> induce fear and loathing. Snakes are not valued, either, for
> the food source they provide for more appreciated owls, ← Opposing
> hawks, herons, and carnivorous mammals. And the fact that Viewpoint
> many poisonous snakes provide venom used in medicines
> and research is ignored by most snake detractors, even
> those who benefit from such medicine. Unfortunately,
> most people's opinions of snakes have been influenced by ← Main Idea
> terrifying myths, fictional media, and negative religious
> stories, resulting in a population that fears these wonderful
> creatures.

This style of passage may occur with any subject area.

If this were an introduction to a Long Passage, can you predict the topic of each supporting paragraph given the last sentence? What predictions can you make about this passage based on the first paragraph? How does the author feel about snakes? Remember to engage the text by reading actively!

9

4. The main idea explains or disputes an opening proverb or quotation.

When a paragraph opens with a proverb, maxim, or.quotation, expect the main idea to be a restatement of the saying or its direct counterargument. The main idea will usually occur in the second half of the first paragraph or in the first sentences of the second paragraph, after a brief explanation of or a commentary on the quotation. Examine a sample:

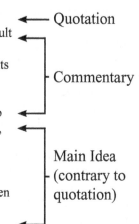

H.L Mencken once remarked, "Looking for an honest politician is like looking for an ethical burglar." It's difficult to believe that even in his day, many politicians did not uphold the very laws and values to which their constituents were held, and it is downright disappointing that changes in our political system were not made then, before the lobbies were so entrenched and the partisan divide was so wide. Yet with the advent of technology and social media, our politicians are facing unprecedented scrutiny and as a result, ethical behavior is a new standard. Unethical politicians are undoubtedly exposed and neither party is willing to take a chance on such candidates; thus, Mencken might be surprised to learn that today's politicians are surprisingly honest.

— Quotation

Commentary

Main Idea (contrary to quotation)

This type of passage is rare on the GRE, and it may occur with humanities, social sciences, or natural sciences texts.

9

These four descriptors of main idea placement do not represent an exhaustive list. The test makers may use a structure not mentioned here, but these four—and most importantly the first two—represent the most common ways the main idea is revealed on the GRE.

Identify the Short Passage Structure Mini-Drill

> In each passage opening below, underline the main idea. Then, diagram the passage, showing contrary opinions, opposing conventional wisdom, personal notes, or other elements as diagrammed in the previous examples. Answers begin on page 218.

PASSAGE 1

Where was Olaudah Equiano born? Since 1999, a debate has raged amongst historians about the birthplace of the author, one of very few slaves of African descent to record his autobiography in English in the eighteenth century. In *The Interesting Narrative of the Life of Olaudah Equiano, or Gustavus Vassa, the African,* Equiano himself claims he was born in Africa, describing life in an African village as a free child. He also provides a first-person account of the arduous journey of the Middle Passage, seemingly something only a captured slave could relate in such detail. In 1999, however, professor and author Vincent Caretta asserted that Equiano was actually born a slave in South Carolina. Caretta argued that Equiano's stories of African life and capture came from oral histories of other slaves and information he gathered in books. The professor provided other evidence, such as a baptismal record and a muster roll, showing that the slave was actually born in the English colony. While the question is far from settled, one thing is certain: members of both sides of the debate possess compelling evidence to support their claims.

PASSAGE 2

Soon after 1900, the oyster industry, which had been expanding since 1885, began to face a much poorer market demand. Owing to a variety of health-related problems in the early 1900's, the United States developed a great concern for good sanitation or, as some termed it, a "pure-food hysteria." Nearly all food dealers were affected including producers of oysters, milk, ice cream, candy, drugs, and many other items.

In the 1800's, oyster packing had been carried out under widely ranging sanitation conditions. Little was known about sanitation, and little thought had been given to the possibility that oysters could pick up diseases in beds and packing plants. But outbreaks of typhoid (Salmonella typhosa) and gastrointestinal disorders were common, and some were tied to the consumption of oysters. Articles about the oyster-typhoid connection were printed frequently in newspapers. Oysters could have picked up the typhoid organism in beds polluted with domestic sewage or during transporting or processing from water, flies, or from the hands of a worker harboring it.

Chapter Summary

There are several strategies you should employ when reading GRE passages:

Adjust your reading speed

- Read most of the passage at your normal reading speed.

- Slow down for main ideas and difficult sections.

- Remember to apply Active Reading strategies, such as paraphrasing difficult sentences.

Plan your attack for Short Passages

- Read the passage before looking at the questions unless there is a single question: in this case, read the question first.

- Take notes as you read.

- Develop a shorthand to speed up your note-taking.

Identify the Short Passage structure

Short Passages are condensed versions of Long Passages

1. Description
   - Point and Example
   - Theory and Critique
2. Comparison
   - Point and Counterpoint
   - Compare and Contrast
3. Cause and Effect
4. Problem and Solution
5. Sequence
6. Combinations of structures

Know common placement patterns for the Main Idea

1. The first sentence is the main idea.
2. The main idea follows an opposing viewpoint.
3. The main idea is the answer to a question.
4. The main idea explains or disputes an opening proverb or quotation.

9

Strategies for Short Passages Answer Key

Identify the Short Passage Structure Mini Drill—Page 216

PASSAGE 1

Where was Olaudah Equiano born? Since 1999, a debate has raged amongst historians about the birthplace of the author, one of very few slaves of African descent to record his autobiography in English in the eighteenth century. In *The Interesting Narrative of the Life of Olaudah Equiano, or Gustavus Vassa, the African*, Equiano himself claims he was born in Africa, describing life in an African village as a free child. He also provides a first-person account of the arduous journey of the Middle Passage, seemingly something only a captured slave could relate in such detail. In 1999, however, professor and author Vincent Caretta asserted that Equiano was actually born a slave in South Carolina. Caretta argued that Equiano's stories of African life and capture came from oral histories of other slaves and information he gathered in books. The professor provided other evidence, such as a baptismal record and a muster roll, showing that the slave was actually born in the English colony. While the question is far from settled, one thing is certain: <u>members of both sides of the debate possess compelling evidence to support their claims.</u>

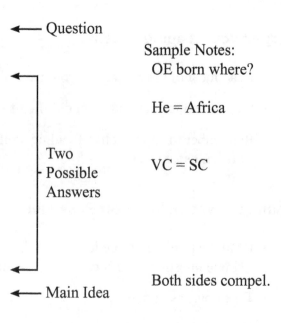

← Question

Two Possible Answers

← Main Idea

Sample Notes:
OE born where?

He = Africa

VC = SC

Both sides compel.

PASSAGE 2

<u>Soon after 1900, the oyster industry, which had been expanding since 1885, began to face a much poorer market demand.</u> Owing to a variety of health-related problems in the early 1900's, the United States developed a great concern for good sanitation or, as some termed it, a "pure-food hysteria." Nearly all food dealers were affected including producers of oysters, milk, ice cream, candy, drugs, and many other items.

In the 1800's, oyster packing had been carried out under widely ranging sanitation conditions. Little was known about sanitation, and little thought had been given to the possibility that oysters could pick up diseases in beds and packing plants. But outbreaks of typhoid (Salmonella typhosa) and gastrointestinal disorders were common, and some were tied to the consumption of oysters. Articles about the oyster-typhoid connection were printed frequently in newspapers. Oysters could have picked up the typhoid organism in beds polluted with domestic sewage or during transporting or processing from water, flies, or from the hands of a worker harboring it.

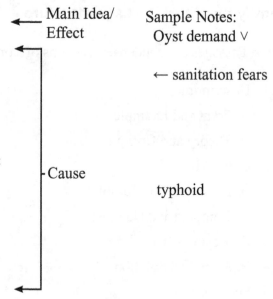

← Main Idea/ Effect

Cause

Sample Notes:
Oyst demand ∨

← sanitation fears

typhoid

9

Reading Comprehension Mastery: Analyze the Answer Choices

Reading Comprehension Mastery:
Analyze the Answer Choices

Introduction

Just like Fill-in-the-Blank questions, Reading Comprehension multiple choice questions have two parts: a question stem and multiple answer choices:

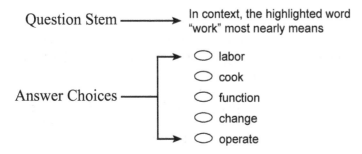

Question Stem ⟶ In context, the highlighted word "work" most nearly means

Answer Choices ⟶
- ◯ labor
- ◯ cook
- ◯ function
- ◯ change
- ◯ operate

Understanding the construction of wrong answers goes a long way in helping you select the right answers.

You are likely wondering why we are "putting the cart before the horse" and discussing the answer choices before covering the question stem. By reviewing answer choices now, you will have more opportunities to practice selecting the right answers and eliminating the wrong ones in the problem sets in the following chapters. We can also point to answers in our explanations for those problem sets and state "This is an Extreme Answer" without explaining that concept over and over because you will know what an Extreme Answer is after reading this chapter. Finally, these strategies are universal to all types of Reading Comprehension questions, so it is convenient to discuss them here before looking at the specific types of questions.

There are two types of answers on the GRE: right answers and wrong answers. But you already knew that, right? In this chapter, we will discuss the characteristics of right and wrong answer choices in greater detail:

1. Right Answers

2. Wrong Answers

   • Copycats

   • Opposites

   • Extremes

   • True But Wrong

   • True To A Point

   • True To You

Let's get started!

The strategies in this chapter apply to all multiple choice questions, whether you are asked to select one or more answers. We will focus most often on Select One answer choice because it allows us to discuss more wrong answer choices. Obviously, though, these tips cannot apply to Select-in-Passage questions, given that answers are not provided in these question types.

10

Right Answers

There is a certain comfort in multiple choice questions, knowing that the right answer is there on the page staring up at you. In Reading Comprehension questions, the right answers are the only answers that can be proven true.

If the question asks you to interpret a phrase or sentence from the passage, **the right answer will be a paraphrase of the actual text from the passage**. Consider an example:

> While the United States was fighting the War of 1812 with Britain, a series of violent incidents occurred when authorities entered Seminole territory to recapture runaway slaves, which aggravated hostility between the U.S. and the Seminole.

1. According to the passage, the "hostility" (line 3) between the United States and the Seminole was intensified by which of the following?

    (A) Wrong answer

    (B) Officials invading Native American territory to reclaim escaped slaves

    (C) Wrong answer

    (D) Wrong answer

    (E) Wrong answer

The correct answer, choice (B), is a reworded version of lines 3 and 4. Compare the wording of the passage and the correct answer:

Words from Passage	Words from Correct Answer
authorities	officials
entered	invaded
Seminole	Native American
territory	*territory*
recapture	reclaim
runaway	escaped
slaves	*slaves*

When adjectives and verbs are used in the original passage, expect the correct answer to use synonyms for these words. Even some of the nouns may be replaced with synonyms, although you should not discount an answer for using the same nouns that were used in the passage. After all, there are only so many ways you can say *spaghetti* or *elephant* or *pants*. If a noun does not have many recognizable synonyms, the test makers will reuse the word in the answer choice. But since adjectives and verbs have many alternatives, they will likely be replaced with different words. Even questions that ask you to draw conclusions about the passage will have right answer choices that prefer synonyms over the actual words from the text. It's one way that the test makers can actually assess whether you understand the passage or are just regurgitating words you happened to read.

The right answer will also include all of the important ideas from the cited line reference, unlike some wrong answers that only provide a portion of the information. Study another example:

Melner attributes the decline in school enrollment to several factors. For one, families are moving out of the area to find work. For another, lackluster test results cause some existing and most new families to choose other districts.

2. According to the passage, enrollment in the school district has decreased because of families'

   Ⓐ Wrong answer

   Ⓑ Wrong answer

   Ⓒ Wrong answer

   Ⓓ Wrong answer

   Ⓔ emphasis on jobs and performance

The correct answer includes both *moving out of the area to find work* (emphasis on jobs) and *lackluster test results* (emphasis on performance). As we will discuss in the next section, wrong answers may address only one of those reasons. The right answer includes all of the important ideas.

Another characteristic of right answers is that **they tend to be more general than wrong answers**:

The festival allowed us to acknowledge our German heritage after hiding our ancestry the rest of the year. For one weekend, my sisters and I could feast on mettwurst and maultaschen, dance the landler, and play Topfschlagen without worrying about the anti-German sentiments permeating the country after the war. It was our most memorable weekend of 1946.

3. According to the passage, the narrator remembers the "festival" with fondness because

   Ⓐ he learned a German dance called the landler

   Ⓑ Wrong answer

   Ⓒ Wrong answer

   Ⓓ it allowed him to celebrate his culture

   Ⓔ German sausages were prepared for the first time that year

10

The correct answer, (D), uses the broad term *culture* to describe the German food, dance, and game that were a part of the festival. The two wrong answers use more specific language. Choice (A) is wrong because it claims the narrator learned a dance; the passage just states that he *danced* the landler, not that he *learned* it. But notice that this answer is quite specific. As is (E). The answer in (E) is wrong because the passage only says that he *ate* mettwurst, not that it was the first time they were *prepared* that year. But again, the use of *German sausages* is quite specific. Sometimes the correct answer is this particular, too, especially if the question asks about a specific event, but when in doubt, select the most general answer choice when guessing.

The right answer is the only answer that can be defended or proven in the text. While many questions ask you which answer best characterizes or most effectively supports an argument in the passage, there is only one choice that completely and correctly answers the question. As we will see, something makes the other four answer choices wrong. When you select an answer, you should be pretty confident that it is correct because you can point to a specific portion of the text that proves the answer.

Now that you know what to look for in the right answers, let's look more closely at common wrong answers!

The right answer can be proven using the passage.

10

Wrong Answers

The test makers carefully write wrong answer choices, intentionally using language and ideas that trick unsuspecting test takers. Learning how these incorrect answers are crafted can help you spot them, which is why eliminating wrong answers can sometimes be easier than determining the right answer.

Copycat Answers

The most common characteristic of wrong answers is that they copy words or phrases from the passage. These are Copycat Answers. Consider an example from earlier in the chapter:

> While the United States was fighting the War of 1812 with Britain, a series of violent incidents occurred when authorities entered Seminole territory to recapture runaway slaves, which aggravated hostility between the U.S. and the Seminole.

1. According to the passage, the "hostility" (line 3) between the United States and the Seminole was intensified by which of the following?

    Ⓐ Wrong answer

    Ⓑ Officials invading Native American territory to reclaim escaped slaves

    Ⓒ Wrong answer

    Ⓓ A violent incident that aggravated the American government

    Ⓔ Wrong answer

We have already looked at how the right answer, choice (B), uses synonyms for words in the text. But consider the choice of words used by answer (D):

Words from Wrong Answer	Words from Passage
violent incident	violent incidents (line 2)
aggravated	aggravated (line 3)

The answer uses two words or phrases directly from the text! Sadly, this simple tactic will trick a lot of test takers into choosing this answer.

The reason that this answer is incorrect is because it expresses an opposite idea, which we will discuss in the next section. The Seminole were aggravated, not the American government as the answer choice states. Copycat Answers are usually combined with another answer trap from the following pages, which is why we discussed Copycats first in this section. Always be leery of answer choices that use several words or phrases from the passage.

Opposite Answers

Just as Fill-in-the-Blank questions often have a wrong answer choice that is opposite of your prephrase, so may Reading Comprehension questions. ETS is playing on students' self-doubt, as many test takers will assume they misunderstood the passage and that it actually said the opposite of what they originally understood. Do not doubt your initial reading unless you reread the text and have a new understanding!

The passage that we studied on the previous page provides a good example of an Opposite Answer, where the statement in the answer choice had the opposite meaning as the passage. Let's look at another from a previous passage:

> The festival allowed us to acknowledge our German heritage after hiding our ancestry the rest of the year. For one weekend, my sisters and I could feast on mettwurst and maultaschen, dance the landler, and play Topfschlagen without
> *Line* worrying about the anti-German sentiments permeating the country after the war.
> 5 It was our most memorable weekend of 1946.

3. According to the passage, the narrator remembers the "festival" (line 1) with fondness because

   Ⓐ he learned a German dance called the landler

   Ⓑ he was able to conceal his German heritage

   Ⓒ Wrong answer

   Ⓓ it allowed him to celebrate his culture

   Ⓔ German sausages were prepared for the first time that year

We have already determined that answer choice (D) is correct: he liked the festival because he was able to celebrate his German heritage. But look at choice (B). This presents an idea opposite of the correct answer: that instead of acknowledging his culture, he hid it. Notice that it also uses the phrase *German heritage* from line 1. Sadly, some students will read this answer choice and assume they misread the passage. They select (B) without ever reading the last three answer choices.

You should note that the test makers often put the most attractive wrong answer choice above the right answer for this very reason. If they can trick you into selecting an answer before reading the correct one, then they helped graduate programs weed out students who are careless and inattentive to detail. Always read all of the answer choices before making your selection. And steer clear of any answer choice that presents an idea directly opposite of your predicted answer.

Extreme Answers

In a GRE answer choice, every word counts, and each of those words should be read literally. Let's analyze the meaning of the following answer choice:

(A) People in the neighborhood think that Mr. Wilson is mean.

Because this answer choice has no modifiers, it states that *ALL* people in the neighborhood think that Mr. Wilson is mean—including Mrs. Wilson, neighboring infants and children, and Mr. Wilson's friends. Because statements like this one are so extreme, the makers of the GRE are likely to use modifiers to subdue the meaning. Consider some examples:

(B) <u>Most</u> people in the neighborhood think that Mr. Wilson is mean.
(C) <u>Many</u> people in the neighborhood think that Mr. Wilson is mean.
(D) <u>Some</u> people in the neighborhood think that Mr. Wilson is mean.

Each of these answer choices added an adjective modifier to *people*, making the answer choices easier to defend than the original answer in (A). However, choices (B) and (C) are still Extreme Answers; the qualifiers *most* and *many* include a lot of people, making these answers difficult to prove. But answer choice (D) is much more moderate. With the use of *some*, you only need to find two people who think Mr. Wilson is mean in order for this answer choice to be true.

Sometimes the right answer will also use *somewhat*:

(E) The neighbor thinks that Mr. Wilson is <u>somewhat</u> mean.

In this answer choice, *somewhat* tempers the meaning of *mean*. Instead of proving that Mr. Wilson is consistently cruel, you only need to find one instance of meanness to make him *somewhat mean*.

Also watch for Extreme helping verbs and verbs. Consider the difference between these three answer choices:

(A) Henry must go to the wedding.
(B) Henry needs to go to the wedding.
(C) Henry should go to the wedding.

It is difficult to defend *must go* and *needs to go*, and it is quite unlikely that the author was that straightforward in the passage. However, *should go* is much easier to prove.

CAUTION: GRE TRAP! Extreme Answers use words that make the answer difficult to defend.

10

For most GRE questions, avoid answers that use *most, many, must, needs*, or these other Extreme words:

- *all, total, only, solely, exclusively, completely, entirely, thoroughly*
- *mainly, chiefly, primarily, largely, mostly*
- *invariably, certainly, absolutely, unquestionably*
- *always, never, not*
- adjectives that end in *-est* (*greatest, largest*, etc.)
- adjectives that end in *-less* (*worthless, useless*, etc.)
- adjectives that are preceded by *most* (*most angry, most important*, etc.)
- adjectives that are preceded by *least* (*least angry, least truthful*, etc.)

Some Extreme Words are more difficult to pinpoint. Consider these two answers:

(A) Penelope was surprised by her mother's <u>vicious</u> reply.
(B) Penelope was surprised by her mother's <u>insensitive</u> reply.

Which answer choice is easiest to defend? The word *vicious* makes answer choice (A) the least likely answer. In order for the reply to be vicious, the mother would have had to have been spiteful, cruel, and severe. But the word *insensitive* is much easier to defend. She simply had to say something that was mildly unkind in order to be called insensitive.

Consider the difference between these moderate and extreme word pairs:

Moderate Word	Extreme Word
unfriendly	hostile
happy	elated
sad	despairing
excited	hysterical
impolite	barbaric
mischievous	sinister
opposition	malice
unrealistic	outrageous
challenge	mock
foolish	ludicrous
anxious	frantic
unlikely	impossible
criticize	chastise

You would be wise to avoid answers with these extreme words and others like them.

Extreme Words are usually modifiers.

One Extreme Word that often avoids detection is *nostalgic*. The definition maintains that a person who is nostalgic desires to return to a happier time in the past. Someone who remembers his childhood is not necessarily nostalgic; he would have to express his longing for the happiness from that childhood in order to be considered nostalgic. So unless an author or narrator plans to build a time machine and return to the past, try to avoid an answer choice with the word *nostalgic* or *nostalgia* on the GRE.

CAUTION: GRE TRAP! Avoid the answer nostalgic on the GRE because it's likely an Extreme answer choice.

Let's look at a previous passage with a question utilizing some Extreme Answers:

> Melner attributes the decline in school enrollment to several factors. For one, families are moving out of the area to find work. For another, lackluster test results cause some existing and most new families to choose other districts.

2. According to the passage, enrollment in the school district has decreased because of families'

   Ⓐ complete confidence in standardized tests

   Ⓑ Wrong answer

   Ⓒ outrage over the lack of employment

   Ⓓ Wrong answer

   Ⓔ emphasis on jobs and performance

We previously determined that the correct answer is (E). But examine choice (A). Aside from being totally inaccurate, it uses the word *complete*. This is an Extreme Word, and so the answer choice should be avoided.

Choice (C) uses the Extreme Word *outrage*. In order to prove this word is justified, the families would have had to have shown powerful feelings of anger and resentment. The passage does not indicate they expressed these feelings, let alone even felt them. Both (A) and (C) are Extreme Answers.

Extreme Answers are almost always incorrect on the GRE. But notice that we've used the modifier *almost* in the previous sentence. That's because there is a slight chance you may encounter an extreme passage. Perhaps you will find a passage where the author detests snakes or adamantly defends the Constitution. If you have an extreme passage, written by an author who is forceful about her beliefs, you can expect some Extreme Answers. These answer choices should be easy to defend, however. If the author states that snakes are wicked and she wishes a plague would wipe them off the face of the Earth, then answer choices with the words *sinister* and *malice* become attractive and defendable. Given the temperate nature of the GRE, though, it is unlikely you will encounter such an extreme passage. When in doubt, avoid all answer choices with extreme words.

GRATUITOUS VOCAB temperate (adj): moderate; not extreme

10

True But Wrong Answers

True But Wrong Answers are especially tricky because they provide a true statement or conclusion based on the passage; however, they do not answer the specific question at hand. They pull a fact or inference from an earlier or later portion of text, but have little to do with the actual question.

Let's consider a question about a passage from the previous chapter:

Where was Olaudah Equiano born? Since 1999, a debate has raged amongst historians about the birthplace of the author, one of very few slaves of African descent to record his autobiography in English in the eighteenth century. In *The Interesting Narrative of the Life of Olaudah Equiano, or Gustavus Vassa, the African*, Equiano himself claims he was born in Africa, describing life in an African village as a free child. He also provides a first-person account of the arduous journey of the Middle Passage, seemingly something only a captured slave could relate in such detail. In 1999, however, professor and author Vincent Caretta asserted that Equiano was actually born a slave in South Carolina. Caretta argued that Equiano's stories of African life and capture came from oral histories of other slaves and information he gathered in books. The professor provided other evidence, such as a baptismal record and a muster roll, showing that the slave was actually born in the English colony. While the question is far from settled, one thing is certain: members of both sides of the debate possess compelling evidence to support their claims.

Line
5

10

15

4. Which of the following best states the author's main point?

    (A) Wrong answer

    (B) Some historians cite a baptismal record as proof that Equiano was born in South Carolina.

    (C) There is significant proof that Equiano was born in both Africa and in the United States

    (D) Wrong answer

    (E) Wrong answer

10

CAUTION: GRE TRAP!
True But Wrong Answers highlight a truth from part of the passage, but they do not answer the question.

Let's start with choice (B). This is a true statement, as indicated in lines 9-12. But *true* is not the same thing as *correct*. The question asks for the author's main point, and choice (B) is simply supporting evidence for half of the main idea. This answer is True But Wrong. Choice (C) provides a true and correct statement that summarizes the main idea of the Short Passage.

As you can see, these True But Wrong answer choices are especially attractive given that they provide a true statement from the passage. Therefore you must be certain that the choice you select answers the question as well.

True To a Point Answers

True to a Point Answers are very attractive choices because they usually start out seemingly correct. Careless test takers might not notice, though, that at some point in the answer choice they become blatantly wrong.

Sometimes these answer choices add new, irrelevant information causing them to be incorrect. For example, if the passage discusses the feeding habits of monarch butterflies, be wary of any answer choice that details the feeding habits of swallowtail butterflies. This answer will appear to be correct when explaining the feeding habits, but once it cites a different butterfly type, it is clearly incorrect. Let's study some examples:

CAUTION: GRE TRAP! True To A Point Answers contain half-truths, but at some point they become indisputably wrong.

Unlike the Tango, a dance which can trace its roots directly back to Argentina and Uruguay, Ballroom Tango saw significant changes in both structure and technique as the dance traveled to the United States and Europe. Film star Rudolph Valentino first brought Ballroom Tango to Hollywood in the early 1920s, and the famous dance instructor Arthur Murray later helped popularize a standardized version which incorporated steps that were common to the US during that period. This incarnation of Ballroom Tango was generally considered somewhat less formal and referred to as the "American Style" by the English, who wished to distinguish this informal approach from their own International Style—a technique that was taught in countries throughout Europe and had already become the de facto standard in competitions around the world.

Line 5

10

GRATUITOUS VOCAB
incarnation (n): act of assuming a body

de facto (adj): recognized

4. The standardized version of the Ballroom Tango features which of the following?

(A) steps that were common in American film
(B) Wrong answer
(C) conventional American movements
(D) Wrong answer
(E) Wrong answer

Choice (A) is appealing because it is True to a Point: *steps that were common*, the phrase in the answer choice, comes right from line 6. But then the answer makes a wrong turn with the phrase *in American film*. The passage does not mention American film in connection with the Ballroom Tango, other than the fact that a film star was responsible for bringing the dance to Hollywood. It does not state that these steps were common in movies, so choice (A) is incorrect.

Astute test takers would also avoid choice (A) because it is a Copycat Answer, using text right from the passage. Choice (C) uses synonyms to express the idea in line 6, and is in fact correct.

10

The most tempting True to a Point Answers have a single word that sabotages the entire answer choice. Consider an example using the same passage:

> Unlike the Tango, a dance which can trace its roots directly back to Argentina and Uruguay, Ballroom Tango saw significant changes in both structure and technique as the dance traveled to the United States and Europe. Film star Rudolph
> *Line* Valentino first brought Ballroom Tango to Hollywood in the early 1920s, and the
> 5 famous dance instructor Arthur Murray later helped popularize a standardized version which incorporated steps that were common to the US during that period. This incarnation of Ballroom Tango was generally considered somewhat less formal and referred to as the "American Style" by the English, who wished to distinguish this informal approach from their own International Style—a technique that was
> 10 taught in countries throughout Europe and had already become the de facto standard in competitions around the world.

5. According to the passage, the Ballroom Tango is different from the Tango because the Ballroom Tango?

   (A) Wrong answer

   (B) was slightly altered once it became popular in America

   (C) Wrong answer

   (D) Wrong answer

   (E) underwent a transformation upon entering the US and Europe

Choice (B) is incorrect because of a single word: *slightly*. The passage states that the Ballroom Tango *saw significant changes* (line 2) making *slightly altered* significantly incorrect. Note, too, that the answer only includes America, omitting Europe as stated in the passage (line 3). Remember, the correct answer will include all of the important ideas, as does choice (E).

Every word counts in a GRE answer choice. You must carefully read each possibility, looking for reasons that the answer choice is incorrect. Be sure to eliminate any answer that is only True to a Point.

10

True To You Answers

One of the biggest mistakes that a student can make is to bring their experience and expectations into the GRE. Your opinions are not relevant on the Reading portion of the test, and you should be careful not to let them influence your understanding of a text.

True to You Answers are designed to take advantage of your personal beliefs and prior knowledge. Let's study an example that plays on a common opinion about slavery:

> By 1750, slavery was a legal institution in all of the American colonies, the profits of which amounted to 5% of the British economy at the time of the Industrial Revolution. The Transatlantic slave trade peaked in the late 18th century, when the largest number of slaves was captured on raiding expeditions into the interior of West Africa. The slaves were shipped to the Americas in the hulls of large boats, where they experienced extremely cramped quarters, lack of ventilation, and unsanitary conditions; a large percentage of the captives died in transit.

Line
5

6. The author of the passage implies that

   (A) the hazardous conditions in which the slaves were shipped resulted in a high mortality rate

   (B) Wrong answer

   (C) Wrong answer

   (D) slavery is uncivilized and immoral

   (E) Wrong answer

10

In the 21st century, we know that slavery is uncivilized and immoral. That is part of the reason why the Civil War was fought and why the 13th amendment to the Constitution was passed. But it is never stated or even implied in the passage, so you cannot assume that the author shares this belief. The passage itself is very matter-of-fact, presenting data and information, but not imparting the author's opinions. Even the sentence about the death of slaves in transit is emotionless and objective. So if the author does not state his opinion, any feelings assigned to him are untrue, no matter how you feel about the subject yourself. After all, the passage could have been written in 1850 by a slave owner in Georgia. Do not apply your personal beliefs to any GRE passage or answer choice!

The test makers might also try to trick you into applying your prior knowledge to a passage:

> In late summer, black bears begin gorging on carbohydrate-rich foods in order to put on significant weight and body fat. They can gain as much as 30 pounds in a single week! Once fall arrives, the bear prepares its den, lining it with leaves and other plants to form a nest.

6. According to the passage, black bears seek "carbohydrate-rich foods" primarily because they

Ⓐ Wrong answer

Ⓑ are preparing to hibernate

Ⓒ need to considerably increase their body mass

Ⓓ Wrong answer

Ⓔ Wrong answer

Unless you skipped kindergarten and most of elementary school, it's likely that you know bears hibernate. Answer choice (B) is depending on this knowledge to seduce you into selecting it as the right answer choice. But you would be wrong.

The passage never mentions hibernation. The reason it provides for the black bears gorging on carbs is *to put on significant weight and body fat*. The correct answer is (C). But many, many test takers would choose (B) because they applied their prior knowledge to the passage and failed to read all of the answer choices.

Remember, if the author does not state or imply an idea, it simply is not true.

Notes:

10

Analyzing the Answer Choices Problem Set

In the following exercise, read the passage and subsequent questions. For each question, select the correct answer choice and, if possible, label the wrong answer choices as Copycats, Opposites, Extremes, True But Wrong, True to a Point, True to You, or a combination of answer types. The first couple have been done for you. Answers begin on page 240.

With Fitzgerald as with no one else in American literature save Poe, the biography gets in the way. Never mind that F. Scott Fitzgerald is the author of one exquisite short novel as perfect as anything in our literature and of another longer, more chaotic novel of tremendous emotional power. Never mind that he has written a couple of dozen stories that by
Line   any standard deserve the designation of "masterful." Ignoring those legacies, much of the general public still tends to
5   think of him in connection with the legends of his disordered and difficult life, and to classify him under one convenient stereotype or another. So diminished in stature, Fitzgerald becomes the Chronicler of the Jazz Age, or the Artist in Spite of Himself, or—most prevalent stereotype of all—the Writer as Burnt-Out Case: a man whose tragic course functions as a cautionary tale for more commonsensical aftercomers. His saga offers an almost irresistible temptation to sermonizers, overt or concealed. It is not right to ride on top of taxicabs or disport oneself in the Plaza hotel's fountain, not right to
10   drink to excess or abuse a "lovely golden wasted talent." Go thou and do otherwise.
   This warning usually remains implicit, of course. It is not the homily but the tale of star-crossed lovers that commands attention—handsome brilliant erratic Scott married for good or ill to beautiful willful unstable Zelda. There is an arresting poignancy in the way the two of them—Scott more than Zelda, perhaps—considered the alternatives and chose the sweet poison. Somehow, in the repeated retellings of this tale, the Fitzgeralds have come to stand for a kind
15   of generic nonspecific glamour, now sadly departed. In 1980 the opening party for an exhibit of Fitzgeraldiana at the National Portrait Gallery drew an enormous crowd determined to celebrate a vanished past. The band played Glenn Miller and Benny Goodman numbers from the 1940s, the decade following Fitzgerald's death. A few women attempted flapper costumes, but for the most part the clothes were as anachronistic as the music. One chap, aiming for colonial elegance, danced in a pith helmet. The details that mattered so much to Fitzgerald, a man precisely in tune with his
20   times, mattered very little to those come to the party to memorialize his legend. Zelda and Scott, Scott and Zelda—they are fixed so securely in the collective mind as lovable reckless youths for whom it all went disastrously wrong that it has been difficult to set that image aside and concentrate on the work that established him as one of the major literary artists of the twentieth century.

Which of the following best states the author's main point?

Ⓐ After Fitzgerald's death, attention to the details of the Jazz Age did not matter to his admirers.

Ⓑ Alcoholism prevented Fitzgerald from becoming a distinguished author.

Ⓒ In many sermons and homilies, Fitzgerald's life continues to serve as a warning against excess.

Ⓓ Fitzgerald is considered one of the most talented writers of the twentieth century.

Ⓔ Fitzgerald's brash behavior and personal hardship over-shadow his literary accomplishments.

(A) *True But Wrong (lines 15-20)*

(B) *Opposite (he __was__ distinguished)*

(C) _____

(D) _____

(E) _____

2. It can be inferred from the passage that the author would agree with which of the following statements?

    [A] The personal life of Poe is scrutinized more than his literary works.

    [B] Fitzgerald's misfortunes are often deemed a warning for new writers.

    [C] Scott had more alternatives to avoiding tragedy than did Zelda.

            Select all answers that apply.

(A) _____

(B) _____

(C) _____

3. The author mentions riding on taxicabs (line 9) primarily in order to

    (A) refute the claim that Fitzgerald's life was disordered and troublesome

    (B) illustrate the reckless actions of Fitzgerald after Zelda was committed to the sanatorium

    (C) identify a possible behavior of a professional author experiencing burn-out

    (D) provide an example of the rash behavior exhibited by Fitzgerald of which others were cautioned against

    (E) lend credibility to the assertion that Fitzgerald had been inappropriately stereotyped

(A) _____

(B) _____

(C) _____

(D) _____

(E) _____

10

4. In lines 18-19 ("One chap . . . helmet"), the author is most likely suggesting that

    (A) Fitzgerald denounced the elegance of the colonial period

    (B) pith helmets were not in fashion during the Jazz Age

    (C) pith helmets were not usually associated with flapper costumes and music from the 1940s

    (D) Fitzgerald was known for always wearing a pith helmet in the 1920s

    (E) the music played at the party was composed twenty years after the era associated with the author

(A) _____

(B) _____

(C) _____

(D) _____

(E) _____

Chapter Summary

There are two types of multiple choice answers on the GRE: right answers and wrong answers.

Right Answers

- Use synonyms.

- Include all of the important ideas from the line reference or passage.

- Tend to use more general language or ideas.

- Can be proven by the text.

- Are provided below the question. You simply have to locate them.

Wrong Answers

- Cannot be proven by the referenced portion of the text.

- Tend to use more specific language but often fail to include all important ideas from the line reference or passage.

- Are often easier to determine than the right answer.

- Are often placed above the correct answer when they are especially attractive to fool you into selecting the wrong answer without reading all five answer choices.

- Come in several styles that are designed to trap you:

☠ **Copycat Answers**

- Use words and phrases directly from the text.

☠ **Opposite Answers**

- Present an idea that is opposite of the right answer and your prephrase.

☠ **Extreme Answers**

- Use words that are difficult to defend. The words may be qualifiers, like *most* and *always*, or adjectives and verbs, like *malicious* and *mock*.

☠ **True But Wrong Answers**

- Make true statements about a portion of the passage that is not the subject of the question.

☠ **True To A Point Answers**

- Provide an answer that is "half-right."

- Often introduce new information not discussed in the passage.

- May have a single word the makes the answer choice wrong.

☠ **True to You Answers**

- Present common beliefs that were not provided in the passage.

- Use facts that are likely a part of your prior knowledge but were not provided in the passage.

Confidence Quotation
"Many of life's failures are people who did not realize how close they were to success when they gave up."
Thomas Edison, American inventor

10

Analyze the Answer Choices Answer Key

Analyzing the Answer Choices Problem Set—Page 236

1. E   Prephrase: Fitzgerald's biography gets in the way of his accomplishments as an author.

    (A) *True But Wrong*. While it is true that the guests at the Fitzgeraldiana party did not seem concerned with the details of the 1920s (lines 15-20), this is not the main idea of the passage.
    (B) *Opposite*. Fitzgerald became a distinguished author (lines 1-4, 22-23) in spite of being an alcoholic (although alcoholism is never specifically mentioned in the passage. True to You?)
    (C) *Extreme and Copycat*. The word *many* needs several instances to be supported. It only says that "his saga offers an almost irresistible temptation to sermonizers." It later says the warning "usually remains implicit," meaning it is unspoken. It copies the words *sermonizers* (line 8), *homily* (11), *warning* (11), and *excess* (10) from the text.
    (D) *True But Wrong*. While the author certainly views Fitzgerald as one of the most talented writers of all of literature (lines 1-4), this is not what the passage is about: the passage discusses how other critics and readers fail to identify Fitzgerald's greatness because they are too busy scrutinizing his personal life.
    (E) *Correct Answer*. This answer most closely matches the prephrase.

2. A and B   Prephrase: Impossible to prephrase.

    (A) *Correct Answer*. In the opening sentence, the author states that Poe's biography also "gets in the way."
    (B) *Correct Answer*. In lines 7 to 8, the author says "a man whose tragic course functions as a cautionary tale for more commonsensical aftercomers."
    (C) *Copycat*. In line 13, the author mentions that Scott perhaps *considered* the alternatives more than Zelda did, but never states that he actually *had* more alternatives from which to choose.

3. D   Prephrase: Show an example of one of the reckless choices made by Fitzgerald

    (A) *Opposite and Copycat*. If anything, this example supports the claim that Fitzgerald had troublesome behaviors. This answer uses *disordered* from line 5.
    (B) *True to a Point and True to You?* This example does illustrate the reckless actions of Fitzgerald. But then the answer takes a wrong turn. The passage does not state if this behavior was before or after Zelda's commitment. In fact, the passage never tells you about her schizophrenia, so this is possibly True To You.
    (C) *Copycat*. This passage is about Fitzgerald specifically, not about other authors. It borrows the words *Burnt-Out* from line 7.
    (D) *Correct Answer*. This example follows the statements about Fitzgerald's life being used as a warning to new authors, so it is obviously an example of the behavior that earned Fitzgerald his reputation.
    (E) *Opposite*. This example provides a reason why Fitzgerald was stereotyped.

4. B   Prephrase: The pith helmet was as anachronistic (out of correct order in time) as the music and the clothing at the party, meaning they were not popular during Fitzgerald's time.

(A) *Copycat*. We have no idea how Fitzgerald felt about the colonial period. This answer uses the words elegance (line 19) and colonial (line 18) from the passage.

(B) *Correct Answer*. This answer most closely matches our prephrase.

(C) *True But Wrong and True to You*. Pith helmets are from the turn of the century; flappers from the 1920s; and the music from teh 1940s. But this is not what the author is suggesting in the sentence that is solely about the pith helmet.

(D) *Extreme*. The word *always* should be a like a red flag on the GRE. If it is correct, it's easy to prove. But the pith helmet was mentioned as something that was not popular during Fitzgerald's heyday in the Jazz Era, not as something he wore.

(E) *True But Wrong*. The sentence in question is about pith helmets, not the music.

10

Reading Comprehension Mastery: Read the Question

Reading Comprehension Mastery:
Read the Question

Introduction

As we noted in the previous chapter, Passage-Based Reading questions have two parts: a question stem and five answer choices.

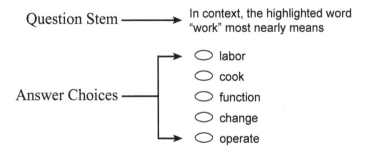

Question Stem ⟶ In context, the highlighted word "work" most nearly means

Answer Choices ⟶
- ○ labor
- ○ cook
- ○ function
- ○ change
- ○ operate

The question stem consists of a question or an incomplete statement.

In paper editions of the GRE practice tests, questions may contain a line reference to the passage, such as "What does the author imply in lines 9-13 ("The house . . . explodes")?" The numbers (lines 9-13) refer to the line numbers of the passage. In this example, the text being considered begins in line 9 and ends in line 13. The portion in parenthesis after the line reference shows the first words of the reference ("The house") and the last word of the reference ("explodes").

In this chapter, we will look at the four steps for attacking each question following a reading comprehension passage:

1. Read the questions.

2. If necessary, return to the passage.

3. Prephrase an answer.

4. Match an answer choice.

Remember to watch for common wrong answer traps throughout the remaining chapters!

11

Strategies for Reading Questions

The steps for attacking questions are the same, no matter what type of passage you have just read. Let's examine each of these steps more closely.

1. Read the questions.

While this may seem like a patronizing imperative, there is more to this step than you may realize.

Consider Every Word

Every word counts on the GRE. This is true for both the questions and the answer choices, but for now, let's look at how this impacts a question. Consider the passage and question below:

> Familiar songs are like cozy blankets. They provide warmth and comfort, never more so than when I feel down and worn out. They wrap around me, assuring me that everything will be okay. My favorite artist is jazz legend Ella Fitzgerald. Her
> *Line* voice is warm honey on a cold day, uplifting my spirits and reminding me how
> 5 beautiful the world can be.

1. The paragraph establishes a comparison between a woman's

   Ⓐ feelings about music and the comfort provided by a blanket
   Ⓑ favorite jazz artist and the beauty of life
   Ⓒ impending depression and the lack of warmth in the world
   Ⓓ familiar music and the arms of a stranger
   Ⓔ melodious voice and the soothing qualities of honey

CAUTION: GRE TRAP!
Failing to carefully read every word of the question can lead to disaster.

Many students will fail to pay attention to the word *woman's* in the question stem. They process the word *comparison* and then completely fail to notice the word *woman's*. The passage does not help you because the comparison between *songs* and *blankets* is a simile, while the comparison between Ella Fitzgerald's *voice* and *honey* is a metaphor. Since similes are much easier to identify than metaphors, most students incorrectly choose choice (A). A closer reading of the question, however, reveals that the test makers are inquiring about the comparison between Ella Fitzgerald's voice and warm honey.

CAUTION: GRE TRAP!
Beware of any gender assumptions you may have to avoid falling into GRE traps.

We should also note that some students miss this question because they assume that the author of the passage is a woman. But where does the passage say this? You should never assume the gender, ethnicity, or age of an author on the GRE.

11

There are some specific words and phrases to watch for in question stems. Many questions will begin with *according to the author* or *according to the passage*, as in the following example:

> According to the author, those who "reject science" are

These questions ask you to provide the author's opinion. In the example above, you are asked to provide the author's opinion on those who reject science. This may not necessarily be what you believe, or what others in the passage believe, but what the author himself believes.

Be careful not to confuse others' beliefs with the author's belief:

> The second sentence indicates that those who "reject science" believe

This question asks about the belief of people who reject science, which is not necessarily the same as the belief held by the author. Pay close attention to whom the question is referring.

Many reading comprehension questions use the words *primarily*, *mostly*, *mainly*, and *chiefly*. In Select One Answer Choice questions, ETS claims that these words indicate that more than one answer may be correct, but that one of the answers is best. We know, however, that this is misleading. Four answers are always wrong and there is a specific reason they are wrong. You do not need to worry about choosing one answer that is "more correct" than another. There is only one right answer.

The final word for which you should watch is *except*. Questions with this word contain four answers that satisfy the question and one that does not:

> According to the passage, all of the following may occur EXCEPT
>
> Ⓐ the use of lacquer paints
> Ⓑ the destruction of the canvas
> Ⓒ an increase in spacial shadowing
> Ⓓ lessons in pencil techniques
> Ⓔ the use of ceramic glaze

In a rare display of leniency, ETS will warn you that the question is tricky by using capital letters for the word EXCEPT. The four answer choices that satisfy the statement in the question can usually be found by combing through the text, making these questions easy but time consuming. Students who notate each paragraph with a 3 or 4 word summary stand to answer these questions much more quickly than those who do not notate as they read.

TIPS and TRICKS
The phrase "according to the passage" means the same thing as the phrase "according to the author."

CAUTION: GRE TRAP!
"Except" questions are traps with a warning sign.

11

Rephrase the Question

Most of the Reading Comprehension questions on the GRE are not really questions—they are actually incomplete statements:

> The third sentence ("Flowing . . . stance") primarily serves to

It is much easier to answer a question than it is to finish a sentence (which is exactly why ETS uses incomplete statements). For this reason, good test takers rephrase the question stem and turn it into an actual question in their heads:

> *What is the purpose of the sentence?*

Notice that the line reference ("Flowing . . . stance") is not included in the paraphrased question. That is because line references are not necessary to understand what the question is asking and the extra information can cause you to forget the question. You can use the line references to return to the text, but you do not need to include them in your rephrased question.

Consider a few more examples of turning incomplete statements into questions:

> In the context in which it appears, "spot" most nearly means
>
> *What does "spot" mean?*

> The author would most likely view the statement of the scientist as
>
> *How would the author view that statement?*

> The author cites an expert primarily in order to
>
> *Why does the author cite an expert?*

Rephrasing is a powerful tool on Reading Comprehension questions, and one that you should practice regularly.

2. If necessary, return to the passage.

Some questions require an understanding of the entire passage, like the following examples:

> The primary purpose of the passage is to

> The passage provides the most information about

> The passage is primarily concerned with

These questions (or incomplete statements) assess your knowledge of the passage as a whole. You cannot return to one specific spot in the passage to find the answer or reread for understanding.

But some Reading Comprehension questions on the GRE Verbal Reasoning section are about a specific line, sentence, or paragraph, and you must return to the passage in order to answer the question. The test makers are even kind enough to refer you back to the specific section with a highlighted word, sentence, or portion of the text.

Line references can be about a single phrase:

> According to the author, the "lost souls" can best be described as

Or they may be about an entire sentence, group of sentences, or paragraph:

> The second sentence functions to

> The four lessons discussed in the passage ("A day . . . rush") serve primarily to

> In the second paragraph, the author is primarily concerned with

For all of these questions, you must return to the passage in order to answer the question.

Remember, the online test will highlight a specific portion of the passage while the paper-based test will include the line reference.

Questions that contain line references require you to return to the passage and reread.

11

3. Prephrase an answer.

Just as with Fill-in-the-Blank questions, where you predict a word to complete a sentence, you should predict an answer to a Passage-Based Reading question before ever looking at the answer choices.

This is by far the most important strategy on reading passages. It helps you connect with the text and ensures that you understand what the question is asking. When you finally look at answer choices, prephrasing prevents you from falling into common traps. Nearly all good readers naturally employ this strategy, but those who read less frequently may need to practice prephrasing until it becomes a habit. Let's examine how prephrasing works:

Sociologist Angela Lieto does not believe that bullying behavior is always fostered in the home. There are thousands of children, she reasons, who exhibit bully behaviors but have not been exposed to such harassment either by the parents or other caretakers. She contends that bullying is a learned habit resulting from
Line
5 the intrinsic rewards of childhood hierarchies. In her view, students who gain confidence and influence by tormenting others will continue to be bullies. It is only when other children determine that bullying is "uncool," thus stripping bullies of their dominant position, that these dominant members of the group will relent.

2. According to the passage, children who bully others primarily do so because of

   Ⓐ genetic factors beyond their control

   Ⓑ physical attributes such as height and weight

   Ⓒ similar harassment from an adult

   Ⓓ the resulting power and self-assurance

   Ⓔ pressure from a parent

You should rephrase the incomplete statement so that it is an actual question: *Why do children bully others?*

Then return to the passage to locate the reason in lines 4-6: "bullying is... resulting from the intrinsic rewards of childhood hierarchies....Students who gain confidence and influence by tormenting others will continue...."

Now prephrase your answer:

Why do children bully others? To gain confidence and influence.

4. Match an answer choice.

Once you prephrase an answer, look at the real answer choices. Find the one that most closely matches your prephrase and select it as the right answer:

Prephrase: *To gain confidence and influence*

2. According to the passage, children who bully others primarily do so because of

    Ⓐ genetic factors beyond their control
    Ⓑ physical attributes such as height and weight
    Ⓒ similar harassment from an adult
    Ⓓ the resulting power and self-assurance
    Ⓔ pressure from a parent

The answer that is closest to your prephrase is (D).

Some students use their hands to cover up the answer choices on the screen while prephrasing. If you find that you are sneaking peeks at the answers, then try this technique until you are more comfortable with the strategy.

You should note that not all answers can be prephrased. Some questions are worded awkwardly or ask about an inference that is difficult to identify. If you find a question with an answer that is impossible to predict, don't panic; you will just have to work through the answer choices without a prephrase.

We cannot overemphasize the importance of prephrasing. Students who prephrase report a higher comfort level with the text and the questions, and they ultimately report higher GRE scores. Active reading creates a running commentary in your head while reading the passage and prephrasing creates a similar commentary while working through the questions.

11

Strategies for Reading Questions Problem Set

> Read the following passage, taking notes about each paragraph. Then rephrase the question stems using your own words and prephrase an answer to that question. Record both your rephrase and prephrase on the lines provided. Finally, select an answer that most closely matches your prephrase, remembering to avoid common answer traps. The first one has been done for you. Answers begin on page 256.

In 1989, Americans and observers all over the world watched in amazement as the Berlin Wall crumbled, bringing down along with it an enormous complex of calcified belief systems. Whether because of synchronicity or simply the deceptive but irresistible human urge to draw connections, an observer of the broad spectrum of classical music in the
Line United States might have detected something similar happening in that world as well. In the way composers operated
5 and the kinds of music they wrote, in the sorts of performing institutions that brought that music and music of the past to the listening public, old models and ways of thinking that had begun to prove decisively unworkable were being chipped away.

Now, almost a decade later, U.S. classical music stands on the verge of an enormous rejuvenation. The process is far from complete—indeed, in some areas it has scarcely begun—but the seeds that have been sown over the past years
10 unmistakably are bearing fruit. The music that is being written today boasts a combination of vitality and accessibility that have been missing from American music for too long. A similar spirit of adventure and innovation can increasingly be found among the country's solo performers and musical organizations.

Artistic liberation, of course, is a slower and more diffuse process than political liberation. In the absence of a single Promethean figure on the order of Beethoven or Picasso, old orthodoxies are more likely to be eroded than exploded. So
15 it is that much of the musical life in the United States still clings to the old ways. Some prominent composers continue to write in the densely impenetrable language forged during the modernist period and clung to in the face of decades' worth of audience hostility or indifference. Some opera companies and symphony orchestras operate as though the United States was still a cultural outpost of Europe, uncertain of the value of anything that doesn't derive from the Old World.

20 But the signs of change are there—among younger composers struggling to find their own voice in defiance of old models, among performers eager to make those voices heard, and among organizations daring enough to give the nation's musical life a distinctively American profile at last.

Nothing is more important to this process than the production of new music, and here is where the picture is at once most heartening and most varied. From the end of World War II until well into the 1970s, the dominant vein in American
25 music was the arid, intricate style that had grown out of early modernism and continued to flourish in the supportive but isolated arena of academia. Much of this music was based on serialism, the system derived from the works of Schöenberg, Webern, and Berg in which the key-centered structures of tonal music were replaced with a systematically evenhanded treatment of all 12 notes of the chromatic scale. Even composers whose works were not strictly serialist, such as Elliott Carter and Roger Sessions, partook of the general preference for intellectual rigor and dense, craggy
30 surfaces. The fact that audiences were nonplused by this music, to say the least, was taken merely as an indication that the composers were ahead of their time.

1. According to the passage, classical music composed between World War II and the fall of the Berlin Wall can be characterized as

  Ⓐ accessible and defiant

  Ⓑ avant-garde and elaborate

  ● dense and banal

  Ⓓ intricate and vivacious

  Ⓔ vapid and innovative

Rephrase the question: _____

How can you characterize classical music composed between WWII and the fall of the Berlin Wall?

Prephrase the answer: _____

Inflexible and dense

2. The second sentence ("Whether . . . as well") suggests that classical music was

Rephrase the question: _____

_____

_____

_____

    Ⓐ deemed unpopular and old-fashioned by the general public

    Ⓑ responsible for a rift between contemporary and conventional composers

    Ⓒ held to rigid standards prior to the 1990s

Prephrase the answer: _____

    Ⓓ lacking a creative individual who could bring change to the genre

_____

    Ⓔ enjoyed only by those in the realm of academia

_____

_____

3. It can be inferred in the third paragraph that Beethoven and Picasso both

Rephrase the question: _____

_____

_____

    Ⓐ compared their Old World art to the art of ancient Greek gods

_____

    Ⓑ preserved old, reliable European techniques when mastering their crafts

Prephrase the answer: _____

    Ⓒ disagreed with composers from previous generations who refused to acknowledge America's influence on classical music

_____

    Ⓓ struggled to gain acceptance among the music and art communities of their times

_____

    Ⓔ brought accelerated changes to the long-standing conventions of their respective disciplines

4. In the context in which it appears, "order" (line 14) most nearly means

Rephrase the question: _____

_____

_____

    Ⓐ command

_____

    Ⓑ arrangement

    Ⓒ discipline

    Ⓓ degree

Prephrase the answer: _____

    Ⓔ request

_____

_____

_____

5. In lines 17-19 ("Some opera...Old World"), it can be inferred that

    Ⓐ many music companies refuse to play music composed by Americans

    Ⓑ the talent of European composers is unrivaled by American composers

    Ⓒ American composers write symphonies that are much more daring and defiant than the symphonies of European composers

    Ⓓ some professional musicians prefer to play European compositions in concert

    Ⓔ professional orchestras find American compositions unworthy

Rephrase the question: _____

_____

_____

_____

Prephrase the answer: _____

_____

_____

_____

6. The fourth paragraph suggests that before changes were made

    Ⓐ orchestras throughout the world were afraid to request new musical styles

    Ⓑ the United States did not have a distinguishable sound to their classical music

    Ⓒ older composers were not sympathetic to younger musicians' plights

    Ⓓ serialists were partial to certain tones

    Ⓔ politicians in Berlin failed to compromise with citizens

Rephrase the question: _____

_____

_____

_____

Prephrase the answer: _____

_____

_____

_____

In the context in which it appears, "process" (line 23) refers to

    Ⓐ the eradication of European influence from American classical music

    Ⓑ the revitalization of American classical music

    Ⓒ the liberation of American composers from public criticism

    Ⓓ the incorporation of modernism and serialism into current classical music

    Ⓔ the erosion of European political control over classical music

Rephrase the question: _____

_____

_____

_____

Prephrase the answer: _____

_____

_____

_____

Note: Remember, most long passages only have four corresponding questions. We have included three more here so you can have extra practice prephrasing.

Chapter Summary

There are several strategies you should employ when answering GRE questions about passages.

Strategies for Passage-Based Reading

1. Read the question.

    - It is important to read every word in the question stem.
    - Know how to tackle an EXCEPT question.
    - Turn an incomplete sentence into a question by rephrasing.

2. If necessary, return to the passage.

    - If the question includes a line reference, you must return to the passage and reread.

3. Prephrase an answer.

    - Prephrasing an answer to the question is the most important strategy in the Reading Comprehension sections.

4. Match an answer choice.

11

Read the Question Answer Key

Strategies for Reading Questions Problem Set—Page 252

1. According to the passage, classical music composed between World War II and the fall of the Berlin Wall can be characterized as

Rephrase the question: How can you characterize classical music composed between World War II and the fall of the Berlin Wall?

Prephrase the answer: Inflexible and dense

Answer: C

2. The second sentence ("Whether . . . as well") suggests that classical music was

Rephrase the question: What does the sentence suggest about classical music?

Prephrase the answer: Classical music was undergoing similar changes, throwing out old ways and accepting new ways

Answer: C

3. It can be inferred in the third paragraph that Beethoven and Picasso both

Rephrase the question: What can you infer about Beethoven and Picasso in this paragraph?

Prephrase the answer: They brought enormous change to their genres.

Answer: E

4. In the context in which it appears, "order" (line 14) most nearly means

Rephrase the question: What does "order" mean in this line?

Prephrase the answer: level, importance

Answer: D

5. In lines 17-19 ("Some opera...Old World"), it can be inferred that

Rephrase the question: What can you infer in these lines?

Prephrase the answer: Note: Difficult to prephrase. Some students might pick up that these orchestras would rather play music by European composers.

Answer: D

6. The fourth paragraph suggests that before changes were made

Rephrase the question: What does this paragraph suggest about the time before changes were made?

Prephrase the answer: Note: Difficult to prephrase. Some students may realize that the nation's musical life did not previously have an American profile.

Answer: B

7. In the context in which it appears, "process" (line 23) refers to

Rephrase the question: What does "process" mean in this line?

Prephrase the answer: change, giving the nation's musical life an American profile

Answer: B

Reading Comprehension Mastery: Vocabulary-In-Context Questions

Reading Comprehension Mastery:
Vocabulary-In-Context Questions

Introduction

There are three main categories of Reading Comprehension questions:

1. **Vocabulary-in-Context Questions** (VIC)

   These questions ask you to define a word from a passage as it is used in the context of a sentence.

2. **Literal Comprehension Questions** (LC)

   Literal Comprehension questions are usually considered the easiest questions in reading comprehension because the answer to the question is directly stated in the passage.

3. **Extended Reasoning Questions** (ER)

   These questions make up the majority of the Reading Comprehension section. They are typically considered more difficult because the answer is not explicitly stated in the passage; you must draw a conclusion based on part or all of the passage to successfully answer these questions.

Each of these categories has question sub-types, which we will examine in detail in the following chapters. This chapter focuses on the first type of question, Vocabulary-in-Context.

Understanding the specific type of question stem can help you determine how to answer the question.

12

Vocabulary-In-Context Questions

Vocabulary-in-Context questions are always Multiple Choice Select One questions, meaning there will be one right answer and four wrong answers. The questions ask you to define a word from a passage as it is used in the context of a sentence. Consider the short passage and simplified question below:

> In the summer of 1967, Warhol asked his agent to book him on a tour of Western colleges, including the University of Oregon. He planned to speak to students about the plot development in his underground films.

1. In the context in which it appears, "book" most nearly means

   Ⓐ dash
   Ⓑ teach
   Ⓒ read
   Ⓓ arrest
   Ⓔ schedule

All five answer choices will be the same part of speech. In this case, they are verbs, so you know that *book* is acting as a verb rather than as a noun. To solve these questions, first prephrase the meaning of the vocabulary word. In this case, *book* means *register* or *schedule*. When you go to match your prephrase, you will see that choice (E) is a perfect fit. Be sure to run your answer choice through the original sentence to ensure it makes sense:

(E) Warhol asked his agent to *schedule* him on a tour

If the answer still escapes you after prephrasing, test all of the answer choices in place of the original word in the sentence:

(A) Warhol asked his agent to *dash* him on a tour
(B) Warhol asked his agent to *teach* him on a tour
(C) Warhol asked his agent to *read* him on a tour
(D) Warhol asked his agent to *arrest* him on a tour
(E) Warhol asked his agent to *schedule* him on a tour

Which one makes sense in the context of the passage? Only answer (E).

In all published example problems from ETS, the wording for these questions is the same: "In the context in which it appears, 'X' most nearly means...." Still, you would be well prepared to expect similar phrasings as well:

In the context in which it appears, "X" is closest in meaning to

In the context in which it appears, "X" is best understood to mean

No matter how the question is asked, the solution method is the same; first prephrase an answer and try to match it to an answer choice, and then, if that doesn't work, try each answer choice in place of the word in the question.

If you are still unable to determine the correct answer, read a few lines above and a few lines below the original word. Often the text will use a synonym. Consider an example:

> The most famous psychologists of the 20th century had varying views of insanity. Carl Jung was of the persuasion that every human being had a story; when this story was rejected or denied by others, derangement was the result. This theory *Line* was widely contended by others, who instead believed that such mental illness was 5 genetic.

1. In the context in which it appears, "persuasion" (line 3) most nearly means

   (A) coercion
   (B) belief
   (C) power
   (D) attraction
   (E) science

TIPS and TRICKS
If you cannot define the word using the context of the sentence, look for synonyms in the surrounding sentences.

This passage is teeming with synonyms for the word *persuasion*: *views* (line 1) and *theory* (line 3) are equivalent nouns, but even the verb *believed* (line 4) indicates that the correct answer is (B), *belief*. If you are unsure of the correct answer for a Vocabulary-in-Context question, be sure to search the surrounding sentences for clues.

12

The overwhelming majority of Vocabulary-in-Context questions ask about the meanings of common words or words with common root words. For these types of questions, do not expect the most common definition to be the answer. For example, one official GRE question asks about the word *coinages*: "In the context in which it appears, 'coinages' most nearly means...." The correct answer is *creations*, but the most common wrong answer is *currencies*. The test makers are playing on the common definition of the root word *coin* to trick test takers into selecting the wrong answer.

TIPS and TRICKS
For Vocabulary-in-Context questions that ask about a common word, avoid the most common definition.

On rare occasion, you may be faced with a Vocabulary-in-Context question that tests vocabulary rather than alternative definitions of common words:

> Thompson was unlike the other students in class. His quiescence was remarkable for his age, reminding me of the Bhikkhus, the Buddhist monks I saw meditating in the village in Nepal.

1. In the context in which it appears, "quiescence" most nearly means

    Ⓐ stillness

    Ⓑ wisdom

    Ⓒ influence

    Ⓓ generosity

    Ⓔ cruelness

Your best solution strategy for questions about difficult vocabulary is to read the surrounding text for clues. In this example, the Buddhist monks are meditating, indicating that Thompson is tranquil and quiet. Answer (A) is best. But the question becomes much more difficult when the vocabulary words appear in the answer choices:

> Thompson was unlike the other students in class. His stillness was remarkable for his age, reminding me of the Bhikkhus, the Buddhist monks I saw meditating in the village in Nepal.

1. In the context in which it appears, "stillness" most nearly means

    Ⓐ quiescence

    Ⓑ sagacity

    Ⓒ prominence

    Ⓓ altruism

    Ⓔ savagery

On questions like this one, you may need to make an educated guess using the strategies for decoding vocabulary you learned in the section on Fill-in-the-Blank questions. Thankfully, these Vocabulary-in-Context questions with vocabulary in the answer choices are quite rare.

If you are running out of time on a Reading Comprehension section, move through the remaining questions to see if you have any Vocabulary-in-Context questions left. Most students consider Vocabulary-in-Context questions the easiest in the section, and you do not have to read the entire passage to answer them correctly.

Expect as few as one or as many as four Vocabulary-in-Context questions on your GRE. On average, most tests have two.

Vocabulary-in-Context Questions Problem Set

Read each short passage below and then answer the corresponding Vocabulary-in-Context question. Answers begin on page 267.

Some critics have asserted that Dylan Thomas' works suffer from several weaknesses, including verbosity and vulgarity. Those who have **championed** his poetry, however, cannot fathom such criticism.

1. In the context in which it appears, "championed" most nearly means

   (A) conquered

   (B) supported

   (C) excelled

   (D) contested

   (E) honored

The skepticism surrounding cold fusion in the 1980s was justifiable, as scientists had become jaded to exaggerated claims of exciting "breakthroughs" that were time and again proven erroneous or premature. They harbored mistrust of such grandiose **professions** and asserted instead that cold fusion was not the answer to the energy crisis.

2. In the context in which it appears, "professions" most nearly means

   (A) deceptions

   (B) embellishments

   (C) declarations

   (D) suspicions

   (E) occupations

With the Gregorian Reforms of the 11th century, many parts of Europe experienced increase of **strictures** for women, who had enjoyed much more opportunity during the Early Medieval period. The convents of the previous era had been led by women and heralded as centers of learning for women, but the new sanctions made them subordinate to male abbots and limited education to select few.

3. In the context in which it appears, "strictures" most nearly means

   (A) liberations

   (B) limitations

   (C) reprimands

   (D) scholarship

   (E) theologies

Jarvis grew up privileged in a wealthy suburb of London. As was the norm with young men of his status, he was **erudite**, having studied at two prestigious universities and learning four languages.

4. In the context in which it appears, "erudite" most nearly means

   (A) affluent

   (B) ingenious

   (C) congruous

   (D) lettered

   (E) pertinent

12

Chapter Summary

Vocabulary-In-Context Questions

- If you cannot determine the meaning of the referenced word, test each answer choice in its place to find the one that makes sense in context.

- Search for synonyms in the surrounding lines of the referenced word.

- For questions that ask about a common word, avoid the most common definition.

- If you are running out of time, scan the questions to find the Vocabulary-in-Context questions and answer them first. You do not have to read the entire passage to answer them correctly.

Confidence Quotation

"We gain strength, and courage, and confidence by each experience in which we really stop to look fear in the face.... We must do that which we think we cannot."
Eleanor Roosevelt, First Lady of the United States

12

Vocabulary-In-Context Questions Answer Key

1. **B** Prephrase: supported

   In this contrast passage, we have critics in the first sentence and supporters in the second sentence.

   Vocabulary:
   verbosity: wordiness   *fathom*: understand

2. **C** Prephrase: claims, assertions

   Watch out for (E), the most common definition of *professions*! The word *such* indicates that these *grandiose professions* are the same as *exaggerated claims*.

   Vocabulary:
   jaded: worn out by overexposure   *grandiose*: exaggerated

3. **B** Prephrase: limitations, restrictions

   The synonym *sanctions* occurs in the third line, and the *strictures* are in contrast to women previously having much more opportunity.

   Vocabulary:
   strictures: restrictions   *heralded*: announced
   sanctions: penalties, rules   *theologies*: religious studies

4. **D** Prephrase: educated

   If you have studied at universities, you are *educated*. Beware of *ingenious*: it means *clever*, not *intelligent*.

   Vocabulary:
   affluent: wealthy   *lettered*: educated
   congruous: appropriate   *pertinent*: relevant
   erudite: educated

Reading Comprehension Mastery: Literal Comprehension Questions

Reading Comprehension Mastery:
Literal Comprehension Questions

Introduction

Literal Comprehension questions ask you to recall facts directly stated in the passage. They play on our human tendencies to make assumptions and draw conclusions, which can cause you to miss these otherwise easy questions. Consider a simplified example:

> After graduating from college, Michelle attended law school in New Mexico.

1. The passage reveals which of the following about Michelle?

   Ⓐ She is intelligent.

   Ⓑ She grew up in New Mexico.

   Ⓒ She is a lawyer.

   Ⓓ She studied pre-law as an undergraduate.

   Ⓔ She pursued a law degree.

There are two facts in the passage: 1) Michelle graduated from college and 2) Michelle attended law school in New Mexico. Therefore, there is only one correct answer: choice (E). Many students, however, will become confused by the assumptions and conclusions they make about Michelle, and the first four answer choices are designed to trick those students:

(A) *She is intelligent.*
The passage never indicates that Michelle is smart. Not every person who attends law school is intelligent. In fact, it's even possible she cheated on her entrance exam.

Never assume anything that cannot be proven on the GRE!

(B) *She grew up in New Mexico.*
Where does the passage say this? She could have moved to New Mexico for law school. We cannot even be sure that she lived in New Mexico while attending law school there. Maybe she lived in Arizona and commuted over state lines.

(C) *She is a lawyer.*
The passage does not reveal whether Michelle actually graduated from law school. And even if she did graduate, maybe she decided to become a teacher or painter or doctor instead.

(D) *She studied pre-law as an undergraduate.*
The passage does not indicate what Michelle's major was in college. It is possible that she studied history or biology and decided after graduation that she wanted to become a lawyer.

The right answer, (E), restates the fact that Michelle attended law school. Notice that it paraphrases the original sentence; most correct answers of Literal Comprehension questions will use synonyms or reworded expressions.

13

Some questions use common phrases that can help you identify them as Literal Comprehension questions:

- According to the author/passage/statement/phrase/line....

- The author/passage/statement/phrase/line indicates....

- The author/passage/statement/phrase/line reveals....

- The author considers

- The author argues

- The author asserts

- Referring to.... or ...refers to....

- Because.... or ...because....

These phrases indicate that the answer is clearly stated right in the passage. You should be excited to find any questions on your test with these phrases because you do not have to draw a conclusion—you simply need to return to the text to find the answer.

There are four specific types of Literal Comprehension questions, making up about 10% of all Reading Comprehension questions:

1. Main Idea

2. Facts and Details

3. Reasons and Results

4. Comparison and Contrast

Understanding each type of Literal Comprehension question will help you more easily identify and answer questions. Let's look at each of these more closely.

Literal Comprehension questions ask you to recall facts from the passage. Those facts are usually rewritten with synonyms in the correct answer.

13

Main Idea Questions

Some test prep materials will group main idea questions with Extended Reasoning questions, the question type we will examine in the next chapter, but ETS generally counts the main idea as literal comprehension. For this reason, and because the main idea of the passage is usually directly stated, we have chosen to discuss Main Idea questions with Literal Comprehension questions.

Questions about the main idea are not as prevalent as some tutors or test prep books make them out to be. In the practice tests of the *Official GRE Study Guide*, less than 3% of the Reading Comprehension questions are about the main idea of a passage. However, identifying the main point of the passage is integral to understanding the finer points of the text, from Facts and Details questions to Extended Reasoning questions. So while actual questions about the main idea are not crucial to your success on the test, understanding the main idea is imperative to your mastery of the passage.

Main Idea questions usually do not include a reference to a word, phrase, sentence, or line. The most common wording of Main Idea questions is the first one below, but you should expect to see any of the four or a variation of these questions:

> The passage is primarily concerned with

> In the passage, the author is primarily concerned with

> Which of the following best states the author's main point?

> Which of the following best describes the central issue with which the passage is concerned?

The answer to these questions is the one that best summarizes the main idea. Remember, the right answer will be a paraphrased version of the main point, and it must be broad enough to cover the entire passage. One or two of the wrong answers will likely be True But Wrong answers, taken directly from the passage, which summarize a specific sentence or paragraph, but not the entire passage.

Main Idea Questions ask you to determine the author's main point. They usually do not include line references.

Because there can only be one Main Idea, expect these questions to only appear as Multiple Choice Select One Answer questions.

13

Let's study an example:

TIPS and TRICKS
If you take notes
as you read,
the main idea
will be easy to
determine.

Most archaeologists believe that Machu Picchu, a pre-Columbian Incan city, was built in the 15th century by the ruler Pachacutec. According to this view, the site was constructed on a mountain ridge as a personal estate for the powerful emperor; he extended his refuge to 1200 of the most elite of Incan aristocracy, who resided in the fortress for at least three generations until the Spanish conquest a century later. Rolf Muller, however, argues that the construction of the city actually started sometime between 2300 and 2100 BC.

Line 5

Muller's theory is based on the alignment of buildings and landmarks in accordance with stars in the sky in the previous millennium. Using advanced mathematical computations, Muller has produced convincing evidence that the most important sites in Machu Picchu were built around the procession of equinoxes that occurred before 2000 BC.

10

Muller also cites architectural anomalies as evidence that the city was built over thousands of years, rather than in a single generation. For example, three of the most famous landmarks—The Hitching Post, The Temple of the Sun, and The Room of Three Windows—were constructed with exacting precision and masterful masonry, skills for which the Incas are well-known. But there are many buildings that were fashioned in a much cruder manner and others that show developing skill, indicating that the city was slowly constructed over long periods of time. A city that was designed by a single architect or even a group of architects working simultaneously would have more architectural consistency.

15

20

Muller, whether right or wrong, has certainly given archaeologists something to think about. I suspect this debate will be discussed in academic papers and in colleges for years to come.

The main idea is stated in the last sentence of the first paragraph: *Rolf Muller, however, argues that the construction of the city actually started sometime between 2300 and 2100 BC.* Now consider a question about the main idea of the passage:

CAUTION: GRE TRAP!
Common wrong
answers for Main
Idea questions
focus on the
point of one
paragraph,
not the entire
passage.

1. The passage is primarily concerned with

    (A) three landmarks that dispute accepted theories about the construction of an Incan city

    (B) the exceptional mathematical skill of Rolf Muller

    (C) the Incan ruler Pachacutec's desire to create a sanctuary for elite members of society

    (D) the lack of architectural consistency in Machu Picchu

    (E) the hypothesis that the construction of Machu Picchu began much earlier and took much longer than previously believed

The best answer is (E). It paraphrases the stated main idea and covers the subject of every paragraph in the passage.

13

Consider the structure of this Theory and Critique passage:

> Theory: Conventional wisdom followed by opposing main idea
>
> Support 1: Evidence that the city was built *much earlier than previously believed*
>
> Support 2: Evidence that the city's construction *took much longer than previously believed*
>
> Author's belief: Acknowledgment that Muller's idea is a *hypothesis*

To review common locations of the main idea in GRE passages, review pages 194-198.

The three supporting paragraphs are incorporated into the main idea.

Let's analyze the wrong answers, too:

(A) *three landmarks that dispute accepted theories about the construction of an Incan city*

True But Wrong: the three landmarks are discussed in lines 14-17, but nowhere else in the passage. The main idea must pervade all paragraphs!

(B) *the exceptional mathematical skill of Rolf Muller*

In lines 9-10, the passage states that Muller used advanced mathematical computations. It does not state that he was the one to do these computations or that he had advanced mathematical abilities. Nor does this idea occur anywhere else in the passage.

(C) *the Incan ruler Pachacutec's desire to create a sanctuary for elite members of society*

True But Wrong: this view is part of the first paragraph's conventional wisdom that Muller attempts to disprove. It is not mentioned elsewhere in the passage.

(D) *the lack of architectural consistency in Machu Picchu*

Copycat/True But Wrong: the last sentence of the third paragraph contains this idea, but it is not present in any of the other paragraphs. The main idea must be supported by each paragraph.

Once you choose your answer, reread the brief notes you took as you read the passage. If your summary supports your answer choice, you have selected the right answer. But if the answer choice does not have anything to do with one or more of the paragraphs, you need to select a new answer.

13

Facts and Details Questions

Questions about the facts and details of a passage ask you to interpret a word, phrase, sentence, or portion of the passage. These are by far the most prevalent Literal Comprehension questions, but still a small portion of the Reading Comprehension questions.

Consider some examples of Literal Comprehension questions:

The passage addresses which of the following issues related to Degner's use of descriptive titles for his novels?

The passage emphasizes which of the following points about frog dissection?

According to the passage, which of the following is true of traveling through Italy?

According to the author of the passage, all of the following are true EXCEPT

Select the sentence that provides Hendrick's opinion about farm-raised tilapia.

The answers to these questions are directly stated in the passage. Remember, when returning to the passage, read the lines above and below the specific sentence or line reference.

As we discussed in the previous chapter, the correct answer will be a paraphrase of part of the actual passage. This is especially true for Literal Comprehension questions because they are interpreting a portion of the passage. Adjectives and verbs from the text are often replaced with synonyms in the correct answer choice, and even some nouns might be altered.

Facts and Details questions ask you to interpret a specific portion of a passage. The answer is directly stated in the passage.

Facts and Details questions come in all shapes and sizes: expect to see them in Select One, Select More Than One, and Select-in-Passage questions.

13

Let's return to our passage about Machu Picchu:

Most archaeologists believe that Machu Picchu, a pre-Columbian Incan city, was built in the 15th century by the ruler Pachacutec. According to this view, the site was constructed on a mountain ridge as a personal estate for the powerful emperor;
Line he extended his refuge to 1200 of the most elite of Incan aristocracy, who resided
5 in the fortress for at least three generations until the Spanish conquest a century later. Rolf Muller, however, argues that the construction of the city actually started sometime between 2300 and 2100 BC.

Muller's theory is based on the alignment of buildings and landmarks in accordance with stars in the sky in the previous millennium. Using advanced
10 mathematical computations, Muller has produced convincing evidence that the most important sites in Machu Picchu were built around the procession of equinoxes that occurred before 2000 BC.

Muller also cites architectural anomalies as evidence that the city was built over thousands of years, rather than in a single generation. For example, three of
15 the most famous landmarks—The Hitching Post, The Temple of the Sun, and The Room of Three Windows—were constructed with exacting precision and masterful masonry, skills for which the Incas are well-known. But there are many buildings that were fashioned in a much cruder manner and others that show developing skill, indicating that the city was slowly constructed over long periods of time. A
20 city that was designed by a single architect or even a group of architects working simultaneously would have more architectural consistency.

Muller, whether right or wrong, has certainly given archaeologists something to think about. I suspect this debate will be discussed in academic papers and in colleges for years to come.

Remember, the correct answer includes all of the important information from the line reference. Wrong answers tend to leave out details.

2. According to the passage, why are the "buildings" in line 17 important to Muller's hypothesis?

(A) They reveal that Machu Picchu was designed to align with equinoxes and stars.

(B) They confirm that an Incan artisan developed his craft slowly throughout his lifetime.

(C) They suggest that the construction of Machu Picchu started before 1400.

(D) They illustrate the masterful skills of Incan builders.

(E) They provide examples of famous landmarks built between 2300 and 2100 BC.

Return to line 17 in the passage: *But there are many buildings that were fashioned in a much cruder manner and others that show developing skill, indicating that the city was slowly constructed over long periods of time.* These buildings were constructed in a crude manner and indicated developing construction skills, unlike the three famous landmarks which were *constructed with exacting precision and masterful masonry* (line 16), so it stands to reason that the crude buildings were built before 1400, because by 1400 the Incans were well-known for their building skills. Only answer choice (C) restates this idea.

13

Once again, let's examine the wrong answers, too:

(A) *They reveal that Machu Picchu was designed to align with equinoxes and stars.*

True But Wrong: Machu Picchu was designed with this alignment in mind per the second paragraph, but this is not why the buildings mentioned in line 17 were important.

(B) *They confirm that an Incan builder developed his craft slowly throughout his lifetime.*

This answer is playing on *developing skill* (line 18-19) and *over long periods of time* (line 19), but this sentence is about the city being built slowly, not the artisan building his personal skills.

(D) *They illustrate the masterful skills of Incan builders.*

Copycat/Opposite: While the buildings constructed after 1400 have *masterful masonry* (line 17), the building they are referencing in the question *were fashioned in a much cruder manner*. Notice, however, that the answer used the word *masterful* to try to trick test takers into selecting it as the right answer.

(E) *They provide examples of famous landmarks built between 2300 and 2100 BC.*

Again, the three famous landmarks referenced in lines 14-16 were built after 1400; the buildings mentioned in the question were older, but the passage never states when they were built or if they are even famous landmarks.

The correct answer will include all of the basic ideas from the text and will not add any new information, as did answer choices (B) and (E). It will likely use synonyms for adjectives, verbs, and even some nouns from the original text, unlike answer choices (A), (B), (C), and (E).

We have already discussed EXCEPT questions earlier in this book, but it bears noting that these queries are usually Facts and Details questions. The answers, which are usually interpreted facts and details, are provided in the text, but you must search for them. Recording short summaries of each paragraph as you read will save you time should you come across an EXCEPT question.

Literal Comprehension questions about Facts and Details simply ask you to choose an answer that restates the original text while maintaining meaning. Once you understand how to avoid the wrong answer choices and zero in on the right one, you will likely find these to be the easiest Reading Comprehension questions.

13 "EXCEPT questions" are usually Facts and Details questions.

Main Idea Questions and Facts and Details Questions Problem Set

Read the short passage below and then answer the corresponding Literal Comprehension questions. Answers begin on page 286.

With access to the Internet suddenly becoming universal, many advertisers have shifted their focus away from traditional mass media and towards online advertising. Recent studies suggest that in the next ten years, the Internet will attract close to $40 billion from advertisers in the United States alone, five times as much as it did a decade earlier.
Line
5 This projected development, coupled with a shrinking share of advertising revenues, has caused traditional mass media companies to increasingly deploy emerging technologies in television advertising, direct marketing, and billboard advertising that promise to help clients tailor their messages to specific demographic groups. Clearly, technological innovations have created a new, consumer-centered model in advertising that may ultimately redefine the very notion of mass communication.

1. According to the passage, all of the following are true EXCEPT

    (A) The new standard in advertising is based on customers and advancements in technology.

    (B) A decrease in revenues at traditional advertising companies is partially responsible for an increase in the use of advertising with technology.

    (C) Revenue from online marketing will significantly increase in the next decade.

    (D) Traditional mass media includes online advertising, direct marketing, and billboard and television advertising.

    (E) Advertisers are using technology to target particular sections of the population who share common characteristics.

2. Which of the following contributed to technology-infused billboards?

    [A] A prediction that online advertising earnings will increase fivefold in the coming decade.

    [B] The loss of market share for traditional advertising companies.

    [C] An increase in demand for demographic-specific marketing.

    Select all answers that apply.

3. The passage is primarily concerned with the

    (A) changes in advertising due to technology

    (B) decline of conventional advertising strategies

    (C) profit loss dealt to traditional advertisers by the use of technology in marketing

    (D) new definition of advertising resulting from online marketing

    (E) increase in advertising revenue since the invention of the internet

13

Reasons and Results Questions

Literal Comprehension questions that fall into this category ask you to provide the reasons for or the results of an action, event, or belief.

Reason questions use Cause and Effect words:

because   since   caused by   due to   resulted from

TIPS and TRICKS
Recognizing common vocabulary can help you quickly determine a question type and best solution method.

Consider some examples:

The author criticizes those who defend their beliefs because

According to the passage, student learning outcomes differ since

According to the passage, the genetic diversity of the population resulted from

The answers to these questions can occur before or after the line reference. Although it seems like the cause should logically come before the effect, an author may introduce a problem before citing the reasons for it.

Result questions, which appear infrequently on the GRE, require you to state the outcome of a situation. They do not use a common vocabulary, but examples include the following:

There is only one Result question featured in all of the officially-published GRE practice tests and questions.

Shelly responds to the accusation in the passage by doing which of the following?

The author shows that he is unaffected by criticism of his theory by

The passage indicates that the vagabonds will eventually

The answers to Result questions usually occur after the line reference because of the natural sequence of events.

Consider an example passage with these two types of questions:

Many patients are hesitant to seek second opinions when making decisions about their health, even when considering major medical procedures. This hesitation is sometimes based on a lack of familiarity with a relatively new physician, but even *Line* where a strong relationship has been developed between doctor and patient, the 5 person being treated often perceives the interest in a second opinion as an affront to the doctor who has provided the first opinion. This tendency is rather unfortunate, given the potential benefits; most patients who seek a second opinion will either receive further confirmation that a particular path represents the proper plan, or a contrary perspective which may suggest alternative methods for treatment.

1. According to the author, many patients fail to seek second opinions because they

    Ⓐ do not realize the potential benefits of dual diagnoses

    Ⓑ worry about offending their original doctor

    Ⓒ seek highly specialized doctors at the onset of treatment

    Ⓓ are unable to make decisions when presented with too much information

    Ⓔ refuse to acknowledge the original diagnosis

In this Reasons question, we are asked to provide the reason that many patients fail to seek second opinions. There are two reasons in the passage:

1. *a lack of familiarity with a relatively new physician* (line 3)

2. *the person...often perceives the interest...as an affront to the doctor who has provided the first opinion* (lines 4-6)

So either reason might be the answer, or the answer might contain both reasons. Answer choice (B) matches the second reason.

> The preferred answer would have BOTH reasons that patients seek second opinions, but since this is not an option, find the answer choice that has one of the reasons listed in the passage.

Answers (A) and (C) are incorrect because they contain ideas not discussed in the passage. Answers (D) and (E) also have irrelevant information, but many students are tempted by them because those students make assumptions. They reason that the patient probably cannot make a decision given two opinions, or that the patient might be scared to admit he has cancer. Remember, never assume on the GRE! The patient could be the CEO of a major corporation who is able to make decisions given hundreds of opinions. And since when did the passage say the patient had cancer? Maybe he's just getting a diagnosis for the common cold! If you found yourself thinking seriously about selecting (D) or (E), you need to work on setting assumptions aside before taking the GRE.

13

Now consider a Results question for the same passage:

Many patients are hesitant to seek second opinions when making decisions about their health, even when considering major medical procedures. This hesitation is sometimes based on a lack of familiarity with a relatively new physician, but even *Line* where a strong relationship has been developed between doctor and patient, the 5 person being treated often perceives the interest in a second opinion as an affront to the doctor who has provided the first opinion. This tendency is rather unfortunate, given the potential benefits; most patients who seek a second opinion will either receive further confirmation that a particular path represents the proper plan, or a contrary perspective which may suggest alternative methods for treatment.

2. The passage indicates that a second opinion most often results in

[A] insulted doctors who stop treatment on patients

[B] more informed decisions about courses of treatment

[C] less hesitation from primary caregivers

Select all answers that apply.

There are two outcomes of second opinions provided in the last sentence of the passage:

1. *patients receive further confirmation that a particular path represents the proper plan* (lines 7-8)

2. *patients receive a contrary perspective which may suggest alternative methods for treatment* (line 9)

Because this is a Select More Than One question, we need to select all of the answers that provide a result of a second opinion. Answer choice (B) effectively summarizes the two outcomes we have identified. They each provide the patient with additional information about courses of treatment, thus leading to more-informed decision-making.

Answer choice (A) might be tempting for students who answered the first question correctly, but it was the *patients* who worried about offending doctors; the passage never said whether the doctors were actually offended by second opinions. Plus, the passage says nothing about doctors stopping treatment. Choice (C), a True to a Point answer, tries to confuse the hesitation of patients (in the passage) with the hesitation of doctors (in the answer choice). Even though this question can have multiple answers, it only has one correct answer choice.

Remember, the answers to Literal Comprehension questions are directly stated in the passage, and the answers to Reasons and Results questions are no different. You should be able to point to a specific portion of the passage and say "The answer is here." The correct answer choice, then, is a paraphrased version of the text.

13

Reasons and Results Problem Set

Read the passage below and then answer the corresponding Literal Comprehension questions. Answers begin on page 287.

James Joyce, the well known Irish writer and poet, credited by many to have played a major role in developing the modernist novel, has long been the subject of intense literary inquiry. A fascinating character himself, Joyce led a hard life which included financial difficulties throughout all but his last few years. He suffered from alcoholism throughout his adult life, a problem that was compounded by other setbacks. As he got older, his eyesight began to fail him,
Line subjecting him to periods of total blindness, and adding to the trauma he suffered as his daughter's psychoses led to her
5 permanent confinement in an asylum.

Perhaps the interesting story of Joyce's own life helps to explain the ongoing fascination with the writer and his works. The author's significant contemporary following is also likely attributable to the fact that his novels, like his perspective, are not conducive to simple interpretation. In a letter, Joyce once described *Finnegans Wake*, one of his best known works, as "an engine with one wheel (and) no spokes."

10 Many of Joyce's phrasings are less than readily decipherable, and as a result his works provide seemingly endless opportunity for speculation about construction and meaning. Consensus among literary scholars is often elusive, which is why outlier academics sometimes gain notoriety in the short term with unsubstantiated but well-publicized claims concerning proper interpretation. For example, Danis Rose, a Joyce scholar in Ireland, recently announced dubious plans to publish "Finn's Hotel," a collection of early notes which he claims to be a previously unknown Joyce work, in
15 spite of the fact that the stories have all been published before, and actually provided the foundation for the later, better known *Finnegans Wake*.

1. According to the author, Joyce "led a hard life" (lines 2-3) because of all of the following EXCEPT

    Ⓐ harsh literary criticism

    Ⓑ mental illness in his family

    Ⓒ monetary hardship

    Ⓓ substance abuse

    Ⓔ health issues

2. According to the passage, the "ongoing fascination" (line 6) with James Joyce is due to the

    Ⓐ notoriety of *Finnegan's Wake*

    Ⓑ odd wording of his short stories

    Ⓒ achievements he attained despite blindness and alcoholism

    Ⓓ possibility of fame for amateur critics who propose unusual theories about the author

    Ⓔ complexity of his life and his works

3. The author indicates that one of the results of Joyce's "less than readily decipherable" phrasings (line 10) is

    Ⓐ the mass marketing of previously-published novels as undiscovered works

    Ⓑ decreased interest in Joyce's personal life

    Ⓒ attention given to the interpretive theories of lesser-known scholars

    Ⓓ agreement among literary critics about the meaning and purpose of Joyce's novels

    Ⓔ expanded readership of Joyce's early notes and short stories

13

Comparison and Contrast Questions

The final type of Literal Comprehension question asks you to find similarities or differences among topics, actions, events, and beliefs. These questions are very rare on the GRE.

Questions that ask you to find similarities between ideas or passages tend to use a few common words:

Comparison and Contrast Questions are extremely rare on the GRE.

both   agree   parallel   is most like   shared by

Consider some sample questions:

Both the author and the critic in line 7 draw attention to which of the following?

What parallel between ice formations and precipitation does the passage reveal?

Questions that ask about differences have their own vocabulary:

unlike   contrast   differ

Let's now look at a couple of examples of Contrast questions:

The "experts" (line 13) and the "advocates" (line 15) differ primarily about whether

According to the passage, the report issued by Renner and the explanation offered by Gray differed on

Pay close attention to the viewpoints of experts, advocates, opponents, or other people and groups mentioned in the passage. You may be asked how these viewpoints compare or contrast with the ideas of the author or other groups of people. As with all Literal Comprehension questions, the answers lie in the text. Jot down the belief of each person separately and then use your notes to draw comparisons.

13

Chapter Summary

Literal Comprehension Questions ask you to recall facts directly stated in the passage. There are four main types of Literal Comprehension Questions:

Main Idea Questions

- The main idea is directly stated in the passage.

- It applies to every paragraph; wrong answers will likely highlight the main idea of a single paragraph.

Facts and Details Questions

- These are the most common Literal Comprehension question.

- The correct answer uses synonyms for the words in the passage and includes all important details.

Reasons and Results Questions

- These questions ask you to interpret the cause or effect of specific actions.

Comparison and Contrast Questions

- You may be asked to draw a comparison or contrast between ideas or viewpoints in the passage.

13

Literal Comprehension Questions Answer Key

Main Idea Questions and Facts and Details Questions Problem Set—Page 279

1. D   Prephrase: Impossible to prephrase EXCEPT questions

   Choice (A): Lines 6-8
   Choice (B): Lines 4-6
   Choice (C): Lines 2-3
   Choice (D): Traditional media does *not* include online marketing, as indicated in lines 1-2. They are shifting from traditional media to online advertising, signifying they are two different things.
   Choice (E): Line 6

2. A and B   Prephrase: Projected increase in online revenue and a shrinking share of advertising revenues

   Line 4-6: *This projected development* [referring to *in the next ten years, the Internet will attract close to $40 billion from advertisers*, line 3] *coupled with a shrinking share of advertising revenues, has caused traditional mass media companies to increasingly deploy emerging technologies in television advertising, direct marketing, and billboard advertising.* Thus, choices (A) and (B) are correct.

   Choice (C) uses some Copycat words (*demographic, specific*), but there is no truth to the statement.

3. A   Prephrase: How advertising is changing with technology

   Only choice (A) matches the prephrase. Even though this is a Main Idea question (and not a Facts and Details question), it's still a Literal Comprehension question.

   (B): True But Wrong. It's implied that traditional media strategies are declining by the fact that these strategies are not incorporating technology. But this is not the main idea of the entire paragraph.

   (C): True But Wrong. They have suffered a revenue loss because they have lost a share of the market to online advertising. But look at the first and last sentence of the paragraph, both of which contain the main idea: neither mentions the revenues, because the earnings are just an example of why the change is occurring.

   (D) Copycat. In the last sentence, the author surmises that a new definition may happen. It has not yet happened, and is not the main idea of the entire paragraph.

   (E) This answer brings in new information about the invention of the internet, which is not mentioned anywhere in the paragraph.

1. A   Prephrase: Impossible to prephrase EXCEPT questions

    The components of his "hard life" are all contained in the first paragraph:

    1. financial difficulties (line 3): Answer (C)

    2. alcoholism (line 3): Answer (D)

    3. eyesight began to fail him...blindness (lines 4-5): Answer (E)

    4. his daughter's psychoses (lines 5-6): Answer (B)

2. E   Prephrase: his interesting life and his complicated novels

    The author provides two reasons for this "ongoing fascination:"

    1. the interesting story of Joyce's own life

    2. the fact that his novels, like his perspective, are not conducive to simple interpretation

    Note that the first statement is from the sentence immediately following the first paragraph, so it is referencing Joyce's personal troubles as the *interesting story*. The author further comments on this *story* when he says *like his perspective* in the second statement. If his novels and his perspective are not conducive to a simple interpretation, then they are the opposite of simple— they are complex. Answer choice (E) is best.

    Copycat: Choice (A) is wrong because the passage does not reveal whether *Finnegans Wake* was notorious (note that the passage does use the word *notoriety* (line 28), tricking some test takers to select this answer.

    True to a Point: Choice (B) is incorrect mainly because of the use of *short stories*. All of his works, including novels, have *less than readily decipherable phrasings*. And while we can infer that there is critical interest in Joyce's works because of these difficult phrasings, it is not stated. Plus, *odd* is not the most synonymous word with *less than readily decipherable*.

    True to a Point: Choice (C) is incorrect because it only contains two of the setbacks faced by Joyce. It omits financial difficulties and his daughter's psychoses (not to mention the complexity of his works). Remember, the right answer will include ALL important ideas, not just some of them.

    True But Wrong: Finally, choice (D) is incorrect. While a portion of this answer rings true elsewhere in the passage, it's not the reason for the fascination for Joyce's works.

13

3.   C   Prephrase: interpretations from outlier academics

The answer comes from lines 13-14: *outlier academics sometimes gain notoriety in the short term with unsubstantiated but well-publicized claims concerning proper interpretation*. This is an example of the *endless opportunity for speculation* cited in lines 10-11.

Notice that the correct answer (C), uses many synonyms: *attention* for *notoriety*; *interpretive theories* for *unsubstantiated claims*; and *lesser-known scholars* for *outlier academics*.

Answer choice (A) is incorrect because of the words *mass marketing* (not discussed in the passage) and *novels* (it was *early notes* that the scholar claimed were undiscovered in the passage).

Opposite: Answer choice (B) is wrong because nothing in the passage indicates that interest has decreased in Joyce's personal life. If anything, it seems to have increased.

Opposite: Answer choice (D) is wrong because it is an opposite answer. The passage states that *consensus among literary scholars is often elusive* (lines 11-12), meaning scholars do not agree.

Answer choice (E) is incorrect because the author does not discuss the increase or decrease in readership. Notice again the use of *short stories*: short stories are not mentioned in the passage at all.

13

Reading Comprehension Mastery: Extended Reasoning Questions

Reading Comprehension Mastery: Extended Reasoning Questions

Introduction

Extended Reasoning questions make up the bulk of Reading Comprehension questions. Roughly 70% of the questions in the *Official Guide to the GRE* are Extended Reasoning questions.

These questions usually cause students the most difficulty because unlike Literal Comprehension questions, the answers to Extended Reasoning questions are not directly stated in the passage. You must draw a conclusion based on information in all or part of the passage.

Let's study a simplified example before looking at specific question types:

> After graduating from law school, Michelle was recruited by the best law firm in the city. She turned them down, however, preferring to work for the non-profit organization, where the underprivileged were able to retain lawyers. The charity
> Line was located a block from where she grew up, so it was a true homecoming and
> 5 success story for one of the neighborhood's own.

1. The paragraph suggests which of the following about "the best law firm in the city?"

    (A) It recruited the most talented graduates.

    (B) It was not located in the city in which Michelle was raised.

    (C) Its job offers were not often turned down.

    (D) Its lawyers were considered the most intelligent in the city.

    (E) It did not typically represent disadvantaged clients.

The inference occurs in lines 2-3: *She turned them down, however, preferring to work for the non-profit organization, where the underprivileged were able to retain lawyers*. This sentence implies that if Michelle had gone to work for the best law firm in the city, she would not be representing underprivileged people because they could not retain lawyers there. The best answer is (E). Notice that it uses the word *typically*, making your argument even more sound. It is easier to defend "It *did not typically represent* disadvantaged clients" than "It *did not represent* disadvantaged clients."

The other four answers are not suggested or stated in the passage. In order for (A) to be correct, the passage would have had to state that Michelle was one of the most talented graduates. Then you could conclude that this is why she was recruited. But without that information, (A) is wrong.

Choice (B) is incorrect because the passage actually implies that the law firm is in the city where Michelle grew up.

While students might be tempted to assume that answer choice (C) is right given what they know about the best law firms from watching TV law shows (such as high salaries, important cases, etc.), the passage does not discuss any other offer besides the one to Michelle. You cannot assume anything on the GRE without evidence to support the assumption.

Finally, choice (D) is incorrect because of the word *intelligent*. While you may conclude that they are the best lawyers (because they work for the best law firm), you do not have enough information to know *why* they are best. Maybe the lawyers win cases because they bribe judges. Or maybe they are the most persistent, refusing to give up on cases. Intelligence was not mentioned in the paragraph, nor was any other reason for the law firm's success.

This example, while simple, demonstrates the difficulty of Extended Reasoning questions and the meticulousness with which you must read each question and answer choice.

There are two main types of Extended Reasoning Questions, but each type can further be broken down into subtypes:

1. Purpose Questions

   • Multiple Choice

   • Select-in-Passage

2. Inference Questions

   • General Inferences

   • Hypothetical Points of View

On the following pages we will explore each type and subtype in more depth. Understanding the question types can help you avoid wrong answers and select the right ones.

14

Purpose Questions

Purpose Questions ask you to explain the function of a particular section of text. Why did the author use this particular word or phrase? Why did the author write this passage? You might be asked about the purpose of a term, phrase, sentence, group of sentences, paragraph, or the entire passage itself.

Many Purpose Questions use common terms in the question:

purpose   functions   serves   because   in order to

The word *because* may be used in other types of questions (like Literal Comprehension Facts and Details questions), but the other terms are most often used in Purpose Questions.

Questions about the passage as a whole are called Primary Purpose Questions and they resemble the following:

The primary purpose of the passage is

The passage primarily serves to

The major purpose of the passage is to

These questions should be easy for you to answer because you will determine the purpose of the passage when identifying the MAPS after reading. Answer choices for Primary Purpose questions tend to use verbs as the first word of the answer choice. Study an example in which the verbs are underlined:

1. The primary purpose of the passage is to

    (A) <u>define</u> the relationship between employee and supervisor
    (B) <u>discuss</u> workplace disobedience
    (C) <u>challenge</u> a management strategy
    (D) <u>illustrate</u> acceptable office behavior
    (E) <u>compare</u> work ethic today to that of the 1950s

Understanding these verbs can help you eliminate wrong answers and select the right one. For example, the verb *challenge* indicates that the author disputes a current theory, and the passage must be written to prove this theory wrong. If the author is not questioning a theory, then you can confidently eliminate this answer in (C). The same goes for *compare*: if two items are not being analyzed for their similarities or differences throughout the entire passage, then answer choice (E) is wrong.

Purpose questions require you to explain the function of a word, phrase, sentence, paragraph, or passage.

Purpose questions use verbs in their answers. Understanding these verbs is important to your success on these questions.

14

There are three common primary purposes on the GRE—to argue against, to argue for, and to explain—and each has a set of verbs that may be commonly used in the correct answer of a Primary Purpose Question. Be sure you understand the meaning of each one and read any accompanying notes about their use on the GRE.

An author's primary purpose is to argue for, argue against, or explain an idea.

Any of these verbs could be used in the correct answer choice, but some are more common than others. Verbs in bold are more likely to be used in correct answers; verbs with an asterisk are less likely.

Verbs That Argue Against:

argue: to present reasons for or against a thing. If an author is arguing throughout a passage, each paragraph will provide a reason for or against the topic.

challenge: to question or dispute. If an author is challenging a topic, each paragraph will present a reason for that challenge.

criticize: to find fault with. If an author is criticizing a topic or theory, he will present reasons why that topic or theory is wrong throughout the passage.

*denounce: to openly condemn. One of the most Extreme verbs that argue against something.

dispute: to argue. See *argue*, above.

*lament: to express sorrow or regret. This verb is less likely to be in the correct answer, but is easy to determine if it is.

object: to argue. See *argue*, above.

oppose: to argue against. If the author argues against a topic, it should be quite clear.

question: to challenge. See *challenge*, above.

rebut: to disprove. If the author rebuts a claim, she will provide evidence to show that claim is wrong.

refute: to disprove. See *rebut*, above.

Verbs That Argue For:

advocate: to support. An author who advocates for a subject will provide reasons for that support.

defend: to support in the face of criticism. Expect an author who is defending a topic to cite reasons the criticism is wrong.

encourage: to support. See *advocate*, above.

endorse: to support. See *advocate*, above.

promote: to support. See *advocate*, above.

14

Verbs That Explain:

address: to discuss. Because all authors discuss their topics on the GRE, this answer is easy to defend.

compare: to find similarities and differences. Note that *compare* can also mean finding differences between two things.

contrast: to find differences. If the author finds similarities between two items, you cannot select *contrast* as an answer.

define: to explain the meaning of. An author may define a term in a sentence or paragraph, but it's unlikely he will spend an entire passage defining something.

describe: to tell in words. Because all authors describe their topics on the GRE, this answer is easy to defend.

discuss: to consider. See *address*, above.

emphasize: to stress a point. Most authors stress their points, so this is another easy answer to defend.

*examine: to investigate closely. A possible answer, but not as likely as *address*, *discuss*, *show*, and other more benign answers that do not have *closely* in their definition.

explain: to provide causes or reasons for. An author who explains a topic will discuss reasons for it.

explore: to look into. See *address*, above.

illustrate: to make clear by use of examples. If an author provides examples of a topic, they are illustrating their point.

note: to mention. See *address*, above.

point out: to indicate. See *address*, above.

present: to introduce. Pay close attention to what the answer choice is presenting; the author may present evidence or theories, but he is unlikely to present an aside or a case study.

*probe: to examine closely. See *examine*, above.

provide: to give. See *present*, above.

show: to indicate. See *address*, above.

*speculate: to conjecture without facts. This answer is always a possibility, but make sure the author is proposing a new idea, not just writing about one that has already been provided.

suggest: to introduce for consideration. See *address*, above.

urge: to persuade. Many GRE passages are written to persuade, so this answer is possible. Just make sure the author is trying to convince people to act in support of or opposition to the topic.

CAUTION: GRE TRAP!
These basic words often cause big problems for GRE test takers! You must understand what each one means before selecting an answer choice containing it. An author may "criticize" a topic, but it's highly unlikely that he will "lament" it!

14

Some Purpose Questions ask you to explain the function of a paragraph. Again, these should not be too difficult to answer if you notate the MAPS of each passage, as the structure of a passage will reveal the function of each of its parts.

Other purpose questions will be about specific portions of the text. Consider some example questions:

1. The quotation in lines 51-53 primarily serves to

2. The author compares "fundamentalists" and "survivors" in order to

3. In line 21, the "winds of change" serve as an example of an action that is

When you rephrase these questions, the first word of your paraphrase should almost always be *why*:

1. Why did the author use a quotation?

2. Why does the author compare "fundamentalists" and "survivors"?

3. Why does the author use the "winds of change"?

Remember, you should always prephrase an answer to each question before looking at the answer choices. Your internal conversation never stops during a GRE passage! *Why did the author use a quotation? Well, it was provided by a dog trainer and it supports his belief that dangerous dogs should be leashed in the city. So he used an expert's opinion to support his thesis. Which answer choice is closest to my prephrase?* Never underestimate the power of the prephrase! Your prephrased answer will lead you to the correct answer choice and steer you away from the wrong ones.

14

The majority of purpose questions ask you to explain the function of a single term, short phrase, or sentence. The answers to these questions are in the lines immediately preceding and following the referenced word or phrase. Consider an example:

> From birth, dolphins are able to squeak, click, whistle, and squawk, all of which serve as a means of communicating with other members of the pod. They also have several methods of non-verbal expression. Jaw claps express aggression; fin-rubbing shows friendship.

1. The author mentions "jaw claps" and "fin-rubbing" in order to

    Ⓐ illustrate forms of non-verbal communication in dolphins
    Ⓑ clarify that dolphin communication is different than human communication
    Ⓒ suggest that dolphins are similar to humans
    Ⓓ explain how verbal cues are misinterpreted
    Ⓔ emphasize the importance of studying dolphins and other marine wildlife

If we were to outline this paragraph, the purpose of those two terms becomes quite clear:

I. Dolphin Communication

   A. Verbal Communication

      1. Squeak
      2. Click
      3. Whistle
      4. Squawk

   B. Non-Verbal Communication

      1. Jaw claps
      2. Fin-rubbing

The jaw claps and fin-rubbing are provided as examples of *several methods of non-verbal expression*, just as the squeaks, clicks, whistles, and squawks are examples of verbal communication. Obviously, you do not need to outline every paragraph on the GRE (nor do you have the time to do so), but we do it here to illustrate how the paragraph is organized, since the organization of the paragraph explains the purpose of those two terms.

The purpose of a term, phrase, or sentence has a wide range of possibilities, from providing an example to defining a term to disproving a theory. Your best strategy for answering questions about the purpose of a passage element is to rephrase the question (*why did the author use this word? this phrase? this sentence?*), reread the portion of the passage that is referenced, and then prephrase an answer to your rephrased question.

TIPS and TRICKS
If you are struggling with a Purpose Question, mentally outline the paragraph to see if the structure reveals the answer.

14

Select-in-Passage Questions

Most of the questions that ask you to select a sentence in the passage are Purpose questions in reverse. Instead of determining the purpose of a sentence, you are provided with the purpose and asked to locate the sentence that fulfills that purpose:

> Select the sentence that provides Fisher's opinion about what caused the independent vote to shift.

TIPS and TRICKS

Most of the "Select-in-Passage" questions are Purpose questions in reverse.

The question tells you the purpose of the sentence: to provide Fisher's opinion about the cause of the voting shift. Your responsibility is to find the sentence with that particular purpose.

Here are some other examples of common Select-in-Passage question formats:

> Select the sentence whose function is to illustrate the relationship between the two layers of sediment.

> Select a sentence that distinguishes between voluntary and involuntary responses.

> Select a sentence in which the author provides examples of the consequences of fracking.

When presented with a Short Passage, expect to search the entire passage for the sentence. But when faced with a Long Passage, the Select-in-Passage question will usually highlight a specific paragraph or portion of the text from which you should conduct your search.

When returning to the passage to locate a sentence, remember that the sentence may be long and complex, covering several ideas at one time. Do not discount a sentence because it contains information unrelated to the purpose in question. Consider an example, in which the sentences are numbered for the sake of discussion:

> (1) Although Charles Kenneth Scott Moncrieff's translation of *À la recherche du temps perdu* is considered by many journalists and writers to be the best translation of any foreign work into the English language, his choice of *Remembrance*
> *Line* *of Things Past* as the general title alarmed the seriously ill Proust and misled
> 5 generations of readers as to the novelist's true intent. (2) It wasn't until 1992 that the title was finally changed to *In Search of Lost Time*. (3) "Remembrance of Things Past" is a beautiful line from William Shakespeare's sonnet 30, but it conveys an idea that is really the opposite of Proust's own. (4) When Scott Moncrieff chose this title, he did not know, of course, where Proust was going with the story and did not
> 10 correctly interpret the title, which might indeed be taken to indicate a rather passive attempt by an elderly person to recollect days gone by.

> 1. Select the sentence that explains how Moncrieff's English title for *À la recherche du temps perdu* might be misunderstood by readers.

14

Which sentence contains information about HOW the title is misinterpreted? Sentence 1 states that the title *misled generations of readers as to the novel's true intent*, but it does not say *how* they were misled. Sentence 3 reveals that the title *conveys an idea that is really the opposite of Proust's own*, but again, does not reveal *how* the title was misunderstood. The answer lies in Sentence 4: *the title...might indeed be taken to indicate a rather passive attempt by an elderly person to recollect days gone by*.

Notice, however, the first part of this sentence: *When Scott Moncrieff chose this title, he did not know, of course, where Proust was going with the story and did not correctly interpret the title*. This has nothing to do with *how* the title was misinterpreted, so some students might eliminate this sentence when searching for a specific purpose. But they would be wrong to dismiss it so quickly. The GRE is filled with complex sentences that contain multiple ideas, and only a small part of a sentence needs to satisfy the purpose in order to be selected as the correct sentence. Be careful not to eliminate a sentence just because part of it is unrelated to the purpose for which you search.

CAUTION: GRE TRAP!
The evidence needed to answer a Select-in-Passage question may come at the end of a complex sentence, where the beginning of the sentence is unrelated to the question. Do not eliminate a sentence just because the first part does not seem to apply!

14

Purpose Questions Problem Set

Read the passage below and then answer the corresponding Purpose questions. Answers begin on page 312.

Line
5

10

15

(1) While emerging information technologies have changed the media landscape in recent years, one of the oldest forms of online advertising—the web banner—continues to be a staple of the Internet age. (2) Banner ads are clearly superior to traditional mass media. (3) Embedded as a small image into a web page, banners allow advertisers to reach millions of customers instantaneously without the geographic limitations inherent in traditional newspaper-based advertising. (4) And unlike television commercials, banner ads can be deployed in association with user input from search engines, which significantly increases their potential for impact.

Perhaps the most attractive feature of banner ads, however, is the transparency with which advertisers can allegedly measure their success. Every time a viewer displays a banner in her web browser, she generates what is commonly known as an "impression." An impression turns into a "click-through event" whenever the viewer clicks on the banner. By dividing the number of click-through events by the total number of impressions generated, advertisers can easily measure the click-through rates of their banner ads and tailor their strategies accordingly.

Some experts have recently argued, however, that the media's focus on click-through rates can be detrimental to the success of their campaigns. For instance, if a banner displayed simultaneously on two different websites generates markedly different click-through rates, many advertisers would be tempted to increase the number of banner ad impressions on the website with the higher click-through rate. Such a strategy does not always work, as click-through events can sometimes increase without generating a higher sales volume. Clearly, click-through rate variability provides an imperfect measure of affinity between the website's audience and the ad campaign's target demographic, and should be used with great deliberation.

1. The primary purpose of the passage is to

   Ⓐ note the benefits and a potential drawback of using a common advertising strategy

   Ⓑ emphasize the importance of using web banners for small businesses

   Ⓒ explore a new information technology

   Ⓓ refute a theory about targeting a demographic

   Ⓔ lament the demise of an obsolete practice

2. Select the sentence in the first paragraph that provides the author's opinion about web banners used in advertising.

3. The author compares "television commercials" with "banner ads" in lines 5-6 primarily in order to

   Ⓐ urge television viewers to patronize advertisers

   Ⓑ challenge a common belief among advertising executives

   Ⓒ point out the limitations of another popular advertising strategy

   Ⓓ explain how one media outlet will eventually replace another

   Ⓔ show how each evolved from a new technology to an economic staple

14

4. The first sentence of the second paragraph functions primarily to

    (A) suggest that a hypothesis has a weakness

    (B) provide support for a claim made earlier in the passage

    (C) dispute evidence previously presented in the passage

    (D) explain how a complicated process works

    (E) speculate about why a doomed technology is so commonly used

5. The final paragraph primarily serves to

    (A) summarize the reasons for a particular theory

    (B) criticize the beliefs of members of the advertising profession

    (C) restate the evidence used to prove a conjecture

    (D) oppose the use of an accepted advertising strategy

    (E) acknowledge a shortcoming of a preferred method of advertising

14

Inference Questions

There are two types of Inference Questions: General Inferences and Hypothetical Points of View.

General Inferences

Most students find inference questions the most challenging Reading Comprehension questions because it is easy to confuse everyday inferences with inferences on the GRE. The test makers take advantage of this confusion by designing answer choices to further stump you.

An inference is a conclusion made by analyzing specific evidence. It's an educated guess, the kind we make every day in our real lives. Consider some common assumptions made from a general statement:

Statement: Scarlett went to the nurse's office.

Frank's Inference: Scarlett is sick.

Gray's Inference: Scarlett is taking her medication.

Hannah's Inference: Scarlett is going home.

All of these inferences are great guesses, and one or all of them may be correct. Other students with more qualified experience or knowledge, might draw different conclusions that are less common:

Izzy's Inference: Scarlett works for the nurse.

Jay's Inference: Scarlett went to check on a sick friend.

Klint's Inference: Scarlett steals from the nurse when the nurse is on his lunch break.

There are many possible conclusions, including some that are more probable than others, when making inferences in our daily lives. On the GRE, however, there is only one right answer. The GRE is a standardized test, so all test takers—including Frank, Gray, Hannah, Izzy, Jay, and Klint—must be able to draw the exact same conclusion. Understanding this difference between real world inferences and GRE inferences can help you avoid selecting the wrong answers on the test.

An inference is a conclusion made by analyzing specific evidence.

14

On the GRE, you should not make regular inferences about a statement. There will be only one conclusion that you can draw—the same conclusion that all other test takers can draw—about a section of text. Consider another general statement:

Statement: Today was the first time Scarlett visited the nurse's office.

There is only a single inference here that can be proven, and thus only one inference that would be correct on the GRE:

> Correct Inference: Scarlett had never been to the nurse's office before today.

You cannot prove any of the following, so these inferences are wrong:

> Incorrect Inference: Scarlett has never been sick at school.
> *Maybe she was sick and went straight home.*
>
> Incorrect Inference: Scarlett is a new student.
> *Maybe she's been at the school for years, but just has never gotten sick.*
>
> Incorrect Inference: Scarlett has never met the nurse.
> *Maybe they met in the hallway.*

Inferences are not direct statements on the GRE, but they can be proven, so avoid drawing any conclusions for which you cannot find any proof.

General inference questions are revealed by common word usage:

suggests   it can be inferred   implies   assumption

While students of formal logic may have very different definitions for these first three words, on the GRE they are used interchangeably. What the author suggests is the same as what he implies which is the same as what can be inferred. Let's look at some examples of inference questions:

> The discussion of volcanoes in the second paragraph primarily suggests that
>
> The author implies that a child's curiosity "might be hindered" (line 12) because
>
> It can be inferred from that passage that Squires' conclusions include which of the following elements?
>
> The author's assumption in the first paragraph is that

TIPS and TRICKS
There is only a single provable inference that can be drawn from a line reference on the GRE.

It is difficult to prephrase many inference questions.

14

Let's examine a GRE-type inference question:

> In August, NASA released the first complete map of ice floes in Antarctica. Researchers can now examine the outward flow of the continent's ice sheets to better help them predict rises in sea level.

1. The passage suggests that

   Ⓐ researchers were unable to predict changes in sea level with early maps

   Ⓑ the technology to delineate the ice floes was not available until recently

   Ⓒ previously published charts were comparably deficient

   Ⓓ the treacherous terrain of Antarctica made it too difficult for researchers to navigate

   Ⓔ changes in sea level interfere with the researchers' ability to chart land masses

One implication lies in the phrase *first complete map*. What does this suggest about earlier maps? That they were incomplete. Choice (C) is best.

Understanding why inference answers are wrong can go a long way to helping you understand why the correct one is right. Look at choice (A): the answer choice uses *unable to predict changes*, while the passage says the new maps *better help them*, indicating that they are already predicting changes in sea level, just not as well as they will be from now on.

TIPS and TRICKS
Sometimes it is easier to eliminate wrong inferences than find the correct inference.

If you chose choice (B), you read too much into the passage. This might be an inference you would make in your real life, like Scarlett going to the nurse's office because she is sick, but it is not one you can make on the GRE. There is no proof in the passage that technology was unavailable until recently.

Choice (D) is a similar assumption that is made without proof. Even if you know that this statement in (D) is True to You, you cannot select it as an answer choice because the passage does not suggest this is so.

Choice (E) is wrong because we were not given any information about how changes in sea level affect charting.

14

Hypothetical Point of View

Questions that ask you to predict a person's response to a hypothetical situation are Hypothetical Point of View questions. You may be asked how an author would respond to a statement or question or you may also be asked to predict the response of a person, expert, group, or opponent mentioned in the text. You can quickly pinpoint some of these questions by the use of *would*:

> The author of the passage would most likely agree that

> The passage suggests that the critics in line 4 would probably agree with which of the following statements?

> It can be inferred that Robinson would be LEAST likely to agree with which of the following?

The best strategy for answering these questions is prephrasing:

> The Antarctic Protocol of 1991 should be amended to allow for mineral prospecting with strict environmental regulations. All mining expeditions would be underground, so the environment and current research projects would not be affected. Scientists around the globe agree that the untapped resources of the Antarctic may hold secrets that are too valuable to ignore.

Line 5

1. The author of the passage would most likely agree with which of the following statements about climate change studies currently occurring on Antarctica?

   Ⓐ Researchers believe their results are less valuable than the discoveries to be made from mining.

   Ⓑ Mineral prospecting would allow the studies to continue without interruption.

   Ⓒ The studies' global impact is over emphasized.

   Ⓓ The studies themselves are polluting the continent just as much as economic exploration would.

   Ⓔ The studies could only be halted with international agreement.

Begin by summarizing the main idea: the author believes that mineral prospecting on Antarctica should be allowed as long as strict environmental regulations are in place. Then address the question: what would the author say about the current climate change studies? The author states that *current research projects would not be affected* by mining. So he would likely say that mining would not stop those studies. Armed with this prephrase, match an answer choice: (B).

If you do not hold a conversation with yourself (like this one) while answering Hypothetical Point of View questions, you will become confused when looking at the answer choices. It is extremely important to prephrase the answer to these questions by asking yourself how the author would likely respond.

CAUTION: GRE TRAP!
Expect a lot of True But Wrong answers for hypothetical inference questions. The test makers will ask you to differentiate between facts in the passage (i.e. the wrong answers) and a person's opinion (i.e. the right answer).

TIPS and TRICKS
Active reading is essential to answering Hypothetical Point of View questions. You must hold a conversation with yourself in order to work out the answers to these questions.

14

Inference Questions Problem Set

Read the passages below and then answer the corresponding Inference questions. Answers begin on page 313.

"Spare the rod and spoil the child," quote many parents today, unaware that they are citing not the Christian Bible, but rather a poem from 1664. Punishments that were also considered acceptable in the 17th century included stoning, drawing and quartering, and drowning, but spanking is the only one still in use in America today. It is an archaic form
Line of punishment that is never acceptable, and research from childhood and parenting experts indicates that spanking is not
5 only ineffective, but also dangerous to the health and welfare of the child.

1. The passage suggests that parents who refer to the adage in line 1 believe that

   Ⓐ they are citing a Biblical reference

   Ⓑ stoning and drowning are still acceptable forms of punishment

   Ⓒ spanking is an unacceptable form of discipline

   Ⓓ spanking is a more effective behavior modification practice than positive reinforcement

   Ⓔ moderate spanking is as harmful to children as whipping with belts and switches

2. The author cites "stoning, drawing and quartering, and drowning" to suggest which of the following?

   Ⓐ Spanking is the only acceptable form of punishment from the 1400s.

   Ⓑ Parents who spank their children are likely to support the death penalty.

   Ⓒ The emotional toll of spanking on children is worse than experts originally predicted.

   Ⓓ Moderate spanking was a preferred method of discipline for parents in the 15th century.

   Ⓔ Spanking is equally as primitive as other 17th century punishments.

Social media has revolutionized how people create and consume information. Unlike the broadcasts of traditional media, which are passively consumed, social media depends on users to deliberately propagate the information they receive to their social contacts. This process, called social contagion, can amplify the spread of information in a social
Line network. Understanding the mechanics of social contagion is crucial to many applications: creating viral marketing
5 campaigns, evaluating the quality of information, and predicting how far it will spread. While the spread of information is often likened to an infectious disease, social contagion differs in that social media users actively seek out information and consciously decide to propagate it.

3. It can be inferred from the passage that compared with propagators of social contagion, which of the following is true of people with infectious diseases?

   Ⓐ They did not pursue the disease.

   Ⓑ They do not purposely disseminate the disease.

   Ⓒ They do not need to understand the fundamentals of the disease.

   Select all answers that apply.

14

Just before Robert Hooke's rightly famous microscopic observations of everything from the "Edges of Rasors" to "Vine mites" appeared in *Micrographia* in 1665, the insatiably curious and incredibly prolific Jesuit scholar Athanasius Kircher published what is in many ways a more spectacular work. *Mundus Subterraneus* (Underground World), a
Line two-volume tome of atlas-like dimensions, was intended to lay out "before the eyes of the curious reader all that is
5 rare, exotic, and portentous contained in the fecund womb of Nature." There is an "idea of the earthly sphere that exists in the divine mind," Kircher proclaimed, and in this book, one of more than thirty on almost as many subjects that he published during his lifetime, he tried to prove that he had grasped it.

As a French writer put it some years later, "it would take a whole journal to indicate everything remarkable in this work." There were extended treatments on the spontaneous generation of living animals from non-living matter, the
10 unethical means by which alchemists pretended to change base metals into gold, and the apparent tricks of nature we now recognize as fossils. The book included detailed charts of "secret" oceanic motions, or currents, among the first ever published. The author's more or less correct explanation of how igneous rock is formed was also arguably the first in print. According to one modern scholar, Kircher "understood erosion," and his entries "on the quality and use of sand" and his "investigations into the tending of fields" had their practical use.

4. The author would most likely agree that *Mundus Subterraneus*

   Ⓐ rivaled *Micrographia* in scope and content

   Ⓑ was inappropriately titled

   Ⓒ repeated themes seen in books previously-published by Kircher

   Ⓓ received little attention upon publication in the 1600s

   Ⓔ introduced original theories that were discredited in time

5. The passage suggests that the French writer in line 8 would probably agree with which of the following statements about Kircher's book?

   Ⓐ It is difficult to evaluate because it includes too many subjects.

   Ⓑ It is one of many books by Kircher on similar subjects.

   Ⓒ It is considered superior to Robert Hooke's publication.

   Ⓓ It contains numerous impressive observations and theories.

   Ⓔ It is the first published work to correctly map ocean currents.

14

Parallel Reasoning Questions

Parallel Reasoning Questions are the rarest of all Reading Comprehension Questions, but you should still be prepared should one appear. These questions ask you to determine which of five situations is most like a scenario in the passage.

Parallel Reasoning questions require you to choose a situation that is most similar to a situation in the passage.

Expect to see some of the following phrases in Parallel Reasoning Questions:

situation   most similar to   most analogous to

additional example   most closely conforms to

Consider some question examples:

Which of the following situations is most analogous to the "relationship" cited in lines 13-14?

The approach to cooking described in lines 54-60 is most similar to which of the following?

Which hypothetical situation involves the same "education" (line 61) discussed by the author?

Now consider a passage and question in more detail:

> The Bowl Championship Series (BCS) in college football was a ranking system that determined the top 10 teams and then matched them in head-to-head games to determine the season's champion. Critics of the system contended that
> *Line* it was inherently unfair because the rankings were partly determined by polls of
> 5 sportswriters, broadcasters, and coaches. This method is subjective, they said, allowing human opinion to have as much or more weight than factual data, namely a team's win-loss record. Many proposed that the NCAA develop a play-off system, much like college basketball's 64-team tournament, to definitively crown a national champion. Such a change was enacted in 2014.

It is impossible to prephrase Parallel Reasoning questions.

1.   Which of the following situations is most analogous to the "system" (line 2) in the passage?

Ⓐ A woman is crowned winner of a pageant because her parents bribed the person who counted votes.

Ⓑ A president of a bank is elected by the bank's investors.

Ⓒ The importance of each sports team at a university is ranked by the revenue it generates.

Ⓓ The most valuable member of a real estate team is determined by comparing the sales generated by each member.

Ⓔ A valedictorian of a high school is chosen based in part on survey results submitted by teachers.

14

To begin, review the argument from the passage about the *system*. You must understand it before you move on to the answer choices: *The Bowl Championship Series (BCS) in college football was a ranking system that determined the top 10 teams and then matched them in head-to-head games to determine the season's champion. Critics of the system contended that it was inherently unfair because the rankings were partly determined by polls of sportswriters, broadcasters, and coaches. This method is subjective, they said, allowing human opinion to have as much or more weight than factual data, namely a team's win-loss record.* Now, consider what you know.

The system was:
- for ranking the top teams (line 2)
- partly determined by polls of people in sports (lines 4-5)
- subjective, using human opinion rather than just win-loss data (lines 5-7)

Now work through each answer choice and look for one that uses similar logic. You will find the correct answer is choice (E).

In choice (E), the situation presented is:
- for ranking the top student
- partly determined by polls of teachers
- subjective, using human opinion rather than just GPA

Choice (E) presents a situation that is similar to the BCS system in the passage.

Choice (A) is incorrect because of the bribe. While you might wonder if some of the people polled for the BCS are bribed, the passage does not state or imply this.

Choice (B) is the most attractive wrong answer. However, an election of a president is not a ranking system nor does it involve any factual data.

Answer choice (C) tricks many people because it is a ranking of sports teams. However, revenue is not mentioned in the passage. Be careful not to apply your personal knowledge of the BCS system (where revenue does play a part in non-BCS bowl games). If it's not stated or implied in the passage, it is irrelevant.

Finally, choice (D) is wrong because the situation uses factual data (sales generated) rather than personal opinion.

Parallel Reasoning questions require you to process five situations, searching for one that is similar to the scenario in the passage. You would be wise to break each down the way that we did here when searching for the correct answer.

Remember, never apply prior knowledge or experience to a GRE question!

14

Parallel Reasoning Questions Problem Set

> Read the passages below and then answer the corresponding Parallel Reasoning questions. Answers begin on page 315.

Harvest of non-targeted animals, or bycatch, is estimated to constitute about one-quarter of the global fish catch. Bycatch comprises all of the animals that are caught but not wanted or used, or are required to be discarded by management regulation. It may include specially protected species such as marine mammals or endangered species, juvenile
Line individuals too small to be marketed, or other species of fish without commercial or recreational value to the fisher.
5 The unwanted species are usually discarded, often dead, either at sea or on shore. Various types of fishing gear are non-selective and can ensnare unwanted catch. Purse seine nets can catch juvenile fish and marine mammals such as dolphins. Longlines catch seabirds, sea turtles, and non-targeted fish along with the targeted catch. Gillnets can also catch seabirds, and lost or discarded gillnets can continue to catch and kill marine animals through what is known as "ghost fishing." Trawls are a particularly non-selective type of gear and can take considerable bycatch of many different
10 species. In addition, concern is also growing about the changes trawls can make to fish habitat. They are often dragged along the bottom of the seabed and may damage habitat.

Overfishing can have broader adverse effects on the ecosystem as well. As noted above, in the 1990s total world catch reached a plateau. In some cases, this plateau in production was maintained by changes in species composition and by "fishing down the food chain." Top predatory species tend to be fished for first. Once depleted, fishing moves down the
15 food chain and can simplify the marine ecosystem. This, along with environmental changes to important habitat areas, can affect future fish production levels.

Overfishing can cause changes in marine food webs, adversely affecting other species. For example, the decline of Steller sea lions in Alaska has been attributed in part to overfishing of the Stellers' main food sources: pollock, cod, and mackerel. Overfishing also has the potential to indirectly change ecosystems such as coral reef ecosystems. When plant-
20 eating fish are removed from coral reef ecosystems, grazing is reduced, allowing the algae that coexist with corals to flourish and potentially take over, especially if the water contains high levels of nitrogen. Because they often reduce light that enters the water, these algae contribute to the loss of corals, which depend upon light.

1. Which of the following situations is most similar to the "harvest of non-targeted animals" in the first sentence?

    Ⓐ A hair stylist takes on a new client who then recommends the salon to three friends.

    Ⓑ A teacher selects an underachieving student to represent the class in the spelling bee.

    Ⓒ A deer hunter intentionally targets a small doe rather than an intended larger buck.

    Ⓓ A farmer accidentally culls part of her immature soybean crop when reaping her wheat crop.

    Ⓔ A veterinarian treats only cats and dogs, refusing to see any other animals in his clinic.

2. The result of "the loss of corals" (line 22) is most similar to a potential issue caused by which of the following types of "fishing gear" (line 5)?

    Ⓐ purse seine nets

    Ⓑ longlines

    Ⓒ gillnets

    Ⓓ discarded gillnets

    Ⓔ trawls

14

Chapter Summary

Extended Reasoning Questions require you to draw conclusions based on information in the passage. There are three types of Extended Reasoning Questions:

Purpose Questions

- You must determine the function of a word, phrase, sentence, paragraph, or passage.

- Understanding purpose verbs can help you eliminate answer choices.

- An author's primary purpose is to argue against, to argue for, or to explain an idea.

- When answering a Select-in-Passage question, do not discount a sentence because it contains extraneous ideas. The right answer is likely a complex sentence that contains more than one idea.

Inference Questions

★ General Inference Questions
- These are the most common Extended Reasoning questions.

- You must draw a conclusion based on a portion of the passage. There is only a single conclusion you can draw on GRE inferences, unlike in real life conversations.

- It may be easier to eliminate wrong inferences than to select the correct one.

★ Hypothetical Point of View Questions
- These questions ask you to predict a person's response to a specific idea.

- Prephrasing is key to answering these questions correctly.

Parallel Reasoning Questions

- These questions ask you to choose a situation that is most similar to a situation in the passage.

- It is impossible to prephrase Parallel Reasoning Questions.

14

Extended Reasoning Questions Answer Key

Purpose Questions Problem Set—Page 300

1. A   Prephrase: to show the advantages and disadvantages of web banners

    Primary Purpose Question: The first two paragraphs are about the benefits of using web banners. The last paragraph presents a potential problem with the technology, however. Only answer choice (A) addresses both ideas. Note that the correct answer is very broad. It uses *common advertising strategy* rather than *web banner*. Most primary purpose questions tend to have correct answer choices that are general, avoiding specifics from the passage.

    Answer choice (B) is incorrect because it adds information about small businesses and it does not emphasize the importance of these banners.

    Choice (C) is the most attractive wrong answer. But it is incorrect because the passage states *web banners are one of the oldest forms of online advertising* (lines 2-3). Notice that it uses the phrase *information technology* from line 1.

    Choice (D) should be suspicious immediately because of *refute*. The author is not arguing against anything. The same is true for (E), as he is not *lamenting*, either.

2. Sentence 2

    Sentences (1), (3), and (4) contain facts that can be proven. Only sentence (2) is an opinion.

3. C   Prephrase: Show why web banners are better than television commercials

    Purpose Question: The author is listing reasons why the web banner is superior to traditional mass media. The first reason is that web banners reach millions instantly (lines 7-8). The second is that it involves user input (line 11), unlike television. This shows the limitation of television commercials.

    The author does not *urge* (A) or *challenge* (B). He does not say that web banners will replace television or vice versa (D). And he does not discuss the development or evolution of either technique (E).

4. B   Prephrase: Show another reason web banners are superior

    Purpose Question: The claim made earlier in the passage is *banner ads are clearly superior to traditional mass media* (lines 2-3). This sentence is providing support for that claim.

    While the third paragraph suggests a weakness of web banners, the line in question does not suggest a weakness about a hypothesis (A). Choice (C) is an Opposite Answer. A process is described later in the second paragraph (D), but whether it is a *complicated* process is a matter of opinion, and it has nothing to do with the topic sentence. Choice (E) is the most commonly chosen wrong answer, but the word *doomed* makes it wrong.

14

5. E Prephrase: Show a drawback of advertising with web banners

Purpose Question: The final paragraph explains a problem that can occur with web banners if advertisers are not careful. Therefore, choice (E) is correct.

(A) is incorrect because no summary is provided. Choice (B) is wildly off-base; the author never criticizes a profession in the passage. Choice (C) is wrong for the same reason that (A) is incorrect. And choice (D) is wrong because the author supports the use of web banners in the first two paragraphs.

Inference Questions Problem Set—Page 306

1. A Prephrase: They are citing the Christian Bible

General Inference: The inference comes from *unaware that they are citing not the Christian Bible, but rather a poem....* This infers that people believe the quote is from the Bible. Notice that (B) leaves out *drawing and quartering*, although it is incorrect based on what it says anyway. No one in the passage believes those punishments are acceptable, which is why they are no longer in use. The parents who quote the adage clearly believe in spanking, so they do not believe (C). Choice (D) introduces positive reinforcement, which is not mentioned in the passage. And choice (E) introduces a new idea about moderate spanking.

2. E Prephrase: This is difficult to prephrase, as many inference questions are.

General Inference: The author notes that these punishments are no longer in use, but that spanking, another form of punishment in the 17th century, still is. He is suggesting that it is equally archaic and barbaric. The best answer is (E). Choice (A) is attractive, but wrong, because the author believes spanking is not acceptable. Don't let your personal beliefs or the beliefs of others influence your choice, or you fall into a True To You trap. For (B), the author pulls in the death penalty, which is not mentioned in the passage. Choice (C) is wrong because no predictions were made in the passage. Finally, (D) is wrong because it brings in a new idea.

3. A and B Prephrase: People with infectious diseases are different than people who contribute to social contagion because they don't actively seek out the disease and they don't consciously decide to spread it.

General Inference: *While the spread of information is often likened to an infectious disease, social contagion differs in that social media users actively seek out information and consciously decide to propagate it.* Choices (A) and (B) match our prephrase. Choice (C) plays on line 4 (*understanding the mechanics of social contagion is crucial*), but is not a part of the inference concerning diseases.

14

4.   A   Prephrase: This is difficult to prephrase, as many inference questions are.

Since you cannot prephrase this question, you have to check every answer choice to see if it provides a correct inference. The first answer (A) is the correct answer. The author stated that Mundus Subterraneus *is in many ways a more spectacular work* [than Micrographia] (line 3). He goes on to explain that the book is extensive in scope and content by giving examples and quoting an authority.

Choice (B) is wrong because the appropriateness of the title was never discussed (although it was in a former passage. Did you get caught?). The author mentions that Kirchner published *more than thirty [books] on almost as many subjects*, but we have no idea if *Mundus* repeated themes in these books, so (C) is out. The popularity of this book—now or in the 1600s—is not discussed, so (D) is wrong. And as for (E), the answer is True to a Point: the book did introduce original theories, but nothing is said about them ever being discredited.

5.   D   Prephrase: *it would take a whole journal to indicate everything remarkable in this work.*

Choice (D) matches our prephrase, which is taken directly from the line about the French writer. Choice (A) is Extreme: the writer says it would take a whole journal to tell you about everything that is remarkable in the book, but he doesn't say this is impossible or that it has too many subjects. Choice (B) is wrong because the passage says Kirchner had books on nearly 30 subjects; we don't know how many were similar and the French author never mentioned the other books. Choice (C) is True But Wrong; this is certainly the author's viewpoint (line 3), but not discussed by the French writer. The same is true of (E). It's partially a true statement (the word *correctly* could be debated), but not the topic of the French writer's comment.

14

1. D   Prephrase: It is impossible to prephrase this question.

Parallel Reasoning Question: Analyze the lines after line 1 to determine what you know about the harvest of non-targeted species.

Bycatch:

- constitutes about 1/4 of the global catch.

- comprises all of the animals that are caught but not wanted or used.

- may include protected species, juvenile individuals, or those without value.

- is discarded.

Now, which answer is most similar? Answer choice (D).

The soybeans:

- were accidentally culled so they are not wanted

- are immature, so they are like juvenile individuals of fish species

2. E   Prephrase: It is impossible to prephrase this question.

Parallel Reasoning Question: What is the result of the loss of corals? The loss or destruction of habitat or ecosystems.

Which type of fishing gear from the fourth paragraph causes the loss or destruction of habitat or ecosystems? The trawls *may damage habitat* (line 11). The other four answer choices only threaten birds or marine life.

Reading Comprehension Mastery: Argument Passages

Reading Comprehension Mastery:
Argument Passages

POWERSCORE
TEST PREPARATION

Introduction

Argument Passages occur with regular Reading Comprehension Passages, and to the untrained eye, they may very well appear to be simple Reading Comprehension Passages. But whereas you are searching for a *main idea* in a Reading Comprehension Passage, you are will be looking for a *conclusion* in an Argument Passage.

Each GRE has 4 or 5 Argument Passages, and since Argument Passages are followed by a single question you can expect 4 or 5 Argument Questions. Most test takers find these questions to be the most intimidating on the GRE. Note, however, that we did not say they actually are the most difficult; once you learn how to identify the elements of an Argument Passage, solving the questions becomes a much easier exercise.

Argument Passages are always followed by a single Select One Multiple Choice question.

Consider a sample Argument Passage and Question before moving on to strategies for attacking these perceived enigmas.

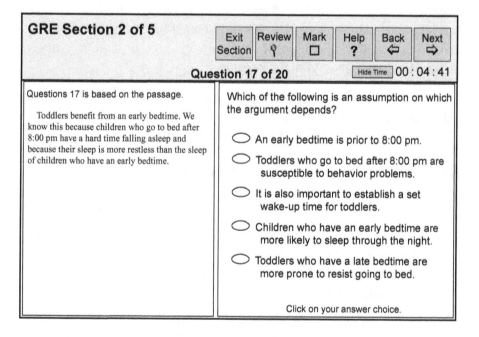

Think you know the answer? We will reveal it later in the chapter when we revisit this argument. In the meantime, let's look at how easy it is to identify these Argument Passages on the next page.

15

Recognize Argument Passages

While Argument Questions can appear with any Reading Comprehension Passage, no matter the length, they most often accompany a short passage that is specifically presented as an Argument Passage. It's important to identify these passages quickly, since your approach to the question will be slightly different than your approach to a regular Reading Comprehension Question. There are a few characteristics of both the passages and the questions to help you swiftly pinpoint an Argument Passage.

Characteristics of an Argument Passage

Argument Passages are easy to identify because of their brevity and single accompanying question.

- **Length**: An argument passage is usually extremely short—even shorter than a typical Short Passage. Most are two to four sentences in length, but some can be as short as a single sentence!

- **Topics**: Regular Reading Comprehension passages typically cover the arts, humanities, or science. Argument Passages often use these subjects, too, but they may also talk about everyday subjects, such as mortgages, blender speeds, and car colors. If the passage includes a fictional name for a company, city, state, country, or similar entity, you can be sure it's an Argument Passage.

- **Elements**: Reading Comprehension passages contain a main idea and supporting evidence, while Argument Passages include premises and conclusions, which we will discuss on the following page.

Characteristics of an Argument Question

- **Number**: Argument Passages are accompanied by a single question.

TIPS and TRICKS
The phrase "if true" in a question always gives away an Argument Passage.

- **Type**: In all of the officially-released GRE tests, argument questions are Select One Multiple Choice questions. It is highly unlikely that you will ever see a Select More Than One or a Select in Passage Question following an Argument Passage.

- **Phrasing**: An overwhelming majority of Argument Questions contain the phrase "if true," as in "Which of the following, if true, most seriously weakens the argument?"

By quickly spotting Argument Passages on the GRE, you will be able to mentally switch gears and prepare to identify premises and conclusions rather than main ideas and supporting evidence.

15

Identify the Elements of the Argument

Once you recognize that a passage is indeed an Argument Passage, you must identify the parts of the argument in order to tackle the corresponding question.

Conclusion

A conclusion is a statement or judgment that follows from one or more reasons. It stands to reason that a conclusion should come at the end of the paragraph, and it often does, but it sometimes occurs in the first sentence as well. Your first task when approaching an Argument Passage is to find the conclusion, which you can do by asking yourself, *"What is the author driving at? What does she want me to believe?"*

Conclusions might also be identified by words or phrases that often accompany them. These conclusion indicators include:

TIPS and TRICKS
It is imperative that you find the conclusion of an argument before answering the question; conclusion indicators can help you tackle this task quickly.

Conclusion Indicators		
thus	therefore	as a result
so	thereupon	resulting
so then	consequently	for this reason
subsequently	as a consequence	accordingly
hence	we can conclude that	leading to
it follows that	it stands to reason that	in consequence

Premises

A premise is a fact, proposition, or statement from which a conclusion is drawn. Premises support and explain the conclusion, literally providing the reasons why the conclusion should be accepted. To identify the premises, ask yourself *"What reasons has the author provided to persuade me? Why should I believe the conclusion? What is the evidence?"*

Premises may also be introduced with common words or phrases, including:

Premise Indicators		
because	since	for
for the reason that	in that	given that
as indicated by	due to	furthermore
owing to	this can be seen from	we know this by

15

Counter Premises

All argument passages contain conclusions and premises, but some will go so far as to include a counter premise—a premise containing an idea that counters the argument. Adding a counter premise that weakens the author's argument may seem like an odd strategy, but by addressing possible complaints, the author can minimize the damage that would be done by the objection if it were raised by a critic. The author basically recognizes potential objections to his argument and then refutes them before they can be used by an opponent.

A counter premise is an author's way of defusing any objections his critics might hurl at his argument. By addressing them up front, he can refute them and lessen their impact.

Counter premises almost always use common indicators:

Counter Premise Indicators

but	although	while
however	though	whereas
not	even though	actually
yet	still	contradictory
paradoxically	despite	at odds
nonetheless	rather than	differ
regardless of	instead of	difference
in contrast	unlike	variation
conversely	in spite of	the reverse
otherwise	except for	even so
on the contrary	contrasting with	contrary
	on the other hand	

Assumptions

An assumption is simply an unstated premise of an argument; that is, an integral component of the argument that the author takes for granted as absolutely true and leaves unsaid. On the GRE, an assumption serves as a necessary piece of the author's opinion, so you must always be on the lookout for information that you know the author believes, even if it is not explicitly stated.

Underlying the process of understanding assumptions is the principle of helping out or supporting the author's position. In order to effectively support an argument, you must always identify the conclusion of the argument and evaluate the validity of that conclusion based on its premises, so our discussion going forward will focus heavily on finding and evaluating premises and conclusions.

Argument Examples

Let's now look at an argument and identify all of its elements:

Although my GRE score is high, my GPA is low. Therefore, I will not be accepted into a top graduate program.

Premise: *My GPA is low*

Counter Premise: [*Although*] *my GRE score is high*

Conclusion: [*Therefore*] *I will not be accepted into a top graduate program*

Assumption: *A low GPA prevents acceptance into a top graduate program*

Notice the conclusion indicator *therefore* and the counter premise indicator *although*. These words can be essential in helping you identify the parts of an argument.

Most arguments contain at least one premise and a conclusion, and the conclusion can come at the beginning or end of the argument. Additional premise, counter premises, and assumptions are optional:

Toddlers benefit from an early bedtime. We know this because children who go to bed after 8:00 pm have a hard time falling asleep and because their sleep is more restless than children who have an early bedtime.

Premise 1: [*We know this because*] *children who go to bed after 8:00 pm have a hard time falling asleep*

Premise 2: [*and because*] *their sleep is more restless than children who have an early bedtime*

Conclusion: *Toddlers benefit from an early bedtime*

Assumption: *An early bedtime is before 8:00 pm*

Notice that this argument does not have any conclusion indicators. It's still relatively easy to find the conclusion because the sentence with two premises starts with the premise indicator *we know this because*. But what if no indicators were used at all?

Did you correctly choose choice (A) for the sample question at the beginning of the chapter?

15

If you struggle with identifying the elements of an argument because there are no indicator words or phrases, force one statement to be the conclusion and the rest to be the premise or premises by inserting conclusion and premise indicators. If the argument makes sense, then you have correctly identified its parts. But if your forced conclusion doesn't seem like a conclusion, then you need to reverse the arrangement and try again. Let's look at an example:

> *The best way to teach these new math concepts will not be easy to determine. Each child has a different learning style and there is very little time for experimentation in a school day replete with the current curriculum.*

Use the conclusion indicator *we can conclude that* and the premise indicator *because* and assign them to the two sentences in the argument:

> Premise: Because *the best way to teach these new math concepts will not be easy to determine*

> Conclusion: We can conclude that *each child has a different learning style and there is very little time for experimentation in a school day replete with the current curriculum*

Does this make a logical argument? Not exactly, so reverse the arrangement:

> Premise: Because *each child has a different learning style and there is very little time for experimentation in a school day replete with the current curriculum*

> Conclusion: We can conclude that *the best way to teach these new math concepts will not be easy to determine*

Now we have a viable argument! The second arrangement makes sense, whereas the first version did not offer a logical conclusion to the premise. You are most likely to struggle with identifying the elements of the argument when there are no premise or conclusion indicators and when the conclusion comes at the beginning of the paragraph. Counter any difficulties by forcing a conclusion and checking the validity of the resulting argument.

15

Diagramming an Argument

As you begin your study of Argument Passages, you may feel the need to take notes about the passage as you read, just as you do during longer Reading Comprehension Passages. The easiest way to do this is with a reverse-T diagram. To begin, draw an upside-down T, labeling the left side with a plus sign and the right side with a minus sign:

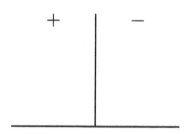

Diagramming an argument obviously takes some time, so while this tool will help you learn to identify the elements of the argument, the ultimate goal is to be able to pinpoint important concepts without a diagram.

When approaching an argument passage, the first step—and the most important undertaking—is to identify the conclusion. The majority of Argument Questions are about the conclusion, so it's important to nail it down early. Record the conclusion under the reverse-T:

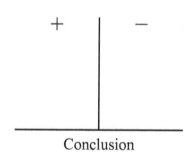

Conclusion

TIPS and TRICKS
Identify the conclusion first, since this is the most important element of the argument.

Then record the premises. Any premise that supports the conclusion should go on the left side, under the plus sign. Any counter premise that contradicts the conclusion is to be recorded on the right side, under the minus sign:

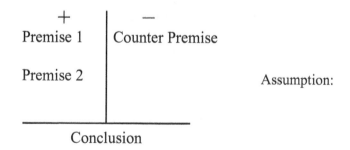

Conclusion

Assumptions, if any, can be jotted down outside the diagram. Remember to use your own shorthand to make your note-taking quick and efficient.

TIPS and TRICKS
Remember to use your own shorthand when diagramming an argument.

15

Let's look at a diagrammed argument:

During last night's robbery, the thief was unable to open the safe. Thus, last night's robbery was unsuccessful despite the fact that the thief stole several documents. After all, nothing in those documents was as valuable as the money in the safe.

Start with the conclusion:

The conclusion indicator "thus" makes the conclusion easy to spot!

$$+ \quad | \quad -$$

robbery was unsuccessful

Now add the premises and counter premise. If you pick up on an assumption central to the argument, jot it down outside of the diagram:

+	−	
1. thief unable to open safe	the thief stole documents	Assumption: A successful robbery is one in which money or something more valuable than money is taken
2. documents not as valuable as money		

robbery was unsuccessful

This is an easy way to keep the information straight and allow you to tackle questions without rereading the passage. Of course, you should use your own shorthand when diagramming. The same diagram made with shorthand might look like this:

Diagramming Argument Passages may seem silly or elementary, but after you attempt a few, you will become much more comfortable with these passages and their corresponding questions. Plus, you will learn the skills needed to organize information when you face more complicated arguments.

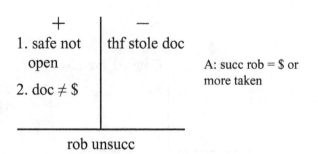

+	−	
1. safe not open	thf stole doc	A: succ rob = $ or more taken
2. doc ≠ $		

rob unsucc

Easy, right? Good! Let's spend some time diagramming Argument Passages before turning our attention to the types of questions that accompany these passages.

Identify the Elements of the Argument Problem Set

Read each argument below and diagram the conclusion, premise(s), and counter premise(s) on a reverse-T plot. If there is an assumption in the argument, jot it down next to your diagram. Answers begin on page 356.

1. Given that the price of grapes is rising, we will no longer offer chicken salad on the menu.

2. The gradual climate change threatens the monetary stability of the nation. As temperatures rise, we are losing millions of dollars in lost crops and profits are plummeting in states that depend on winter tourism.

3. The downtrend of the economy has concluded owing to prudent economic reforms by the government.

4. In Victona, the number of cases of "teacher burnout" has increased 20 percent in the last decade. However, part of the increase may be attributed to extended maternity or paternity leave: many teachers have taken 2 or 3 years off of work to attend to their young children, but fully intend to return to work after their leave. Since the statistics simply look at the number of new teachers who are no longer working in Victona after 5 years of employment, they may not reflect the actual number of teacher burnout cases.

5. While researchers acknowledge that nurses' reactions and words play a critical role in the well-being and recovery of cancer patients, the nurses' dialogue with their patients about the expression of feelings is often problematic. These nurses are frequently untrained about the best ways to use metaphors and figurative language to console patients. As a result, oncology departments must provide instruction to nurses concerning appropriate language with cancer patients as well as provide perennial supervision by a psychoanalytically-trained administrator.

15

Weaken Questions

Strengthen and Weaken Questions are the most common types of GRE questions to accompany Argument Passages.

There are five types of questions that accompany Argument Passages: Weaken Questions, Strengthen Questions, Resolve the Paradox Questions, Method of Reasoning Questions, and Assumption Questions.

Weaken Questions ask you to select an answer choice that most challenges the conclusion in a passage. These questions often use hypothetical situations with the phrase *if true*, as well as some specialized vocabulary. You can recognize a Weaken Question if it uses one of the following terms:

weakens	undermines	disproves
detracts	challenges	refutes

Consider several examples:

> Which of the following, if true, most seriously weakens the argument?
>
> Which of the following, if true, would most effectively undermine the "original idea" (line 25)?
>
> Which of the following discoveries would most strongly challenge the claim made by "researchers" in line 3?
>
> Which of the following statements directly contradicts the information presented?

Weaken questions tend to occur with Argument Passages that contain one of the following features:

Weaken Questions ask you to choose an example that disproves the argument.

1. **Incomplete Information**
   The author fails to consider all of the possibilities or relies upon evidence that is incomplete. This flaw can be attacked by bringing up new possibilities or damaging information.

2. **Improper Comparison**
   The author attempts to compare two or more items that are essentially different.

3. **Qualified Conclusion**
   The author qualifies or limits the conclusion in such a way as to leave the argument open to attack. This same flaw often appears in incorrect answer choices.

While these three scenarios are not the only ways an argument can be weak, they encompass a large proportion of the errors that appear in GRE stimuli.

15

Let's now take a look at a Weaken Question:

> The owner of the bird seed store in Izzone has spent years educating residents about the danger of outdoor cats to local sparrow populations. When cats are kept inside, sparrows are safe from their most threatening predator. In particular, nesting
> *Line* females that rely on backyard feeders for sustenance are not preyed upon so their
> 5 nestlings survive to fledging. As a result, sparrow population numbers must be increasing, and the sales of bird seed for sparrows is bound to increase as well.

1. Which of the following, if true, most seriously weakens the argument?

    Ⓐ It takes only 25 days from the time an egg is laid to produce an independent juvenile sparrow.

    Ⓑ Outdoor cats help control the population of king snakes which feed mainly on sparrow eggs.

    Ⓒ Great horned owls are known to prey on sparrows.

    Ⓓ Some nesting female sparrows avoid backyard feeders and prefer to forage for the seeds of grains and weeds.

    Ⓔ Local chickadee populations have not been affected by cats being left outside.

Weaken Questions are almost always about the conclusion, so start there when assessing the argument:

CAUTION: GRE TRAP!
Focus on the conclusion when answering Strengthen and Weaken Questions. The wrong answers will use the premises and counter premises to attempt to trick you.

$$+ \qquad -$$

Sparrow population numbers must be increasing, and the sales of bird seed for sparrows is bound to increase as well

Then consider the premises and counter premises (if any):

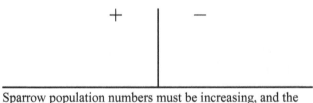

$+ \qquad -$

1. The owner of the bird seed store has spent years educating residents about the danger of outdoor cats to local sparrow populations
2. When cats are kept inside, sparrows are safe from their most threatening predator
3. Nesting females that rely on backyard feeders for sustenance are not preyed upon so their nestlings survive to fledging

Sparrow population numbers must be increasing, and the sales of bird seed for sparrows is bound to increase as well

15

Our task is to determine the answer choice that contradicts the conclusion: *that sparrow populations and sparrow bird seed sales are increasing*. The rest of the text provides premises for the conclusion, but it will be used against you when selecting an answer. Focus only on the conclusion and ask yourself if each statement provides new evidence to threaten it.

Choice (A) contends that sparrows become independent quickly. Does this detract from the fact that sparrow populations are increasing? No. And it has nothing to do with the cats—the cats have been killing mother birds despite the fact that the sparrows grow quickly.

Choice (B) is the correct answer. The argument says that the bird population is going to increase because its biggest predator—the cat—is no longer a factor. But according to (B), if the cats are reigned in, the king snake population will grow and thus more sparrow eggs will be eaten. All the eggs that are eaten by snakes will affect the population. It may still rise, but it may drastically decline, too. This statement weakens the conclusion.

In choice (C), we are given another predator that affects the sparrow population. But these owls were eating sparrows whether the cats were let out or not; the number of sparrows affected by owls is not going to decrease when the cats are kept inside.

Similarly, in choice (D), some sparrows are not eating at backyard feeders, but these same sparrows will forage whether the cats are in or out.

Choice (E) is probably the most common wrong answer because we want to rationalize that if cats aren't affecting the population of one type of bird then they won't affect a similar type of bird. But this rationalization is dangerous because it relies on outside knowledge, not on what is stated in the passage. Maybe cats do not like the taste of chickadees or maybe chickadees have developed a wicked defense against cat attacks. Either way, their population numbers have nothing to do with the sparrow population numbers.

When searching for the answer to a Weaken Question, think of a debate scenario. Your opponent has just delivered a speech that includes all of the text in the passage. It is your turn to speak, and you need to prove him wrong. Which answer choice can you fire at him to show that his argument is weak? Or conversely, if you were defending the author's argument, which answer choice would you most fear because it proves your argument wrong?

15

There are three types of answer choices to avoid when faced with a Weaken Question:

1. **Opposite Answers**

   As previously discussed in the Reading Comprehension section, these answers do the exact opposite of what is needed. In this case, they strengthen the argument as opposed to weakening it. Although you might think answers of this type are easy to avoid, they can be very tricky. To analogize, have you ever gotten on a freeway thinking you were going south when in fact you later discovered you were going north? It is easy to make a mistake when you head in the exact opposite direction. In the same way, Opposite answers lure the test taker by presenting information that relates perfectly to the argument, but just in the wrong manner.

2. **True to a Point Answers**

   True to a Point Answers are like the old fashion Shell Games of street magicians. With a little sleight of hand, the test makers can trick you into selecting the wrong choice. Remember, a True to a Point Answer occurs when an idea or concept is raised in the stimulus and then a very similar idea appears in the answer choice, but the idea is changed just enough to be incorrect but still attractive. In Weaken questions, the Shell Game is usually used to attack a conclusion that is similar to, but slightly different from, the one presented in the stimulus.

CAUTION: GRE TRAP!
Some of the answer traps that exist in Reading Comprehension also exist in Argument Passages!

3. **Out of Scope Answers**

   These answers simply miss the point of the argument and raise issues that are either not related to the argument or tangential to the argument.

While these three answer types are not the only ways an answer choice can be attractively incorrect, they appear frequently enough that you should be familiar with each form.

Some students find that Weaken Questions are among the most difficult on the GRE because they require our brains to work "backwards."

15

Cause and Effect Weaken Questions

Humans naturally seek to explain why things happened. "Everything happens for a reason," we quip when searching for the purpose of events that may seem senseless. This search often takes the form of cause and effect reasoning, which asserts or denies that one thing causes another, or that one thing is caused by another. On the GRE, cause and effect reasoning appears in a number of Argument Passages, often in the conclusion where the author mistakenly claims that one event causes another. Consider an example:

> Last year, a governmental health agency instituted a nationwide anti-tobacco campaign and the number of deaths resulting from lung cancer decreased by twenty percent. Thus, the health agency's campaign must have caused the drop.

Most causal conclusions like the one above are flawed because there can be alternate explanations for the stated relationship: some other cause could account for the effect (such as a new medication that increases lung cancer survival rates); some third event could have caused both the stated cause and effect (such as a lung cancer epidemic two years ago which scared many smokers into quitting and prompted the government to create an anti-tobacco campaign); the situation may in fact be reversed (as would be the case if the government created the anti-tobacco campaign as a result of being encouraged by the decrease in lung cancer deaths); the events may be related but not causally (as would be the case if the events happened simultaneously); or the entire occurrence could be the result of chance.

In short, causality occurs when one event is said to make another occur. The cause is the event that makes the other occur; the effect is the event that follows from the cause. By definition, the cause must occur before the effect, and the cause is the "activator" or "igniter" in the relationship. The effect always happens at some point in time after the cause. Because a cause and effect relationship has a signature characteristic—the cause makes the effect happen—there is an identifiable type of expression used to indicate that a causal relationship is present. The following list contains a number of the phrases used by the makers of the GRE to introduce cause and effect relationships, and you should be on the lookout for these when reading an Argument Passage:

Cause and Effect Indicators		
caused by	because of	responsible for
reason for	leads to	induced by
is an effect of	determined by	produced by

Whenever you identify a causal relationship in the conclusion of a GRE problem, immediately prepare to either weaken or strengthen the argument. Attacking a cause and effect relationship in Weaken questions almost always consists of choosing an answer that performs one of the following tasks:

1. **Provides another possible reason for the effect**. For example, if the argument states that obesity causes high blood pressure, look for an answer choice that provides another cause—such as heredity, gender, or age—of high blood pressure. Because the author believes there is only one cause, identifying another cause weakens the conclusion.

2. **Refutes the cause and effect relationship, usually by showing that when one occurs, the other does not**. For example, if the argument states that obesity causes high blood pressure, look for an answer that shows obesity occurs in a patient but high blood pressure does not. This type of answer often appears in the form of a counterexample. Because the author believes that the cause always produces the effect, any scenario where the cause occurs and the effect does not—or any scenario where the effect occurs and the cause does not—weakens the conclusion.

3. **Suggests the possibility of a reverse cause and effect situation**. For example, if the argument states that obesity causes high blood pressure, look for an answer choice in which high blood pressure caused obesity. Because the author believes that the cause and effect relationship is correctly stated, showing that the relationship is backwards (the claimed effect is actually the cause of the claimed cause) undermines the conclusion.

4. **Undermines or disproves the data used in the premises**. For example, if the premise states that 90% of the obese patients in the study had high blood pressure, an answer choice might inform you that all of those patients were genetically predisposed to high blood pressure because they all had a parent with the condition. If the data used to make a causal statement is in error, then the validity of the causal claim is in question.

TIPS and TRICKS
The correct answer to a causal Weaken Question will usually accomplish one of these tasks!

15

Strengthen Questions

Strengthen Questions ask you to select an answer choice that best supports the conclusion in a passage; they also use *if true* and their own terms to indicate the question type:

supports   strengthens   substantiates

Examples of these questions include the following:

> Which of the following, if true, most strengthens the argument?
>
> Which of the following, if true, would best support the "original idea" (line 25)?
>
> Which of the following discoveries would most strongly support the claim made by "researchers" in line 3?
>
> Which of the following statements directly supports the information presented?

As you can see, Strengthen questions are very similar to Weaken questions except for the word designating whether you are to strengthen or weaken an argument.

Let's examine these questions more closely:

> Cleeves, a country in Matine, requires its residents to undergo a yearly magnetic resonance imaging test (MRI) in order to promote early disease detection. In the other countries of Matine, residents receive MRIs only when symptoms of disease are already present. Obviously, Cleeves' more vigilant program is the explanation
> *Line 5* for the fact that the life expectancy of the citizens of Cleeves is far higher than that of the residents of the other countries, even though the single oldest person living in Matine is not from Cleeves.

1. Which of the following, if true, most strengthens the argument?

 (A) The MRIs can detect only 50% of all life-threatening diseases.

 (B) Different countries have different criteria for determining what constitutes a symptom worthy of an MRI test.

 (C) All residents of Cleeves are required to exercise with a certified personal trainer for a minimum of two hours each week.

 (D) There are more residents with life-threatening diseases living in Cleeves than in any of the other countries of comparable or greater population.

 (E) About 25% of the life-threatening diseases detected by MRI cannot be cured and ultimately result in loss of life.

Like Weaken Questions, Strengthen Questions are almost always about the conclusion, so identify it quickly. If needed, you can construct a diagram:

+	−

Obviously, Cleeves' more vigilant program is the explanation for the fact that the life expectancy of the citizens of Cleeves is far higher than that of the residents of the other countries

Then add the premises and counter premises:

+	−
1. Cleeves requires its residents to undergo a yearly MRI in order to promote early disease detection. 2. In the other countries, residents receive MRIs only when symptoms of disease are already present	The single oldest person living in Matine is not from Cleeves

Obviously, Cleeves' more vigilant program is the explanation for the fact that the life expectancy of the citizens of Cleeves is far higher than that of the residents of the other countries

The question requires us to select the statement that best strengthens the conclusion, which is *Obviously, Cleeves' more vigilant program is the explanation for the fact that the life expectancy of the citizens of Cleeves is far higher than that of the residents of the other countries.*

Remember, the rest of the text provides premises for the conclusion, but it will be used against you when selecting an answer. Focus only on the conclusion and ask yourself if each statement provides new evidence to support it.

Choice (A) states "*The MRIs can detect only 50% of all life-threatening diseases.*" Does this support the idea that Cleeves' more vigilant program—with annual MRIs—is responsible for higher life expectancy? No. If anything, it weakens the argument, because the MRIs are not doing a very good job at finding disease.

Choice (B) is about the other countries and their policies in determining who gets an MRI. This does not strengthen Cleeves' case at all.

In Choice (C), we are given another reason that Cleeves' residents might be healthy. This answer choice does not indicate what the other countries

15

do, so no comparison can be made as to the vigilance of the program. Plus, this answer weakens our conclusion because the annual MRIs are not fully responsible for the good health of the residents of Cleeves.

Choice (D) is the correct answer. It strengthens the conclusion—that Cleeves' vigilant program is responsible for higher life expectancy—because not only do the people of Cleeves live longer than the people in the other countries, but there are *more* people in Cleeves who are seriously ill than those in other countries. The assumption is that these annual MRIs help identify the illnesses early so that doctors can take life-saving measures.

Choice (E) is wrong because it contradicts the idea that annual MRIs raise life expectancy.

Sometimes the best way to choose an answer is to imagine writing an outline for a research paper for school. If your main idea is the conclusion—in this case, *Cleeves' more vigilant program is the explanation for the fact that the life expectancy of the citizens of Cleeves is far higher than that of the residents of the other countries*—which answer choice would you select as evidence to prove your main idea?

Correct answers for Strengthen Questions have great range; to put it in numerical terms, any answer choice that strengthens the argument, whether by 1% or 100% is correct.

Cause and Effect Strengthen Questions

Because Strengthen and Weaken questions require you to perform opposite tasks, to strengthen a causal conclusion you take the exact opposite approach that you would in a Weaken question.

In Strengthen questions, supporting a cause and effect relationship almost always consists of choosing an answer choice that performs one of the following tasks:

1. **Eliminates any alternate causes for the stated effect**. For example, if the argument states that obesity causes high blood pressure, look for an answer choice that eliminates other causes—such as heredity, gender, and age—of high blood pressure. Because the author believes there is only one cause (the stated cause in the argument), eliminating one or more of the other possible causes strengthens the conclusion.

2. **Proves the cause and effect relationship, usually by showing that when one occurs, the other occurs or by showing that when one does not occur, the other does not occur**. For example, if the argument states that obesity causes high blood pressure, look for an answer that shows obesity always results in high blood pressure or one that shows healthy weight always results in people with normal blood pressure. Because the author believes that the cause always produces the effect, any scenario where the cause occurs and the effect follows—or any scenario where the cause does not occur and the effect does not follow—lends credibility to the conclusion. This type of answer can appear in the form of an example.

3. **Eliminates the possibility of a reverse cause and effect situation**. Because the author believes that the cause and effect relationship is correctly stated, eliminating the possibility that the relationship is backwards (the claimed effect is actually the cause of the claimed cause) strengthens the conclusion. For example, if the argument states that obesity causes high blood pressure, an answer choice could strengthen that by showing that high blood pressure did not cause obesity.

4. **Strengthens or proves the data used in the premises**. For example, if the premise states that 90% of the obese patients in the study had high blood pressure, an answer choice might inform you that all of those patients were not genetically predisposed to high blood pressure and had normal blood pressure before becoming obese. If the data used to make a causal statement are in error, then the validity of the causal claim is in question. Any information that eliminates error or reduces the possibility of error will support the argument.

It is important to note that Strengthen and Weaken Questions may also appear with a regular Reading Comprehension passage. When this happens, the question will point you toward a particular argument in the longer passage and then ask you to support or undermine that argument. Use the same techniques you have learned here to answer Strengthen and Weaken Questions that occur with longer Reading Comprehension texts.

15

Weaken Questions and Strengthen Questions Problem Set

> Read each argument below and use scratch paper to diagram the conclusion, premise(s), and counter premise(s) on a reverse-T plot if needed. Then answer the corresponding question. Answers begin on page 358.

There is an increased interest among hobbyists in creating three dimensional (3-D) content given the recent surge of 3-D movies, television, and other media. Despite this amateur interest, the generation of such 3-D content is still dominated by trained professionals due to the high costs associated with 3-D motion capture instruments. Therefore, the inception of an inexpensive motion capture system will not only advance the production of content by novice users, but also stimulate the development of the 3-D industry.

1. Which of the following, if true, most seriously weakens the argument?

    Ⓐ The inexpensive motion capture system requires its users to have an advanced knowledge of graphics and design.

    Ⓑ The idea for the most successful 3-D blockbuster film was conceived by an amateur to motion capture instruments.

    Ⓒ Most 3-D designers have completed post graduate degrees.

    Ⓓ The 3-D market has very few job openings each year for new content generators.

    Ⓔ The animation industry was unaffected when developers released inexpensive computer software to help novice users learn to animate videos.

Research has proven that the majority of the chemicals in sunscreen are endocrine disrupters which interfere with the normal function of hormones. Laboratory tests on animals have shown chemicals such as oxybenzone, 4-MBC, and octinoxate are absorbed through the skin and converted to synthetic hormones, resulting in abnormally high or low levels of natural hormones, which can cause reproductive disorders and developmental interference. For this reason, endocrinologists recommend using mineral-based *sunblocks*—those containing zinc oxide and titanium dioxide—which do not penetrate the skin.

2. Which of the following, if true, most strengthens the argument?

    Ⓐ One study suggested that minerals such as zinc oxide are an endocrine disrupter when ingested.

    Ⓑ Mineral based sunblocks must be reapplied every two hours in order to remain effective against UVA rays.

    Ⓒ When used in eye shadow, oxybenzone has been shown to increase estrogen levels in women.

    Ⓓ One study found that men who applied sunscreen for a week experienced a significant drop in testosterone levels.

    Ⓔ Most dermatologists recommend the use of sunscreen to their patients.

Children under five years of age who spend significant time screen-viewing (SV)—that is, watching TV, playing video games, and using computers and handheld devices—are at an increased risk for obesity, psychological difficulties, and metabolic disorders in later childhood. Studies have found that toddlers and preschoolers model the amount of time they spend SV by observing the length of their parents' SV time; when parents spend more than two hours SV each day, children were 3.4 times more likely to also spend more than 2 hours SV per day. Parents must decrease their own SV time in order to decrease the amount of time spent SV by their children.

3. Which of the following, if true, most effectively undermines the argument?

    Ⓐ Children older than five years of age are not nearly as affected by their parents' SV habits.

    Ⓑ Parents and children both spend less time watching TV during the week than on the weekend.

    Ⓒ The sources of SV for children under five years of age are largely composed of educational material

    Ⓓ Only 5% of children under five years of age spend more than 2 hour SV each day.

    Ⓔ Children are unaware of the amount of time their parents spend SV after the children go to bed.

15

Resolve the Paradox Questions

Resolve the Paradox questions also use hypothetical situations with the phrase *if true*, as well as specific vocabulary. Each question will ask you to take an action to fix a problem, using the following vocabulary:

Resolve the Paradox Questions require you to explain a set of seemingly contradictory facts.

Action	Problem
	paradox
resolves	discrepancy
reconciles	contradiction
explains	conflict
	puzzle

Here are some examples of how those words might be used in Resolve the Paradox Questions:

> Which of the following, if true, would help resolve the apparent paradox?

> Which of the following, if true, best reconciles the apparent discrepancy?

> Which of the following, if true, best explains the increase in the rate of the chemical reaction?

A paradox is a statement that seems to contradict itself, such as "Don't go near the water until you take swim lessons." At first, this seems illogical—in order to learn to swim, you have to practice *in the water*. But the author might offer up a statement to help the paradox make sense, such as "The first four swim lessons occur in a classroom, not in the water."

On the GRE, the paradoxes are a bit more subtle and often involve critical reasoning. Let's look at an example.

> With progressive cell phone technology, driving is becoming more dangerous. Text messaging, cellular internet use, and phone calls are distractions that have been proven to impair a driver's ability to operate a motor vehicle. Yet the number of fatalities resulting from distracted driving due to cell phone use has decreased by 10% in the last three years.

Resolve the Paradox Questions usually accompany passages that do not contain a conclusion. Did you notice that this argument only offers three premises but no conclusion? Let's diagram it on the next page.

TIPS and TRICKS
Passages that are followed by a Resolve the Paradox Question usually do not contain a conclusion.

15

With progressive cell phone technology, driving is becoming more dangerous. Text messaging, cellular internet use, and phone calls are distractions that have been proven to impair a driver's ability to operate a motor vehicle. Yet the number of fatalities resulting from distracted driving due to cell phone use has decreased by 10% in the last three years.

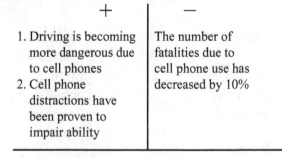

+	−
1. Driving is becoming more dangerous due to cell phones 2. Cell phone distractions have been proven to impair ability	The number of fatalities due to cell phone use has decreased by 10%

Do you see the paradox? Cell phones are making driving more dangerous, but the number of deaths due to cell phone use while driving are decreasing. Logically, if cell phones are making driving more dangerous, you would expect the number of fatalities due to cell phone use to be *increasing*, not decreasing.

Your task on the GRE is to select a statement that helps the paradox make sense.

1. Which of the following, if true, best reconciles the apparent contradiction?

    (A) There was a 9% increase in the number of people injured due to distracted driving during the last three years.

    (B) The overall fatality rate due to vehicular accidents has decreased by 10% in the last three years.

    (C) A teenager's reaction time is seven times faster than that of an adult over age 40.

    (D) The number of drivers using cell phones has increased by only 5% in the last three years.

    (E) Vehicles produced within the last three years have new safety features that protect occupants better than those in older automobiles.

CAUTION: GRE TRAP! Stay away from answers that only explain one of the premises. The correct answer must resolve both sides of the paradox.

Let's analyze each answer choice now. Answer choice (A) supports the first premise, that cell phones, a form of distracted driving, are making driving more dangerous because there is an increase in the number of injuries. But this only addresses one of the premises and does not confront the contradictory premise. Answers that only explain one side of the argument are common wrong answer traps in Resolve the Paradox Questions.

15

Choice (B) uses a piece of data from the passage—10%—to try and trick you into selecting it as the correct answer. This Copycat answer provides another paradox for the first two premises. If driving is becoming more dangerous due to cell phones, it stands to reason that the overall fatality rate—no matter the reason for those fatalities—should be increasing, not decreasing.

In answer choice (C), we are given a fact about two different types of drivers. If the statement is true, you would expect there to be fewer accidents with teenage drivers than with adult drivers, but this does nothing to explain the decreasing rates of fatal accidents among ALL drivers.

Choice (D) might be an attractive wrong answer choice, but if you were tricked by this one, you were employing faulty reasoning. According to this answer, there is a slight increase in the number of drivers using a cell phone while driving. So it stands to reason that there will also be a slight increase in the number of fatalities due to cell phone use while driving, *not* a 10% decrease.

The last answer, choice (E), is the correct answer. Given that cell phone use makes driving more dangerous, we should expect more fatalities. But this answer explains why that is not the case—new safety features make the cars safer, so even if there is an increase in accidents, these safety features are better at preventing fatalities.

The correct answer to any Resolve the Paradox question has some common characteristics:

1. **The correct answer contains active resolution.**
   The correct answer will actively resolve the paradox—it will allow both sides to be factually correct and it will either explain how the situation came into being or add a piece of information that shows how the two ideas or occurrences can coexist.

2. **The correct answer shows how the situation arose.**
   Because you are not seeking to disprove one side of the situation, you must select the answer choice that contains a possible cause of the situation. So when examining answers, ask yourself if the answer choice could lead to the situation in the passage. If so, the answer is correct.

3. **The correct answer addresses the facts.**
   When attempting to resolve the problem in the stimulus, you must address the facts of the situation. Many answers will try to lure you with reasonable solutions that do not quite meet the stated facts. These answers are incorrect.

15

Similarly, the wrong answers can sometimes be eliminated based on common characteristics:

1. **A wrong answer may explain only one side of the paradox.**
   If an answer supports or proves only one side of the paradox, that answer will be incorrect. The correct answer must show how both sides coexist.

2. **A wrong answer may misstate the facts.**
   Any answer choice that does not conform to the facts as stated in the passage is incorrect.

3. **A wrong answer may point out similarities and differences.**
   If the passage contains a paradox where two items are different, then an answer choice that explains why the two are similar cannot be correct.

   Conversely, if the passage contains a paradox where two items are similar, then an answer choice that explains a difference between the two cannot be correct.

   In short, a similarity cannot explain a difference, and a difference cannot explain a similarity.

Remember, your objective when faced with a Resolve the Paradox is to first find that paradox. Diagramming the argument may make this apparent for those new to Argument Passages, but your ultimate goal is to identify the argument elements without extra notation. Once the paradox is determined, search for the answer that helps the paradox make sense, being sure to avoid any answer choice that explains only one side of the paradox or uses data and facts from the argument to mislead you.

15

Resolve the Paradox Problem Set

> Read each argument below and use scratch paper to diagram the conclusion (if applicable), premise(s), and counter premise(s) on a reverse-T plot. Then answer the corresponding question. Answers begin on page 360.

In the country of Bengalia, men who live in the province of Anders have lower reported rates of major depression than men who live in the province of Collings. The men of Anders, however, are at a much higher risk of exposure to social stressors, which are known to be risk factors for depression.

1. Which of the following, if true, best reconciles the apparent discrepancy?

    Ⓐ The men of Collings are required to follow a strict exercise regimen.

    Ⓑ The men in Anders are more likely to face unemployment, poverty, and divorce than men in Collings.

    Ⓒ The doctors in Anders require three visible symptoms in order to diagnose major depression while the doctors of Collings only require two such symptoms for the same diagnosis.

    Ⓓ The health organizations in both Anders and Collings have identical definitions of major depression.

    Ⓔ The women of Collings are more likely to be diagnosed with major depression than are the women of Anders.

Officials at Fitzpatrick Pharmaceuticals announced last year that they expected a 75% decrease in the cost of producing the drug Judizen when an inexpensive substitute for one of its main ingredients was discovered. This original ingredient, found in nature, was scarce and thus caused a high production cost for Judizen. Yet despite this new discovery, the average price paid by consumers for Judizen has increased by 5%.

2. Which of the following, if true, would help resolve the apparent paradox?

    Ⓐ The price of drugs in other developed countries is significantly lower because the governments of those countries set price limits.

    Ⓑ The substitute ingredient is abundantly found in nature.

    Ⓒ Shortly after the announcement, a new health care law passed which created high taxes for drug companies.

    Ⓓ In the last ten years, the price of Judizen has increased 5% to 10% per year.

    Ⓔ There has been a 41 percent increase in the price of the top 200 brand-name drugs in the last five years.

Refined carbohydrates are the primary cause of obesity; these carbohydrates are broken down by the body very quickly, which causes insulin levels to rise and in turn increases fat storage in fat cells. Despite this fact, the people of China consume a diet rich in refined carbohydrates (specifically white rice and noodles) and vegetables while maintaining one of the lowest obesity rates in the world.

3. Which of the following, if true, best explains the low rate of obesity in China despite carbohydrate consumption?

    Ⓐ White rice and noodles break down in the body at a rate similar to that of whole grains.

    Ⓑ The overall obesity rate in China is 5% but soars to 20% in some major cities.

    Ⓒ Eaten in combination, the fiber in vegetables slows the breakdown of refined carbohydrates.

    Ⓓ Brown rice has a lower metabolic breakdown rate than that of white rice.

    Ⓔ Fat cells use fewer calories to store fat than to convert glucose to fat.

15

Method of Reasoning Questions

The last two types of questions—Method of Reasoning and Assumption Questions—do not appear as frequently as the other three types of questions on the GRE. For this reason, we will present a combined problem set at the end of the two sections.

Method of Reasoning Questions ask you to identify the role played by a particular portion or portions of the argument. These questions may resemble one of the following examples:

> In the argument, the highlighted sentence serves which of the following roles?

> In the argument, the highlighted portions play which of the following roles?

The answer choices will then describe possible roles of the statements, often using the terms we discussed in the previous section such as *premise* and *conclusion*.

Instead of identifying the facts and details of the argument as in the previous questions we studied, you must identify the underlying logical organization of the argument. Answer choices can be proven or disproved by directly referring to the content of the passage. For example, if an answer choice claims there is a contradiction in the passage, search the passage to see if a contradiction is present. If not, the answer choice is incorrect.

If you can locate a contradiction, make certain the contradiction is correctly described by the answer choice. Incorrect answer choices in Method of Reasoning questions often begin by describing something that occurred in the passage but end by describing something that did not occur in the passage. Justify your answer choice by looking at what was actually said by the author.

The arguments that accompany these questions, though, are usually more complex than the average Argument Passage, so it may be helpful to diagram the argument at first, paying particular attention to words indicating premises, counter premises, and conclusions, with the goal of mentally isolating these elements in the future. You may find that these arguments contain more than one conclusion in an attempt to confuse you. If you diagram carefully, however, you will avoid any traps and likely be able to answer the question without any extra effort.

Method of Reasoning Questions are similar to Purpose Questions in regular Reading Comprehension; in both, you must identify the role played by a specific portion of the text.

Passages that accompany Method of Reasoning Questions are often complicated, so you must rely on conclusion indicators to locate all possible conclusions in the passage.

15

Let's first look at such an argument and diagram its elements:

> Collisions of warm air and cold air create instability, leading to strong, long-lived thunderstorms. The most common location for these collisions in the United States is the central plains. During these thunderstorms, the cold air drops as the warm air rises, and the warm air often twists into a spiral, creating a tornado. It stands to reason then that tornados are prevalent in the central plains. The front will continue east. As it does, it encounters more warm air, stabilizing the front and causing the thunderstorms to lose strength. Therefore, tornadoes are not as common along the East coast as they are in the central plains.

Line 5

Can you spot the TWO conclusions? The first is what the GRE calls an intermediate conclusion, in the middle of the passage. It follows the conclusion indicator *it stands to reason then that*: **tornadoes are prevalent in the central plains**. The second conclusion is the main conclusion, occurring at the end of the passage and following *therefore*: **tornadoes are not as common along the East coast as they are in the central plains.**

Armed with two conclusions, you will need two reverse-T diagrams:

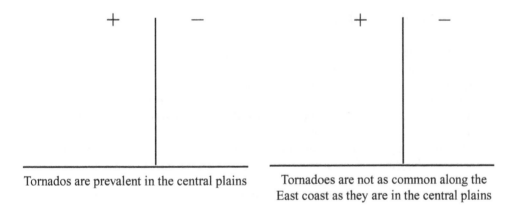

Tornados are prevalent in the central plains

Tornadoes are not as common along the East coast as they are in the central plains

Now add the premises that led to the intermediate conclusion:

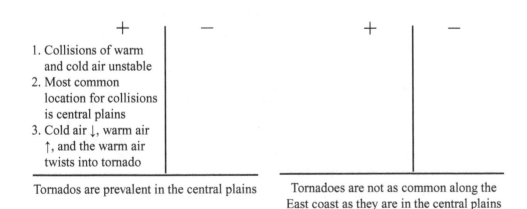

1. Collisions of warm and cold air unstable
2. Most common location for collisions is central plains
3. Cold air ↓, warm air ↑, and the warm air twists into tornado

Tornados are prevalent in the central plains

Tornadoes are not as common along the East coast as they are in the central plains

Remember to use your own personal shorthand if you choose to diagram an argument. We have used more robust labeling methods here and in subsequent diagrams for your understanding and for the ease of discussion.

15

And finally, include the premises that preceded the final conclusion:

+	−	+	−
1. Collisions of warm and cold air unstable 2. Most common location for collisions is central plains 3. Cold air ↓, warm air ↑, and the warm air twists into tornado		1. Front goes east 2. It encounters more warm air, stabilizing the front and causing the thunderstorms to lose strength	

Tornados are prevalent in the central plains | | Tornadoes are not as common along the East coast as they are in the central plains

Not included in the diagram are the assumptions that the author must make in order to draw these conclusions, such as *the air in the east is warmer*. You may or may not automatically pick up on assumptions while reading a passage. In this type of Method of Reasoning Question, however, they will not be addressed because they are not stated and thus not able to be highlighted.

Now consider the question and answer choices:

Collisions of warm air and cold air create instability, leading to strong, long-lived thunderstorms. The most common location for these collisions in the United States is the central plains. During these thunderstorms, the cold air drops as the
Line
5 warm air rises, and the warm air often twists into a spiral, creating a tornado. It stands to reason then that **tornados are prevalent in the central plains**. The front will continue east. **As it does, it encounters more warm air, stabilizing the front and causing the thunderstorms to lose strength**. Therefore, tornadoes are not as common along the East coast as they are in the central plains.

1.   In the argument given, the two portions in boldface play which of the following roles?

   Ⓐ The first provides evidence that supports an objection to the conclusion; the second serves as an intermediate conclusion that supports another conclusion later in the argument.

   Ⓑ The first states an intermediate conclusion that supports another conclusion later in the argument; the second provides support for that later conclusion.

   Ⓒ The first serves as evidence that undermines a premise in the argument; the second provides a position that the argument as a whole contradicts.

   Ⓓ The first provides support of an intermediate conclusion that supports another conclusion later in the argument; the second is that intermediate conclusion.

   Ⓔ The first asserts the conclusion of the argument as a whole; the second offers support for that conclusion.

Consider the diagram again, where the two portions in boldface in the text are highlighted:

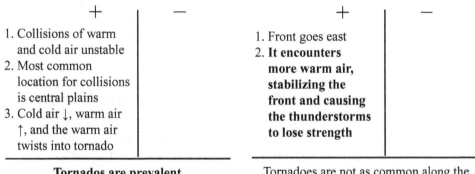

+	−		+	−
1. Collisions of warm and cold air unstable 2. Most common location for collisions is central plains 3. Cold air ↓, warm air ↑, and the warm air twists into tornado			1. Front goes east 2. **It encounters more warm air, stabilizing the front and causing the thunderstorms to lose strength**	

Tornados are prevalent in the central plains | Tornadoes are not as common along the East coast as they are in the central plains

We can prephrase the answer before looking at the choices: *the first bold portion is the first conclusion; the second bold portion is a premise that supports the second conclusion.* Can you find an answer that matches our prephrase?

We can eliminate choice (A) because there are no objections or counter premises in the argument.

Choice (B) is the correct answer. Compare it to our prephrase:

Prephrase:
1. The first is the first conclusion;

2. The second is a premise that supports the second conclusion

Answer:
1. The first states an intermediate conclusion that supports another conclusion later in the argument;

2. The second provides support for that later conclusion.

Choice (C) is wrong for the same reason that (A) is wrong; there are no counter premises.

Answer choice (D) might trip up test takers who do not keep close track of the conclusion indicators. But the first bold portion *is* the intermediate conclusion, not support for it.

Choice (E) may trick those who do not realize there are two conclusions.

Remember, watching for conclusion indicators is an extremely important strategy when attacking Method of Reasoning questions. If you miss a conclusion indicator, you might miss a second conclusion, and the answer choices are poised to take advantage of such mistakes.

CAUTION: GRE TRAP!
Many Method of Reasoning passages have two conclusions!

15

Assumption Questions

Assumption questions on the GRE are extremely rare, but because they are often the most difficult type for students, and because assumptions in general can play a critical role in argumentation, it is important that you fully understand how to attack them.

Let's review how assumptions function in an argument. An assumption is simply an unstated premise of an argument; that is, an integral component of the argument that the author takes for granted as absolutely true and leaves unsaid. In our daily lives we make assumptions all the time, but generally we leave them unaddressed because they make logical sense: they follow from the context of what is being discussed and our experience with the way the world works.

When you encounter assumptions in GRE questions they can be challenging to identify because, unlike the commonsense assumptions we make in life, you must identify them explicitly, as concrete statements directly related to the argument at hand. So you are faced with the difficult task of figuring out the author's mindset and determining exactly what unstated belief(s) he or she held when formulating the argument.

To help, think of an assumption as the foundation of the argument, a statement that the premises and conclusion rest upon. If a statement is something that the author might only think could be true, or if the statement contains additional information that the author is not committed to, then that statement is not an assumption. So in a way, assumptions may appear to be somewhat minimalist, as they are restricted only to what the author can be known to believe, and nothing more.

We have addressed a number of arguments in this chapter that contain assumptions, so let's revisit one of those examples and take a closer look at the role of its central assumption:

> *My GPA is low. Therefore, I will not be accepted into a top graduate program.*
>
> Premise: *My GPA is low*
>
> Conclusion: *Therefore, I will not be accepted into a top graduate program*
>
> Assumption: *A low GPA prevents acceptance into a top graduate program*

Remember, assumptions are not stated, but the argument depends upon them. The author relies on these beliefs in order to build his argument.

Consider some examples of the phrasing involved in Assumption Questions:

Which of the following is an assumption on which the argument depends?

Which of the following is an assumption made in drawing the conclusion?

The argument in the passage depends on which of the following assumptions?

The argument in the passage assumes that...

The conclusion of the argument cannot be true unless which of the following is true?

On the GRE, assumptions can play one of two roles—the Supporter or the Defender. The Supporter role is the traditional linking role, as in the example above, where an assumption connects the pieces of the argument. Because Supporters often connect "new" or "rogue" pieces of information in the argument, Supporter assumptions are often relatively easy to identify because they simply close an argument's gaps. Should you ever see a missing connection or a new element in the conclusion, a Supporter assumption answer will almost certainly close the gap or link the new element back to the premises. This is the most common type of assumption on the GRE.

Let's look at a Supporter Assumption question:

Despite the fact that many professional writers consider travel writing a lesser form of journalism, it is in fact a legitimate journalistic enterprise, since it employs classical journalism techniques such as detailed research into the history of a given locale and extensive interviews with local residents.

1. Which of the following is an assumption on which the argument depends?

    Ⓐ If a literary work is crafted via extensive interviews of noteworthy subjects, it should be viewed as legitimate.

    Ⓑ Since travel writing follows the methods of traditional journalism, it will produce intriguing material for readers.

    Ⓒ Any writing that does not employ classical techniques is a lesser form of journalism.

    Ⓓ If a literary pursuit involves classical journalism techniques, then it would be considered a journalistic enterprise.

    Ⓔ The interview process used by travel writers can provide further information about the history of a region.

Supporter Assumptions link together "new" or "rogue" elements in the text or fill logical gaps in the argument.

Confidence Quotation
"I can win an argument on any topic, against any opponent. People know this, and steer clear of me at parties. Often, as a sign of their great respect, they don't even invite me."
Dave Barry, author

15

If you choose to diagram the argument, it should look like this:

TIPS and TRICKS
For Supporter
Assumption
Questions, you
can eliminate
an answer
that adds new
information.

+	−
Since it employs classical journalism techniques such as detailed research into history of a locale and extensive interviews with local residents	Despite the fact that many professional writers consider travel writing a lesser form of journalism

it is in fact a legitimate journalistic enterprise

Do you detect a Supporter Assumption in this argument?

+	−	
Since it employs classical journalism techniques such as detailed research into history of a locale and extensive interviews with local residents	Despite the fact that many professional writers consider travel writing a lesser form of journalism	Assumption: Anything that employs classical journalism techniques is a legitimate journalistic enterprise.

it is in fact a legitimate journalistic enterprise

In answer choice (A), the author does not discuss "noteworthy subjects," and hence this is not an assumption of the argument. Since an assumption fills in a gap between two pieces of the text, the correct answer must contain information that was stated in the text. You can eliminate any answer that adds new information not in the original passage.

For (B), the first part of this answer is extremely attractive, but the second half of the answer addresses "intriguing material," another subject that was not discussed in the argument. Like (A), this is not an assumption of the argument.

Answer choice (C) is the most popular wrong answer. The answer connects two pieces of the argument, but those pieces are from the premise and the counter-premise. The author only discusses the fact that travel writing uses classic techniques, but the author makes no assumption about writing that does not use those techniques.

If you were able to identify the assumption before looking at the answer choices, then you have the perfect prephrase for Choice (D). This is the correct answer. The answer acts as a Supporter and connects the elements in the conclusion to the elements in the final sentence.

15

Finally, in choice (E), the answer attempts to falsely combine two of the methods used by classical journalism: research and interviews. There is no indication that the interviews with the residents reveal the history of the locale.

The Defender role is entirely different, and Defender assumptions protect the argument by eliminating statements that would harm the conclusion. In this sense, they "defend" the argument by showing that a possible avenue of attack has been eliminated (shown not to exist). In a typical argument, there are usually a large number of Defender assumptions possible, as any potential weakness could be the source of the assumed "defense." Fortunately, this type of Assumption question is even less common than the Supporter, so while it is unlikely you will see one on test day we would be remiss not to mention it.

Return to our previous example:

> *My GPA is low. Therefore, I will not be accepted into a top graduate program.*

What are some ideas that could weaken this argument?

> An applicant with a perfect GRE score is guaranteed acceptance to a top graduate school.
>
> A legacy applicant is guaranteed acceptance to a top graduate school.
>
> A celebrity is guaranteed acceptance to a top graduate school.

The author of the argument assumes that any idea that could weaken his statement is impossible and cannot occur, thus the statements on the previous page are not applicable. To defend his argument, he assumes all of the following:

> An applicant with a perfect GRE score is NOT guaranteed acceptance to a top graduate school.
>
> A legacy applicant is NOT guaranteed acceptance to a top graduate school.
>
> A celebrity is NOT guaranteed acceptance to a top graduate school.

These are Defender Assumptions; they protect the argument against statements that would undermine the conclusion.

15

Let's examine a sample question:

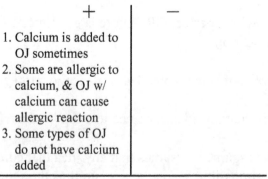

During the production of orange juice, calcium is sometimes added as a nutritional supplement. Certain individuals are allergic to calcium, and drinking orange juice fortified with calcium can cause an allergic reaction. Fortunately, some types of orange juice do not have calcium added during production, so calcium-allergic individuals can drink these orange juices without inducing an allergic reaction to calcium.

Defender Assumptions are nearly impossible to prephrase or identify before looking at the answer choices.

1. The argument in the passage depends on which of the following assumptions?

    Ⓐ There are no other substances besides calcium that are typically present in orange juice that cause allergic reactions.

    Ⓑ Orange juice has the same nutritional value whether calcium is added or not.

    Ⓒ Calcium-allergic individuals cannot ingest any calcium without having an allergic reaction.

    Ⓓ Calcium is often added to other beverages besides orange juice.

    Ⓔ In orange juice that does not have calcium added during production, calcium is not naturally present in quantities that cause an allergic reaction.

Consider a diagram of the argument:

+	−
1. Calcium is added to OJ sometimes	
2. Some are allergic to calcium, & OJ w/ calcium can cause allergic reaction	
3. Some types of OJ do not have calcium added	

So calcium-allergic individuals can drink these OJs
without inducing an allergic reaction to calcium

Unlike Supporter Assumptions, Defender Assumptions can be extremely hard to identify before looking at the answer choices because there are so many possibilities for the test makers to choose from. Since there is no "missing link" in this case, we can see that this is a Defender Assumption question.

In answer choice (A), the author does not conclude that orange juice is free of all allergens—the far more limited conclusion present in the stimulus is that people who are allergic to *calcium* could safely consume orange juice that has not had calcium added.

With choice (B), the nutritional value of orange juice is not at issue in this question, and the argument does not require this assumption.

Answer choice (C) simply provides that people who are allergic to calcium are *very* allergic. That is, any amount will trigger an allergic reaction. Since the author's conclusion indicates that non-calcium-added orange juice is safe for such people to consume, this is not an assumption on which the argument relies.

Choice (D) is outside the scope of the issue under discussion. The author's comments are limited to orange juice and its safety for people who are allergic to calcium. The existence of other calcium-supplemented products is irrelevant, so this is not an assumption on which the author's argument relies.

The correct answer choice is (E); it provides an assumption that is required of the author's argument. The author must be assuming that orange juice has no naturally present calcium—if it does have some calcium naturally that would cause an allergic reaction, then this would destroy the author's conclusion that, as long as calcium has not been added, calcium-allergic people could safely drink orange juice.

15

Method of Reasoning Questions & Assumption Questions Problem Set

> Read each argument below and use scratch paper to diagram the conclusion (if applicable), premise(s), and counter premise(s) on a reverse-T plot. Then answer the corresponding question. Answers begin on page 362.

Free radicals are highly reactive, oxygen-rich molecules that contribute to the growth of cancerous tumors. An antioxidant, on the other hand, is a molecule that inhibits oxidation and precludes cell damage. It follows then that cancerous growth should be delayed or prevented with antioxidant treatment. The results of research studies with such treatment, however, have suggested otherwise; **the use of vitamin E and N-acetylcysteine, two antioxidants, has been proven to fuel the growth of lung cancer**. For this reason, doctors do not recommend antioxidant supplements for cancer patients.

1. In the argument, the two portions in boldface serve which of the following roles?

    Ⓐ The first asserts the conclusion of the argument as a whole; the second undermines that conclusion.

    Ⓑ The first states a position that provides support for the conclusion of the argument as a whole; the second provides an intermediate conclusion that supports that conclusion of the argument as a whole.

    Ⓒ The first serves as evidence that contradicts an intermediate conclusion that disputes a further conclusion stated in the argument; the second is that further conclusion.

    Ⓓ The first provides a premise of an intermediate conclusion that contradicts a further conclusion stated in the argument; the second provides evidence that contradicts that intermediate conclusion.

    Ⓔ The first presents evidence that supports a contradiction to the intermediate conclusion; the second is that intermediate conclusion.

Xani and Yata are the only two languages spoken in the country of Zorba, with Xani spoken by the majority of Zorba's residents. Thus, by learning Xani prior to visiting Zorba, tourists can feel confident that they have done the most that they can to assist in communicating with Zorba's locals.

2. Which of the following is an assumption made in drawing the conclusion?

    Ⓐ Travelers to ZXorba will not visit other countries in addition to Zorba.

    Ⓑ Xani is easier to learn than Yata.

    Ⓒ Most tourists are committed to effectively communicating with the residents of the countries that they visit.

    Ⓓ Learning both Xani and Yata would not allow tourists to better communicate with the residents of Zorba than would only learning Xani.

    Ⓔ Xani and Yata are both commonly spoken in countries other than Zorba.

In the state of Alpha, public schools that do not receive satisfactory academic scores above a certain percentage on a district-wide standardized test are taken over by the governor, who may choose to close the school or bring in a special team of charter school administrators in an attempt to increase student achievement. On this year's district wide standardized test, Beta School scored 73%, Gamma School scored 82%, Delta School scored 70%, and Epsilon School scored 77%. Thus, none of the four schools will be taken over by the governor.

3. Which of the following is an assumption on which the argument depends?

    Ⓐ Charter schools have higher district wide standardized test scores than do public schools.

    Ⓑ Delta School would have been taken over by the governor if its score had been 1% lower.

    Ⓒ When a school is closed, its students have to be divided up and absorbed by schools with satisfactory scores.

    Ⓓ Charter school administrators have more experience with satisfactory test scores than do public school employees.

    Ⓔ Scores of 70% or above on the district wide standardized test are considered satisfactory academic scores.

15

Chapter Summary

Argument Passages are easily identified because they are extremely short and have a single question, which often uses the phrase "if true." Your initial task is to diagram the argument, identifying the premise(s), counter premise(s), assumption(s), and conclusion(s) using indicator words as guides. There are four types of questions to look for with Argument Passages:

Strengthen and Weaken Questions

- Strengthen Questions ask you to select an answer choice that best supports the conclusion in a passage.
- Weaken Questions require you to choose an answer that challenges the position in the passage.
- These are the most common question types to accompany Argument Passages.

Resolve the Paradox Questions

- These questions ask you to select a statement that "fixes" a contradiction in the passage.
- Passages with Resolve the Paradox Questions usually do not have conclusions.
- These questions are the second most common question type to follow Argument Passages.

Method of Reasoning Questions

- These questions ask you to identify the role played of a particular portion or portions of the argument.
- Passages with Method of Reasoning Questions are typically more complicated than the average Argument Passage. Be sure to diagram the argument carefully.
- These questions are rare on the GRE.

Assumption Questions

- Assumption Questions ask you to identify an assumption on which the argument is based.
- Supporter Assumption Questions ask you to close the gap in the line of reasoning by linking elements together; Defender Assumption Questions require you to locate a statement that protects the argument by eliminating ideas that could weaken it.
- These questions are also rare on the GRE.

15

Argument Passages Answer Key

Identify the Elements of the Argument Problem Set—Page 327

1. Given that the price of grapes is rising, we will no longer offer chicken salad on the menu.

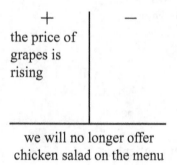 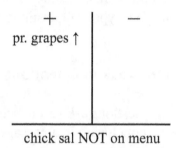

2. The gradual climate change threatens the monetary stability of the nation. As temperatures rise, we are losing millions of dollars in lost crops and profits are plummeting in states that depend on winter tourism.

3. The downtrend of the economy has concluded owing to prudent economic reforms by the government.

15

4. In Victona, the number of cases of "teacher burnout" has increased 20 percent in the last decade. However, part of the increase may be attributed to extended maternity or paternity leave: many teachers have taken 2 or 3 years off of work to attend to their young children, but fully intend to return to work after their leave. Since the statistics simply look at the number of new teachers who are no longer working in Victona after 5 years of employment, they may not reflect the actual number of teacher burnout cases.

+	−
1. Part of the increase may be attributed to extended maternity or paternity leave: many teachers have taken 2 or 3 years off of work to attend to their young children, but fully intend to return to work after their leave 2. the statistics simply look at the number of new teachers who are no longer working in Victona after 5 years of employment	the number of cases of "teacher burnout" has increased 20 percent in the last decade

The statistics may not reflect the actual number of teacher burnout cases in Victona

+	−
1. Part ↑ may be from ext mat/pat leave: int to rtrn to work 2. stats only look at # new teach who aren't there aft 5 yrs	"teach burnout" ↑ 20% in dec.

stats not accurate

5. While researchers acknowledge that nurses' reactions and words play a critical role in the well-being and recovery of cancer patients, the nurses' dialogue with their patients about the expression of feelings is often problematic. These nurses are frequently untrained about the best ways to use metaphors and figurative language to console patients. As a result, oncology departments must provide instruction to nurses concerning appropriate language with cancer patients as well as provide perennial supervision by a psychoanalytically-trained administrator.

+	−
1. the nurses' dialogue with their patients about the expression of feelings is often problematic 2. these nurses are frequently untrained about the best ways to use metaphors and figurative language to console patients	researchers acknowledge that nurses' reactions and words play a critical role in the well-being and recovery of cancer patients

oncology departments must provide instruction to nurses concerning appropriate language with cancer patients as well has perennial supervision by a psychoanalytically-trained administrator.

+	−
1. nurses' dial. re feelings is prblm 2. nurses untrained re mtphor and fig lang	nurses' react & wds help cancer pat

oncol dept must teach nurses right lang & prov. superv by trained admin.

15

1. **A**

+	−
Increased interest by amateurs due to media	Industry dominated by professionals due to cost

Inexpensive system will increase production of content by amateurs and stimulate industry

The conclusion: The inception of an inexpensive 3D motion capture system will not only advance the production of content by novice users, but also stimulate the development of the 3-D industry

Weaken Answer: The inexpensive motion capture system requires its users to have an advanced knowledge of graphics and design.

The author is arguing that a cheap system will help novice users and promote the industry, but the complicated system won't help if the novices cannot figure out how to use it, no matter how cheap it is.

Choice (B) tries to trick you by discussing a novice, but this novice conceived the film—the answer does not indicate that he created the content. And even if he did, this is one person, so it does not affect the conclusion.

Choices (C) and (D) strengthen the idea that the industry is limited and dominated by professionals.

Choice (E) tries to present a parallel situation, but does nothing to prove or disprove the argument.

2. **D**

+	−
1. Chemicals in sunscreen = endocrine disrupters 2. Absorbed through skin—converted to synthetic hormones, so abnormal high or low levels of natural hormones, cause reproductive & developmental issues	

endocrinologists recommend using mineral-based sunblocks which do not penetrate the skin

The conclusion: Endocrinologists recommend using mineral-based sunblocks—those containing zinc oxide and titanium dioxide—which do not penetrate the skin.

Strengthen Answer: One study found that men who applied sunscreen for a week experienced a significant drop in testosterone levels.

The author is arguing that non-absorbing sun*block* must be used because absorbing sun*screen* changes hormone levels. If men who applied sunscreen had a decrease in testosterone, a male hormone, then this evidence supports the conclusion.

Choice (A) may seem like it's trying to weaken the conclusion, but since the author never says that sunblock should be ingested, it's a moot point. It has nothing to do with applying sunblock to the skin.

15

Choice (B) presents a disadvantage of sunblock, but again, it has nothing to do with why the author says sunblock should be used (hormone disruption).

Choice (C) is probably the most attractive wrong answer. It provides further evidence that oxybenzone changes hormone levels. However, it has nothing to do with the conclusion regarding sunscreen vs. sunblock.

Choice (E) discusses a different type of doctor and their recommendation.

3. E

+	−
1. Children under five who spend significant time SV at increased risk for health issues 2. Children model the amt of time SV after parents' SV time; 3.4 times more likely to spend 2+ hrs per day if parent did 2+ hrs	

Parents must decrease their own SV time in order to decrease the amount of time spent SV by their children.

The conclusion: Parents must decrease their own SV time in order to decrease the amount of time spent SV by their children

Weaken Answer: Children are unaware of the amount of time their parents spend SV after the children go to bed.

The author is arguing children model their SV time after their parents' SV time, so parents must decrease their time SV. But if these parents choose to SV when their children are asleep, the kids have no idea, so they can't model that time. Therefore, parents do not have to decrease their SV time—they can SV as many hours as they want after the kids are asleep.

For choice (A), you should ask "As who?" This comparison is not complete. And since the argument is about children under five, this statement has no bearing on the argument.

Choice (B) presents a fact that does not support or disprove the fact that parents must decrease their own SV time in order to decrease the amount of time spent SV by their children.

Choice (C) is probably the most attractive wrong answer. It provides a reason why it may be okay for children under five to SV. But the argument is not about what content is viewed—it's about the health consequences of SV, no matter what content is viewed. Also, it has nothing to do with the parents' SV time reflecting on children.

Choice (D) tells us that only a small percent of the population is affected by the phenomena. But the argument is not concerned with this detail—it never says if it's 5% or 95% of the population. It just says that parents must decrease their SV time in order to affect a decrease in their children's SV time in order to alleviate the health concerns.

15

1. C

+	−
Men in Anders have lower rates of major depression	Men in Anders are at higher risk for depression

The paradox: Men in Anders have a higher risk of depression but have lower rates of depression in comparison to the men in Collings.

Answer choice (A) would provide a reason why the men in Collings are less depressed, rather than the men in Anders.

Choice (B) proves that men in Anders are at a higher risk of exposure to social stressors. But it does nothing to show why their depression rates are lower. Remember, stay away from answers that only support one side.

Choice (C) is the correct answer. If there are different standards for the diagnosis, and Anders has stricter standards, it stands to reason that there will be fewer diagnoses in Anders than in Collings.

Choice (D) would strengthen the paradox and Choice (E) is about the women, which does nothing to explain the paradox surrounding the men.

2. C

+	−
Officials expected 75% decrease in cost of production	The price paid by consumer increased by 5%

The paradox: Officials expected a 75% decrease in production costs but consumers are actually paying 5% more.

In (A), we are presented with a fact about foreign countries, but this does nothing to explain the prices in this country.

Choice (B) supports the first premise, that there will be a 75% decrease in production cost because the substitute ingredient is not only inexpensive, but abundant.

Choice (C) is the correct answer. If Fitzpatrick Pharmaceuticals is hit with new taxes, these taxes may be higher than the money saved by using a substitute ingredient, thus raising the cost of the medication.

Choice (D) provides the cost history of Judizen, but does not explain why the price continued to increase when it was expected to decrease. Still, this is an attractive wrong answer choice.

Finally, in (E), we are presented with information about top medications. The prices of these drugs have all increased. But we don't even know if Judizen is one of those top 200, and even if it is, this answer does not explain why the price went up when it was expected to go down.

15

3. C

+	−
Refined carbs are broken down quickly, raising insulin and fat storage, so they are responsible for obesity	The Chinese eat refined carbs but have a low obesity rate

The paradox: Refined carbs break down quickly, thus causing obesity, but people in China who eat a lot of refined carbs have a low obesity rate.

Choice (A) tries to trick you with your prior knowledge. If you know that whole grains break down slower than refined carbs, you might be tempted to choose this answer. But remember, leave your prior knowledge at the door when you take the GRE! The rate of breakdown of whole grains does not explain the Chinese low obesity rate.

Choice (B) tells us more about the obesity rate in China, but does not explain how their diet of refined carbohydrates keeps their overall obesity rate low.

Choice (C) is the correct answer. Since obesity happens when refined carbs are broken down quickly, obesity will not happen when the fiber slows down that break down.

Choice (D) would work if the passage said that Chinese people ate brown rice, but it specifically states that they eat white rice and noodles.

Finally, in (E), we are given a complicated fact to trick us. But this fact does nothing to explain the low obesity rate in China.

15

1. D

Let's diagram the first half of the argument:

+	−
Free radicals are highly reactive, oxygen-rich molecules that contribute to the growth of cancerous tumors	An antioxidant, on the other hand, is a molecule that inhibits oxidation and precludes cell damage

It follows then that cancerous growth should be delayed or prevented with antioxidant treatment

The second half of the argument provides a counter premise to the first conclusion, so the two reverse-T diagrams overlap:

+	−
Free radicals are highly reactive, oxygen-rich molecules that contribute to the growth of cancerous tumors	An antioxidant, on the other hand, is a molecule that inhibits oxidation and precludes cell damage

+ It follows then that cancerous growth should be delayed or prevented with antioxidant treatment	**The use of two antioxidants has been proven to fuel the growth of lung cancer** −

For this reason, doctors do not recommend antioxidant supplements for cancer patients.

Once you diagram the argument, identify the two pieces that are highlighted. Now you can prephrase the role of these two sentences: *the first provides a premise for the first conclusion, and the second is a premise that contradicts that first conclusion.* Now match your prephrase to an answer choice.

15

Prephrase: *the first provides a premise for the first conclusion, and the second is a premise that contradicts that first conclusion.*

Answer choice (A): The first <u>asserts the conclusion</u> of the argument as a whole; the second undermines that conclusion. *No.*

Answer choice (B): The first states a position that provides support for the conclusion <u>of the argument as a whole</u>; the second provides an <u>intermediate conclusion</u> that supports that conclusion of the argument as a whole. *No.*

Answer choice (C): The first serves as evidence that <u>contradicts</u> an intermediate conclusion that disputes a further conclusion stated in the argument; the second is that further <u>conclusion</u>. *No.*

Answer choice (D): The first provides a premise of an intermediate conclusion that contradicts a further conclusion stated in the argument; the second provides evidence that contradicts that intermediate conclusion. *YES!*

Answer choice (E): The first presents evidence that supports a <u>contradiction</u> to the intermediate conclusion; the second is that intermediate <u>conclusion</u>. *No.*

2. D

Consider the diagrammed argument:

$+$ | $-$

1. Xani & Yata are only 2 languages spoken in Zorba
2. With Xani spoken by the majority of Zorba's residents

Thus, by learning Xani prior to visiting Zorba, tourists can feel confident that they have done the most that they can to assist in communicating with Zorba's locals

At first glance the argument does not seem to have any gaping holes. This would suggest a Defender answer is coming, and indeed that is the case.

Answer choice (A): The author does not need to assume this statement because the stimulus is specifically about visitors visiting Zorba and communicating with Zorba's locals.

Answer choice (B): The ease of learning a particular language is not under examination in this question. This answer is thus irrelevant to the argument.

Answer choice (C): The author's argument concerns what tourists can do to assure themselves that they have done the most they can in order to assist in communicating with Zorba's locals. Whether tourists are committed to taking those steps is not part of the argument. When faced with the negation of the answer choice, the author would likely reply: "They may not be committed, but if they want to do the most they can, they should learn Xani prior to visiting Zorba." As you can see, the negation has not undermined the author's position, and so this answer is incorrect.

Answer choice (D): This is the correct answer. The key to this answer is the conclusion of the argument, where the author states that "tourists can feel confident that they have done *the most they can do* to assist in communicating with Zorba's locals" (italics added for emphasis). Because the author states that learning just the one language spoken by the majority of Zorbans is doing the "most they can do," this answer defends the conclusion by indicating that it would *not* be better to learn both Zorban languages. If this answer did not make sense at first glance, you should have noted the negative language and then negated the answer. Applying the Assumption Negation Technique produces a statement that would clearly attack the conclusion: "Learning both Xani and Yata *would* allow tourists to better communicate with the residents of Zorba than would only learning Xani." If learning both languages provides better communication, then learning just Xani would not be the most that a tourist could do to assist in communicating with Zorba's locals.

Answer choice (E): This answer is incorrect because the argument is about visiting Zorba and communicating with Zorba's locals. The fact that the two languages are spoken in other countries is not relevant.

3. E

Consider the diagrammed argument:

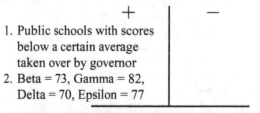

Answer choice (A): The scores of charter schools have nothing to do with the conclusion that no public schools are being taken over.

Answer choice (B): This True to You answer might trick you, but the score that necessitates a takeover is never given or implied.

Answer choice (C): Again, an answer that is not reflective of the conclusion and may play on your prior knowledge.

Answer choice (D): While this may be an inference readers make, it is not an inference on which the conclusion depends.

Answer choice (E): The correct answer. The passage states that schools that do not receive a satisfactory academic score above a certain percentage will be taken over. The four schools mentioned are not being taken over. Therefore, the lowest score of the four—70—must be high enough to be considered satisfactory.

15

Verbal Reasoning Mastery: Problem Sets

POWERSCORE®
TEST PREPARATION

Verbal Reasoning Mastery: Problem Sets

Review

Now that you have read about Fill-in-the-Blank questions, reading strategies, passage formats, and question and answer analysis, it is time to test your knowledge with passage problem sets. But before you begin, take a few minutes to review the most important points from the previous chapters.

Fill-in-the-Blank: The Four Step Solution Method

1. Read the question stem.
   For difficult questions, use the following strategies:
   • Remove irrelevant words and phrases.
   • Rephrase the sentence.
   • Read in chunks.
   • Relate the sentence to your own life.
2. Prephrase the answer(s).
   • It is imperative that you prephrase an answer *before* looking at the answer choices.
   • If you are unable to prephrase, test each answer choice in the blank(s).
3. Match the answer choice(s).
4. Backplug your selection(s).

Fill-in-the-Blank: Sentence Equivalence Strategies

• Eliminate an answer choice that does not have a synonym or a word with a closely-related meaning.
• Be wary of synonym pairs that do not fit the meaning of the sentence.
• Understand that your prephase can lead you in the general direction of the correct answers, but it may not always be a perfect match.

Fill-in-the-Blank: Recognize the Question Type

• Contrast Questions
• Similarity Questions
• Definition Questions
• Cause and Effect Questions
• Combination Questions

16

Fill-in-the-Blank: Analyze the Answer Choices

Wrong Answer Traps
    Double Definition Answers
    Opposite Answers
    Related Answers
    "Kind Of" Answers
    Multiple Blank Answers

Fill-in-the-Blank: Decode the Vocabulary

Vocabulary in the Question Stem
- Determine if the word is relevant to the context, and if so, search for synonyms in the sentence.
- Eliminate wrong answers before guessing.

Vocabulary in the Answer Choices
1. Selecting an Unknown
   - Do not eliminate a word if you cannot define it.
   - Trust yourself to eliminate wrong answer choices.
2. Vocabulary Roots and Affixes
   - Know some basic, common prefixes and affixes.
   - Consider related words.
   - Use your knowledge of words in foreign languages.
   - Watch for common Imposter Answers.
3. Word Sense
   - As a last resort, make a guess based on a word's "feeling."

Reading Comprehension: Employ Reading Strategies

1. Adjust your attitude.
2. Adjust your reading speed according to the passage length.
3. Read the passage before reading the questions, unless the passage is accompanied by a single question.
4. Practice active reading, including taking notes as you read.
5. Identify the passage MAPS.
6. Recognize patterns on the GRE.
7. Read each question.
8. If necessary, return to the passage.
9. Prephrase an answer.
10. Match an answer choice.

Reading Comprehension: Recognize the Question Type

Vocabulary-In-Context Questions
    Define a vocabulary word in the passage.

Literary Comprehension Questions
    Main Idea Questions
    Facts and Details Questions
    Reasons and Results Questions
    Comparison and Contrast Questions

Extended Reasoning Questions
    Purpose Questions
    Inference Questions
        General Inferences
        Hypothetical Points of View
    Parallel Reasoning Questions

Reading Comprehension: Analyze the Answer Choices

Right Answers
Wrong Answers
    Copycat Answers
    Opposite Answers
    Extreme Answers
    True But Wrong Answers
    True to a Point Answers
    True to You Answers

Reading Comprehension: Argument Passages

1. If needed, diagram the argument.
2. Look for indicator words to help identify the conclusion, premises, and counter premises.
3. Note any assumptions that you may encounter as you read.
4. Recognize the five types of Argument Questions:
    Weaken Questions
    Strengthen Questions
    Resolve the Paradox Questions
    Method of Reasoning Questions
    Assumption Questions

Confidence Quotation

"There are admirable potentialities in every human being. Believe in your strength and your youth. Learn to repeat endlessly to yourself, 'It all depends on me.'" André Gide, Nobel Prize-winning French author

16

Fill-in-the-Blank Problem Set

> Each of the sentences or paragraphs below has a word or set of words that has been omitted. From the answer choices, choose the word or set of words that best completes the meaning of the sentence. Choose one answer from each box for the questions that have oval answer choices and two answers from each box for questions that have square answer choices. Answers begin on page 386.

1. The study, which examined the _____ between altitude and hypertension, was based on one hundred patients, all of whom lived at moderate to high altitudes and had been diagnosed with high blood pressure.

Ⓐ juncture
Ⓑ grievance
Ⓒ correlation
Ⓓ succession
Ⓔ contrition

2. Despite having similar elevation, size, and water temperature to Lake Huron, Lake Michigan has not been _____ by the algae problem faced by the other Great Lake, likely because Lake Michigan is deeper and has a natural pollution filtration system along the Chicago River.

Ⓐ enhanced
Ⓑ disclosed
Ⓒ cowed
Ⓓ plagued
Ⓔ depleted

3. With low rates of diabetes and other obesity-related diseases, the Netherlands is consistently (i)_____ to be one of the healthiest countries in the world, a(n) (ii)_____ that is largely due to a national diet that emphasizes vegetables and dairy products.

Blank (i)	Blank (ii)
Ⓐ contemplated	Ⓓ resolution
Ⓑ deemed	Ⓔ designation
Ⓒ envisioned	Ⓕ endowment

4. Both Abigail Adams and Eliza Wilkinson worried about the rights of women during the American Revolution and the Critical Period after the war, but without a public forum or receptive audience, each of the women was _____ to expressing her concerns in letters to trusted loved ones.

Ⓐ	stretched
Ⓑ	reduced
Ⓒ	driven
Ⓓ	accustomed
Ⓔ	partial

5. Engineering interns at the automotive corporation are often surprised at the (i)_____ of their first responsibilities, which may include filing completed reports or retrieving coffee, but the CEO believes that all of her employees should equally participate in the most (ii)_____ undertakings.

Blank (i)		Blank (ii)	
Ⓐ	whimsy	Ⓓ	elemental
Ⓑ	gravity	Ⓔ	intricate
Ⓒ	triviality	Ⓕ	somber

6. An increase in the number of teachers with graduate degrees and a (i)_____ in enrollment in education programs at colleges nationwide suggests that teacher education programs are not as (ii)_____ as the magazine article originally reported.

Blank (i)		Blank (ii)	
Ⓐ	surge	Ⓓ	inaccessible
Ⓑ	variation	Ⓔ	permissive
Ⓒ	slump	Ⓕ	instructive

16

7. The groundwork for the secession of South Carolina, which was home to several radical pro-slavery politicians known as "Fire-Eaters," was laid throughout the 1850s, when slavery became a (i)_____ issue amongst members of the union. Northern states held abolitionist persuasions and resisted the westward expansion of slavery, while southern states held pro-slavery (ii)_____ and supported the spread of the institution into the western territories. Fearing a lack of (iii)_____, the Fire-Eaters began to call for the separation of the southern states into a new nation.

Blank (i)	Blank (ii)	Blank (iii)
Ⓐ sovereign	Ⓓ distinctions	Ⓖ reconciliation
Ⓑ copious	Ⓔ hostilities	Ⓗ discord
Ⓒ divisive	Ⓕ sentiments	Ⓘ veracity

8. In his 1651 book *Leviathan*, English philosopher Thomas Hobbes argued that an absolute monarchy was the ideal form of government because people were inherently _____; because of such evil natures, they could not be trusted to govern other people.

Ⓐ cavalier
Ⓑ genteel
Ⓒ esoteric
Ⓓ audacious
Ⓔ malevolent

9. After the death of his first wife, which he suspected occurred at the hands of his trusted advisors, Ivan the Terrible left Moscow and gave up the Russian throne. Most historians believe this (i)_____ was intended to manipulate the aristocracy since Ivan quickly returned to power at the request of his court members when they agreed to grant him an absolute monarchy. He was known for such (ii)_____ and other (iii)_____ behavior, such as torturing animals, displacing innocent families, and mutilating and murdering his adversaries.

Blank (i)	Blank (ii)	Blank (iii)
Ⓐ abdication	Ⓓ remunerations	Ⓖ contemptible
Ⓑ relegation	Ⓔ machinations	Ⓗ regal
Ⓒ platitude	Ⓕ corpulence	Ⓘ intractable

10. While previous United States Presidents had been able to _____ the media to propagandize earlier conflicts and wars, neither Lyndon Johnson nor Richard Nixon succeeded in his attempts to spin the media during the Vietnam War.

A	reinforce
B	exploit
C	dissuade
D	manipulate
E	dispense
F	embrace

11. After years of complaints from customers and former clients, the insurance commissioners finally acknowledged that the failing automotive insurance company exhibited poor customer service and _____ tactics, including shameful settlement amounts and delayed claim payments.

A	adept
B	slothful
C	underhanded
D	lethargic
E	righteous
F	unscrupulous

12. When creating the city's charter, the residents argued that their interests were better represented by smaller, local jurisdictions than by a large, _____ central ministry, so the metropolis was divided into seven distinct districts, each with its own government.

A	restricted
B	meddlesome
C	boundless
D	authoritative
E	exclusive
F	sweeping

16

13. Even though the variegated shell ginger, a colorful plant native to India, prefers full sun over full shade, gardeners have reported that it _____ in shade gardens throughout the southern United States.

A	languishes
B	thrives
C	compensates
D	shrivels
E	recovers
F	flourishes

14. The legislation, which at one time was believed to be a certainty, is now being stymied by partisan politics; members of the majority party have vowed that the bill will not be passed because the backlash could sway election results in November.

A	stymied
B	impeded
C	sanctioned
D	transcended
E	elicited
F	sullied

15. Although Governor Sam Houston was averse to abolition, he adamantly opposed Texas's _____ and secession from the Union; as a result, he resigned from office rather than pledge allegiance to the Confederacy, the legality of which he refused to recognize.

A	complaisance
B	ratification
C	insurrection
D	sedition
E	acclimatization
F	subordination

Read the following passages and then answer the corresponding questions. Remember, questions with an oval next to the answer choices have a single correct answer; questions with a square next to the answer choices may have one, two, or three correct answers. Answers begin on page 390.

The theory of continental drift existed for several hundred years before a comprehensive understanding of plate tectonics in the 1960s provided a sufficient explanation of the movement of continents relative to each other. The key principle of plate tectonics is that the lithosphere, a rigid layer of the earth's crust that "floats" on top of the fluid-like asthenosphere,
Line
5 is comprised of several plates, which move against one another at their boundaries. These plate boundaries are often quite volatile, and produce earthquakes, mountain ranges, oceanic trenches, and the majority of the world's active volcanoes. Clearly, continued investigation of plate movement is warranted as we strive to better understand not only the geological history of our planet, but also the powerful, and often destructive, forces associated with plate boundaries.

1. The author suggests that the "theory" (line 1) was

   (A) a comprehensive explanation of continental drifting

   (B) proven wrong by the discovery of plate tectonics

   (C) sufficient for predicting natural disasters

   (D) lacking information to adequately explain the shifting of large land masses

   (E) the only conjecture about continental movement until the 1960s

2. According to the passage, "continued investigation" (line 6) is necessary in order to

   (A) map out the ocean's deepest trenches

   (B) form a sufficient explanation of plate tectonics

   (C) better predict earthquakes and volcano eruptions

   (D) further comprehend the history and potential power of the Earth

   (E) determine the geological composition of the lithosphere and asthenosphere

For many, America's annals of race are written in black and white. Certainly United States history since the great civil rights initiatives of the 1950s and 1960s has been framed largely from that point of view. This bipolar perspective, however, is challenged by some critics as inaccurate and inadequate, given the historic presence of other groups in our nation, and
Line
5 their growing numbers on the American landscape. Indeed, many observers believe a more comprehensive view of history and a more equitable shaping of effective public policy will result from a refined concept of race embracing this broader view of the roles of culture and ethnicity.

3. The author suggests that the "perspective" (line 2) is insufficient because

   (A) the history of civil rights is not embraced by all Americans

   (B) racism is still occurring in the United States

   (C) it does not include some of America's ethnic groups

   (D) it is held by white Americans who make up the majority of the population

   (E) critics contend that African Americans are not given a voice in public policy

16

Faulkner lived a good deal of his life in opposition to many of the things Mississippi has come to represent; his life and a good deal of his work are frontal assaults on its middle-class pretensions, its cultural backwardness, and its racist politics. Mississippians, of course, resented their collective portrayal in his works, and returned his implicit criticism with a combination of indifference and calumny. It swallowed hard and reacted negatively when he analyzed its racist traditions in
Line
5 *Light in August* (1932), *Absalom, Absalom!* (1936), *Go Down, Moses* (1942), and *Intruder in the Dust* (1948); but when in the mid fifties he carried his criticism to the public arena, "official" Mississippi began to return the antagonism with all the power its newspapers and pulpits, bully and religious, could muster. During his lifetime and for some years beyond, official Mississippi was hard put indeed to find anything nice to say about him either publicly or privately, and there were times when a public ceremony in his home state connected with him and his work would have more likely been an assembly to
10 burn his books than to have his portrait hung or his books discussed. Faulkner has long since had the last laugh, and it may be too easy, this side of the tumultuous days of the Civil Rights movement, to undervalue his personal struggle in taking the public stands he took. If we do, though, we will miss a good deal of the significance of his life and work as it grew out of the complex combination of powerful emotions that Mississippi evoked in him and, thanks to him, in us. Indeed, Faulkner scholars and readers in other countries tell me that part of his continuing appeal to them lies precisely in his love of and his
15 commitment to his own country, so that part of what makes him international seems to be his very localness in Mississippi.

In a 1933 essay, Faulkner suggested that a writer in Mississippi had two alternatives: to escape or to indict. He tried the former by simply leaving as frequently as he could: to Canada, where he enlisted in the Royal Air Force, in an unsuccessful effort to get into World War I; to New Haven and New York in the early twenties; to New Orleans and Europe in the mid twenties; to Hollywood sporadically to try to make a living when his novels weren't selling. He often indicted his home
20 region in several novels and stories, which frequently depicted the South's and Mississippi's people as backward, violent, oppressive, and ignorant.

4. The passage is primarily concerned with Faulkner's

    Ⓐ criticism of the middle class in the South

    Ⓑ relationship with the state of Mississippi

    Ⓒ involvement in the Civil Rights movement

    Ⓓ attempts to move away from his homeland

    Ⓔ acceptance of his heritage

5. The passage suggests which of the following about Faulkner? (Select all answers that apply.)

    Ⓐ His portrayal of Mississippians angered residents who retaliated with public criticism of Faulkner.

    Ⓑ His public stance against oppression caused conflict in his personal life.

    Ⓒ His works were successfully turned into movies because his depiction of local Mississippi appealed to viewers.

6. The sentence in lines 10-12 ("Faulkner . . . took") suggest that

    Ⓐ Mississippi acknowledged its racist politics after the Civil Rights movement

    Ⓑ Faulkner was amused by the public reaction to his books

    Ⓒ time has tempered the perceived difficulty for Faulkner in criticizing Mississippi

    Ⓓ Faulkner was an active participant in the Civil Rights Movement

    Ⓔ the emotional toll on the people of Mississippi and on Faulkner was a consequence of exposing racism

7. In the context in which it appears, "lies" (line 14) most nearly means

    Ⓐ reposes

    Ⓑ feigns

    Ⓒ prevails

    Ⓓ spans

    Ⓔ entombs

The soil pH determines the color of the flowers for most French Hydrangeas (*Hydrangea macrophylla*). In soil that is strongly acidic, the flowers will bloom blue or purple, but in soil that is alkaline and free of aluminum, the flowers will be pink. Gardeners can make soil more acidic by adding garden sulfur and they can create more alkaline soil by adding lime. Thus, a French Hydrangea planted in a garden with lime added will bloom with pink flowers.

8. The conclusion of the argument cannot be true unless which of the following is true?

    Ⓐ The garden soil was not alkaline prior to the addition of lime.

    Ⓑ The hydrangea had blue blooms in the previous growing season.

    Ⓒ The gardener must reapply lime every growing season.

    Ⓓ The garden does not have any aluminum occurring naturally in the soil.

    Ⓔ The garden soil must be neutralized before adding lime.

While advocates of wind energy often cite environmental concerns as a reason for their argument to replace fossil fuels, they disregard the negative impact that wind turbines have on birds, bats, and their environment. Wind turbines are so lethal to birds that Germany halted a wind project over the potential risk to species with threatened populations. In America, the best localities for wind farms happen to coincide with the direct migration corridor of the seriously endangered whooping crane. Wind farms along their route not only present the risk of death, but also of confused or lost birds; lights on wind turbines have been known to disrupt the migratory routes of birds because they use stars as their migration map. Unfortunately, birds are unable to differentiate between natural and unnatural light sources. As a result of these environmental impacts, more research must be completed before wind energy is selected as the renewable energy source to replace nonrenewable fossil fuels.

9. Which of the following statements, if true, would best support the argument made in the passage?

    Ⓐ Wind power is inconsistent and depends on fossil fuels for backup on days that are not windy.

    Ⓑ Whooping cranes are not known to migrate at night, and instead use the sun as a guide.

    Ⓒ The cost of manufacturing and transporting wind turbines is extremely high.

    Ⓓ New wind turbines operate at such an extremely slow speed that birds are seldom injured by them.

    Ⓔ Pine trees in a forest are dying from holes bored by beetles because the population of beetle-eating bats has been decimated by wind turbines.

The study of past climates and ecological changes in Alaska are an important key to understanding the likely consequences of future climate changes in high latitude ecosystems. Future climate changes, whether triggered by human-induced changes in the atmosphere or by natural climate cycles, will result in changes in the species composition and
Line distribution of vegetation types. On the basis of the fossil record and climate history of Alaska, we can expect that future
5 periods of cooler, drier climate will result in shrinkage of forest boundaries, lowering of altitudinal tree line, and expansion of tundra vegetation into lower elevations. A future change to warmer, moister climates will result in expansion of Alaska's forests into areas now occupied by tundra. The past record also shows that the magnitude of future global scale climate changes and ecological responses will be greater at high latitudes than at lower latitudes.

10. Which of the following statements about climate change in Alaska is supported by the passage?

    Ⓐ The total area occupied by tundra will decrease if there is a climate shift toward warmer, moister air.

    Ⓑ The most consequential threat to vegetation growth in Alaska comes from climate changes induced by humans.

    Ⓒ Climate changes generate more significant ecological changes in mountains and higher altitudes than in areas at or near sea level.

    Ⓓ By studying the past climates of Alaska, scientists are able to predict the pattern of future climate cycles in Alaska.

    Ⓔ If a cooler, drier climate prevails, the forest perimeter will expand into area currently covered by tundra.

As Virginia Woolf's letters and diaries amply record, music was a central part of her social life as it was for many of her contemporaries and she was at her best as a humorist writing about these occasions. She records with glee the various mishaps that befall musicians and audiences—a prima donna throwing down her music in a rage; a button popping off the plump Clive Bell's waistcoat during the slow movement of a piano sonata; an elderly man crashing loudly but astonishingly
Line
5   unhurt down the stairs at Covent Garden. The social conventions, artifice and pretensions governing these performances intrigue her and allow her to sharpen her wit, but music wasn't only an occasion for slapstick humour or social satire. It played a central part in the political vision of Woolf's writing, shaping her understanding and representations of feminism and sexuality, pacifism and cosmopolitanism, social class and anti-Semitism. And it informed, too, the formal experiments of her prose. Woolf learned many of her astonishing literary innovations from music—adopting from Wagner's operas, for
10   example, the technique of shifting from one narrative perspective to another in order to represent the unspoken thoughts and feelings of her characters.

11. According to the passage, music was important to Virginia Woolf for all of the following reasons EXCEPT

Ⓐ it introduced her to musical methods from which she derived new literary elements

Ⓑ it allowed her to avoid social conventions and instead conduct formal social experiments on her contemporaries

Ⓒ it granted her opportunities for socializing in her community

Ⓓ it provided her with material that she could write as humorous anecdotes

Ⓔ it helped mold her view of contemporary politics

12. In the context in which it appears, "informed" (line 8) most nearly means

Ⓐ permeated

Ⓑ encumbered

Ⓒ apprised

Ⓓ condoned

Ⓔ expunged

Clues to the origin of Pluto's moons are found in the shapes and orientations of their orbits. All four appear to be co-planar and nearly circular. If the moons were gravitationally captured objects they would more likely have inclined and elliptical orbits, like the outermost moons of Jupiter. They are also in nearly resonant orbits, that is, the orbital period of
Line
one body is related to that of another by a simple fraction—something that develops via small perturbations over time.
5   This evidence indicates that the moons had plenty of time to interact gravitationally with each other, and therefore were probably born together. This would be the case if the moons formed in a single titanic collision between Pluto and another Kuiper belt object billions of years ago. This collision scenario is supported by increasingly sophisticated computer simulations that predict the aftermath of such planetary encounters. The simulations show that the orbits of Pluto's moons would have circularized quickly, perhaps in only a few hundred million years. The simulations have not explained,
10   however, why the moons' orbits are so mysteriously close to exact resonance—but not precisely so—after all this time.

13. Which of the following can be inferred from the passage regarding Jupiter? (Select all answers that apply.)

Ⓐ It has moons whose orbits are in exact resonance.

Ⓑ It collided with Pluto billions of years ago.

Ⓒ Its outermost moons were gravitationally captured.

14. Select the sentence in the passage that presents a possible origin of Pluto's moons.

16

John Martin, born in the week that the Bastille was stormed in July 1789, was an instinctive revolutionary. His generation may have suffered from a misty-eyed envy of new-found liberties in America and France, but they understood what practical revolution might mean at home and they strove to achieve liberation from repression and tyranny without bloodshed; very largely they succeeded.

Line 5   Martin has often, and wrongly, been seen as a religious fanatic by a comprehensive misunderstanding of his paintings and by false association with his schizophrenic arsonist brother. He has also been portrayed as a Luddite (by critics who should have known better) and by Ruskin, a late contemporary, as a mere artisan in lamp-black. Poor Martin. Despite his very evident technical deficiencies as a painter—he inevitably suffers by comparison with his friends and contemporaries Turner and Constable—he was equally adept at creating a theatrical sense of a world undergoing irreversible change, and

10 more fervent than either in his desire to be an engine of that change. If there were dramatists better placed to portray the dilemmas of the human condition, and one immediately thinks of Shelley and Byron, of Delacroix and Dickens, no-one came closer than Martin to designing the perfect sets on which to act out the drama: he was the supreme architect and engineer of the sublime.

15. The passage indicates that the author would agree with which of the following statements? (Select all answers that apply.)

    A John Martin's painting skills were insufficient compared to other painters of the time period.

    B Some critics have incorrectly labeled John Martin as a religious zealot and Luddite.

    C John Martin's contemporaries demanded governmental changes that resulted in the French Revolution.

16. Which of the following can be inferred from the passage regarding Martin's participation in the theater?

    Ⓐ He was sought-after as a set designer because famous authors approved of his design for their novels.

    Ⓑ He used set design to illustrate the need for nonviolent revolution to gain freedom from government control.

    Ⓒ He created sets that had religious undertones.

    Ⓓ He lacked the technical art skills needed as a painter to design successful theater sets.

    Ⓔ He was compared to highly respected contemporary playwrights because he wrote plays that accurately illuminated problems in society.

The Greek-speaking rhetorician and writer Lucian of Samosata, born around 125 CE in what is now known as Syria, has had a somewhat mixed reception through the ages. Scholars agree that his contemporaries and successors viewed him with a great deal of respect. Early Christians were less admiring of Lucian and his pagan and vitriolic pen, though by the time of

Line the renaissance, he had regained favor among learned people. Italian humanists translated him from Greek, and thus Lucian

5 went on to influence the post-renaissance modern world.

    While scholars divide themselves over whether Lucian's greatest contribution lies in his preservation of classical rhetoric or his innovative force as a satirist, in either case what continues to interest casual readers and scholars alike is his profound sense of humor in investigating what are serious philosophical subjects: the moral life, epistemology, and politics. It is perhaps epistemology which can be seen as Lucian's main focus of satire in what has become his best known work, Vera

10 Historia (in English, True Story), a detailed and elaborate fantasy about travelling to the moon.

17. Select the sentence in the passage that presents the author's opinion about why people still read Lucian's works today.

Given the wealth of available information about Civil War soldiers, the comparative poverty of such knowledge about Civil War sailors borders on the astonishing. Two explanations account for this imbalance. First, the broad narrative of presidential leadership and the clash of armies in Virginia that Ken Burns's *The Civil War* told so powerfully all but
Line
5 excludes naval forces from the tale. Second, existing accounts of the naval Civil War have focused on the strategic role of naval forces in the contest, the governmental architects of naval policy, the naval officers who masterminded operations, and the innovations in technology and weaponry to the near exclusion of the enlisted sailors' war. No image of "Jack Tar" comparable to Bell I. Wiley's classic portraits of "Billy Yank" and "Johnny Reb" fills the popular imagination or the works of Civil War historians.

Because the navy, unlike the army, was racially integrated, understanding the history of black sailors requires some effort
10 but even more interpretive caution to unravel it from that of all Civil War sailors. Exploring the similarities and differences in the experiences of black and white enlisted men must avoid viewing the racial groups in strictly monolithic terms that do not allow for internal complexity and diversity and shifting, if not altogether porous, borders. The work must also beware currently popular understandings of the black soldiers' experience. Often framed around the Fifty-fourth Massachusetts Volunteer Infantry, that tale depicts stoic sacrifice and daunting perseverance in pursuit of freedom and equality that in
15 the end was crowned with "Glory," the impression conveyed by the popular feature film. The black sailors' story fits awkwardly, if at all, within that image.

18. In the context in which it appears, "borders" (line 2) is best understood to mean

  Ⓐ verges

  Ⓑ imposes

  Ⓒ settles

  Ⓓ depends

  Ⓔ surrounds

19. The author suggests which of the following about the "image" (line 6) of Jack Tar?

  Ⓐ It is omitted from Civil War history because the Navy was not involved in many conflicts.

  Ⓑ It was not created until years after the Civil War.

  Ⓒ It is not as glorified as the representations of Civil War soldiers.

  Ⓓ It depicts a black sailor while other images focus on white Civil War soldiers.

  Ⓔ It was not created by a famous author.

20. The discussion about "popular misunderstandings" (line 13) suggests that

  Ⓐ the Navy was considered more elite than the army

  Ⓑ the public mistakenly assumes that all black enlistees fought for the Union

  Ⓒ few black soldiers enlisted to pursue freedom and equality

  Ⓓ the experience of black sailors was not worthy of retelling in a feature film

  Ⓔ accounts of black soldiers in the Civil War are often romanticized

21. Select the sentence in the second paragraph that describes a popular allegory of black soldiers' experiences in the Civil War.

Online learning is a relatively new development in K-12 education but is rapidly expanding in both number of programs and participants. Given this expansion and a dearth of existing research on the topic, it is critical to conduct rigorous evaluations of online learning in K-12 settings to ensure that it does what people hope it will do: help improve student learning.

Line
5   However, those undertaking such evaluations may well encounter a number of technical and methodological issues that can make this type of research difficult to execute. For example, the scant research literature on K-12 online learning evaluation provides few existing frameworks to help evaluators describe and analyze programs, or tools, such as surveys or rubrics, they can use to collect data or assess program quality. Another common challenge when students are studying online is the difficulty of examining what is happening in multiple, geographically distant learning sites. And multifaceted
10 education resources—such as vast Web sites offering a wide range of features or virtual schools that offer courses from multiple vendors—are also hard to evaluate, as are programs that utilize technologies and instructional models that are new to users.

    Furthermore, evaluations of online learning often occur in the context of a politically loaded debate about whether such programs are worth the investment and how much funding is needed to run a high-quality program; about whether online
15 learning really provides students with high-quality learning opportunities; and about how to compare online and traditional approaches. Understandably, funders and policymakers—not to mention students and their parents—want data that show whether online learning can be as effective as traditional educational approaches and which online models are the best. These stakeholders may or may not think about evaluation in technical terms, but all of them are interested in how students perform in these new programs. At the same time, many online program leaders have multiple goals in mind, such as
20 increased student engagement or increased student access to high-quality courses and teachers. They argue that test scores alone are an inadequate measure for capturing important differences between traditional and online learning settings. And, like educators in any setting—traditional or online—they may feel a natural trepidation about inviting evaluators to take a critical look at their program, fearing that it will hamper the progress of their program, rather than strengthen it.

22. The passage is primarily concerned with

    Ⓐ pointing out the disadvantages of online learning

    Ⓑ defending the vastness of online learning tutorials

    Ⓒ explaining the difficulties of evaluating online learning programs

    Ⓓ summarizing the policies that prevent online learning from expanding

    Ⓔ establishing the superiority of online schools in comparison to traditional schools

23. Which of the following situations is most analogous to the issues presented in lines 6-9 ("For example . . . sites")?

    Ⓐ An airline executive assesses an under-researched flight training program that is operating in many different cities.

    Ⓑ A biologist attempts to determine the different components of soil samples from all seven continents.

    Ⓒ A traditional classroom teacher fails to measure his students' progress with a standardized test.

    Ⓓ A lawyer and an incarcerated client, who are unable to meet in person, use web cameras to discuss trial strategy.

    Ⓔ An author who is intimidated by technology writes her novels in a notebook.

24. According to the passage, which of the following is a reason it is difficult to evaluate online learning programs? (Select all answers that apply.)

    Ⓐ Students are spread out in numerous locations instead of being together in a central classroom.

    Ⓑ Some online education leaders who have goals in addition to increased test scores are hesitant to allow scrutiny of their programs.

    Ⓒ There is a dearth of current literature and resources to help analysts effectively evaluate programs.

25. Select the sentence in the third paragraph in which the author introduces examples of objectives for students that cannot be measured by test scores.

16

The religious views of Charles Darwin, the venerable Victorian naturalist and author of the *Origin of Species* (1859) never cease to interest modern readers. Bookshops and the internet are well-stocked with discussions of Darwin's views and the implications of his theory of evolution for religion. Many religious writers today accuse Darwin of atheism. Some popular proponents of atheism also enlist Darwin to their cause. Even while Darwin was still alive there were widely varying descriptions of his religious opinions—which he kept mostly private. In 1880 the Austrian writer Ernst von Hesse-Wartegg visited Darwin at his home, Down House, in Kent. The coachman who drove Hesse-Wartegg from the train station at Orpington opined of the famous Mr. Darwin: "Ha es en enfidel, Sar- yes, an enfidel—an unbeliever! and the people say he never went to church!". The passage quoted here was actually marked in Darwin's copy of this German newspaper (the Frankfurter Zeitung und Handelsblatt)—no doubt it amused Darwin as much as the German attempt to capture the Kentish accent through phonetic spelling.

Other commentators were more generous in their interpretations of Darwin's religiosity. The modern myth of a timeless conflict of science and religion was far from the reality experienced by Victorian readers who first turned the pages of Darwin's *Origin of Species* and *Descent of Man* (1871). It is now widely forgotten that the scientific debate over the theory of evolution was over within twenty years of the publication of *Origin of Species*. Yet how could that be given that the Victorians were, by and large, far more religious than people generally are today and the scientific evidence for evolution was far less complete than it is now? The explanation is that for very many Victorians the choice was not between God and science, religion or evolution, but between different notions of how God designed nature. It was already widely accepted that fixed natural laws (or secondary laws) had been discovered that explained natural phenomena from astronomy and chemistry to physiology and geology. Darwin, it was believed, had simply discovered a new law of nature designed by God. And it seems this was how Darwin himself viewed at least part of the religious implications of his evolutionary theory. This also makes it all the more understandable that Darwin was buried by the nation in Westminster Abbey in 1882.

Line 5

10

15

20

26. The author cites the coachman's quotation (lines 7-8) primarily in order to

 Ⓐ support the claim that Victorians were more religious than the people of today

 Ⓑ provide an example of one of the commonly held perceptions about Darwin during his lifetime

 Ⓒ suggest that Germans had a difficult time understanding English accents

 Ⓓ support the claim of modern writers that Darwin was an atheist

 Ⓔ challenge the theory that Darwin believed in God

27. In the context in which it appears, "capture" (line 9) is best understood to mean

 Ⓐ possess

 Ⓑ mock

 Ⓒ represent

 Ⓓ seize

 Ⓔ acquit

28. Which of the following differences between modern readers of the *Origin of Species* and Victorians readers of the *Origin of Species* is indicated by the passage? (Select all answers that apply.)

 Ⓐ Modern readers are generally less interested in Darwin's religious views than were Victorian readers.

 Ⓑ Modern readers are generally less religious than were Victorian readers.

 Ⓒ Modern readers are aware of more scientific evidence supporting evolution than were Victorian readers.

29. The author of the passage would probably agree with which of the following statements?

 Ⓐ The debate between religion and science concerning evolution waged for more than two decades after the publication of the *Origin of Species*.

 Ⓑ The religious views of Darwin were of little interest to the public in Victorian era England.

 Ⓒ Some modern atheists cite Darwin as a supporter of their cause because he believed evolution was created by God.

 Ⓓ It would be unusual for an atheist to be entombed by England in Westminster Abbey.

 Ⓔ Darwin entertained atheists from all over the world at his home in Kent.

Twins. triplets, and higher-order multiples are more frequently conceived by women undergoing assisted reproductive techniques, women under 20 or over 35, and women with a family history of multiple gestations than other women in the general population. In the two decades surrounding the new millennium, the number of women pregnant with multiples rose substantially. This was attributed to the increase of pregnancies resulting from in vitro fertilization (IVF) in which the doctor transferred multiple embryos back into their patients. Starting in 2010, however, most doctors practicing IVF reduced transfers to a single embryo because of the high risk and increased medical costs of multiple gestations. Yet the ratio of the number of women pregnant with multiples to the number of women pregnant with a singleton has remained level and not decreased.

30. Which of the following, if true, would help resolve the apparent paradox?

Ⓐ The number of women undergoing IVF has increased significantly since 2010.

Ⓑ The number of triplet pregnancies has decreased since 2010.

Ⓒ In 2010, researchers discovered that men with a family history of identical twins have a higher chance of fathering identical twins.

Ⓓ The success rate of IVF leading to live births has increased by over 40% in twenty years.

Ⓔ The number of women over 35 who have conceived since 2010 has risen sharply.

Problem Sets Answer Key

Fill-in-the-Blank Problem Set—Page 372

1. C   Possible Prephrases: relationship, connection, link

    The answer that best matches the prephrases is *correlation*.

    Vocabulary:
    juncture: point in time or place   *succession:* the use of sequence or order
    grievance: complaint   *contrition:* remorse

2. D   Possible Prephrases: affected, harmed, hindered

    Because the algae is a problem, it's likely a negative word that fits in the blank. The best choice is (D), *plagued*.

    Vocabulary:
    cowed: frightened or intimidated

3. (i) B (ii) E   Possible Prephrases: (i) thought, named (ii) title, description, classification

    The first blank is Cause and Effect; if the country has low rates of diseases, it is going to be considered a healthy country. Choice (B) is best. The second blank is a Definition blank, as it is defined by the description that precedes it. The best answer is (E).

    Vocabulary:
    contemplated: thoughtfully considered   *resolution:* a formal opinion or decision
    deemed: regarded; judged   *designation:* an identification
    envisioned: pictured mentally   *endowment:* a monetary gift or award

4. B   Possible Prephrases: forced, only able

    Having to express their concerns to loved ones was a consolation; they would rather have had a public forum or receptive audience. Thus, *reduced* is the best answer.

5. (i) C (ii) A   Possible Prephrases: (i) insignificance, basics (ii) basic, simple

    The two blanks have similar meanings. The first blank is defined by the tasks—filing and retrieving coffee—which are basic responsibilities that might surprise someone majoring in a complicated field like engineering. Both (C) and (A) describe the basic nature of the tasks.

    Vocabulary:
    whimsy: excessively playful notion   *elemental:* basic
    gravity: seriousness   *intricate:* complicated
    triviality: insignificance; commonness   *somber:* serious

16

6. (i) A (ii) D   Possible Prephrases: (i) increase (ii) difficult, declining

The first blank is going to be similar in meaning to *increase*. Choice (A), *surge*, means *swelling*.

The second blank is a Contrast Question Stem, filled with a word that would show the increase in teachers with advanced degrees and in education programs proves the magazine article wrong. While it's not quite possible to prephrase the blank perfectly, you get a sense that we are looking for a word with a negative meaning to oppose the increase idea expressed earlier. Choice (E) has a meaning that is positive and sort of opposite of the *difficult* or *declining* prephrase, while (F) makes no sense. Choice (D), *inaccessible*, is best.

Vocabulary:
inaccessible: not easy to enter

7. (i) C (ii) F (iii) G
Possible Prephrases: (i) dividing, disagreement (ii) persuasions (iii) agreement, a solution

The first blank is defined by the second sentence, in which we learn the two sides are divided on or disagree about an issue. Thus it is a *divisive* issue, choice (C). Beware of *sovereign* in the first blank, as some students may associate the term *popular sovereignty* with the topic and erroneously pick this Related Word. The second blank is similar to *persuasions* because *the North believed X and the South believed Y*, where *X* and *Y* are similar in form. Choice (F) is closest in meaning to *persuasions*. Given this disagreement (the cause), the Fire-Eaters feared a lack of agreement or a lack of a solution (the effect). Choice (G) is best for the third blank.

Vocabulary:
sovereign: supreme; indisputable
copious: abundant
divisive: creating division
hostilities: abundant
sentiments: opinions
reconciliation: agreement; settlement
discord: disagreement
veracity: honesty; truthfulness

8. E   Possible Prephrases: bad, untrustworthy

In this Definition and Cause and Effect sentence, the blank is defined by *evil natures*. Also, the cause is that people are naturally bad and the effect is that they *should not be trusted to govern other people*. The best answer is *malevolent*, as it is defined as *evil*.

Vocabulary:
cavalier: arrogant and snobbish
genteel: elegant and refined
esoteric: secret or confidential
audacious: bold and fearless
malevolent: evil

16

9. **(i) A (ii) E (iii) G**
   Possible Prephrases: (i) leaving, giving up (ii) manipulations (iii) bad, wicked, evil

   The first blank is defined by the previous sentence, as indicated by the word *this*: *gave up the Russian throne*. The definition of *abdication* is *the act of giving up a throne*. The second blank is similar to the word *manipulate*, and choice (E), *machinations*, means *schemes* or *crafty plots*. The final blank is defined by the three examples of Ivan's behavior at the end of the passage, all of which are *contemptible—or despicable—*acts. Choice (G) is the answer.

   Vocabulary:
   relegation: demotion   *corpulence:* obesity; fatness
   platitude: remark repeated too often   *regal:* relating to a king
   remunerations: payments   *intractable:* stubborn

10. **B and D**   Possible Prephrases: use, spin

    The word in the blank is similar to *spin*, meaning that previous presidents were able to manipulate the media. The best answers are (B) and (D). Choice (C), *dissuade*, has a meaning that is somewhat opposite of our prephrase. The remaining three answer choices do not make sense.

11. **C and F**   Possible Prephrases: poor, shameful, sneaky

    The blank continues in similar manner to *poor customer service* and can be defined by *shameful settlement amounts* and *delayed claim payments*. The best answers are (C) and (F).

    Vocabulary:
    adept: very skilled   *lethargic:* drowsy; sluggish
    slothful: lazy   *righteous:* morally right; virtuous
    underhanded: dishonorable   *unscrupulous:* not abiding by morals

12. **C and F**   Possible Prephrases: non-local, all-inclusive, all-encompassing

    This is a Contrast and Cause and Effect Sentence. The contrast comes from *smaller, local jurisdictions*. The blank is the opposite of this. And the sentence states that the districts were divided up (the effect) because the residents did not want a large, non-local, central ministry (the cause). The best two answers are *boundless* and *sweeping*.

13. B and F   Possible Prephrases: grows well

In this Contrast sentence, the word in the blank is going to show that the plant does well in shade gardens despite its preference for full sun. The best answers are (B), *thrives*, and (F), *flourishes*.

Vocabulary:
languishes: to become weak or feeble   *compensates*: to offset or counterbalance

14. A and B   Possible Prephrases: stopped, blocked

We can solve this question through Contrast (*at one time was believed to be a certainty*) or through the Definition (*members...have vowed that the bill will not be passed*) methods. If the bill was once certain, it is now not certain. Thus, it is being stopped or blocked. And the blank is being defined by *not be passed*. The best answers are (A) and (B).

Vocabulary:
stymied: hindered   *transcended*: risen above; exceeded
impeded: hindered   *elicited*: called forth; brought out
sanctioned: approved   *sullied*: made dirty

15. C and D   Possible Prephrases: rebellion, uprising

In this Similarity sentence, the word in the blank is similar to secession. The best answers are (C) and (D).

Vocabulary:
complaisance: being agreeable   *sedition*: rebellion against a government
ratification: the act of approving   *acclimatization*: adaptation
insurrection: rebellion; resistance   *subordination*: the act of placing lower in rank

16

1. D   Prephrase: was not comprehensive or a sufficient explanation

    General Inference Question
    (A) Opposite Answer
    (B) Most attractive wrong answer. But the theory was not proven wrong; it was actually confirmed with evidence that helped better explain the theory.
    (C) The theory was not sufficient as an explanation; the passage did not say whether it was sufficient or insufficient for predicting disasters.
    (E) Extreme Answer (*only*)

2. D   Prephrase: better understand not only the geological history of our planet, but also the powerful, and often destructive, forces associated with plate boundaries.

    Reasons and Results Question
    (A) Not discussed in passage.
    (B) Copycat Answer. The sufficient explanation was made in the 1960s.
    (C) True to You. While this is a viable reason for continuing investigation, the author does not state it explicitly. Plus, the answer omits information about mountain ranges and oceanic trenches, which were also included in the same portion of text.
    (E) Not discussed in passage and somewhat of a Copycat Answer.

3. C   Prephrase: other ethnic groups are not included

    Main Idea Question
    (A) True To You (?) and Copycat. This answer uses several words from the passage to distract test takers from the fact that its point is never made in the passage.
    (B) True To You (?). The passage never implies or states this.
    (D) Not discussed in the passage.
    (E) True to a Point, Opposite and Copycat. The phrase *critics contend* seems to be heading in the right direction but then it turns into an Opposite Answer. The author says that public policy is shaped by white and black histories, but that it should include all of America's races.

4. B   Prephrase: The antagonism between Faulkner and Mississippi

    Main Idea Question
    (A) True to a Point/Copycat: The first paragraph mentions *middle-class pretensions*, but Faulkner's criticism of the South involves many other factors.
    (C) Copycat: This is never indicated in the passage, but the phrase *Civil Rights movement* is used.
    (D) True to a Point: Only one-half of the third paragraph deals with Faulkner's *escape*.
    (E) The last paragraph suggests that Faulkner eventually does *face* and *deal with* his culture, but that is only at the end; the rest of the passage is about his antagonism towards his culture.

5.   A and B   Prephrase: Difficult to prephrase

General Inference Question
(C)   Copycat: The passages mentions both Hollywood and the appeal of the Faulkner's "localness," but there is no indication that he was in Hollywood to work on movie adaptations of his novels.

6.   C   Prephrase: The Civil Rights movement makes it easy to undervalue his personal struggle

General Inference Question
(A)   This idea is not indicated in the passage
(B)   Copycat: This answer plays on *laugh* in the sentence before the line reference.
(D)   While Faulkner criticized Mississippi for its racial politics, the article does not indicate whether Faulkner participated in the Civil Rights movement
(E)   Copycat: This answer plays on *emotions* in line 13, but is never stated in the passage. Plus, Faulkner did not expose racism, he simply commented on it.

7.   C   Prephrase: exists

Vocabulary-In-Context Question
(A)   reposes: lies down
(B)   feigns: lies; fakes
(C)   prevails: exists generally
(D)   spans: stretches
(E)   entombs: buries

8.   D   Prephrase: Difficult to prephrase

Argument Passage Assumption Question
The passage states that flowers will be pink when the soil "is alkaline and free of aluminum." It doesn't matter how much lime the gardener adds to create alkaline conditions; if there is aluminum in the soil, the blooms will not be pink.

9.   E   Prephrase: Impossible to prephrase

Argument Passage Strengthen and Question
The author's argument is that wind energy must be studied more because it is harmful to birds, bats, and their environment. Only answer choice E presents a scenario in which one of these items is harmed (and actually both bats and the environment are harmed).

10. A   Prephrase: Impossible to prephrase

Facts and Details Question
(A)   The correct answer, supported by the fourth sentence of the passage (lines 6-7)
(B)   Copycat: The passage is more about changes to Alaska vegetation than about threats to it; the passage uses human-induced which is similar to the phrase in this answer choice.
(C)   This answer plays on the word *latitude* in the last sentence, hoping you mistake it for *altitude*. Remember, every word counts in a GRE answer choice!
(D)   Copycat/True to a Point: Studying the past climates of Alaska is a *key to understanding the likely consequences of future climate changes*, not the pattern of future climate *cycles*.
(E)   Opposite: If there is a cooler climate, there will be *shrinkage of forest boundaries*.

16

11. B   Prephrase: Impossible to prephrase

Facts and Details Question
(A)   True: Lines 8-11
(B)   Copycat: This answer uses *allowed*, *social conventions*, and *formal...experiments*, which are all words used in the passage.
(C)   True: Line 1
(D)   True: Lines 2-5
(E)   True: Lines 6-8

12. A   Prephrase: influenced; penetrated; filled

Vocabulary-In-Context Question
(A)   permeated: penetrated
(B)   encumbered: burden
(C)   apprised: gave notice to
(D)   condoned; approved
(E)   expunged: erased

13. C   Prephrase: Difficult to prephrase

General Inference Question
(A)   The passage states that Pluto's moons are nearly resonant, but nothing is mentioned or inferred about the resonance of Jupiter's moons.
(B)   The passage states that Pluto collided with another Kuiper belt object; there is no inference that this object was Jupiter.
(C)   In lines 2 to 3, the sentence suggests that Pluto's moons were not gravitationally captured because their shapes are round and their orbits resonant. Jupiter, on the other hand, has outer moons with inclined and elliptical orbits because they were gravitationally captured. This correct answer uses a lot of the same words from the text, as do the other two answers, likely because there are not a lot of synonyms that can be used to adequately explain this science concept.

14. Sentence: *This would be the case if the moons formed in a single titanic collision between Pluto and another Kuiper belt object billions of years ago.*

Purpose Question
The phrase *this would be the case* refers to *probably born together*, so imagine the sentence reading as follows: *The moons were probably born together and formed in a single titanic collision between Pluto and another Kuiper belt object billions of years ago.*

15. A and B   Prephrase: Impossible to prephrase

Facts and Details Question

(A) True: The passage states "Despite his very evident technical deficiencies as a painter—he inevitably suffers by comparison with his friends and contemporaries Turner and Constable...."

(B) True: The passage states "Martin has often, and wrongly, been seen as a religious fanatic" and "He has also been portrayed as a Luddite (by critics who should have known better)...."

(C) False: Martin was born when the Bastille was stormed *during* the French Revolution. The passage states that he and his contemporaries looked for a "practical revolution" "without bloodshed" unlike the recent French Revolution.

16. B   Prephrase: Difficult to prephrase

General Inference Question

(A) The famous authors are cited for being exemplars of dramatists who best "portray[ed] the dilemmas of the human condition." They did not seek Martin out to design sets for their stories.

(B) This is the correct answer. The passage indicates that Martin's generation "strove to achieve liberation from repression and tyranny without bloodshed" and that the "instinctive revolutionary" Martin was able to be "an engine of that change" by designing the "perfect sets on which to act out the drama" of a "world undergoing irreversible change."

(C) Opposite Answer: Martin was mislabeled as a religious fanatic; nothing indicates his sets had any religious influence.

(D) True to a Point: Martin had "very evident technical deficiencies as a painter," but "no-one came closer than Martin to designing the perfect sets."

(E) Martin was a set designer, not a playwright.

17. Sentence: *While scholars divide themselves over whether Lucian's greatest contribution lies in his preservation of classical rhetoric or his innovative force as a satirist, in either case what continues to interest casual readers and scholars alike is his profound sense of humor in investigating what are serious philosophical subjects: the moral life, epistemology, and politics.*

Purpose Question
The opinion comes at the end of this complex sentence: *what continues to interest casual readers and scholars alike is his profound sense of humor in investigating what are serious philosophical subjects.*

18. A   Prephrase: nears; approaches

Vocabulary-In-Context Question
(A) verges: borders

19. C   Prephrase: the image of a sailor is not comparable to the images of soldiers

General Inference Question
(A)   It was not *omitted*; it just wasn't comparable to the other two. The other part of this answer that is untrue is *the Navy was not involved in many conflicts*. If you selected this answer, you are assuming incorrectly.
(B)   This statement is partially true about the other two images, not of Jack Tar. They were created during the Civil War, but later depicted by Wiley.
(D)   This is not suggested.
(E)   Selecting this answer is inferring too much.

20. E   Prephrase: people think only of the story from a movie when they imagine black enlistees

General Inference Question
(A)   Not stated in the passage; if anything, the army was more glorified than the Navy, since there is a lack of information.
(B)   True to You?
(C)   Extreme. *Few* makes this hard to defend, and actually the opposite was true in most cases. But neither side is indicated about African American sailors.
(D)   This is not stated.

21.   Sentence: *Often framed around the Fifty-fourth Massachusetts Volunteer Infantry, that tale depicts stoic sacrifice and daunting perseverance in pursuit of freedom and equality that in the end was crowned with "Glory," the impression conveyed by the popular feature film.*

Purpose Question
An allegory is a material representation of an abstract idea, and the black soldiers of the Civil War are represented by the characters in *Glory*.

22. C   Prephrase: The problems with evaluating online learning

Main Idea Question
(A)   The author never says online learning is ineffective; he just cites problems with making those judgments.
(B)   True but Wrong: The author does state that there are vast websites, but this is not the central idea throughout the passage.
(D)   This is untrue and not discussed.
(E)   The author remains neutral, describing online learning but not judging it in comparison to traditional classrooms.

23. A   Prephrase: Impossible to prephrase, but you should note the line reference. It says that it is hard to evaluate a program without existing research and with learning taking place at different sites.

Parallel Reasoning Question
(B)   Nothing is noted about existing research in this situation.
(C)   Nothing is noted about existing research or distance learning in this situation.
(D)   Nothing is noted about existing research in this situation.
(E)   Nothing is noted about existing research or distance learning in this situation.

24. **A, B, and C** Prephrase: There are reasons listed throughout the second and third paragraph.

    Facts and Details Question
    (A) True. Lines 8-9: *Another common challenge when students are studying online is the difficulty of examining what is happening in multiple, geographically distant learning sites.*
    (B) True. Lines 20-23: *They argue that test scores alone are an inadequate measure for capturing important differences between traditional and online learning settings. And, like educators in any setting—traditional or online—they may feel a natural trepidation about inviting evaluators to take a critical look at their program, fearing that it will hamper the progress of their program, rather than strengthen it.*
    (C) True. Lines 6-8: *For example, the scant research literature on K-12 online learning evaluation provides few existing frameworks to help evaluators describe and analyze programs, or tools, such as surveys or rubrics, they can use to collect data or assess program quality.*

25. Sentence: *At the same time, many online program leaders have multiple goals in mind, such as increased student engagement or increased student access to high-quality courses and teachers.*

    Purpose Question
    The purpose of this sentence is to provide examples of goals that cannot be assessed by test scores.

26. **B** Prephrase: Give an example of someone alive during Darwin's time who thought he was an atheist

    Purpose Question
    (A) True but Wrong: The author does say that Victorians were generally more religious (line 15) but this is not the purpose of the quotation in the previous paragraph.
    (C) The author suggests that the Germans' attempt to phonetically write the accent was comical, but he does not suggest that the Germans couldn't understand the accent.
    (D) Modern writers discuss Darwin's views, but not all of them believe he was atheist.
    (E) The author believes that Darwin believed in God (lines 19-21), but the coachman is just an example of a Victorian who did not share his belief.

27. **C** Prephrase: portray; represent

    Vocabulary-In-Context Question

28. **B and C** Prephrase: Difficult to prephrase

    Compare and Contrast Question
    (A) False: This is never indicated in the passage; if anything, the opposite is true because Victorian readers quit debating the issue within twenty years. We are still debating the issue today.
    (B) True: Lines 14-15
    (C) True: Lines 15-16

16

29. D   Prephrase: Impossible to prephrase

Hypothetical Inference Question
(A)   The debate *was over within twenty years* (line 14).
(B)   Extreme: The term little interest is hard to prove given that *Even while Darwin was still alive there were widely varying descriptions of his religious opinions* (lines 4-5).
(C)   True to a Point: Some modern atheists do cite Darwin as a supporter, but it's NOT because he believed in God.
(D)   True: The last two sentences of the passage state that if Darwin believed in God, it would support the state burying him in Westminster Abbey, inferring that if he didn't believe in God, this would be inconceivable.
(E)   There is no indication that Ernst von Hesse-Wartegg was an atheist.

30. E   Prephrase: Impossible to prephrase

Argument Passage Resolve the Paradox Question
The paradox exists in the fact that the suspected reason for multiple pregnancies has decreased, but the number of multiple pregnancies has not decreased as a result. So what could cause the numbers to stay the same? If there was an increase in something else that results in multiple pregnancies, such as a higher number of women over 35 conceiving.

Test Readiness

17

Test Readiness

POWERSCORE
TEST PREPARATION

Are you ready to take the GRE? If so, follow these guidelines for your final preparation.

The Day Before the GRE

The day before the test can be a stressful time. Try to relax as much as possible; read a book, see a movie, or relax with friends. Engage in activities that will get your mind off of the GRE.

Take a Study Break

You should not study the day (or the night) before the GRE! Professional athletes call this "tapering." After weeks or even months of training for a competition, athletes take a day or two off before the race or the game to give their muscles a chance to rest and rejuvenate. Your brain works the same way. Cramming the day before the GRE can cause fatigue and poor performance on test day. So taper your "workout" the day before the GRE by skipping the study session. In doing so, you will be alert and mentally ready to tackle the ten-section test.

Eat Dinner

Approach the GRE the way athletes approach an important game. Trained athletes eat a meal containing complex carbohydrates the night before competition. Carbohydrates are stored by the athletes' bodies and used for energy the following day, but carbohydrates aren't just fuel for your muscles—they are fuel for your brain, too. You will need to eat a dinner rich in complex carbohydrates, such as baked potatoes, bread, and pasta. A well-balanced meal the night before the test can help you stay sharp and focused on the day of the test.

Find the Test Center

Avoid any added stress on test day by finding the test center in advance if you do not already know where it is located. Drive by the test center and check out the parking situation. Also make sure that you don't need to stop for gasoline in the morning. These two simple precautions will prevent you from arriving late and being denied admission on test day.

Gather Your Materials

Get your test materials organized in advance. Gather up everything that you need for the test the night before to avoid running around the next morning. Assemble the following:

Confidence Quotation

"You have to have confidence in your ability, and then be tough enough to follow through," Rosalyn Carter, First Lady of the United States

- Your GRE Confirmation Email: This was emailed to you upon registration for the GRE. Paper-based test takers should bring their admission ticket instead.

- A Photo ID: You can use your driver's license or your passport. For a more detailed list of acceptable identification, visit ETS's website.

- A Snack: The entire test day takes approximately four hours, which might overlap with your normal lunch hour. There is an optional 10-minute break after the third section, at which time you will be able to eat a snack outside of the testing room. Take a granola bar or a bag of carrot sticks to avoid losing concentration when the hunger pangs arrive. Try to avoid a snack containing excess sugar.

- A Bottle of Water: You are also encouraged to drink water during each break. Take your own bottle of water in case the test center does not have drinking fountains.

- A Bag or Backpack: You will be asked to place your personal items in a designated area outside of the testing room, so keeping them together in a small bag or backpack is a good idea.

Get a Good Night's Sleep

Go to bed early the night before the test. The entire GRE experience is four very long hours, and if you don't get a decent night's sleep, you are guaranteed to fade halfway through the exam.

The Morning of the GRE

After a great dinner and a good night's sleep, you should be ready to conquer the one little test that will help you gain admission to the graduate school of your choice.

Eat Breakfast and (if applicable) Lunch

It's a proven fact that breakfast increases your concentration, mood, and memory. Eat a healthy breakfast on the morning of the GRE. Many former morning test takers have complained about the distraction caused by grumbling stomachs—both their own and those of other students—so save yourself any embarrassment or discomfort by eating a breakfast and taking a snack. If you are taking the test in the afternoon, be sure to eat breakfast and lunch.

Getting an adequate amount of sleep the night before the test can help your concentration and stamina.

Follow Your Normal Routine

If you wake up every morning and watch TV while you get ready for work, don't stop on account of the GRE! Similarly, if you've never had a cup of coffee, don't start on the morning of the test. Consistency in your routine will allow you to focus on your primary objective—performing well on the test.

Dress in Layers

The temperature of the room can have an effect on your GRE results. If you are too hot or too cold, you may have trouble concentrating. To help control the temperature, dress in layers; peel down to a t-shirt if you're warm or add a sweatshirt if you're cold. Note, however, that the test center supervisor has the right to inspect hats, scarves, jackets, outerwear, and other personal items taken into the test room.

Leave Your Cell Phone in the Car

If cell phones are seen or heard in the testing center, you will be asked to leave. ETS is very specific about this rule, and does not allow any electronic devices (music players, timers, cameras, etc) in the test center. Avoid any temptation—and any risk—by leaving your cell phone and other electronic devices in the car.

Arrive on Time

Arrive at the test center thirty minutes prior to the test time indicated on your email confirmation or admission ticket. Don't forget to bring all of the following:

- Your email confirmation
- Photo ID
- A snack
- A bottle of water

Students who arrive after the time on the admission ticket will not be admitted to the test center!

Believe In Yourself

Confidence can go a long way, and since you have read the *PowerScore GRE Verbal Reasoning Bible*, you should feel confident and able. As you wait at the test center, visualize yourself writing exceptional essays and knowing the answers to all of the Quantitative and Verbal Reasoning questions. Many athletes use this same technique before a competition. Your performance will be a reflection of your own expectations.

At the Test Center

Upon entering the testing facility, you will be asked to stow your personal items in a designated area at the test center, outside of the test room. Many facilities have lockers for this purpose. You will check in with your test administrator, who will ask you to complete pre-test paperwork. Once finished, you will sit down with the test administrator and complete an electronic check-in process, where he or she will ask to see your photo ID. Administrators are instructed to deny admission to anyone who does not have valid ID or to anyone who does not match the photo on the ID. In addition, the administrator will take your picture to submit to ETS with your test results.

Snacks and drinks are allowed at the testing center, but must be consumed outside of the testing room during breaks.

Once you are ready to begin testing, you will be assigned a specific test room and a specific seat.

If you engage in any misconduct or irregularity during the test, you may be dismissed from the test center. Actions that could warrant such consequences include creating a disturbance, giving or receiving help, cheating, removing scratch paper from the room, eating or drinking in the testing room, and using a cell phone.

If you encounter a problem with the test or the test center itself, report it to the test supervisor. Reportable problems include power outages, clock malfunctions, and any unusual disturbances caused by an individual or group.

If you feel anxious or panicked for any reason during the test, close your eyes for a few seconds and relax by taking a deep breath. Think of other situations where you performed with confidence and skill.

After the Test

At the completion of the GRE, the test supervisor will collect your scratch paper. You will be asked whether you want to report or cancel your scores. If you choose to report them, you will receive an unofficial score on the Quantitative Reasoning and Verbal Reasoning sections, although a printout of these scores will NOT be provided. You will not know your Analytical Writing score until you receive the official results two to three weeks later.

Once you see your scores, you have the option to electronically report them to up to four colleges for free. If you wait to report these scores at a later date, there will be a fee to do so.

If you are tempted to cancel your score at the testing side, you must make this decision without the benefit of knowing how you scored. We caution you to cancel your score only when necessary. Some valid reasons to cancel your score include becoming sick during the test or being affected by a test center distraction. Once a score is cancelled, it cannot be reinstated and you do you receive a refund of your test fee.

Scores are mailed about three weeks after the test.

The official scores are mailed in two to three weeks.

Afterword

Thank you for choosing to purchase the PowerScore GRE Verbal Reasoning Bible. We hope you found this book useful and enjoyable, but most importantly, we hope this book helps you raise your GRE score.

In all of our publications we strive to present the material in the clearest and most informative manner. If you have any questions, comments, or suggestions, please do not hesitate to email us at:

 **gre@powerscore.com**

We love to receive feedback, and we do read every email that is sent to us.

Also, if you have not done so already, we strongly suggest you visit the website for this book at:

 **powerscore.com/grevrbible**

This free online resource area contains supplements to the book material, provides updates as needed, and answers questions posed by students. There is also an official evaluation form we encourage you to use.

If we can assist you in any way in your GRE preparation or in the college admissions process, please do not hesitate to contact us. We would be happy to help.

Thank you and best of luck on the GRE!

Appendix A
Roots and Affixes
Dictionary

18

Appendix A: Roots and Affixes Dictionary

POWERSCORE
TEST PREPARATION

Prefixes   (A prefix is placed at the beginning of a word to alter the meaning of the root)

a-, ab-, abs-: away, down, from. Examples: *alee, absent, abdicate, abstract*

ad-: toward, addition to. Examples: *advance, adjacent, adjoin, advocate*

age-, agere-, agi-: act. Examples: *agenda, agile*

ambi-, amphi: both, around. Examples: *ambidexterous, ambiguous, ambivalent. amphitheater*

a-, an-: not, without. Examples: *anarchy, against, atypical*

ante-: before. Examples: *antecedent, anteroom, anterior, antechamber, antebellum*

anthro-: human. Examples: *anthropology*

anti-: against. Examples: *antipathy, anti-aging, antibiotic, antihistamine*

aqua-: water. Examples: *aqueduct, aquatic, aqualung*

archa, arch, archi-: ancient. Examples: *archaic, archetype, archeology, archive*

arch-: leader, chief, first. Examples: *archbishop, archduke, archenemy*

auto-: self. Examples: *autobiography, autograph, automate*

be-: completely. Examples: *bewitch, bejewelled, bedazzle, bestow*

bi-: two, double. Examples: *bicycle, bicentennial, biweekly, biplane*

bible-: book. Examples: *bibliography, bibliophile, Bible*

bene-: good. Examples: *benefit, benevolent, beneficiary*

circum-: around, circular. Examples: *circumference, circumvent, circumnavigate*

contra-, counter-: against, opposite. Examples: *contraband, contraceptive, counterattack, contradict*

de-: 1. down. Examples: *descend, degenerate, decrease*
2. reversal. Examples: detoxify, de-ice, derail

di-: two, double. Examples: *dilemma, digress, dichotomy*

dia-: across, through. Examples: *diagram, dialect, diameter*

dis-: not, apart. Examples: *disappoint, dissect, disproportionate, disable, disinclined*

dyna-: power, ability. Examples: *dynamic, dynasty, dynamite*

ego-: self. Examples: *egotistical, egocentric*

en-, em-: to bring into the condition of. Examples: *enlighten, embitter, encircle, enroll, employ, embody*

equ-, equi-: equal. Examples: *equidistant, equivocal, equivalent*

Prefixes

ex-: out of, from. Examples: *excommunicate, exterminate, expel, extrovert*

hetero-: different. Examples: *heterogeneous, heterozygous, heterosexual*

homo-: same. Examples: *homogeneous, homozygous, homosexual*

in-, il-, im-, ir-,: 1. in, Examples: *incarcerate, introvert, illuminate, imbibe, immigrant, irrigate*
      2. not, Examples: *inexpensive, illegal, impossible, irresponsible*

inter-: between. Examples: *interstate, interact, interrupt, interlock, intersperse*

iso-: similar, equal. Examples: *isosceles, isocracy, isometric*

medi-: middle, between. Examples: *mediator, median, medium, mediocre, media*

miso-: hate. Examples: *misanthrope, misogyny*

mono-: one, single. Examples: *monopoly, monochrome, monocle, monotony*

multi-: many, much. Examples: *multitude, multiple, multicolor, multitask*

neo-: new. Examples: *neophyte, neonatal, neoclassical*

non-: not. Examples: *nonessential, noncompetitive, nontoxic, nonreciprocal*

ob-, oc-, of-, op-: 1. blocking, against. Examples: *obstruct, occult, offend, opponent*
      2. toward, to. Examples: *observe, occupy, opt*

omni-: all, every. Examples: *omnipotent, omnipresent, omniscient, omnivore*

pan-: all. Examples: *panacea, pandemic, panorama, panoply, panoptic*

para-: beside. Examples: *paralegal, parallel, paramount, parasite, paragraph*

per-: through, thoroughly. Examples: *perennial, pervade, perfect, perceive, permeate*

peri-: around. Examples: *perimeter, periscope, periphery*

philo-: love. Examples: *philosophy, philanthropy, bibliophile*

poly-: many. Examples: *polygon, polyglot, polygraph*

post-: after. Examples: *postscript, postpartum, postdate, postpone, postseason*

pre-: before. Examples: *preview, preseason, preapprove, precaution, preconceived, predestined, preliminary*

pro-: 1. before, moving forward. Examples: *prologue, provision, progress, procreate, propel, promote*
      2. in favor of. Examples: *proponent, pro-life, prohibition, protagonist*

re-: again. Examples: *repaint, reappraise, return, redo, redirect, recant, refurbish, regenerate*

syn-: acting together. Examples: *synchronize, syncopate, synonym, syndicate*

sol-, solo-, soli-: alone, single. Examples: *solely, soliloquy, solitary, solitude. soloist*

sub-, suf-, sup-, sur-, sus-: under, lower, nearly. Examples: *subsidiary, subway, subjugate, subliminal, subordinate, subtle, sufficient, supplant, suppress, susceptible, sustain*

super-: above, greater than. Examples: *superficial, supersede, supervise, superb, superfluous*

Prefixes

trans-: across, over. Examples: *transaction, translate, transcontinental, transport, transpose, transcended*

uni-: one. Examples: *unicycle, unicorn, union, universe, unitarian, unique, unify*

Roots (A root word is the basic form of a word containing the central meaning)

ace, acer, acri: bitter, sharp, sour. Examples: *acerbic, acetate, acrid*

acu: sharp. Examples: *acute, acumen, acupuncture*

ag, agi, act: do, move, go. Examples: *agitate, agile, actuate*

ali, allo, alter: other, different. Examples: *alien, allocate, alteration, alternate, altruism*

alt: high, deep. Examples: *altitude, altimeter, alto*

am, amor: love, friendship. Examples: *amiable, amicable, enamored, paramour*

anni, annu, enni: yearly. Examples: *annual, perennial, anniversary, annuity, centennial*

antiqu: old. Examples: *antique, antiquated, antiquity*

apt, ept: fitting, suitable. Examples: *adapt, aptitude, inept, adept*

arch: chief, rule. Examples: *monarchy, matriarch, patriarch, architect*

aster, astr: star. Examples: *asterisk, astronomy, asteroid, disaster*

aud, audio: hear, listen. Examples: *audiobook, auditory, auditorium, audible*

aug: increase. Examples: *augment, august*

bas: low. Examples: *bass, basement, abase, debase*

bell, belli: war, antagonism. Examples: *belligerent, antebellum, bellicose, rebellion*

brev: short. Examples: *brevity, abbreviate, brief*

caco: bad, harsh. Examples: *cacophony, cacography*

cad, cas, casc: to fall. Examples: *cadence, cascade, casualty*

cand: shining. Examples: *candle, incandescent, candidate, candid*

cap, cip, cept: to take. Examples: *capture, disciple, precipitate, concept, decept, intercept*

capit, capt: head. Examples: *decapitate, captain, capital*

carn: flesh. Examples: *carnivore, carnal, carnage, incarnate, reincarnate*

caus, caut: burn, heat. Examples: *caustic, cauterize*

cause, cuse, cus: cause, reason. Examples: *because, excuse, accuse*

ced, ceed, cede, cess: 1. go, move. Examples: *process, secede, succeed, exceed*
2. yield, surrender. Examples: *concede, intercede*

celer: fast. Examples: *accelerate, celerity, decelerated*

Roots

centr, centri: center. Examples: *central, centrifugal, eccentric, anthropocentric, egocentric, concentrate*

chrom: color. Examples: *monochrome, chromatography*

chron: time. Examples: *chronicle, chronological, anachronistic, synchronize*

cid, cide: kill. Examples: *homicide, genocide, insecticide, herbicide, suicide*

cis: cut. Examples: *scissors, precise, incision, concise, decision, excise*

cit: call, start. Examples: *incite, elicit, solicit*

civ, civil: citizen, same group. Examples: *civilian, civic, civility*

clam, claim: verbalize, say. Examples: *exclaim, proclaim, clamor, reclaim, acclaim*

clin: bend, lean. Examples: *recline, incline, inclination*

clud, clus, claus: shut, closed. Examples: *seclude, include, exclusive, recluse, clause, claustrophobic*

cogn, gnos: know. Examples: *cognition, recognize, agnostic, incognito, diagnose*

corp, corpus: body. Examples: *corporation, corpulent, incorporate, corpse*

cosm, cosmo: universe, world. Examples: *cosmopolitan, cosmos, microcosm, cosmonaut*

crea: create, origin. Examples: *creative, miscreant, procreate, recreation*

cred: believe. Examples: *incredible, credit, credence, credibility, credulous*

creas, cresc, cret, cru: rise, grow. Examples: *increase, crescendo, secrete, accrue*

crit: separate, choose. Examples: *criteria, critic, mediocrity*

cur, curs: run, happen. Examples: *incur, concur, occurrence, current, procure*

cycl, cyclo: wheel, circular. Examples: *Bicycle, cyclone, recycle*

deca, deci: ten. Examples: *decade, decathlon, decimal, decimate*

dem, demi, demo: people. Examples: *democracy, demonstration, endemic, pandemic*

dict: say, speak. Examples: *diction, edict, dictionary, contradict, predict, indict, malediction*

dign: worthy. Examples: *dignify, dignitary, indignant, dignity*

doc, doct: teach. Examples: *indoctrinate, doctor, document*

domin: master. Examples: *dominate, indomitable, dominion*

don: give. Examples: *donate, condone, donor*

dox: opinion, praise. Examples: *orthodox, paradox*

duc, duct: lead, bring. Examples: *induce, conductor, abduct, reduction, produce, transducer*

dura: hard, lasting. Examples: *durable, duration, endure, obdurate, duration*

fac, fact, fic, fect: do, make. Examples: *facilitate, facsimile, factory, efficient, effect*

Roots

fall, fals: deceive. Examples: *fallacy, falsify*

fid, fide, feder: faith, trust. Examples: *fidelity, confide, confidence, Fido, perfidious, federal*

fin: finish, completed. Examples: *infinite, final, definite*

fix: fasten, fix. Examples: *affix, fixture, prefix, suffix, crucifix, transfixed*

flex, flect: bend. Examples: *reflex, reflect, flexible, inflection, deflect*

flu, fluc, fluv: flowing, not fixed. Examples: *fluent, fluctuate, fluid, fluvial, influence, mellifluous*

form: form, shape. Examples: *transform, formation, uniform, formal, information*

forc, fort: strong. Examples: *fortify, comfort, fortitude, force, reinforce*

fract, frag: break. Examples: *fracture, fragment, fraction, infraction*

frater: brother. Examples: *fraternal, fraternize, fraternity*

fus: pour. Examples: *confusion, infuse, profuse, transfuse, diffuser*

gam, gamy: marriage, union. Examples: *monogamy, amalgamation, bigamy*

gen: origin, birth, race, kind. Examples: *genetics, generic, regenerate, genesis, pathogen*

gest: carry, bear. Examples: *congest, gestation, digest, suggest*

glu, glo: bond together. Examples: *conglomerate, glue, agglomerate, globe*

grad, gress: step, move forward. Examples: *graduate, progress, digress, biodegradable, gradual, aggressive*

graph, gram: written. Examples: *paragraph, diagram, grammar, graphic, biography, telegram*

grat: pleasing. Examples: *gratitude, congratulations, grateful, gratuitous*

grav: heavy, weighty. Examples: *gravity, gravitate, grave, gravel*

greg: group. Examples: *segregation, aggregate, congregation, gregarious*

here, hesi: stick. Examples: *adhesive, adhere, hesitate, coherence, heretic, cohesion*

hum, human: earth, man. Examples: *inhumane, humanity, exhume, humble, posthumous*

idio, idios: one's own. Examples: *idiom, idiosyncrasy, idiot, idiopathic*

ject: throw. Examples: *object, eject, abject, conjecture, deject, injection, project, reject, subjective, trajectory*

join, junct: join. Examples: *conjunction, conjoin, juncture, adjoin, joint, junction, subjunctive, adjunct*

juven: young. Examples: *juvenile, rejuvenate*

leg, legis: law. Examples: *legal, legislation, illegitimate*

levi: light. Examples: *levitate, levy, levin, levity, alleviate, levigate*

lexi: word. Examples: *dyslexic, lexicography, lexicon*

liber, liver: free. Examples: *liberate, deliverance, libertine, liberal, deliberate, livery*

liter: letters, words. Examples: *literacy, illiterate, literal, obliterate, literature, literary*

Roots

loc, loco: place. Examples: *location, local, relocate*

log: 1. study. Examples: *biology, anthropology, psychology,*
    2. word. Examples: *monologue, epilogue, catalog, logic*

loqu, locut: talk, speak. Examples: *eloquent, locution, soliloquy, loquacious*

luce, lumi, luna: light. Examples: *illuminate, luminary, translucent, luminous, lunar*

magn: great, bigger. Examples: *magnificent, magnanimous, magnify, magnate*

man: hand. Examples: *manufacture, manually, manipulate, manage, mangle, manifest*

mand: command. Examples: *commandment, mandatory, demand*

mar, mari, mer: sea. Examples: *marina, maritime, mariculture, marinade, mermaid,*

mater, matri: mother. Examples: *maternity, matriarch, mama, maternal, matrimony*

ment: mind. Examples: *mental, mentor, mention, dementia*

merg: sink, dip. Examples: *submerge, merge, emergency*

meter: measure. Examples: *metric, symmetry, altimeter, centimeter, geometry*

migr: wander, change locations. Examples: *migrate, emigration, migrational*

mir: look. Examples: *mirror, admire, mirage*

mit, miss: send. Examples: *submit, remit, submission, missionary, permission, commission, commit*

mobi, moto, mov: move. Examples: *automobile, motion, immobilize, mobile, motor, movie, removable*

mon: warn, remind. Examples: *admonish, monitor, monument, premonition*

mort: death. Examples: *mortuary, immortal, mortify, postmortem, mortician, amort*

nat: born, from. Examples: *nativity, natural, innate, nationality, natal, prenatal*

neg: deny. Examples: *negate, negative, renege, abnegate, neglect*

nomen, nomin: name. Examples: *nominate, nomenclature, nominee, denominator, nominative, ignominious*

nov: new. Examples: *novice, novel, novelty, innovate, nova, renovate, novitiate*

opti, opic: sight. Examples: *optical, myopic, optimist, optimum, panoptic*

ortho: straight, proper. Examples: *orthodox, orthopedic, orthodontics*

par: equal. Examples: *compare, disparity, separate, parity*

pater, patri: father. Examples: *paternal, patriot, paternity, patriarch, papa, expatriate, patrician*

path, pathy: feeling. Examples: *sympathy, empathy, antipathy, sympathize, telepathy, empathetic,*
    psychopath

ped: 1. foot. Examples: *pedestrian, pedal, impede, pedicure*
    2. child Examples: *pediatrician, pedantic, pedagogical, pedigree*

pel, puls: drive, urge. Examples: *propel, dispel, repulse, compel, compulsive, repel, impulse, pulsate*

pend, pens, pond: hang, weigh. Examples: *suspend, pendant, pensive, propensity, ponder, dependence,*
    suspense

Roots

phon: sound. Examples: *phonics, symphony, cacophony, telephone, homophone*

plac: please, settle. Examples: *placate, complacent, implacable, placebo, placid*

plic, ply: bend, fold. Examples: *complicate, implicate, explicate, plate, reply, implicit*

poli, polis: city. Examples: *metropolitan, metropolis, politician, policy, political*

pon, pos, pound: place, put. Examples: *exponent, impound, compound, position, deposit, dispose*

pop, pub: people. Examples: *population, populace, pop-culture, popular, publish, republic, publicity*

port: carry. Examples: *import, transportation, porter, deported, portable, exportation, support*

poten: power. Examples: *potent, potentate, omnipotent, potential, potency*

prehend, prehens: seize, grasp. Examples: *comprehend, apprehend, reprehensive, prehensile*

prima, prot: first. Examples: *primal, primary, primate, primer, prototype, protagonist, protozoan*

psych: mind. Examples: *psychiatrist, psychology, psychic, psychopath*

rect, recti: to make straight, right. Examples: *rectangle, rectify, rectitude, direction, resurrect, erect, insurrection*

reg, rig: rule. Examples: *regulate, register, regent, regal, regiment, rigor, rigid*

rid, ris: laughter. Examples: *ridicule, ridiculous, derisive, deride, riddle, risable*

rog, roga: ask. Examples: *interrogate, prerogative, derogatory, arrogant, rogation*

rupt: break. Examples: *rupture, interrupt, bankrupt, corrupt, erupt, abrupt, disrupted*

sacr, sanc, secr: sacred, holy. Examples: *sacrifice, sanctity, sacrilegious, sacrosanct, sanctify, sanctimonious, sanction, consecrate, secret, desecrate*

salv, salu: safe, healthy. Examples: *salvation, salutary, salvage, salubrity, salubrious*

sate, satis: enough. Examples: *satisfied, satiated, satisfactory, insatiable, sated, compensate*

sci, scio: know, knowledge. Examples: *science, subconscious, conscience, omniscient*

scrib, script: write. Examples: *prescribe, inscription, scribble, circumscribe, describe, transcribe, conscribe, conscription, descriptive, subscription*

scop: watch, see. Examples: *scope, periscope, microscopic, horoscope, endoscopy, kaleidoscope*

sec, sect: cut. Examples: *dissect, bisect, intersection, sect, sectarian, section*

sed, sid, sess: sit, settle. Examples: *sedate, sedentary, resident, sediment, insidious, preside, possess, obsess*

sen: old. Examples: *senior, senator, senile*

sent, sens: feel. Examples: *sentimental, sensible, sensor, sensual, desensitize, sensory*

sequ, secut, sue: follow, pursue. Examples: *consequence, sequential, sequel, consecutive, pursue, obsequious, sequester, prosecute*

serv: save, keep. Examples: *conserve, preserve, reserve, observe, service, deserve, conservation, preservative*

sign: sign, mark. Examples: *signature, insignia, consign, signatory, assign, signal, signify, design*

Roots

simil, simul: like, at the same time. Examples: *similar, simultaneous, assimilation, facsimile, simile, verisimilitude, simulator*

sist, sta, stit: stand. Examples: *assist, persist, constituent, stance, stamina, static, stationary, resist, consist*

solv, solu: loosen, come apart. Examples: *dissolve, solution, insolvent, soluble, resolute*

somn: sleep. Examples: *insomnia, somniferous, somnolent*

soph: wise. Examples: *sophomore, philosophy, sophistication, sophistry, sophist*

spec, spect, spic: look. Examples: *respect, inspect, conspicuous, specify, spectator, perspicacious, suspicion, spectacle, specimen, prospect*

stat, stab: stand, resist. Examples: *status, static, stable, establish, station*

string, strict: draw tight, close. Examples: *constrict, stringent, astringent, restriction, district, stricture*

stru, struct: build. Examples: *construe, construction, destructive, structure, instrument, obstruct*

sum, sumpt: take. Examples: *presume, presumptuous, assume, assumption, consume, sumptuous*

tact, tag, tang, tig, ting: touch. Examples: *contact, tactile, tangent, contingent, contiguous, contagious*

tele: distance. Examples: *television, telephone, telepathy, telescope, telecommuter, telegraph*

tempo: time. Examples: *temporary, contemporary, extemporize, temporal*

ten, tain: hold. Examples: *attention, tenacious, contain, maintain, sustainable, attain, tenant*

term: end, final. Examples: *termination, terminal, intermit, exterminate*

ter, terr, terra: earth. Examples: *territory, terrace, inter, terrier*

test: witness. Examples: *testimony, testify, contest, attest*

theo: god. Examples: *theology, theocracy, pantheon, theory, theocentric*

thesis, thet: to put forth. Examples: *hypothesis, antithesis, epithet, synthesis, aesthetics*

tort, tors: twist. Examples: *contortionist, torsion, distort, extort, torture*

tract: pull, draw. Examples: *tractor, attract, retract, extraction, contraction, traction*

trib: pay, give. Examples: *tribute, tribunal, tributary, diatribe, distribute, tribulation*

trud, trus: to thrust. Examples: *intrude, intrusion, abstruse, obtrude, extrude, protrusive*

turb: disturb. Examples: *disturbance, perturb, turbid, turbinate, turbulent*

urb: city. Examples: *urban, suburban, suburb, urbane, urbanite*

util: useful. Examples: *utilize, futile, utilitarian, utility, mutilate*

vac, vacu: empty. Examples: *vacuum, vacate, vacuous, evacuation*

vad, vas: go. Examples: *evasive, evade, invasion, invade, pervasive, pervade*

val, vail: strength. Examples: *prevail, valiant, valuable, avail, validate, valedictorian, convalescent*

ven, vent: come. Examples: *prevent, intervene, event, intervention*

Roots

ver, veri: truth. Examples: *veritable, veracity, aver, verify, verisimilitude*

verb: word. Examples: *verbose, verbal, verbatim, reverberate, verbalize*

vert, vers: turn. Examples: *convert, averse, reversal, divert, diversion, revert, inadvertent, diverse*

vinc, vict: conquer, win. Examples: *invincible, victorious, convict, evict, convince, victim*

viv, vit: live. Examples: *lively, vivacious, vitality, vivid, revive, survive*

voc, vok: call. Examples: *vocal, invoke, evoke, revoke, vocabulary, vocation, provoke*

vor: devour, eat. Examples: *carnivore, voracious, savory*

Suffixes   (A suffix is placed at the end of a word to create a new word or part of speech)

-able, -ible, -ile: able, capable of. Examples: *durable, accessible, fallible, reconcilable, infertile, versatile*

-acious, -ary, -ery, -ory, -hood, -ine, -ity, -ty, -ive, -ness, -ious, -ous, -ship, -tude: having the quality of. Examples: *mendacious, sagacious, legendary, robbery, sensory, neighborhood, masculine, temerity, brevity, kindness, quaintness, generous, ingenious, friendship, scholarship, exactitude, multitude*

-ade, -age, -ance, -ancy, -ency, -cy, -dom, -ice, -ion, -ment, -mony, -sion, -tion, -ure: act of, condition of, state of. Examples: *blockade, carnage, sustenance, flippancy, infancy, transparency, freedom, cowardice, champion, improvement, matrimony, tension, motivation, failure*

-al, -an, -ian: belonging to. Examples: *banal, informal, median, suburban*

-ary, -ate, -ee, -eer, -er, -or, -ist: one who. Examples: *secretary, potentate, advocate, absentee, employee, auctioneer, privateer, camper, mentor, activist*

-cule, -ling, -ette, -let: little. Examples: *miniscule, hatchling, cassette, anklet,*

-escent, -ize: becoming. Examples: *adolescent, putrescent, luminescent, crystallize, epitomize, specialize*

-en, -fic, -fy, -mize: to make, making. Examples: *broaden, scientific, beautify, mortify, minimize, optimize*

-esque, -ic, -id, -ish, -ly, -y: of, like. Examples: *picturesque, generic, intrepid, stylish, happily, flowery*

-ful, -ose : full of. Examples: *bountiful, plentiful, beautiful, bellicose*

-ism: belief in. Examples: *idealism, baptism, globalism, postmodernism*

-less: without. Examples: *homeless, hopeless, fearless, thoughtless*

-some: characteristic of. Examples: *troublesome, delightsome, quarrelsome*

-ward: in a direction. Examples: *westward, wayward, backward*

Appendix B
Vocabulary: Repeat Offenders

Appendix B
Vocabulary: Repeat Offenders

Top 700 Repeat Offenders

The following vocabulary list contains 700 of the most commonly-occurring GRE vocabulary words. Only study the words that are unfamiliar to you. Once you know a word, place a check mark next to it to avoid redundant studying. These words are also available in a printable format on our website at www.powerscore.com/greVRbible. For tips on studying vocabulary words, return to page 152.

☐ **abdicate**: (*vb*) to give up, often in a formal manner
King Edward VIII abdicated the throne in order to marry Mrs. Wallis Simpson, a divorced American.
Word Forms: abdicable, abdicative, abdicator, abdication   Antonym Form: unabdicative

☐ **aberrant**: (*adj*) unusual
My dog displayed aberrant behavior when he refused to greet me at the door or eat any of the treats I offered.
Word Forms: aberrance, aberrancy, aberrantly, aberrate, aberrational

☐ **abeyance**: (*n*) temporary suspension
The council voted to place the decision in abeyance for a month while more research was conducted.
Word Forms: abeyant, abeyancy

☐ **abjure**: (*vb*) to give up, often in a formal manner
King Edward VIII abjured the throne in order to marry Mrs. Wallis Simpson, a divorced American.
Word Forms: abjuratory, abjurer, abjuration   Antonym Forms: unabjuratory, unabjured, nonabjuratory

☐ **abstemious**: (*adj*) sparing in consumption, especially of food and drink
Abby's emaciated figure was the result of her abstemious lifestyle; she never ate breakfast or lunch, and rarely ate dinner.
Word Forms: abstemiously, abstemiousness

☐ **abstruse**: (*adj*) hard to understand
Mr. Abbot tried to teach us how to solve an abstruse math problem, but it was too complicated for us to understand.
Word Forms: abstrusely, abstruseness, abstrusity

☐ **accretion**: (*n*) an increase
Akeem's gradual accretion of duties at work did not go unnoticed; he was given a raise for taking on the extra work.
Word Forms: accrete, accretive, accretionary   Antonym Forms: nonaccretion, nonaccretive

☐ **acerbic**: (*adj*) sour; harsh
Sour Patch Kids candy tastes like acerbic gummy bears.
Word Forms: acerbically, acerbate, acerbity   Antonym Forms: unacerbic, unacerbically

☐ **acidulous**: (*adj*) sour; sharp
Her acidulous criticism of my paper on Shakespeare was disappointing since I had invested many hours in research.
Word Forms: acidulent, acidulation   Related Words: subacidulous, acid

☐ **acme**: (*n*) the highest point
The Roman Empire reached its acme of power around 11 AD, but a slow decline occurred over the next four centuries.
Word Forms: acmic, acmatic,

☐ **acumen**: (*n*) good judgment
The judge was respected for his acumen when sentencing convicted defendants.
Word Forms: acuminous, acuminate, acumination   Antonym Form: unacuminous

☐ **adroit**: (*adj*) highly skilled, especially with one's hands
The adroit mechanic was able to fix Addy's old car, even though six other mechanics said it couldn't be repaired.
Word Forms: adroitly, adroitness

☐ **aerie**: (*n*) a nest; a home high on a mountain
Our aerie atop Roan Mountain was a cozy escape from the hustle and bustle of city life.
Related Word: aerial

☐ **aesthetic**: (*adj*) relating to beauty
Alaina chose this church because of its aesthetic qualities; it was the most beautiful wedding chapel she had ever seen.
Word Forms: aesthetically, aesthetics (*n*.), aestheticize, aesthete, aesthetician   Antonym Form: unaesthetic

☐ **affable**: (*adj*) friendly
In the fable, the affable princess was adored by all except for her three stepsisters who were angered by her friendliness.
Word Forms: affably, affability, affableness   Antonym Forms: inaffable, inaffibility

☐ **affected**: (*adj*) fake; phony
Afton had never traveled outside of the United States, but he used an affected French accent to attract attention.
Word Forms: affectedly, affectedness

☐ **aggrandize**: (*vb*) increase in size
Agatha, an avid baseball enthusiast, used her inheritance to aggrandize her collection of baseball cards.
Word Forms: aggrandizement, aggrandizer, aggrandizable   Related Words: aggrade, grand

☐ **alacrity**: (*n*) liveliness and eagerness
Alaina impressed her new boss by accepting the task with alacrity; she was both eager and excited to get started.
Word Form: alacritous

☐ **alchemy**: (*n*) magical power; process of turning base metals into gold
Al uses alchemy in the kitchen, turning simple ingredients into delicious culinary works of art.
Word Forms: alchemic, alchemical, alchemistic, alchemistical, alchemically, alchemist, alchemistry   Related: chemistry

☐ **amalgamation**: (*n*) a combination
Amy's new dance routine is an amalgamation of styles, including ballet and jazz.
Word Forms: amalgam, amalgamate, amalgamable, amalgamative, amalgamator

☐ **ameliorate**: (*vb*) to make better
Amelia was an outstanding caregiver; she could ameliorate a patient's discomfort just by smiling kindly.
Word Forms: ameliorable, ameliorableness, ameliorant, ameliorative, amelioratory, ameliorator

☐ **amenable**: (*adj*) agreeable
Amy was amenable to changing my schedule at work so that I could attend my son's baseball games.
Word Forms: amenability, amenableness, amenably   Antonym Forms: nonamenable, nonamenability, nonamenableness

☐ **amiable**: (*adj*) friendly
The amiable celebrity was known for his willingness to sign autographs and visit with his fans.
Word Forms: amiably, amiability, amiableness   Antonym Form: unamiable   Related Word: amicable

☐ **amortize**: (*vb*) to eliminate debt by making payments
For most borrowers, it takes thirty years to amortize their mortgage.
Word Forms: amortized, amortizable, amortizement, amortization   Antonym Forms: unamortized

☐ **amulet**: (*n*) magical charm to ward off evil
Amos placed a small amulet in his pocket, a charm that he believed helped him advance to the state tennis finals.
Word Form: amuletic

☐ **anachronistic**: (*adj*) out of chronological order
Today's announcement about the impending demolition of the baseball stadium is anachronistic; the stadium was razed early last week.
Word Forms: anachronistically, anachrony, anachronic, anachronism, anachronous, anachronously
Related Word: chronological, chronology

☐ **analgesic**: (*adj*) capable of relieving pain
Although Andy was in the most painful stages of the disease, his daughter's visit was analgesic; he was so happy to see her that his pain was significantly reduced.
Word Forms: analgesic (n.), analgetic   Related Word: analgesia

☐ **anodyne**: (*n*) something that relieves pain
The comedy club was an anodyne to Annika's grief; while she was there, she could forget her pain and sadness.
Word Form: anodynic

☐ **anthropocentrism**: (*n*) theory that regards humans as the central element of the universe
People who support the theory of anthropocentrism have a difficult time believing in intelligent life on other planets.
Word Forms: anthropocentric, anthropocentrically, anthropocentricity   Related Word: anthropology

☐ **antipathy**: (*n*) strong dislike
Antonio's antipathy for reporters stemmed from his childhood, when journalists hassled him about his father's trial.
Word Forms: antipathist, antipathize, antipathic   Related Words: sympathy, empathy, apathy

☐ **apathy**: (*n*) an absence of emotion or enthusiasm
The teacher was disappointed in the students' apathy toward the field trip; she had mistakenly believed that this trip would finally excite them about learning.
Word Forms: apathetic, apathetical, apathetically, apathist   Related Words: sympathy, empathy, antipathy

☐ **apocryphal**: (*adj*) fake; untrue
April told an apocryphal tale about my mother; I wanted so much to believe it even though I knew it wasn't true.
Word Forms: apocryphally, apocryphalness, apocryphalist

☐ **apostate**: (*n*) person who abandons their religion or cause
I had been an apostate from my religion for years, but recently had started thinking about rejoining the church.
Word Forms: apostatic, apostatical, apostatically, apostasy, apostatize

☐ **approbation**: (*n*) approval
Apollo's proposal for new lighting on campus was met with approbation, as the board agreed there was a safety issue.
Word Forms: approbate, approbative, approbator, approbatory   Related Word: preapprobation, subapprobation

☐ **archaic**: (*adj*) so extremely old as seeming to belong to an earlier period
The college cannot have sorority or fraternity houses because of an archaic town law that does not allow unmarried people to live together.
Word Forms: archaically, archaism, archaistic, archaist   Related Word: archaeology

☐ **ardor**: (*n*) intense passion
Mrs. Armstrong, my English teacher, is known for her ardor for the literature of William Faulkner; last summer she even visited his hometown in Mississippi in order to better visualize the settings of his books.

☐ **arrogate**: (*vb*) to claim without rights
The government arrogated Arianna's land, so she hired a lawyer to prove it did not have any rights to her property.
Word Forms: arrogatingly, arrogation, arrogator, arrogative   Antonym Forms: unarrogated, unarrogating

☐ **ascertain**: (*vb*) to make certain
The detective was able to ascertain the suspect's whereabouts on the night of the burglary through surveillance video.
Word Forms: ascertainable, ascertainableness, ascertainably, ascertainment, ascertainer

☐ **ascetic**: (*n*) a person who practices self-denial as a spiritual discipline
To prove his devotion to the religion, the ascetic did not own anything that might provide comfort or pleasure, such as a mattress or television set.
Word Forms: ascetic (adj.), ascetical, ascetically, asceticism

☐ **assail**: (*vb*) to attack
Asa was determined to master the GRE Verbal Reasoning section, so she assailed vocabulary words with determination.
Word Forms: assailable, assailableness, assailer, assailment, assailant   Antonym Form: unassailed

☐ **assiduous**: (*adj*) constant and attentive
Ashley is an assiduous researcher; she was able to find articles on the poet that even the librarian could not locate.
Word Forms: assiduously, assiduousness, assiduity

☐ **assuage**: (*vb*) to relieve or ease
The shoplifter assuaged his guilt by confessing to the crime.
Word Forms: assuagement, assuager   Antonym Forms: unassuaged, unassuaging

☐ **attenuate**: (*vb*) to weaken
Atticus' muscles slowly attenuated when he quit working out at the gym.
Word Forms: attenuation, attenuator, attenuatedly   Antonym Forms: unattenuated, unattenuatedly
Related Words: overattenuate, subattenuate, tenuous

☐ **audacious:** (*adj*) bold and fearless
Audrey asked audacious questions that most people would be scared to ask.
Word Forms: audaciously, audaciousness, audacity   Antonym Forms: unaudacious, unaudaciously, unaudaciousness

☐ **augment:** (*vb*) to enlarge or increase
In an effort to augment her paper on William Faulkner, Aubrey added three pages about the author's childhood.
Word Forms: augmentation, augmentable, augmentative, augmentatively, augmenter

☐ **augury:** (*n*) divine prediction
Augustus believed the groundhog's shadow was an augury of a delayed springtime.
Word Forms: augural, augurate, auguration, augur

☐ **august:** (*adj*) noble and dignified
The august king was admired for his good work.
Word Forms: augustly, augustness

☐ **auspicious:** (*adj*) favorable; fortunate
Austin waited for an auspicious time to ask his father to borrow the car; he finally had his chance on the day that his dad received a sizable raise at work.
Word Forms: auspiciously, auspiciousness

☐ **austere:** (*adj*) 1. strict; disciplined; serious 2. simple; undecorated
Mr. Aston is the most austere teacher at school; he does not tolerate any talking nor does he accept late assignments.
Word Forms: austerely, austereness, austerity

☐ **autonomy:** (*n*) independence
The Confederate states fought to gain autonomy from the Union during the Civil War.
Word Forms: autonomous, autonomously, autonomist

☐ **avarice:** (*n*) extreme greed for material wealth
Avery amassed million-dollar homes, luxury cars, and exquisite jewelry to satisfy her avarice, but still wanted more.
Word Forms: avaricious, avariciously, avariciousness

☐ **avuncular:** (*adj*) resembling an uncle in kindness or indulgence
Mr. Avery developed an avuncular affection for his neighbor's children after having spent so many years next door.
Word Forms: avuncularly, avuncularity   Related Word: uncle

☐ **axiom:** (*n*) principle or rule
The golden rule is a good axiom to live by.
Word Forms: axiomatic, axiomatical, axiomatization   Antonym Forms: nonaxiomatic, nonaxiomatical, unaxiomatic

☐ **banal:** (*adj*) repeated too often; overfamiliar through overuse
The plot of the movie is banal; everything that takes place in this film has happened in a dozen other movies.
Word Forms: banally, banalize, banality

☐ **belfry:** (*n*) a bell tower
No one volunteered to clean out the belfry because of all the bats that live in it.

☐ **benevolent:** (*adj*) charitable; kind
The benevolent nun spent her entire life working with the poor.
Word Forms: benevolently, benevolentness, benevolence   Related Words: benefactor, benefit

☐ **bevy:** (*n*) a large group
The picnic lunch on the beach attracted a bevy of birds.

☐ **bifurcate:** (*vb*) to divide into two branches
Biff's family tree bifurcated in 1946 when his grandmother remarried, thus creating a second branch of relatives.
Word Forms: bifurcately, bifurcation, bifurcous   Related Word: fork

☐ **bilk:** (*vb*) to cheat or swindle
Bill was bilked out of $10,000 when he invested in the phony scheme.
Word Form: bilker

☐ **blight**: (*n*) any factor that causes decay or deterioration
The blight that killed Blake's corn was responsible for the destruction of crops throughout the county.
Word Form: blightingly   Antonym Forms: unblighted, unblightedly, unblightedness

☐ **blithe**: (*adj*) cheerful
Blythe was known for her blithe spirit; she was always happy and cheerful.
Word Forms: blitheful, blithefullly, blithely, blitheness, blithesome   Related Word: overblithe

☐ **bombast**: (*n*) pompous or pretentious talk or writing
Be sure that your speech isn't pretentious or inflated, as the audience has no time to listen to bombast.
Word Forms: bombastic, bombastically, bombaster

☐ **bonhomie**: (*n*) friendliness
Bonnie had many friends who admired her kind nature and bonhomie.
Word Form: bonhomous

☐ **boor**: (*n*) a person who is rude, clumsy, and lacking social manners
Boris was a boor at the dinner party; after telling the host that her house was cheaply decorated, he ate his steak with his fingers and burped during the meal.
Word Forms: boorish, boorishly, boorishness
Note: Be careful not to confuse a boor (a rude person) with a bore (a boring person).

☐ **bromide**: (*n*) a common saying
As true as the old bromides are, such as "It is better to have loved and lost than never to have loved at all," none of them are much comfort to a newly-broken heart.
Word Forms: bromidic, bromidically

☐ **bucolic**: (*adj*) relating to country life; rural
The farmer lived a bucolic lifestyle, rising with the sun to tend the farm and retiring at sundown.
Word Forms: bucolical, bucolically

☐ **burgeon**: (*vb*) to flourish
Under the mayor's direction, the quiet town burgeoned into an active city.

☐ **burnish**: (*vb*) to polish
In preparation for his dinner party, Bernie burnished the silverware and serving platters.
Word Forms: burnishable, burnishment, burnisher   Antonym Form: unburnished

☐ **byzantine**: (*adj*) highly complex or intricate
In a home loan, the byzantine language and unfamiliar terminology can be intimidating to a first-time home buyer.

☐ **cabal**: (*n*) a secret group of plotters or schemers
The cabal met in a church basement to plan the overthrow of the government.
Word Form: caballer   Related Word: cabala

☐ **cacophony**: (*n*) harsh, jarring sound
On the first day of school, the band's output was a cacophony of trumpets and horns; however, by the end of the year, the horn section blended well with the rest of the ensemble.
Word Forms: cacophonic, cacophonous, cacophonously

☐ **cajole**: (*vb*) to influence by gentle urging, caressing, or flattering
Caleb cajoled his mother into letting him borrow the car by telling her how young and pretty she looked today.
Word Forms: cajolement, cajolingly, cajolery, cajoler

☐ **callous**: (*adj*) insensitive; emotionally hardened
The senator's callous indifference to the suffering of the people in the war-torn country cost him reelection.
Word Forms: callously, callousness   Related Word: callus

☐ **calumny**: (*n*) a false statement intended to harm someone's reputation
Callie delivered the calumny about Brittany to an audience in the cafeteria; she hoped the lie would keep the other girl from becoming Prom queen.
Word Forms: calumniate, calumniation, calumnious, calumniously, calumniatory, calumniator

☐ **canard**: (*n*) false story or rumor
The belief that Napoleon was short is a canard; he was actually 5'7", an above average height for a Frenchman in 1800.

☐ **canonical**: (*adj*) authorized or accepted
Pluto is no longer a canonical planet; due to its small mass, it was reclassified as a "dwarf planet" in 2006.
Word Forms: canonically, canon, canonic   Antonym Forms: uncanonical, uncanonically

☐ **cantankerous**: (*adj*) ill-tempered and unwilling to cooperate
The cantankerous old man took the little boy's sucker and refused to give it back.
Word Forms: cantankerously, cantankerousness

☐ **capricious**: (*adj*) apt to change suddenly
Cane's capricious personality made him a fun friend but a terrible boss; social spontaneity was exciting but workplace unpredictability was frustrating.
Word Forms: capriciously, capriciousness, caprice

☐ **cartographer**: (*n*) a person who makes maps
Amerigo Vespucci was one of the first cartographers to create a map of North America.
Word Forms: cartography, cartograph, cartographic, cartographical, cartographically

☐ **castigate**: (*vb*) to criticize or punish severely
Cassie was castigated by her parents and the school principal for her role in the cheating scam.
Word Forms: castigation, castigative, castigatory, castigator

☐ **cataclysm**: (*n*) a violent upheaval
The political uprising against the dictator is a cataclysm that will hopefully result in a more democratic regime.
Word Forms: cataclysmic, cataclysmically, cataclysmal   Related Word: catastrophe

☐ **cathartic**: (*adj*) inducing a release of tense emotions
Painting was a cathartic exercise for Cathy; through her paintings she was able to release anger and fear.
Word Forms: cathartically, catharticalness

☐ **catholic**: (*adj*) universal; liberal
Cathy had very catholic tastes, enjoying a wide array of food and drink.
Word Forms: catholically, catholicly, catholicalness, catholicness

☐ **caustic**: (*adj*) burning or stinging
Cosette's caustic remark stung Kent; he could handle criticism about his job, but her bitter words were personal.
Word Forms: caustically, causticly, causticness, causticity

☐ **cavalier**: (*n*) a man who is chivalrous and gallant
The young cavalier was rewarded for his gallant behavior when he was chosen to escort the princess to the ball.
Word Forms: cavalier (adj.), cavalierly, cavalierness, cavalierism

☐ **censure**: (*n*) strong disapproval
High school teachers voiced their censure of the new novel due to mature themes and profanity.
Word Forms: censurer, censureless   Related Words: miscensure, precensure, procensure

☐ **charlatan**: (*n*) a person who falsely claims to possess skills or knowledge; an imposter
The charlatan tricked the unsuspecting customers out of money by pretending to be able to predict the future.
Word Forms: charlatanic, charlatanish, charlatanical, charlatanically, charlatanistic, charlatanry, charlatanism

☐ **chary**: (*adj*) cautious; timid; choosy
Charlie was chary of sitting on the wobbly chair; he was afraid it would break under his weight.
Word Form: charily   Antonym Form: unchary

☐ **chicanery**: (*n*) the use of tricks to deceive someone
The con artist relied on chicanery to get his victims to reveal their Social Security numbers; he promised them a tropical vacation for simply listing their personal information.
Word Forms: chicane, chicaner

☐ **churlish**: (*adj*) rude and vulgar
Cheryl did not think the man's churlish jokes were appropriate, and asked that he apologize for his vulgarity.
Word Forms: churlishly, churlishness, churl

☐ **circumlocution**: (*n*) an indirect way of expressing something
Sergio hoped that his circumlocution would stall the reporters long enough to think of a better answer to their question.
Word Forms: circumlocutory, circumlocutorily, circumlocutional, circumlocutionary

---

☐ **circumscribed**: (*adj*) restricted
Her driving privileges are circumscribed by the state; she is only allowed to drive at night if she is returning from work.
Word Forms: circumscribable, circumscriber   Related Word: circle

☐ **circumspect**: (*adj*) cautious; discreet
Given the recent theft of passwords, you need to be circumspect when sharing personal information on the internet.
Word Forms: circumspectly, circumspectness   Antonym Forms: noncircumspect, noncircumspectly, noncircumspectness

☐ **clandestine**: (*adj*) secret
The school administrators held clandestine meetings about the school uniform policy; they were afraid that if the public knew they were contemplating a new policy, the outcry would squash the issue.
Word Forms: clandestinely, clandestineness, clandestinity

☐ **cloying**: (*adj*) wearying through excess
Her perfume smelled sweet at first but became cloying after sitting in the car with her for an hour.
Word Forms: cloy, cloyingly   Antonym Form: uncloying

☐ **coalesce**: (*vb*) to blend into one
The two streams coalesced into a river.
Word Forms: coalescence, coalescent   Antonym Forms: noncoalescence, noncoalescent

☐ **coffer**: (*n*) a box for storing valuables; funds
Keifer depleted the organizations coffers, but his plan was to replenish the funds.
Word Form: cofferlike

☐ **cogent**: (*adj*) convincing; telling
Craig presents a cogent argument through sound evidence and logical conclusions.
Word Forms: cogency, cogently   Antonym Form: noncogent, noncogently, uncogent, uncogently

☐ **collusion**: (*n*) a secret agreement; conspiracy
The founding fathers worked in collusion to revolt against the British government.
Word Forms: collusive, collusively, collusory   Antonym Forms: noncollusion, noncollusive   Related Word: collude

☐ **conciliate**: (*vb*) to win over; to make peace
The manager was able to conciliate the angry customer by offering her a fifty dollar gift certificate.
Word Forms: conciliable, conciliation, conciliatory, conciliatorily, conciliatoriness   Related Word: reconcile

☐ **concomitant**: (*adj*) existing or occurring at the same time
Building a home can be an exciting process, but it also has concomitant stress associated with difficult decisions.
Word Forms: concomitant (n.), concomitantly, concomitance

☐ **conflagration**: (*n*) a destructive fire
The fire department determined that the conflagration in the old warehouse was a result of faulty wiring.
Word Forms: conflagrative, conflagrate, conflagrant

☐ **conspicuous**: (*adj*) obvious
The realtor put the "For Sale" sign in a conspicuous spot in the front yard so that people in traffic could easily see it.
Word Forms: conspicuously, conspicuousness, conspicuity
Antonym Forms: inconspicuous, inconspicuously, inconspicuousness

☐ **consummate**: (*adj*) perfect and complete
Constantine is the consummate host; he greets his guests, makes sure they are comfortable and enjoying themselves, and introduces new friends to everyone.
Word Forms: consummate (vb.), consummately, consummatory, consummation, consummator

☐ **contrite**: (*adj*) feeling guilty and remorseful
The contrite criminal broke into sobs as he apologized to the victim's family for the suffering he had caused.
Word Forms: contritely, contriteness, contrition

☐ **contumacious**: (*adj*) willfully disobedient
The contumacious convict spat at the judge and refused to acknowledge his sentence.
Word Forms: contumaciously, contumaciousness, contumacity   Antonym Form: noncontumacious, noncontumaciously, noncontumaciousness   Related Words: contumely, contumelious, contumeliously, contumliousness

convoluted: (*adj*) complicated
Connor was unable to finish the seventeenth-century novel due to the convoluted language of the period.
Word Forms: convolutedly, convolutedness   Related Word: involuted

corpulent: (*adj*) excessively fat
The corpulent man purchased two adjacent airline seats in order to have a more comfortable flight.
Word Forms: corpulently, corpulence, corpulency

corroborate: (*vb*) to confirm or support with evidence
Coral's thesis was corroborated by three supporting paragraphs, each presenting an example that proved her main idea.
Word Forms: corroborated, corroboration, corroborative, corroboratively, corroboratory, corroborant, corroborator
Antonym Form: uncorroborated

cosset: (*vb*) to pamper
Cossette cosseted the puppy, providing him with diamond collars, caviar dinners, and doggy massages.
Word Form: cosseted   Antonym Form: uncosseted

coterie: (*n*) an exclusive group of people; a clique
The town's wealthiest socialites formed a coterie and few people were able to gain entrance to the circle.

craven: (*adj*) cowardly
Rather than face her landlord and explain the damage to the house, the craven tenant packed up and moved in the night.
Word Forms: craven (n), cravenly, cravenness   Antonym Form: uncraven

crescendo: (*n*) peak of growth
The cheers in the audience reached a crescendo when the concert headliner was introduced.
Antonym Form: decrescendo   Related Word: crescent

culpable: (*adj*) worthy of blame
The jury found the suspect culpable for the break-ins.
Word Forms: culpability, culpableness, culpably   Antonym Form: nonculpable, nonculpableness, nonculpably
Related Word: exculpate, culprit

cumbersome: (*adj*) clumsy, awkward, and heavy
The old television set was cumbersome, making it difficult to move into the other room.
Word Forms: cumbersomely, cumbersomeness   Related Words: cumber, encumber

cupidity: (*n*) excessive greed
Cullen's downfall was his cupidity; he couldn't walk away with the money he had already embezzled and was caught when he went back for more.
Word Form: cupidinous

curmudgeon: (*n*) cranky, difficult person
The old curmudgeon complained about every part of his meal.
Word Form: curmudgeonly   Related Word: cur

cynical: (*adj*) distrusting and pessimistic
Cyndi's cynical attitude made it hard for her to believe in anyone's good intentions.
Word Forms: cynically, cynicism, cynic

dalliance: (*n*) the deliberate act of delaying and playing instead of working
Dalton's dalliance at the basketball court kept him from working on the term paper that was due tomorrow.
Word Forms: dally, dallyingly, dallier   Related Word: dilly-dally

daunt: (*vb*) to cause to lose courage
Don had finally worked up the courage to ride the roller coaster when he was daunted by the pale faces of the riders who had just completed the ride.
Word Forms: dauntingly, dauntingness   Antonym Forms: dauntless, dauntlessly, dauntlessness, undaunted, undauntedly

dearth: (*n*) a lack in supply
During the Second World War, the dearth of male baseball players led to the creation of a women's baseball league.

debunk: (*vb*) to prove untrue
The reporter debunked the urban legend about the witch in the woods by revealing wild goats as the sources of the noises.
Word Form: debunker

debutante: (*n*) a young woman making her debut into society
The debutantes were introduced at a formal ball, after which they were considered members of the aristocratic society.

declivity: (*n*) a downward slope
The backyard's declivity caused rainwater to wash down it, creating a pool of standing water at the bottom of the slope.
Word Forms: declivitous, declivous, declivent   Antonym Form: acclivity

decorous: (*adj*) proper and dignified
The decorous host made sure that she had proper table settings; each was arranged correctly for the five-course meal.
Word Forms: decorously, decorousness   Antonym Forms: indecorous, indecorously, indecorousness
Related Word: decorum

deject: (*vb*) to lower someone's spirits; make downhearted
The news of her father's declining condition dejected Denise, as she had been sure his health was starting to improve.
Word Forms: dejected (adj.), dejectedly, dejectedness, dejectory, dejection   Related Words: reject, eject

deleterious: (*adj*) harmful
The deleterious effects of cigarette smoking, such as lung cancer, are highlighted in the public service campaign.
Word Forms: deleteriously, deleteriousness   Related Word: delete

delineate: (*vb*) to outline
In her speech, Delilah clearly delineated her plans for changing several policies should she be elected class president.
Word Forms: delineable, delineative, delineation, delineament, delineatory, delineator   Antonym Form: undelineated

demagogue: (*n*) a political leader who seeks support by appealing to popular passions and prejudices
Hitler was a demagogue who gained power by exploiting religious prejudices in Germany.
Word Forms: demagoguery, demagogism, demagogic, demagogical, demagogically

demarcate: (*vb*) to set, mark, or draw the boundaries of something
The twins demarcated the room after their fight; Demarcus was only allowed access to the right side of their room, while Demonte had to stay on the left side.
Word Forms: demarcation, demarcator

demur: (*vb*) to object
I was surprised when my father did not demur to me attending the rival college of his alma mater.
Word Forms: demurrable, demurral, demurrer   Antonym Form: undemurring

denigrate: (*vb*) to damage the reputation of
The candidate hoped to denigrate his opponent's character by exposing the embezzlement scandal.
Word Forms: denigration, denigrative, denigratory, denigrator

derelict: (*n*) a person without a home, job, or property
The derelict spent his days begging on the street corner and his nights sleeping in the alley.
Word Forms: derelict (adj.), derelictly, derelictness, dereliction   Related Word: relinquish

deride: (*vb*) to ridicule
The unsupportive team captain derided Desiree's attempts to make the volleyball squad.
Word Forms: deridingly, derision, derisive, derisible, derider

derivative: (*n*) something that came from an original
The Pilates exercise system is a derivative of the ancient Indian practice of yoga.
Word Forms: derivative (adj.), derivatively, derivativeness, derive, derivation

☐ **desiccate**: (*vb*) to dry up
When the flowers in my bouquet desiccate, I can preserve them as dried flowers.
Word Forms: desiccation, desiccative, desiccated, desiccator

☐ **despoiler**: (*n*) a person who steals goods
The despoilers from the pirate ship stripped the village members of all their possessions.
Word Forms: despoil, despoilment   Related Word: spoils (n.)

☐ **despot**: (*n*) a ruler with complete power
The despot was a harsh ruler who imposed outrageous taxes and unreasonable upon against his subjects.
Word Forms: despotic, despotical, despotically, despotism

☐ **destitute**: (*adj*) completely wanting or lacking (usually money, food, and shelter)
The homeless man wasn't always destitute; he once had a job, but poor money management led to bankruptcy.
Word Forms: destitutely, destituteness, destitution

☐ **desultory**: (*adj*) disconnected and random
People wondered about Desiree's mental state when her conversation turned desultory; she jumped from topic to topic with seemingly no connection.
Word Forms: desultorily, desultoriness, desultorious

☐ **diaphanous**: (*adj*) sheer; nearly translucent
Daphne would be wise to wear a slip under that diaphanous skirt.
Word Forms: diaphanously, diaphanousness, diaphaneity   Antonym Forms: nondiaphanous, nondiaphanously

☐ **diatribe**: (*n*) bitter criticism; verbal attack
It was clear from Diana's diatribes against her mother that their relationship was beyond repair.
Word Form: diatribist

☐ **dictum**: (*n*) a formal statement
The president released a dictum forbidding texting while at work.

☐ **didactic**: (*adj*) educational
The children's book is not only entertaining, but also didactic; the story teaches the dietary habits of marine animals.
Word Forms: didactical, didactically, didacticism, didact   Related Words: autodidactic, autodidact

☐ **diffident**: (*adj*) shy; reserved
Daphne was diffident when she first made the team, but by the end of the season, she was clearly a leader on the court.
Word Forms: diffidently, diffidence   Antonym Forms: nondiffident, nondiffidently, undiffident

☐ **dilatory**: (*adj*) intending to delay
Dillon asked nearly twenty dilatory questions at the start of class in an attempt to postpone the scheduled math test.
Word Forms: dilatorily, dilatoriness   Related Word: delay

☐ **dilettante**: (*n*) a person who engages in an activity (such as art) without serious intentions or inquiry
Although Dylan started painting, he was merely a dilettante; his paintings were amateur attempts at a part-time hobby.
Word Forms: dilettantish

☐ **dirge**: (*n*) a funeral song
As the dirge played, mournful cries could be heard throughout the funeral.
Word Forms: dirgeful

☐ **disabuse**: (*vb*) to free someone from false ideas
Dixon believed tomatoes were vegetables but I disabused him of that idea when I revealed they are actually fruits.
Word Form: disabusal

☐ **discern**: (*vb*) to perceive or understand with sight or other senses
The captain discerned another ship in the fog.
Word Forms: discernible, discernibly, discernment, discernibility, discernableness, discerner
Antonym Forms: indiscernible, indiscernibly, indiscernibility, indiscernibleness

☐ **disdain**: (*n*) a lack of respect accompanied by a feeling of intense dislike
The suspect was looked upon with disdain by the detectives who investigated the terrible crime.
Word Forms: disdain (vb.), disdainful, disdainfully, disdainfulness   Related Word: deign

☐ **disenfranchise**: (*vb*) to deprive of voting rights
American citizens who are convicted of a felony are disenfranchised, losing their right to vote in any election.
Word Forms: disenfranchisement, disfranchise   Antonym Forms: enfranchise, franchise

☐ **disillusion**: (*vb*) to free from false beliefs
As a young politician, Dane believed he could stop the corruption that ran through the county government, but he was quickly disillusioned by the extent of the illegal activity.
Word Forms: disillusionment, disillusive, disillusionize, disillusionist

☐ **disingenuous**: (*adj*) insincere
Denise's disingenuous apology was just an attempt to get out of her punishment; she was not truly sorry for going to the concert without permission.
Word Forms: disingenuously, disingenuousness, disingenuity   Antonym Forms: ingenuous, ingenuously, ingenuousness
Related Word: genuine

☐ **disparage**: (*vb*) to belittle or criticize
My mom's feelings were hurt when I disparaged her cooking skills.
Word Forms: disparagement, disparaging (adj.), disparagingly, disparager

☐ **disparate**: (*adj*) different and distinct
The mixture of three disparate styles—jazz, rock, and country—created a unique sound and a diverse audience.
Word Forms: disparately, disparateness   Related Word: disparity

☐ **dissembler**: (*n*) a person who conceals his real feelings by professing false beliefs
The dissembler pledged allegiance to the rebel group, but he was really working undercover for the opposing army.
Word Forms: dissemble, dissemblingly, dissemblance   Related Words: resemble, semblance

☐ **disseminate**: (*vb*) to spread widely
The police hoped the information about the suspect would disseminate quickly; the more people who knew, the better chances of apprehending the wanted man.
Word Forms: dissemination, disseminative, disseminator

☐ **dissonance**: (*n*) harsh, jarring sound
On the first day of school, the band's output was a dissonance of trumpets and horns; however, by the end of the year, the horn section blended well with the rest of the ensemble.
Word Form: dissonancy   Antonym Form: consonance   Related Words: assonance, resonance

☐ **distaff**: (*n*) the female part of a family
Driving skills clearly fell on the distaff side of the family; the ladies had clean driving records but the men had sixteen traffic tickets among them.

☐ **dither**: (*vb*) to be indecisive
Dillon dithered on whether to go to business school or law school.
Word Forms: ditherer, dithery

☐ **diurnal**: (*adj*) daily; daytime
Humans are diurnal creatures, so working the night shift can disrupt our natural sleep rhythms.
Word Forms: diurnally, diurnalness   Antonym Forms: undiurnal, undiurnally   Related Word: nocturnal

☐ **divert**: (*vb*) to turn away from a course
Traffic was diverted through side streets in order to avoid an accident on the main road.
Word Forms: divertedly, diversion, divertible   Related Words: invert, convert, revert

☐ **divine**: (*vb*) to predict using supernatural means
Devina asked the psychic to divine her future using the crystal ball.
Word Forms: divinable, divinely, divineness, divination, divinator   Related Word: divine (adj)

☐ **doctrinaire**: (*adj*) impractical; insistent about one's own theory
The doctor believed that the lack of exercise was the single cause of high blood pressure and was doctrinaire in his inability to accept genetic factors.
Word Forms: doctrinaire (n), doctrinairism   Antonym Forms: nondoctrinaire, undoctrinaire

☐ **dogmatic**: (*adj*) characterized by assertion of unproved or unprovable principles
The dogmatic scientist continued to publish his theory, despite the fact that it was unproven.
Word Forms: dogmatically, dogmaticalness, dogmatize, dogmatism, dogmatist   Related Words: dogma

☐ **draconian**: (*adj*) harsh and severe
In the novel, the king used draconian forms of punishment—such as torture or starvation—on anyone caught plotting against the monarchy.
Word Forms: draconic, draconically

☐ **droll**: (*adj*) amusing; comical
The droll little man amused the children with his odd gait and his quaint way of speaking.
Word Forms: drollness, drolly, drollery

☐ **dubious**: (*adj*) doubtful; questionable
The candidate's dubious past came back to haunt her in the election.
Word Forms: dubiously, dubiousness, dubitable   Antonym Forms: indubious, indubiously   Related Word: doubt

☐ **dupe**: (*vb*) to deceive
Dupree was duped into investing in the scam.
Word Forms: dupe (n), dupable, dupability, duper, dupery   Antonym Form: undupable

☐ **dyspeptic**: (*adj*) irritable and gloomy
Dyson was dyspeptic about his acceptance into business school; everyone tried to cheer him up, but he was convinced he would be rejected.
Word Forms: dyspeptically   Antonym Forms: nondyspeptic, nondyspeptical, nondyspeptically

☐ **earnest**: (*adj*) serious; sincere
The earnest student took the SAT seriously; he bought several study guides, and dedicated two hours a day to practice.
Word Forms: earnestly, earnestness

☐ **ebullient**: (*adj*) extremely excited or enthusiastic
The ebullient child clapped her hands and jumped up and down as she waited to ride the pony at the party.
Word Forms: ebulliently, ebullience

☐ **eclectic**: (*adj*) made up of choices from diverse sources
Mrs. Eckert has an eclectic music collection; her albums span from classic jazz to hip hop to disco.
Word Forms: eclectically, eclecticist   Related Word: select

☐ **edify**: (*vb*) to benefit by instruction
The art teacher edified his students by taking them to a premier art gallery to teach about painting techniques.
Word Forms: edifier, edifyingly, edifying, reedify   Antonym Forms: nonedified, unedified

☐ **efficacious**: (*adj*) effective
The pest repellent was efficacious in keeping the mosquitoes away; none of the guests were bothered by the bugs.
Word Forms: efficaciously, efficaciousness, efficacy, efficacity
Antonym Forms: inefficacious, inefficaciously, inefficaciousness, inefficacy, inefficacity
Related Words: effect, effective

☐ **effigy**: (*n*) a representation of someone
The mayor's effigy was unveiled as a sculpture in the park, erected to honor his lifelong service.
Word Form: effigial

☐ **effrontery**: (*n*) shameless boldness
She had the effrontery to imply that I was pregnant when in fact I had just gained some weight.

☐ **effusive**: (*adj*) excessive enthusiasm or emotion
Effie's effusive praise was so excessive and over-the-top that it almost seemed insincere.
Word Forms: effusively, effusiveness   Related Words: effuse, infuse

☐ **egalitarian**: (*adj*) characterized by the belief in equal rights for all people
Edgar's egalitarian beliefs made him an excellent husband; he divided the housework equally, helping his wife with cooking, cleaning, and childcare.
Word Forms: egalitarian (n.), egalitarianism, egality   Related Word: equality

☐ **egregious**: (*adj*) outrageously bad or offensive
Edie made the egregious mistake of asking the slightly overweight woman if she were expecting a baby.
Word Forms: egregiously, egregiousness

☐ **elegy**: (*n*) a sad poem or song
"To An Athlete Dying Young" is a heartbreaking elegy written by A. E. Housman.
Word Forms: elegize, elegist

☐ **elicit**: (*vb*) to call or bring out
The woman elicits sympathy from her audience by telling the story of her difficult childhood.
Word Forms: elicitation, elicitor   Related Word: solicit
Note: *elicit* is often confused with *illicit*, which means illegal

☐ **eloquent**: (*adj*) expressing oneself powerfully and effectively
The minister's eloquent sermon stirred the members of the church.
Word Forms: eloquently, eloquence   Antonym Forms: ineloquent, ineloquently, ineloquence

☐ **elucidate**: (*vb*) to make clear by explanation
The story in the newspaper elucidated some of the details of the mystery that had previously raised questions.
Word Forms: elucidation, elucidative, elucidatory, elucidator   Related Word: lucid

☐ **embroil**: (*vb*) to bring into an argument or negative situation
Emory is embroiled in a lawsuit with his former landlord over the condition of the apartment when he moved out.
Word Forms: embroilment, embroiler

☐ **eminent**: (*adj*) distinguished and prominent
The eminent professor has taught at distinguished colleges, which is why he is such a remarkable addition to the faculty.
Word Forms: eminently, eminence   Note: *eminent* is often confused with *imminent*, which means about to occur

☐ **emissary**: (*n*) a person sent on a mission to represent the interests of someone else
The general sent an emissary to the enemy's camp to inquire about the terms of surrender.
Related Words: emission, emissive, emit

☐ **emollient**: (*n*) that which has a softening or soothing effect, especially to the skin
Emmaline applied an emollient lotion to the rough calluses on her hands.
Word Form: emollient (adj.), emollience

☐ **empirical**: (*adj*) resulting from an experiment
As a scientist, Emmie relied on empirical data every day, which is why it was hard for her to trust her intuition.
Word Forms: empirically, empiricalness

☐ **emulate**: (*vb*) to imitate in order to match or excel
Emily hoped to emulate her older sister's success on the tennis court.
Word Forms: emulative, emulatively, emulation, emulator

☐ **encomium**: (*n*) high praise
The chairwoman delivered an encomium about Enzo before introducing him as the employee of the month.
Word Form: encomia

☐ **endemic**: (*adj*) natural to a local area
Fire ants are endemic to the southeastern coastal plains, but they have started to migrate to the interior.
Word Forms: endemically, endemism   Antonym Forms: nonendemic, unendemic   Related Words: epidemic, pandemic

☐ **enervated**: (*adj*) lacking strength or vigor
After an entire weekend of moving furniture, Enrico was enervated; he would need to rest to get his strength back.
Word Forms: enervate (vb.), enervation, enervative, enervator

☐ **engender**: (*vb*) to produce
Divorce can engender feelings of anger, loss, and powerlessness.
Word Forms: engenderer, engenderment   Antonym Form: unengendered   Related Word: generate

☐ **enigma**: (*n*) a puzzle
The dog's escape from the pen is an enigma; no one can figure out how she broke out of the locked enclosure.
Word Forms: enigmata (plural), enigmatic, enigmatical, enigmatically

☐ **ennui**: (*n*) boredom
The monotony of my job produces utter ennui.

enumerate: (*vb*) to count; to name one by one
The blog enumerated the top five study tips for the GRE.
Word Forms: enumerative, enumerator, enumerable   Antonym Forms: nonenumerated, nonenumerative
Related Words: numeral, number

ephemeral: (*adj*) lasting a very short time
Effie's sadness over her breakup is ephemeral; she will quickly find a new boyfriend to help her forget the last.
Word Forms: ephemeral (n.), ephemerally, ephemeralness, ephemerality, ephemerous, ephemeron

epicure: (*n*) a person with refined tastes, particularly of food and wine
The reality show features several epicures judging the cooking skills of America's best chefs.
Word Forms: epicurean, epicureous, epicurism

epistolary: (*adj*) relating to letters
The couple has an epistolary relationship; although they have never met, they communicate regularly through letters.
Word Forms: epistle, epistolatory, epistolic, epistolical, epistolize, epistoler, epistolist

equanimity: (*n*) steadiness of mind under stress
Eva made an excellent emergency room doctor because she handled trauma with equanimity; she was clear-headed during the most stressful situations.
Word Forms: equanimous, equanimously, equanimousness   Related Word: longanimity

equivocal: (*adj*) uncertain; open to multiple interpretations
The politician's equivocal statement about the environment could support either side of the issue.
Word Forms: equivocality, equivocacy, equivocally, equivocalness
Antonym Forms: unequivocal, unequivocally, unequivocalness

ersatz: (*adj*) artificial; serving to substitute
Aspartame is an ersatz sugar that has caused a lot of controversy in recent years.

erudition: (*n*) knowledge gained from study
Erik's erudition is sure to help him win a lot of money on the trivia-based quiz show.
Word Forms: eruditional, erudite, eruditely, eruditeness

eschew: (*vb*) to avoid; to shun
Attempting to follow a low carb diet, Essie eschewed all foods containing sugar.
Word Forms: eschewal, eschewer   Antonym Form: uneschewed

esoteric: (*adj*) intended for a select group of people; secret or confidential
Esteban was a member of an esoteric club, whose membership consisted strictly of men over fifty who lived in the city.
Word Forms: esoterically, esotericism, esotericist   Antonym Forms: exoteric, exoterically, exotericism

espouse: (*vb*) to adopt or marry (such as an idea or cause)
Although Esmerelda had never practiced a formal religion, she espoused her fiancé's faith in order to join his church.
Word Forms: espousal, espouser   Related Word: spouse

ethos: (*n*) the spirit or attitude of a group
The ethos of 4-H is education resulting in positive change for the community.

eulogy: (*n*) a formal expression of praise (often delivered at funerals)
The director delivered a eulogy about the center's most helpful volunteer, praising her for helping the needy.
Word Forms: eulogize, eulogist

euphemism: (*n*) an inoffensive word or phrase used in place of one that is hurtful or harsh
In the hospital's yearly report, the euphemism "negative patient outcome" is used instead of "death."
Word Forms: euphemistic, euphemistically, euphemist, euphemistical, euphemious, euphemously, euphemize
Antonym Forms: uneuphemistic, uneuphemistical

euphony: (*n*) pleasant sound
When the orchestra started to play, a euphony ensued that made audience members smile.
Word Forms: euphonize, euphonious, euphoniously, euphoniousness
Antonym Forms: noneuphonious, noneuphoniously

☐ **evanescent**: (*adj*) vanishing
Many people believe that youth is evanescent, quickly vanishing before it can be truly appreciated.
Word Forms: evanescently, evanesce, evanescence   Related Word: vanish

☐ **exacerbate**: (*vb*) to increase the harshness or bitterness of
My headache was exacerbated by the child playing drums on the pots and pans.
Word Forms: exacerbatingly, exacerbation   Related Word: acerbate
Note: *exacerbate* is often confused with *exasperate* (meaning to irritate).

☐ **exasperate**: (*vb*) to intensely irritate
The airline passenger was exasperated by the last minute cancellation of his flight.
Word Forms: exasperatedly, exasperatingly, exasperation, exasperator
Related Word: asperate
Note: *exasperate* is often confused with *exacerbate* (meaning to increase).

☐ **exculpate**: (*vb*) to clear from blame
The arson suspect was exculpated when forensics revealed that the fire had been the result of faulty wiring.
Word Forms: exculpable, exculpation, exculpatory   Related Words: culpable, culprit
Related Words: inculpate, inculpable, inculpation, inculpably, inculpatory, inculpability, inculpableness

☐ **exegesis**: (*n*) an explanation or critical interpretation (especially of the Bible)
The minister is delivering an exegesis on the first two books of the Bible, where he will interpret the lessons from Genesis and Exodus and apply them to modern times.
Word Forms: exegetic, exegetical, exegetically, exegete, exegetist

☐ **exigent**: (*adj*) urgent; demanding
This is an exigent matter: if you don't reach the client in time, we stand to lose millions of dollars.
Word Forms: exigently, exigence   Antonym Forms: nonexigent, nonexigently, unexigent, unexigently

☐ **exonerate**: (*vb*) to clear from blame
The use of DNA helped exonerate the innocent man; twenty years after he was sent to prison, he was released.
Word Forms: exoneration, exonerative, exonerator

☐ **exorbitant**: (*adj*) greatly exceeding bounds of reason or moderation
I am forced to stop shopping at that grocery store until the owners lower the exorbitant prices on meats and produce.
Word Forms: exorbitantly, exorbitance

☐ **expatriate**: (*n*) a person who lives outside his own country, often to renounce allegiance
The little village in Costa Rica is filled with American expatriates who moved there for a more relaxed lifestyle.
Word Forms: expatriate (vb.), expatriation   Related Word: patriot

☐ **explicator**: (*n*) a person who explains or interprets
My attorney was an excellent explicator; he clearly interpreted each clause of the legal contract.
Word Forms: explicate, explication, explicative, explicatively, explicatory   Related Word: explicit

☐ **explicit**: (*adj*) clearly expressed or demonstrated
Mr. Jones left explicit directions for the substitute so he was surprised when they were not followed.
Word Forms: explicitly, explicitness   Antonym Forms: inexplicit, inexplicitly, implicit, implicitly, implicitness

☐ **exponent**: (*n*) one who explains or interprets
The teacher was an exponent of turn of the century literature, explaining the themes that populated novels at that time.
Word Forms: exponent (adj), exponential, exponentially   Antonym Forms: nonexponential, nonexponentially

☐ **expurgate**: (*vb*) to revise by removing offensive text; to purify by cleansing
Recent versions of <u>Huckleberry Finn</u> *have been expurgated to remove racial slurs and references.*
Word Forms: expurgated, expurgation, expurgator   Antonym Form: unexpurgated

☐ **extemporaneous**: (*adj*) done without advance preparation
I was not expecting to be called to the stage, so I gave an extemporaneous speech.
Word Forms: extemporary, extemporaneity, extemporaneously, extemporarily, extemporaneousness, extemporariness

☐ **extol**: (*vb*) to praise highly
The critic extolled the works of Shakespeare, citing them as the most important contribution to the English language.
Word Forms: extollingly, extolment, extoller

extraneous: (*adj*) not relevant or essential
When studying for the SAT, be sure to ignore the extraneous information in the book, such as the history of the test.
Word Forms: extraneously, extraneousness   Related Word: extra

exuberant: (*adj*) overflowing, especially with joy
The young wife was exuberant when her husband returned safely from the military after a year-long tour of duty.
Word Forms: exuberantly, exuberance, exuberate

facetious: (*adj*) not intended to be taken seriously
Fatima, who hated getting her teeth cleaned, was being facetious when she said, "I love going to the dentist!"
Word Forms: facetiously, facetiousness

fallacy: (*n*) a false idea
Many textbooks teach the fallacy that George Washington cut down a cherry tree; it is widely believed that an author made up that story to increase the sales of his book.
Word Forms: fallacious, fallaciously, fallaciousness

fallible: (*adj*) capable of making a mistake
Fallon knew that her boyfriend was fallible, but she was still disappointed to learn that he had lied to her.
Word Forms: fallibly, fallibility, fallibleness   Antonym Forms: infallible, infallibly, infallibility, infallibleness
Related Word: fall

fallow: (*adj*) not in use
The fallow field had not been used for crops in over a decade so the farmer had to till and aerate the soil.
Word Forms: fallowness   Antonym Form: unfallowed

fastidious: (*adj*) giving careful attention to detail; hard to please
Mrs. Foster, my teacher, is a fastidious grader; she deducts points for any error in grammar, punctuation, or spelling.
Word Forms: fastidiously, fastidiousness   Antonym Form: unfastidious

fatuous: (*adj*) foolish and silly
The professor made a fatuous argument that everyone dismissed due to its extreme foolishness.
Word Forms: fatuously, fatuousness

fawn: (*vb*) to seek attention through flattery
The associate fawned over his supervisor in an attempt to receive a raise.
Word Forms: fawner, fawningly, fawningness

fecund: (*adj*) productive; fruitful
The fecund field has been producing record-setting crops for many years.
Word Forms: fecundity, fecundate, fecundator, fecundatory

felicity: (*n*) pleasing and appropriate style; happiness
The book review highlighted both the felicities and the imperfections of the novel.
Word Forms: felicitous, felicitously, felicitousness   Antonym Forms: infelicity, infelicitous, infelicitously

fervid: (*adj*) hot or passionate
The fervid senator fought passionately for victim's rights.
Word Forms: fervidity, fervidly, fervidness Antonym Form: nonfervid, nonfervidly, nonfervidness Related Word: fervent

fetid: (*adj*) stinky; smelling of decay
I hated turning the compost pile because of its fetid smell.
Word Forms: fetidly, fetidness, fetidity

flippant: (*adj*) disrespectful; lacking seriousness
Floyd was grounded for making flippant remarks about the new rules his father set for him.
Word Forms: flippantly, flippantness, flippancy

flotsam: (*n*) floating wreckage or useless, discarded items
In the filthy city, the gullies are filled with flotsam that finds its way into the sewer after a heavy rain.
Related Word: jetsam   Note: *Flotsam* originally referred to the floating wreckage of a boat, while *jetsam* referred to the items discarded by a ship in distress. Both are loosely used today to refer to useless, discarded items.

foible: (*n*) a minor flaw or weakness of character
Foster's only foible is his inability to make a decision.
Related Word: feeble

☐ **fomentation**: (*n*) a push for trouble or rebellion
The juniors would not have participated in skip day if it weren't for the fomentation of their senior friends.
Word Forms: foment, fomenter

☐ **foppish**: (*adj*) affecting extreme elegance in dress and manner
The foppish fellow wore a three piece suit and a top hat to the wedding.
Word Forms: foppishly, foppishness, foppery, fop

☐ **ford**: (*n*) a shallow portion of a river used for crossing
Pioneers often would travel miles out of their way in order to find a ford that would allow them to safely cross a river.
Word Forms: ford (vb), fordable

☐ **formidable**: (*adj*) causing fear due to powerful strength
Forrest is a formidable opponent on the tennis court; he has not lost a set in his last twenty games.
Word Forms: formidably, formidableness, formidabilty

☐ **fortuitous**: (*adj*) fortunate; by chance
Getting stuck in an elevator with a head hunter on my way to a job interview turned out to be a fortuitous event.
Word Forms: fortuitously, fortuitousness, fortuity   Antonym Form: nonfortuitous, nonfortuitously,
nonfortuitousness   Related Word: fortunate

☐ **foster**: (*vb*) to encourage or care for
The arts foundation hopes to foster art education in the schools by donating supplies and materials.
Word Forms: fostered (adj.), fosteringly, fosterer

☐ **fractious**: (*adj*) unruly; irritable
Fido was a fractious dog who refused to cooperate even after months of obedience classes.
Word Forms: fractiously, fractiousness   Antonym Form: unfractious, unfractiously, unfractiousness

☐ **frenetic**: (*adj*) frantic
The castaways were frenetic in waving down the rescue plane.
Word Forms: frenetically, frenetical   Antonym Form: nonfrenetic, nonfrenetically

☐ **frivolous**: (*adj*) not serious; silly
The author's new novel is a frivolous look at life in the city; although it lacks the serious tones of his previous novels, it's a fun and enjoyable story.
Word Forms: frivolously, frivolousness, frivolity, frivol, frivoler

☐ **frugal**: (*adj*) characterized by the avoidance of excessive spending
A frugal shopper will always wait for items to go on sale or clearance before purchasing them.
Word Forms: frugally, frugalness, frugality

☐ **fulminate**: (*vb*) to explode loudly or to loudly pronounce
Phil was angry at his boss and fulminated his frustrations to his coworkers at lunch.
Word Forms: fulminator, fulminatory, fulmination   Antonym Form: nonfulminating, unfulminated,
unfulminating

☐ **furtive**: (*adj*) sneaky
Frank devised a furtive plan in which he would sneak onto the rival's campus and steal their school flag.
Word Forms: furtively, furtiveness

☐ **gambol**: (*n*) to skip and frolic
Grandma was a fun friend; she gamboled through the field with me, collecting flowers and chasing butterflies.

☐ **garner**: (*vb*) to earn or to collect
Garrett garnered a reputation as a fierce lawyer after winning the trial amid national scrutiny.
Antonym Form: ungarnered

☐ **garrulous**: (*adj*) excessively talkative or wordy
The garrulous hairdresser talked the entire time he cut my hair.
Word Forms: garrulously, garrulousness, garrulity

☐ **genial**: (*adj*) polite and friendly
It's important for a kindergarten teacher to be genial; young children respond positively to a friendly adult.
Word Forms: genially, genialness, geniality   Related Word: congenial

germane: (*adj*) related to; relevant
I have some ideas germane to the discussion that might resolve some of the issues we are having.
Word Forms: germanely, germaneness　　　Antonym Forms: nongermane, ungermane

glib: (*adj*) fluent and talkative, often insincerely so
The glib salesman promised me that the car had been inspected, but the transmission blew two days after I bought it.
Word Forms: glibly, glibness　　　Antonym Forms: unglib, unglibly

glower: (*vb*) to stare with dislike or anger
Mr. Glover glowered at me after I walked on his flowers.
Word Form: gloweringly　　　Antonym Forms: unglowering, ungloweringly

gradation: (*n*) gradual or successive changes
The bumble bee can see subtle gradations in color that humans are unable to notice.
Word Forms: gradational, gradationally　　　Related Word: regradation

gratuitous: (*adj*) free; given without reason
On Monday, our supervisor announced that all employees were receiving two gratuitous tickets to this weekend's concert.
Word Forms: gratuitously, gratuitousness, gratuity

gregarious: (*adj*) sociable
Greg is a gregarious student who finds it difficult to avoid socializing during class.
Word Forms: gregariously, gregariousness　　　Antonym Form: ungregarious

grievous: (*adj*) causing grief or very serious
During the war, families feared news from a grievous telegram indicating that their loved one had been injured or killed.
Word Forms: grievously, grievousness　　　Antonym Forms: nongrievous, nongrievously, nongrievousness

grovel: (*vb*) lowering oneself as in asking forgiveness or showing respect
Grover groveled for forgiveness from his mother after he broke her favorite vase.
Word Forms: groveler, grovelingly　　　Antonym Form: ungroveling

guile: (*n*) a skillful deception
The sneaky woman used guile to get close to the withdrawn millionaire; she pretended to have known his brother who died in the war.
Word Forms: guileful, guilefully, guilefulness　　　Antonym Forms: guileless, guilelessly, guilelessness
Related Words: guise, disguise

gustatory: (*adj*) relating to the sense of taste
The restaurant provides a gustatory experience by offering skewers of beef, pork, and poultry marinated in exotic oils.
Word Forms: gustatorily, gustation, gustative, gustativeness

hackneyed: (*adj*) repeated too often; overfamiliar through overuse
Instead of relying on hackneyed clichés in your essay, try to create original metaphors and similes.
Word Form: hackney (vb.)

halcyon: (*adj*) joyful, peaceful, or prosperous
During the company's halcyon days, the employees were making higher than average wages and enjoying benefits unmatched by other corporations.
Word Forms: halcyonian, halcyonic

hapless: (*adj*) unlucky
The hapless fellow was in a car accident on the same day he lost the winning lottery ticket.
Word Forms: haplessly, haplessness

harangue: (*n*) a long, pompous speech
At the assembly, the principal delivered a harangue on the merits of perfect attendance and good behavior.
Word Forms: harangue (vb.), harangueful, haranguer

hedonist: (*n*) a person dedicated to the pursuit of pleasure
After working for years as a hospice nurse, Heidi had no respect for the hedonist who lived next door; by only seeking pleasure, he left the more unpleasant activities to caretakers like Heidi.
Word Forms: hedonist (adj.), hedonistic, hedonistically, hedonism, hedonic, hedonically

☐ **hegemony**: (*n*) leadership
The country exerted its hegemony over the smaller territories.
Word Forms: hegemonic, hegemonical Antonym Form: antihegemony

☐ **heretical**: (*adj*) characteristic of an opinion at odds with accepted beliefs
Many people in the church believe the heretical teaching of evolution should be banned.
Word Forms: heresy, heretic, heretically, hereticalness Antonym Forms: nonheretical, nonheretically

☐ **hermetic**: (*adj*) isolated and protected
Many of the sea islands were hermetic during the Civil War, making them a safe place for runaway slaves to hide.
Word Forms: hermetical, hermetically Antonym Form: unhermetic Related Word: hermit

☐ **histrionic**: (*adj*) overly dramatic
The histrionic patient pretended to faint when he saw the needle used for the vaccination.
Word Forms: histrionic (n.), histrionics, histrionical, histrionically

☐ **hoary**: (*adj*) old or stale
Harry tells the same hoary stories at every dinner party.
Word Forms: hoarily, hoariness Antonym Form: unhoary

☐ **hubris**: (*n*) pride; arrogance
If pride goes before a fall, hubris goes before a downfall.
Word Form: hubristic Antonym Forms: nonhubristic, unhubristic

☐ **husband**: (*vb*) to manage wisely or thriftily
Henry husbanded his finances so that he would have plenty to live on in retirement.
Word Form: husbander Antonym Form: unhusbanded Related Word: husband (n)

☐ **iconoclast**: (*n*) a person who attacks cherished ideas or traditional institutions
Many religious leaders accused the author of being an iconoclast for presenting evidence that contrasted with the religion's long-standing beliefs.
Word Forms: iconoclastic, iconoclastically, iconoclasm

☐ **idiosyncrasy**: (*n*) a characteristic that is peculiar to a specific person
Some people found Ida's idiosyncrasy a source of humor, but I never made fun of her for wearing her shirt backwards.
Word Forms: idiosyncratic, idiosyncratically

☐ **idolatrous**: (*adj*) great adoration
The young girl's idolatrous worship of the teen heartthrob began to worry her mother.
Word Forms: idolatry, idolatrously, idolatrousness
Antonym Forms: nonidolatrous, nonidolatrously, nonidolatrousness Related Words: idol, idolize

☐ **ignoble**: (*adj*) dishonorable; common
Your ignoble behavior at the dinner party will keep you off of invitation lists in the future.
Word Forms: ignobility, ignobleness, ignobly Antonym Forms: noble, nobility, nobly

☐ **ignominious**: (*adj*) disgraceful and shameful
Izzy's ignominious crime brought shame and embarrassment to her entire family.
Word Forms: ignominiously, ignominiousness, ignominy

☐ **illusory**: (*adj*) creating illusions; deceiving
The illusory sweepstakes isn't really a contest at all; "winners" think they have won a free cruise, but the trip actually costs several hundred dollars and requires attendance at marketing seminars.
Word Forms: illusorily, illusoriness, illusive Related Word: illusion

☐ **imbue**: (*vb*) to inspire
After the seminar, our supervisor was imbued with the teachings of the keynote speaker, a management expert.
Word Form: imbuement Antonym Form: unimbue

☐ **immutable**: (*adj*) unchangeable
We are born with some immutable characteristics, such as race, gender, height, and eye color.
Word Forms: immutability, immutableness, immutably Antonym Form: mutable Related Word: mutation

☐ **impasse**: (*n*) blocked progress; deadlock
We came to an impasse in our discussion about our wedding colors; we both refused to compromise.

☐ **impecunious**: (*adj*) poor
In less than a year, Imogen had lost all of her money, going from a wealthy businesswoman to an impecunious beggar.
Word Forms: impecuniously, impecuniousness, impecuniosity

☐ **imperturbable**: (*adj*) calm; incapable of agitation
Imelda had imperturbable composure, which is why she was selected to tackle the nerve-wracking feat.
Word Forms: imperturbability, imperturbableness, imperturbably   Antonym Forms: perturb, perturbable

☐ **impervious**: (*adj*) not capable of being affected
Ima was impervious to Jack's insults; nothing he said seemed to affect her.
Word Forms: imperviously, imperviousness, imperviable   Antonym Forms: pervious, perviously, perviousness

☐ **impetuous**: (*adj*) impulsive
While at the airshow to see old war planes, Ivan made an impetuous decision to go skydiving.
Word Forms: impetuously, impetuousness, impetuosity   Related Word: impetus

☐ **impious**: (*adj*) lacking respect or devotion, usually for a god or religion
Imogene had a difficult time convincing her impious husband to attend church with the family.
Word Forms: impiously, impiousness   Antonym Forms: pious, piously, piousness

☐ **implacable**: (*adj*) incapable of being pacified or appeased
Inez was so upset at the waiter that she became implacable; nothing the manager offered was going to make her happy.
Word Forms: implacability, implacableness, implacably   Antonym Forms: placable, placably, placability
Related Word: placid

☐ **implicit**: (*adj*) implied though not directly expressed
Although we never mentioned the fight, there seemed to be an implicit agreement not to talk about it.
Word Forms: implicitly, implicitness, implicity   Antonym Forms: explicit, explicitly, explicitness

☐ **imprecation**: (*n*) a curse
The old woman dabbled in voodoo, and was known for casting imprecations on her enemies.
Word Forms: imprecate, imprecator, imprecatory   Antonym Form: unimprecated

☐ **impugn**: (*vb*) to attack as false or wrong
The candidate impugned his opponent's voting record, proving that she had voted against reform she now supports.
Word Forms: impugnable, impugnability, impugnment, impugner   Related Word: oppugn

☐ **impute**: (*vb*) to attribute or credit to
The doctors imputed her sudden weight loss to a problem with her thyroid gland.
Word Forms: imputable, imputably, imputative, imputatively, imputativeness, imputedly, imputer   Related Word: putative

☐ **incarnadine**: (*adj*) red or pink; flesh-colored
For Valentine's Day, I gave my girlfriend incarnadine carnations since red is the color of love and passion.
Word Form: incarnadine (vb)   Related Word: carnation

☐ **inchoate**: (*adj*) in the early stages of development
Your inchoate plan for the fund-raiser has a lot of potential, but we need to discuss some details before moving forward.
Word Forms: inchoately, inchoateness, inchoation, inchoative, inchoatively

☐ **incipient**: (*adj*) beginning; just starting
The zinc lozenges will help an incipient cold, but do nothing for a well-established virus.
Word Forms: incipiently, incipience, incipiency

☐ **incontrovertible**: (*adj*) unquestionable; impossible to deny
Protesters demanded the release of the imprisoned woman, saying there was incontrovertible proof of her innocence.
Word Forms: incontrovertibly, incontrovertibility, incontrovertibleness
Antonym Forms: controvertible, controvertibly, controvertibility, controvertibleness, controvert

☐ **incorrigible**: (*adj*) incapable of being corrected or punished
The incorrigible child continued to throw his vegetables even after the mother threatened to send him to his room.
Word Forms: incorrigibly, incorrigibleness, incorrigibility
Antonym Forms: corrigible, corrigibly, corrigibleness, corrigibility

☐ **incredulous**: (*adj*) skeptical; not willing to believe
The incredulous car buyer did not believe the dealer's claim that the car was accident-free; he insisted on seeing a report on the car's history.
Word Forms: incredulously, incredulousness, incredulity   Related Word: incredible
Antonym Forms: credulous, credulously, credulousness, credulity

☐ **inculcate**: (*vb*) to teach through persistent repetition
Ms. Ingles inculcated her students with a love of reading; many years later, an overwhelming majority reported that they were still voracious readers.
Word Forms: inculcation, inculcative, inculcator

☐ **indigenous**: (*adj*) native to
Although the flower can now be found all over the eastern United States, it is indigenous to Florida.
Word Forms: indigenously, indigenousness, indigeneity, indigen, indigene

☐ **indignant**: (*adj*) displaying anger due to unfairness
The seniors were indignant over their disqualification in the homecoming contest, claiming that the decision was unfair.
Word Forms: indignantly, indignation

☐ **indolent**: (*adj*) lazy
India was an indolent worker, and was thus fired when it was discovered that she was lazy.
Word Forms: indolently, indolence

☐ **ineffable**: (*adj*) incapable of being put into words
Effie's joy at being reunited with her long-lost brother was ineffable; words could not explain her happiness.
Word Forms: ineffably, ineffableness, ineffability   Antonym Form: effable

☐ **inexorable**: (*adj*) unyielding
Mary Ingalls was aware that she would lose her sight before she began her inexorable decline into blindness.
Word Forms: inexorability, inexorably, inexorableness   Antonym Form: exorable

☐ **ingenious**: (*adj*) clever and inventive
Jeannie invented an ingenious device for the beach that combined a cooler, radio, and portable fan.
Word Forms: ingeniously, ingeniousness, ingenuity   Related Word: genius

☐ **ingenue**: (*n*) an artless, innocent young girl (especially as portrayed on the stage)
The young actress will play the part of the ingenue, an innocent girl who becomes caught up in the plot in Act II.
Related Word: ingenuous

☐ **ingrate**: (*n*) an ungrateful person
Inga came off as an ingrate when she failed to thank her hosts for dinner.
Word Form: ingrately   Related Word: grateful

☐ **ingratiate**: (*vb*) to put oneself in another's good graces
Ingrid's boyfriend ingratiated himself with her father by sharing a love of classic movies and old cars.
Word Forms: ingratiation, ingratiatory, ingratiating

☐ **inherent**: (*adj*) existing as a natural and essential characteristic
The abused dog had an inherent distrust of men, so only female volunteers at the shelter could get close to him.
Word Forms: inherently, inhere, inherence   Related Word: inherit

☐ **inimical**: (*adj*) harmful or hostile
Oscar cast an inimical sneer at Melissa when she took credit for his idea.
Word Forms: inimically, inimicalness, inimicality, inimicable   Related Word: enemy

☐ **iniquity**: (*n*) wickedness
The wicked witch's iniquity kept Dorothy from returning to Kansas.
Word Forms: iniquitous, iniquitously, iniquitousness

☐ **innocuous**: (*adj*) harmless
No one had to be evacuated after the tanker spill, as the gas released was innocuous.
Word Forms: innocuously, innocuousness, innocuity   Antonym Forms: nocuous, nocuously, nocuousness
Related Word: inoculate

insidious: (*adj*) intended to entrap, deceive, or harm
Sid devised an insidious plan to get the witness to admit he hadn't really witnessed the crime.
Word Forms: insidiously, insidiousness

insipid: (*adj*) bland, dull, or uninteresting
When I left for college, the insipid cafeteria food made me miss my father's home-cooked meals.
Word Forms: insipidly, insipidness, insipidity   Antonym Forms: sipid, sipidity

insolence: (*n*) rudeness
The headmaster said that insolence would not be tolerated; rude behavior towards a teacher would result in suspension.
Word Forms: insolent (n.), insolently, insolence

insular: (*adj*) narrow-minded; isolated
The culture is criticized for its insular ideas, such as the belief that women should not be allowed to attend school.
Word Forms: insularly, insularism, insularity

insurrection: (*n*) a rebellion or uprising
King George ordered British troops to quash the colonist's insurrection, but the uprising led to the Revolutionary War.
Word Forms: insurrectional, insurrectionally, insurrectionism, insurrectionist

inter: (*vb*) to bury
James Garfield, the 20th President of the United States who was assassinated in 1881, was interred in Cleveland, Ohio.
Word Form: reinter   Antonym Form: uninterred

interlocutor: (*n*) a person who takes part in a conversation
At the apartment complex, the two interlocutors continued to debate the merits of television outside my bedroom window until well after midnight.
Word Forms: interlocution, interlocutory   Related Words: locution, eloquent

interregnum: (*n*) a period of time free from authority
When the king died, there was a two week interregnum as the prince returned from abroad for his coronation.
Word Form: interregnal

intractable: (*adj*) stubborn; difficult to manage
The intractable child refused to let the babysitter into the room.
Word Forms: intractability, intractableness, intractably

intransigent: (*adj*) refusing to yield or compromise
When it came to Edgar's hunting trophies, Enid was intransigent; she refused to hang the deer heads on the wall.
Word Forms: intransigent (n.), intransigently, intransigence, intransigency

inundate: (*vb*) to flood
After the newspaper ran the controversial story, the editor was inundated with calls from hundreds of angry subscribers.
Word Forms: inundation, inundatory, inundator

inure: (*vb*) to become used to
People in Alaska were inured to cold weather.
Word Forms: inuredness, inurement   Antonym Form: uninured

invective: (*n*) violent criticism
The governor was quick to issue an invective denouncing the show that portrayed her state's residents as vulgar and obscene.
Word Forms: invective (adj), invectively, invectiveness   Antonym Form: uninvective

inveigle: (*vb*) to persuade with smooth talk
Vicki inveigled Vivianne into playing checkers, even though Vivianne would have rather played chess.
Word Forms: inveiglement, inveigler   Antonym Form: uninveigled

investiture: (*n*) ceremony for bestowing an official title
At the investiture, the detective was promoted to sergeant.
Word Form: investitive

☐ **invidious**: (*adj*) intended to hurt, offend, or discriminate
Ivan's invidious remarks to his wife shocked their guests; they had no idea that he could be so cruel.
Word Forms: invidiously, invidiousness

☐ **invoke**: (*vb*) to summon into action or bring into existence
The psychic claimed that he could invoke the spirits in the house through an old-fashioned séance.
Word Forms: invocable, invocation, invocational, invoker   Related Words: evoke, provoke, revoke

☐ **irascible**: (*adj*) quickly aroused to anger
The irascible old lady caused a scene at the restaurant by yelling at the manager when her hamburger was overcooked.
Word Forms: irascibly, irascibleness, irascibility   Related Word: ire

☐ **itinerant**: (*adj*) traveling from place to place to work
The itinerant pastor was transferred to our church from a ministry in Ohio; he will stay with us for six months before going to New Hampshire.
Word Forms: itinerant (n.), itinerantly, itinerate, itineration   Related Word: itinerary

☐ **jettison**: (*vb*) to throw away
Jett was arrested when he jettisoned old boat fuel into the harbor.
Word Form: jettisonable

☐ **jingoism**: (*n*) noisy and excessive patriotism for one's country
The candidate's jingoism cost him the election, as constituents did not believe he could tactfully handle foreign policy.
Word Forms: jingo, jingoish, jingoist, jingoistic, jingoistically

☐ **jocular**: (*adj*) characterized by joking
Jack's speeches were always entertaining because they were peppered with jocular anecdotes.
Word Forms: jocularly, overjocular, jocularity   Related Word: joke

☐ **juncture**: (*n*) a critical point in time
At this juncture, I think it's important to merge the Human Resources and Marketing departments.

☐ **juxtapose**: (*vb*) to place side by side
When Justin's picture was juxtaposed with his father's picture, the resemblance between the two was remarkable.
Word Form: juxtaposition   Related Word: pose

☐ **keen**: (*adj*) sharp as in a point, or sharp as in intelligence
It will take a keen mind to solve this difficult puzzle.
Word Forms: keenly, keenness

☐ **kindle**: (*vb*) to light up or to excite
The novel "Jurassic Park" kindled his interest in dinosaurs.
Word Form: kindler   Related Word: kindling

☐ **kinetic**: (*adj*) characterized by motion
Some students are kinetic learners who learn best when they are moving around.
Word Form: kinetically   Antonym Form: nonkinetic   Related Words: telekinesis, kinetics

☐ **knell**: (*n*) sound of a bell at a funeral or a sign of looming death or destruction
The town was quiet, with boarded up buildings and no sign of life, a knell of the impending war.
Word Form: knell (vb)

☐ **lachrymose**: (*adj*) tearful; sad
Lakeisa tends to get lachrymose over animal rescue commercials depicting cats and dogs in abusive situations.
Word Forms: lachrymosely, lachrymosity

☐ **laconic**: (*adj*) expressing much in few words
A laconic essay will be scored higher than an essay with unnecessary words or sentences.
Word Forms: laconically, laconism   Antonym Form: unlaconic

☐ **lament**: (*vb*) to express grief; to mourn
When Lamont left for college, his little sister lamented his absence for weeks.
Word Forms: lament (n.), lamentingly, lamentable, lamentably, lamenter   Antonym Form: unlamented

A

☐ **lampoon**: (*vb*) to mock in a satire
The actors of "Saturday Night Live" make a living by lampooning current events.
Word Forms: lampoon (n), lampooner, lampoonist, lampoonery   Antonym Form: unlampooned

☐ **languid**: (*adj*) lacking in energy or spirit
My boss's languid response to my proposal wasn't expected; I thought he'd be excited about my initiative and creativity.
Word Forms: languidly, languidness   Antonym Forms: unlanguid, unlanguidly, unlanguidness
Related Word: languish

☐ **lapidary**: (*adj*) relating to polished stones; characterized by exactness and extreme polishing
The author's lapidary manuscript was so carefully crafted that editors could find no mistakes.
Word Forms: lapidarian, lapidarist

☐ **largess**: (*n*) generous gift-giving
Larissa's largess at the twins' birthday party would not soon be forgotten; she gave them enough toys to keep them busy for a year.
Related Word: large

☐ **lassitude**: (*n*) lack of energy; weariness
One symptom of the illness was lassitude; Leslie learned early on that she had no energy during an attack.

☐ **latent**: (*adj*) existing but not visible or obvious
Latika clearly had latent ability in math, but she failed to put forward any effort in the subject so no one knew how bright she really was.
Word Forms: latently, latency

☐ **laud**: (*vb*) to praise, glorify, or honor
Landon was lauded for his achievements at the laboratory; he had made more progress in a year than most scientists had made in a decade.
Word Forms: laudable, laudably, laudation, laudative, laudatory, laudator

☐ **lavish**: (*adj*) very generous or extravagant
The lavish wedding reception had a steak and lobster dinner, several intricate ice sculptures, and a famous jazz band.
Word Forms: lavishly, lavishness, lavishment, lavisher

☐ **legerdemain**: (*n*) trickery; sleight of hand
The magician employed legerdemain to fool the audience into believing he pulled a rabbit from his hat.
Word Form: legerdemainist

☐ **levity**: (*n*) inappropriate lack of seriousness
The teenagers' levity during the assembly on drinking and driving cost them six Saturdays in detention.

☐ **lexicography**: (*n*) the act of writing dictionaries
Noah Webster's career in lexicography developed from his dissatisfaction with British school books; he wrote his first dictionary to help his elementary students learn to spell.
Word Forms: lexicographic, lexicographical, lexicographically, lexicographer   Related Words: lexicon, dyslexic

☐ **liberate**: (*vb*) free; unrestrained
When the farmer accidentally left the stall door open, the liberated horse sprinted for the woods.
Word Forms: liberated, liberative, liberatory, liberation, liberator   Antonym Form: unliberated

☐ **libertine**: (*adj*) unrestrained by morals
Libby had no scruples and thus made libertine choices, never worrying about those affected or what others would think.
Word Forms: libertine (n), libertinage, libertinism

☐ **licentious**: (*adj*) unrestrained by morals
Libby had no scruples and thus made licentious choices, never worrying about those affected or what others would think.
Word Forms: licentiously, licentiousness   Antonym Form: nonlicentious, nonlicentiously, nonlicentiousness
Related Word: license

☐ **limpid**: (*adj*) clear; calm
The limpid waters provided opportunity for the anglers to sight cast directly to the fish they could see in the clear water.
Word Forms: limpidity, limpidness, limpidly

☐ **lissome**: (*adj*) flexible
The lissome gymnast dazzled the audience with her tumbling routine.
Word Forms: lissomely, lissomeness

☐ **listless**: (*adj*) lacking energy or spirit
My boss's listless response to my proposal wasn't expected; I thought he'd be excited about my initiative and creativity.
Word Forms: listlessly, listlessness

☐ **loquacious**: (*adj*) extremely talkative
Lance was disappointed in his loquacious date; she talked so much that she never had time to listen to any of his stories.
Word Forms: loquaciously, loquaciousness, loquacity   Related Words: eloquent, ventriloquist, soliloquy

☐ **lucid**: (*adj*) clear; easy to understand
If your directions had been more lucid, I might have made it to the party on time.
Word Forms: lucidly, lucidness, lucidity   Related Word: elucidate

☐ **lugubrious**: (*adj*) excessively mournful; sad and gloomy
Lucy's lugubrious behavior has started to annoy her friends; it has been two months since her breakup with Josh, but she is still as gloomy as if it had happened yesterday.
Word Forms: lugubriously, lugubriousness, lugubriosity

☐ **luminous**: (*adj*) radiating light; enlightening; easily understood
The meeting was luminous because we finally figured out the reason that the mayor was backing the construction project.
Word Forms: luminously, luminousness   Antonym Forms: nonluminous, nonluminously, nonluminousness
Related Words: luminary, illuminate, luminescent

☐ **machination**: (*n*) a crafty plot
The fairy tale follows the machinations of an evil stepsister who is out to steal the prince from the heroine.
Word Forms: machinate, machinator

☐ **maelstrom**: (*n*) a powerful whirlpool or turbulent chaos
When the manager was fired, he left the office in a maelstrom; there was frequent infighting and little leadership.

☐ **magnanimous**: (*adj*) noble and generous in spirit
The magnanimous donor has given over ten million dollars to children's charities in the city.
Word Forms: magnanimously, magnanimousness, magnanimity

☐ **magnate**: (*n*) an important person in a field of business
Henry Ford was an automotive magnate, manufacturing the first automobile that was affordable to the middle class.
Word Form: magnateship

☐ **malediction**: (*n*) a curse
The members of the team feared that the old woman had placed a malediction upon their season because they hadn't won a game since accidentally shattering her windshield with a foul ball.
Word Forms: maledictive, maledictory, maledict   Antonym Forms: benediction, benedictive, benedictory
Related Words: diction, dictate, dictionary

☐ **malevolent**: (*adj*) evil
The malevolent old man plotted the demise of his neighbor's barking dog.
Word Forms: malevolently, malevolence, malevolency

☐ **malice**: (*n*) a desire to make others suffer
Malika's sharp comment was delivered with malice; she knew that her words would hurt her mother's feelings.
Word Forms: malicious, maliciously, maliciousness   Antonym Form: unmalicious

malinger: (*vb*) to fake an illness to avoid responsibility
Malinda claims to have strep throat, but since she has been known to malinger in the past make sure she brings a doctor's note when she returns to work.
Word Form: malingerer

malleable: (*adj*) capable of being shaped or influenced
Mallory worried that her malleable son would learn inappropriate behavior from the older boys he played with at school.
Word Forms: malleably, malleableness, malleability   Antonym Forms: unmalleable, unmalleability

malodorous: (*adj*) having an unpleasant smell
My malodorous shoe smelled so terrible that my mom threw it away.
Word Forms: malodorously, malodorousness   Related Words: odor, odorously

mar: (*vb*) to make imperfect; to disfigure
My nearly-perfect report card was marred by a low grade in speech class.
Word Forms: mar (n.), marred (adj.)   Antonym Form: unmarred

martial: (*adj*) relating to war
The mayor was in favor of taking a martial approach to the problem, preferring to send soldiers into the abandoned houses to remove the squatters and drug dealers.
Word Forms: martialism, martialist, martially, martialness   Antonym Form: nonmartial

martinet: (*n*) a person who rigidly demands that rules are followed; a strict disciplinarian
Marty realized that the drill sergeant was a martinet, so his best course of action was to closely follow all the rules.
Word Forms: martinetish, martinetism

matriarch: (*n*) the female head of a family
As the matriarch of the family, Grandma sat at the head of the Thanksgiving dinner table.
Word Forms: matriarchal, matriarchic, matriarchalism, matriarchy
Antonym Forms: patriarch, patriarchal, patriarchic, patriarchalism, patriarchy   Related Words: ma, maternal

maudlin: (*adj*) foolishly emotional
When Maude drinks too much, she becomes maudlin, crying over silly things like her shoelaces coming untied.
Word Forms: maudlinism, maudlinly, maudlinness   Antonym Forms: unmaudlin, unmaudlinly

maverick: (*n*) a person who chooses to be independent in behavior or thought
Even though the other ranchers were branding their cattle, Sam was a maverick who believed he did not need to follow the rules set by his associates.

melange: (*n*) a mixture
Melanie's walls are decorated with a mélange of surfing posters and beach photographs.

mendacious: (*adj*) lying, false, or untrue
The mendacious girl said that she didn't take her mother's lipstick, but the bright red evidence was all over her face.
Word Forms: mendaciously, mendaciousness, mendacity

mendicant: (*adj*) begging
In the poverty-stricken country, mendicant children approach tourists to ask for food and money.
Word Forms: mendicancy, mendicity

mercurial: (*adj*) apt to change; volatile; lively
Meryl was known for her mercurial moods; she could be charming and kind one minute and caustic and hateful the next.
Word Forms: mercurially, mercurialness   Antonym Forms: unmercurial, unmercurially, unmercurialness
Related Word: mercury

meretricious: (*adj*) insincere; flashily attractive
Meredith bestowed meretricious praise upon Mark on-camera, but she had nothing nice to say about him off-camera.
Word Forms: meretriciously, meretriciousness   Antonym Form: unmeretricious, unmeretriciously, unmeretriciousness

meritocracy: (*n*) a form of social system in which power goes to those with superior abilities
Critics argue that a meritocracy cannot be fairly created, as intelligence and ability are difficult to measure accurately.
Word Form: meritocratic   Related Word: merit

☐ **meticulous**: (*adj*) extremely careful and precise with details
Miss Walter demanded meticulous essays; perfect spelling and punctuation were essential for a high grade.
Word Forms: meticulously, meticulousness, meticulosity

☐ **militate**: (*vb*) to have substantial influence
Millie's grandfather's significant donations to the university militated for her acceptance in the admissions process.
Word Form: militation   Related Words: military, militia

☐ **mirth**: (*n*) laughter or merriment
Even the old scrooge could not resist the mirth of the holiday season, as he eventually joined in the celebration.
Word Forms: mirthful, mirthfully, mirthfulness,   Antonym Forms: mirthless, mirthlessly, mirthlessness

☐ **misanthrope**: (*n*) a person who hates and distrusts mankind
The main character is a bitter misanthrope who learns to trust again through her friendship with the children next door.
Word Forms: misanthropist, misanthropic, misanthropical, misanthropically, misanthropy

☐ **miscreant**: (*n*) a person who is evil or villainous
The miscreant came to town with the intention of creating strife and commotion, as he enjoyed watching others argue.
Word Forms: miscreant (adj.), miscreance, miscreancy

☐ **miser**: (*n*) a stingy person who lives in miserable conditions in order to save money
The old miser lives in a rat-infested apartment even though he has more than enough money to live in a nice home.
Word Forms: miserly, miserliness   Related Words: misery, miserable

☐ **missive**: (*n*) a letter
The governor sent out missives to her supportive constituents, thanking them for their contributions to her campaign.

☐ **mitigate**: (*vb*) to make less intense or severe
Mitch was grounded for a week when he broke curfew, but his mom mitigated his punishment by several days when she learned that he had been late because he was taking a sick friend to the hospital.
Word Forms: mitigable, mitigatedly, mitigation, mitigative, mitigatory, mitigator
Antonym Forms: immitigable, immitigably, immitigability, unmitigable, unmitigated, unmitigatedly

☐ **mollify**: (*vb*) to soften or soothe
Molly was able to mollify the crying child by offering him an ice cream cone.
Word Forms: mollification, mollifier, mollifyingly, mollifiable

☐ **molt**: (*vb*) to shed feathers
The cockatoo molted every spring in preparation for new feathers.
Word Form: molter

☐ **monastic**: (*adj*) relating to monasteries or relating to a dedicated way of life
Mona lived a monastic life, refraining from sensual pleasures and the accumulation of material possessions.
Word Form: monastically   Antonym Forms: nonmonastic , nonmonastically
Related Words: pseudomonastic, monastery

☐ **morass**: (*n*) 1. a swamp 2. a difficult situation
After Morgan accepted Jill's invitation to the dance, he found himself in a morass; his friend offered him a ticket to a concert that he really wanted to see, but it happened to be on the same night as the dance.

☐ **moratorium**: (*n*) suspension of an ongoing activity
When many students were late returning from lunch, the principal placed a moratorium on off-campus lunch privileges.
Word Form: moratory

☐ **mores**: (*n*) important customs or beliefs of a group
The advertisements in the housekeeping magazine from 1950 reflect the social mores of the time.

☐ **morose**: (*adj*) gloomy
After his girlfriend moved away, Morris became morose and depressed.
Word Forms: morosely, moroseness, morosity

☐ **multifarious:** (*adj*) having many parts and much variety
The school offers multifarious activities after school; children should have no problem finding a program that matches their interests.
Word Forms: multifariously, multifariousness

☐ **mundane:** (*adj*) ordinary and somewhat boring
While a trip to the beach had once been exciting, we went so often that it had become mundane.
Word Forms: mundanely, mundaneness, mundanity

☐ **munificent:** (*adj*) very generous
The munificent donor gave the hospital enough money to build a specialized center for heart patients.
Word Forms: munificently, munificentness, munificence

☐ **myopic:** (*adj*) lacking long-term vision
Maya has a myopic outlook when it comes to investment; she complains about the money she is investing now, rather than focusing on the money she will make in the future.
Word Forms: myopically, myopia

☐ **nadir:** (*n*) the lowest point
Nadia entered the nadir of despair when she lost her job and her fiance called off the wedding.
Word Form: nadiral

☐ **naïve:** (*adj*) inexperienced and gullible
Nan was naïve in thinking that no one looked at her online social page except her friends; her father looked at it daily.
Word Forms: naïvely, naïveness, naïveté

☐ **narcissist:** (*n*) a person who has excessive love or admiration of oneself
Nancy is a narcissist who is unable to love her husband or her children as much as she loves herself.
Word Forms: narcist, narcissism, narcistic, narcissistic, narcissistically

☐ **nascent:** (*adj*) being born or beginning
The nascent hockey team did not have much experience, as this was their first year in the league.
Word Forms: nascence, nascency

☐ **nebulous:** (*adj*) vague or cloudy
When I woke up in the hospital, I only had a nebulous memory of the accident.
Word Forms: nebulously, nebulousness   Antonym Forms: nonnebulous, nonnebulously, nonnebulousness

☐ **nefarious:** (*adj*) extremely wicked
In the novel, the nefarious character plotted to financially destroy the hero.
Word Forms: nefariously, nefariousness

☐ **neologism:** (*n*) a new word
Each year Merriam Webster decides which neologisms will be granted entry into their dictionaries.
Word Forms: neologist, neologistic, neologistical, neology

☐ **neophyte:** (*n*) a beginner
Neil is a neophyte at downhill skiing, so he should stick to the smaller hills today.
Word Forms: neophytic, neophytish, neophytism

☐ **nettle:** (*vb*) to irritate
I was nettled by her annoying voice.
Word Forms: nettle (n), nettler, nettly   Antonym Form: unnettled

☐ **nihilism:** (*n*) belief in the rejection of rules and the destruction of social and political order
During the rebellion, the followers of nihilism were the first to break the laws in the city.
Word Forms: nihilistic, nihilistically, nihility, nihilist

☐ **noisome:** (*adj*) offensive (especially odors)
My noisome shoe smelled so terrible that my mom threw it away.
Word Forms: noisomely, noisomeness

☐ **nominal:** (*adj*) in name only; minimal
The president was a nominal leader; the real people making the important decisions were his advisors.
Word Form: prenominal   Antonym Forms: unnominal, unnominally

☐ **noxious**: (*adj*) harmful
The danger of a carbon dioxide leak is that the noxious fumes are odorless.
Word Forms: noxiously, noxiousness

☐ **nuance**: (*n*) a subtle difference
The nuances between the two fonts are often missed by the untrained graphic designer.
Word Form: nuanced

☐ **numismatic**: (*adj*) pertaining to coins or medals
The archeologist found numismatic evidence of the ancient civilization, including three coins with depictions of animals.
Word Forms: numismatics, numismatical, numismatically

☐ **obdurate**: (*adj*) stubborn
The obdurate child refused to eat his vegetables and sat at the dinner table with the untouched broccoli until bedtime.
Word Forms: obdurately, obdurateness, obduracy   Related Word: indurate

☐ **obfuscate**: (*vb*) to confuse or make unclear
If a solution to a math question requires units to be in inches, the test makers may obfuscate the question by using feet.
Word Forms: obfuscation, obfuscatory

☐ **oblique**: (*adj*) slanting; not straight; indirect or evasive
The politician made oblique comments about his opponent, hinting at corruption but not actually saying it was an issue.
Word Forms: obliquely, obliqueness

☐ **obstreperous**: (*adj*) noisily defiant or aggressive
The obstreperous students crowded the school board meeting to protest the new dress code.
Word Forms: obstreperously, obstreperousness, obstreperosity

☐ **obscure**: (*adj*) not clearly understood or expressed
Most of the movie audience did not understand the obscure reference to the other movie.
Word Forms: obscure (vb.), obscurely, obscureness, obscuredly, obscurity

☐ **obsequious**: (*adj*) overly flattering or obedient
The new employee was distrusted by his co-workers because of his obsequious behavior; he agreed with everything the boss said and laughed at all of her bad jokes.
Word Forms: obsequiously, obsequiousness, obsequence

☐ **obstinate**: (*adj*) extremely stubborn
Mr. O'Brien was obstinate about eating at the bistro; he refused to eat anywhere else.
Word Form: obstinately, obstinateness, obstinacy

☐ **obstreperous**: (*adj*) noisily defiant or aggressive
The obstreperous students crowded the school board meeting to protest the new dress code.
Word Forms: obstreperously, obstreperousness, obstreperosity

☐ **obstructionist**: (*n*) a person who purposely blocks progress
Alberta worried that obstructionists would interfere with her environmental bill, ending her efforts to save the eagles.
Word Forms: obstructionistic, obstructionism   Related Words: obstruct, obstruction, obstructive

☐ **obtuse**: (*adj*) intellectually slow; dull
You might have to simplify your explanation of photosynthesis because Obie is a bit obtuse.
Word Forms: obtusely, obtuseness

☐ **obviate**: (*vb*) to prevent any perceived difficulty
The car seat manufacturer obviated the risk of injury by removing the cup holder from the most recent model.
Word Forms: obviable, obviation, obviator, preobviate   Antonym Form: unobviable

☐ **occlude**: (*vb*) to shut or block
Plaque buildup in the arteries can occlude the flow of blood resulting in heart disease.
Word Forms: occludent, occlusion, occlusal   Antonym Forms: include, nonocclusion

odious: (*adj*) offensive; hateful
The majority of Americans view dog fighting as an odious crime.
Word Forms: odiously, odiousness   Related Word: odium

officious: (*adj*) aggressively forward
My officious neighbor insisted on helping me after my accident, but I really just wanted to be left alone.
Word Forms: officiously, officiousness, overofficious

ominous: (*adj*) threatening or foreshadowing evil
The dark clouds in the distance were ominous and threatened to ruin the picnic.
Word Forms: ominously, ominousness   Related Word: omen

onerous: (*adj*) oppressive; burdensome
Cinderella was saddled with onerous household duties while she lived with her wicked stepmother.
Word Forms: onerously, onerousness, onerosity   Antonym Forms: nononerous, nononerously, nononerousness

opaque: (*adj*) not clear; not allowing light to pass through
The glass on the bathroom shower has an opaque layer that prevents people from seeing through it.
Word Forms: opaquely, opaqueness   Related Word: opacity

opine: (*vb*) to express an opinion
The editor opined about the evils of genetically modified foods in today's opinion section of the newspaper.
Antonym Form: unopined   Related Word: opinion

opprobrium: (*n*) disgrace or severe criticism due to shameful behavior
The team owner faced public opprobrium when he was caught making racial remarks.
Word Forms: opprobrious, opprobriously, opprobriousness   Antonym Form: nonopprobrious

opulent: (*adj*) rich and luxurious
The opulent kitchen had marble countertops and solid gold fixtures.
Word Forms: opulently, opulence, opulency

oration: (*n*) a formal speech
The political candidate delivered an oration about the benefits of her universal health care plan.
Word Forms: orate, oratorical, orator

ornate: (*adj*) highly decorated
The ornate palace had colorful paintings and intricate wood carvings in every room.
Word Forms: ornately, ornateness   Related Word: ornament

orotund: (*adj*) a rich voice or pompous speech
The millionaire's orotund speech at the graduation ceremony was shocking; he was not normally known for being pompous and pretentious.
Word Form: orotundity   Related Word: rotund

orthodox: (*adj*) customary; traditional
Maria and Bryan chose an orthodox ceremony with the standard wedding vows and the typical progression of events.
Word Forms: orthodoxly, orthodoxness, orthodoxal, orthodoxical, orthodoxy
Antonym Forms: unorthodox, unorthodoxical, heterodox

ossify: (*vb*) to harden like bone; to become inflexible in habits or beliefs
Oscar was open-minded prior to college, but after graduation he began to ossify concerning politics.
Word Form: ossifier   Antonym Form: unossifying

ostensible: (*adj*) pretended
Austin's ostensible excuse for missing school was that his grandmother was in the hospital; the real reason, however, was that he went to the beach.
Word Forms: ostensibly, ostensive   Related Word: ostentatious

overt: (*adj*) open and observable; not secret or hidden
The candidate's overt support of stem cell research was unusual; he made it clear that if elected, he would work to increase research efforts.
Word Forms: overtly, overtness   Antonym Forms: covert, covertly, covertness

overwrought: (*adj*) extremely excited or disturbed
Eva became overwrought when she lost her cell phone.
Related Word: overwork

☐ **pacify**: (*vb*) to calm; to bring peace
The babysitter used a teething ring to pacify the crying baby.
Word Forms: pacifiable, pacifyingly, pacific, pacifier, pacifist

☐ **paean**: (*n*) a song of praise
The ancient Greeks sang paeans to Apollo and other gods.
Word Form: paeanism

☐ **palatial**: (*adj*) like a palace; magnificent
Polly bought a palatial home that had eight bedrooms, two kitchens, a ballroom, and a six car garage.
Word Forms: palatially, palatialness   Antonym Form: unpalatial

☐ **palliate**: (*vb*) to relieve or lessen
Aloe will palliate the pain from a sunburn.
Word Forms: palliation, palliator, palliative   Antonym Forms: nonpalliation, unpalliated

☐ **pallid**: (*adj*) pale; lacking energy
Palmer did not look healthy; his pallid skin had lost all trace of color.
Word Forms: pallidly, pallidness

☐ **panacea**: (*n*) a cure for all diseases, or a solution to all problems
The manager believed the new software was a panacea for all of the company's computer problems, but Pam was skeptical of its ability to improve the entire system.
Word Form: panacean

☐ **panache**: (*n*) dashing style, flair, or manner
Penny only dates men with panache; she prefers to be seen with flamboyant boyfriends.

☐ **panegyric**: (*n*) a formal expression of praise
The director delivered a panegyric about the center's most helpful volunteer, praising her for helping the needy.
Word Forms: panegyrical, panegyrically, panegyrist, panegyrize, self-panegyric

☐ **panoply**: (*n*) complete or impressive array
Penelope has managed to attract a panoply of bird species to her backyard bird feeder.
Word Form: panoplied   Antonym Form: unpanoplied

☐ **paradox**: (*n*) a statement that contradicts itself but nevertheless may still be true
Parker said, "I always lie," but this is a paradox; if the statement is true, then he must be lying.
Word Forms: paradoxal, paradoxical, paradoxically, paradoxicalness, paradoxicality, paradoxology

☐ **paragon**: (*n*) a perfect example
Parmida is a paragon of professionalism; she arrives on time, treats co-workers with respect, and refrains from gossip.
Word Forms: paragon (vb.), paragoned

☐ **parenthetical**: (*adj*) characterized by the use of parenthesis
A remark in parenthesis is called a parenthetical remark, which is usually used to explain the sentence.
Word Forms: parenthetic, parenthetically, parentheticalness   Related Word: parentheses

☐ **pariah**: (*n*) a person who is rejected; an outcast
Pamela became the pariah of the company when she was caught stealing money from her co-workers.
Word Forms: pariahdom, pariahism

☐ **parley**: (*vb*) to talk or confer
The two generals met to parley their demands for surrender.
Word Forms: parley (n), parleyer

☐ **parody**: (*n*) a humorous imitation
The awards show opened with a parody of a movie; all of the characters were played by monkeys dressed like the actors.
Word Forms: parody (vb.), parodiable, parodic, parodist

☐ **parry**: (*vb*) to ward off, avoid, or evade
The senator parried any questions about the scandal by focusing on the state of the economy.
Word Forms: parriable, parrier   Antonym Forms: unparried, unparrying

☐ **parsimonious**: (*adj*) extremely reluctant to spend money; frugal and stingy
The parsimonious woman told her grandchildren that the gumballs in the candy machine were too expensive.
Word Forms: parsimoniously, parsimoniousness, parsimony

☐ **partisan**: (*adj*) tending to favor one group or one way of thinking
Gun control is a partisan issue; one party favors government management while the other prefers individual authority.
Word Forms: partisanship, partisanry, partisan (n.)   Antonym Forms: nonpartisan, bipartisan   Related Word: party

☐ **pastiche**: (*n*) a work that is a mixture of styles, materials, or sources
Patsy's composition was truly a pastiche, borrowing musical elements from Bach, Beethoven, and Mozart.
Word Forms: pasticcio, pasticheur, pasticheuse

☐ **patriarch**: (*n*) the male head of a family
As the oldest of the seven, Uncle Pat was the patriarch of the family and thus gave the toasts at all family gatherings.
Word Forms: patriarchal, patriarchic, patriarchalism, patriarchy
Antonym Forms: matriarch, matriarchal, matriarchic, matriarchalism, matriarchy   Related Words: pa, paternal

☐ **paucity**: (*n*) an insufficient quantity or number
Pam realized there was a paucity of hamburger buns.

☐ **peccadillo**: (*n*) a minor fault or sin
Mr. Peck brought a bottle of white wine instead of a bottle of red wine to the dinner, but was forgiven for this peccadillo when he also produced a box of luxurious European chocolates.

☐ **pedagogical**: (*adj*) relating to education or teaching
The course for new teachers taught the pedagogical principal that all children could learn.
Word Forms: pedagogy, pedagogic, pedagogically, pedagogism, pedagogery, pedagogish, pedagog, pedagogue

☐ **pedantic**: (*adj*) overly focused on small details while teaching or learning
It was difficult to be Penny's partner because she was pedantic about recording every single step of the scientific method.
Word Forms: pedantical, pedantically, pedanticalness, pedanticism, pedantism, pedantry, pedant, pedantesque

☐ **pejorative**: (*n*) a word that is derogatory or belittling
At one time, 'imbecile' meant weak, but it has since become a pejorative to describe a person who is intellectually slow.
Word Forms: pejorative (adj), pejoratively, pejoration
Antonym Forms: nonpejortaive, nonpejoratively, unpejorative, unpejoratively

☐ **penchant**: (*n*) a strong liking
Penny has a penchant for poetry; she has filled two notebooks with poems and poetic lines.

☐ **penitent**: (*adj*) feeling or expressing remorse for misdeeds
The penitent criminal asked for forgiveness from the family he had robbed.
Word Forms: penitently, penitence   Antonym Forms: impenitent, impenitently, impenitence
Related Words: repentant, penance, penitentiary

☐ **penurious**: (*adj*) extremely reluctant to spend money; stingy and frugal or extremely poor
The penurious old man refused to donate his spare change to the charity.
Word Forms: penuriously, penuriousness, penury

☐ **peregrinate**: (*vb*) to travel
After high school, Perry chose to peregrinate through Europe before attending college.
Word Forms: peregrinator, peregrination   Related Words: peregrine, peregrinity

☐ **perfidious**: (*adj*) tending to betray
The perfidious soldier was selling classified secrets to the army's enemies.
Word Forms: perfidiously, perfidiousness, perfidy

☐ **perfunctory**: (*adj*) done only as a matter of routine, with indifference and a lack of enthusiasm
The principal gave a perfunctory speech about attendance, even though the students had heard the same speech a dozen times before.
Word Forms: perfunctorily, perfunctoriness

☐ **peripatetic**: (*adj*) traveling about
Perry had a peripatetic nature, so after high school, he spent several years traveling Europe before attending college.
Word Forms: peripatetic (n), peripatetically, peripateticism

☐ **permeate**: (*vb*) to spread throughout
The smell of sweet apples permeated the room when Grandma pulled the apple pie from the oven.
Word Forms: permeation, permeative, permeator, interpermeate   Antonym Form: nonpermeation

☐ **pernicious**: (*adj*) exceedingly harmful
The pernicious rumor could ruin several lives if permitted to spread.
Word Forms: perniciously, perniciousness

☐ **perquisite**: (*n*) a payment or benefit in addition to one's regular pay
While working at the marina, my perquisites included free boat storage, a discount at the tackle shop, and daily tips.

☐ **perspicacity**: (*n*) intelligence manifested by being astute
My accountant's perspicacity saved me thousands of dollars on my tax returns because he found hidden rebates.
Word Forms: perspicacious, perspicaciously, perspicaciousness   Related Words: perspicuity, perspicuous

☐ **peruse**: (*vb*) to read
After the lawyer perused the motion to suppress evidence, she declared it was a flimsy attempt that no judge would grant.
Word Forms: perusable, peruser, preperuse, reperuse

☐ **pervasive**: (*adj*) spreading or spread throughout
The pervasive odor of garlic quickly spread throughout the entire house.
Word Forms: pervasively, pervasiveness, pervade, pervadingly, pervadingness, pervasion, pervader
Related Words: invade, invasive

☐ **petulant**: (*adj*) easily irritated over small issues
The petulant actress stormed off the set when she discovered that her dressing room did not have bottled water.
Word Forms: petulantly, petulance, petulancy   Related Word: petty

☐ **phalanx**: (*n*) a closely massed group
The soldiers formed a phalanx to protect the building from the protestors.

☐ **philanthropist**: (*n*) a person who makes charitable donations intended to increase human well-being
As a young philanthropist, Phillip used to donate his allowance to the homeless shelter.
Word Forms: philanthropy, philanthropic, philanthropical, philanthropically

☐ **philistine**: (*n*) a person who resists culture, the arts, or intellectual pursuits
Phil is such a philistine; he'd rather sit at home and watch reality shows than go see a play or visit a museum.
Word Forms: philistine (adj), philistinism

☐ **phlegmatic**: (*adj*) unemotional; calm
I thought the kids would be excited about our trip to the amusement park, but their reaction was much more phlegmatic.
Word Forms: phlegmatical, phlegmatically, phlegmaticalness   Antonym Forms: unphlegmatic, unphlegmatical

☐ **picayune**: (*adj*) small and of little importance
The man is a fool to let a picayune argument destroy his friendship with his neighbor.
Word Forms: picayunish, picayunishly, picayunishness

☐ **pious**: (*adj*) religiously devoted
The pious woman attended a church service seven days a week.
Word Forms: piously, piousness   Antonym Form: impious

☐ **pith**: (*n*) the essential part
The pith of the argument was that Ren wanted Grayden's toy.
Related Word: pithy

☐ **pithy**: (*adj*) brief but meaningful
The pastor made a pithy remark about integrity that made me reflect on my own habits long after the short sermon.
Word Forms: pithily, pithiness   Related Word: pith

☐ **placid**: (*adj*) calm
When the wind died down, the lake became placid, with hardly a ripple disturbing the surface.
Word Forms: placidly, placidness, placidity

platitude: (*n*) remark repeated too often
"The customer is always right" is just a platitude in which very few service-industry workers believe anymore.
Word Forms: platitudinous, platitudinarian, platitudinize

plebeian: (*adj*) of the common people; lacking sophistication
The queen looked down upon her plebeian subjects who did not know anything about refinement or sophistication.
Word Forms: plebeianism, plebeianly, plebeianness   Antonym Form: unplebeian   Related Word: plebe

plethora: (*n*) overabundance
At 300 applications, there are a plethora of qualified applicants for the program, but only 100 spots to fill.
Word Forms: plethoric, plethorically

pliant: (*adj*) capable of being bent or capable of being influenced
The pliant plastic can be easily molded into any shape, size, or design.
Word Forms: pliantly, pliantness, pliancy   Related Word: pliable

plucky: (*adj*) brave
The plucky little duck jumped right into the water without waiting for its mother to lead the way.
Word Forms: pluckily, pluckiness

polemical: (*adj*) controversial; causing opposition
Polly published a polemical article about vaccinations that caused much debate among her readers.
Word Forms: polemic, polemically, polemicist, polemicize   Antonym Forms: nonpolemic, nonpolemical, nonpolemically

politic: (*adj*) ingenious, wise, or diplomatic
Paul made a politic manager; he kept employees happy and productive using tactful approaches and strategies.
Word Form: politicly   Related Word: political

polyglot: (*adj*) able to speak, read, or write in many languages
The polyglot woman was an asset to the company; she could speak with customers in Japan, Germany, Spain, and Italy.
Word Forms: polyglot (n.), polyglotism   Related Word: monoglot

populist: (*n*) a person who supports the rights and powers of the common people
The candidate is a populist who believes in promoting the causes of the working classes.
Word Forms: populist (adj.), populistic, populism

posit: (*vb*) to assume as fact; to put in place
The teacher posited that the children had cheated without hearing their side of the story.
Word Form: posit (n)   Related Word: deposit

potentate: (*n*) a powerful ruler
The potentate was born into the power of the monarchy; his family had ruled the country for over six hundred years.
Related Word: potent

pragmatic: (*adj*) practical; guided by practice rather than theory
When her bobby pin broke, Penelope found a pragmatic solution; she used a paper clip to hold back her stray hair.
Word Forms: pragmatical, pragmatically, pragmaticalness, pragmatism, pragmatistic, pragmatist

prattle: (*vb*) to babble
The child prattled on about his love of robots.
Word Forms: prattler, prattlingly

precipitate: (*vb*) to bring about abruptly
Prescott's sudden decision to move to a smaller apartment was precipitated by the loss of his job.
Word Forms: precipitate (adj.), precipitately, precipitateness, precipitative, precipitator   Related Word: precipitous

precis: (*n*) a short summary
Rather than submit the entire manuscript, I sent the publishing company a precis of my novel.
Word Form: precis (vb)

precocious: (*adj*) advanced in development or maturity (especially in mental aptitude)
The precocious little boy was able to solve the algebraic equation without any help from his teacher.
Word Forms: precociously, precociousness, precocity

☐ **predilection**: (*n*) a preference
Preston has a predilection for cheddar so be sure not to serve mozzarella when he visits.

☐ **prescience**: (*n*) knowledge of events before they happen
Grandma had an eerie prescience about my accident before it happened but I was too foolish to listen to her warnings.
Word Forms: prescient, presciently

☐ **pretense**: (*n*) a false act intending to deceive
He got an interview with the pretense that he had a doctorate from Yale, but the interviewer quickly discovered the lie.
Word Forms: pretenseful, pretension, pretentious, pretentiously   Antonym Forms: pretenseless, unpretentious
Related Word: pretend

☐ **prevaricate**: (*vb*) to lie or deceive
Presley prevaricated about her grades, claiming to have a 3.5 GPA even though it was below 2.0.
Word Forms: prevarication, prevaricative, prevaricatory   Antonym Form: unprevaricating

☐ **pristine**: (*adj*) pure, clean, or unused
The interior of the old car was in pristine condition; the upholstery was spotless and the equipment worked perfectly.
Word Form: pristinely

☐ **probity**: (*n*) honesty and integrity
Prudence was often selected as hall monitor because of her probity; the teacher knew he could trust her.

☐ **proclivity**: (*n*) a natural tendency
Prescott had a proclivity to lie, so few people trusted him.

☐ **prodigal**: (*adj*) recklessly wasteful or lavishly abundant
The prince was criticized when his prodigal spending was documented by the tabloid.
Word Forms: prodigal (n), prodigally

☐ **prodigy**: (*n*) a person, often a child, who is extraordinarily gifted or talented
The musical prodigy could play the most complicated Mozart composition on a piano by the time he was five years old.
Related Word: prodigious

☐ **profligate**: (*adj*) shamelessly immoral or recklessly wasteful
The profligate prince was criticized when his wasteful spending was documented by the tabloid.
Word Forms: profligate (n), profligately, profligateness

☐ **progenitor**: (*n*) a direct ancestor or originator
Although dogs now come in all shapes, sizes, and temperaments, the progenitor of their species was the wild wolf.
Word Forms: progenitorial, progenitorship   Related Word: genitor

☐ **proletarian**: (*adj*) of the working class
Education is an important proletarian value; working class parents believe that a college degree will offer their children many more career choices.
Word Forms: proletarian (n.), proletarianly, proletarianness, proletarianism, proletary, proletariat

☐ **proliferate**: (*vb*) to grow rapidly
The franchise has proliferated; there were just two restaurants ten years ago, but now there are more than two hundred.
Word Form: proliferative, proliferation

☐ **propensity**: (*n*) a natural tendency
Mrs. Petty loved to talk to friends and neighbors, so it was no surprise that she had a propensity to gossip.

☐ **propitiate**: (*vb*) to calm or pacify
The king was able to propitiate the mob by agreeing to meet with their leader.
Word Forms: propitiable, propitiatingly, propitiative, propitiator   Antonym Form: nonpropitiable

☐ **propriety**: (*n*) accepted or appropriate standards
When traveling abroad, it is important to observe the proprieties of your host country.
Antonym Form: nonpropriety

prosaic: (*adj*) dull and lacking excitement
Pam claimed the movie was predictable and prosaic, causing her to fall asleep halfway through.
Word Forms: prosaical, prosaically, prosaicness, prosaicism

proselytize: (*vb*) to convert someone to another belief, religion, party, or cause
Prewitt spent the summer proselytizing for the governor's re-election campaign.

provincial: (*adj*) unsophisticated and limited; associated with the country
The officer judged Prescott by his provincial dress; she assumed he was unsophisticated just because he wore overalls.
Word Forms: provincially, provincialism, provincialize, provincialist   Related Word: province

prudent: (*adj*) careful and sensible
Perry made a prudent decision when he chose not to ride home with his friend who had been drinking.
Word Forms: prudently, prudence, prudency, prudential
Antonym Forms: imprudent, imprudently, imprudence, imprudential   Related Word: prude

puerile: (*adj*) childish; immature
Your puerile jokes are suitable for the playground, but they won't get many laughs in a comedy club.
Word Forms: puerilely, puerilism   Antonym Forms: nonpuerile, nonpuerilely

pugilist: (*n*) a person who fights with his fists; a boxer
The two pugilists entered the ring for the first round of the boxing match.
Word Forms: pugilistic, pugilistically, pugilism

pugnacious: (*adj*) tending to quarrel or fight easily
Paul cannot walk his pugnacious dog in the park because she always starts fights with the other dogs.
Word Forms: pugnaciously, pugnaciousness, pugnacity   Related Word: pugilistic

pulchritude: (*n*) beauty
The model's pulchritude earned her the coveted spot on the cover of the magazine.
Word Form: pulchritudinous

punctilious: (*adj*) marked by precise accordance with details
Mr. Putnam is punctilious about punctuation; all of his students must correctly use periods, commas, and semicolons.
Word Forms: punctiliously, punctiliousness, punctilio   Related Word: punctual

pundit: (*n*) a critic or expert
The political pundits are employed by newspapers and television networks to evaluate the actions of the President.
Word Forms: punditic, punditically, punditry, punditocracy

pungent: (*adj*) sharp; biting
Cosette's pungent remark stung Kent; he could handle criticism about his job, but her bitter words were personal.
Word Forms: pungency, pungently   Antonym Forms: nonpungency, nonpungent, nonpungently

pusillanimous: (*adj*) timid; cowardly
The pusillanimous lion asked the wizard for courage in the old fairy tale.
Word Forms: pusillanimously, pusillanimity

putrefy: (*vb*) to decay
The forgotten vegetables putrefied in the hot sun.
Word Forms: putrefiable, putrefier   Antonym Forms: unputrefiable, unputrefied   Related Word: putrid

quaff: (*vb*) to drink a beverage
Quinn quaffed three sodas as if she had an unquenchable thirst.
Word Forms: quaffer, quaffable   Antonym Form: unquaffed

quell: (*vb*) to put an end to
The coach quelled the rumor that he was taking another job by signing an extension of his current contract.
Word Forms: quellable, queller

querulous: (*adj*) complaining
Quentin's querulous tone irritated Nina; he always found something about which to complain.
Word Forms: querulously, querulousness

☐ **quiescent**: (*adj*) being quiet or still or inactive
When the mine closed, the once-bustling town became quiescent and forlorn.
Word Forms: quiescently, quiescence, quiescency   Related Word: quiet

☐ **quixotic**: (*adj*) not sensible about practical matters; idealistic and unrealistic
I let Quincy make his quixotic plans for our summer vacation; he would soon realize that his itinerary was too expensive and unrealistic.
Word Forms: quixotical, quixotically, quixotism, quixote   Related Name: Don Quixote

☐ **quotidian**: (*adj*) daily or commonplace
The teacher completed a quotidian report that tracked her student's absences.
Word Forms: quotidianly, quotidianness

☐ **raconteur**: (*n*) a skilled storyteller
Raquel was a true raconteur; by the time she finished telling the story about her vacation, everyone in the room was intently listening.
Word Form: raconteuse   Related Word: recount

☐ **raiment**: (*n*) clothes
Raymond brought a change of raiment with him so that he could shower and dress after basketball practice.
Related Word: array

☐ **rancorous**: (*adj*) showing deep-seated resentment
In the fairy tale, the rancorous stepmother is jealous of the young maiden's beauty, youth, and innocence.
Word Forms: rancor, rancorously, rancorousness   Related Word: rancid

☐ **raucous**: (*adj*) unpleasantly loud and harsh
Rachel's raucous laughter often drove people away.
Word Forms: raucously, raucousness, raucity

☐ **raze**: (*vb*) to tear down
The old abandoned buildings were razed in preparation for the construction of the new baseball stadium.
Word Form: razer

☐ **rebuke**: (*vb*) to sharply criticize or reprimand
The principal rebuked the three students who wandered away from their chaperone on the field trip.
Word Forms: rebuke (n.), rebukingly, rebukable, rebuker

☐ **rebut**: (*vb*) to prove false using evidence
The lawyer rebutted the witness's testimony by providing contrary evidence.
Word Forms: rebuttable, rebuttal, rebutter   Related Word: but (conj.)

☐ **recalcitrant**: (*adj*) stubbornly resistant to authority or control
The recalcitrant protesters were not fazed by the presence of the campus security officer, and only a handful of them disbanded when the police arrived.
Word Forms: recalcitrant (n.), recalcitrance, recalcitrancy, recalcitrate, recalcitration

☐ **recondite**: (*adj*) difficult to understand without special knowledge
The recondite blueprints were meant to be understood by architects, not by the layperson.
Word Forms: reconditely, reconditeness

☐ **redoubtable**: (*adj*) worthy of fear and respect
Forrest is a redoubtable opponent on the tennis court; he has not lost a set in his last twenty games.
Word Forms: redoubtableness, redoubtably, redoubted

☐ **redress**: (*vb*) to correct or to relieve
The newspaper redressed the issue by offering an apology and printing the correct name of the suspect.
Word Forms: redress (n), redressable, redresser   Antonym Form: unredressable

☐ **refulgent**: (*adj*) radiant; shining
The movie star's refulgent dress sparkled in the lights on the red carpet.
Word Forms: refulgence, refulgency, refulgentness, refulgently   Antonym Forms: unrefulgent, unrefulgently

☐ **refute**: (*vb*) to prove to be false; to deny as true
The senator refuted claims he was arrested for careless driving by publishing his flawless driving record in the paper.
Word Forms: refutable, refutably, refutability, refutation, refutal, refuter
Antonym Forms: irrefutable, irrefutably, irrefutability

☐ **rejoinder**: (*n*) a response
Reggie's rejoinder did not sufficiently answer the question.
Antonym Form: nonrejoinder

☐ **relegate**: (*vb*) to assign to a less important position; to demote
Rae Ann was relegated to dishwashing when she was caught being rude to the restaurant customers she was serving.
Word Forms: relegable, relegation   Antonym Forms: unrelegated

☐ **remiss**: (*adj*) careless and neglectful
Rebekkah was criticized for being remiss in her work; she had made many careless mistakes this week.
Word Forms: remissly, remissness

☐ **remuneration**: (*n*) payment
Each of the workers received remuneration for helping Remy paint his house.
Word Forms: remunerate, remunerable, remunerability, remunerably, remunerative, remuneratively, remunerativeness,
remuneratory, remunerator

☐ **renounce**: (*vb*) to give up; to turn away from
The king renounced the thrown when he married a woman who was not accepted by the royal family.
Word Forms: renounceable, renouncement, renouncer   Related Words: announce, denounce

☐ **repast**: (*n*) a meal
We sat down to a repast of fried chicken, corn on the cob, and coleslaw.
Word Form: repast (vb)

☐ **replete**: (*adj*) filled; complete
My professor returned my essay replete with comments, suggestions, and criticisms.
Word Forms: repletely, repleteness, repletive, repletively   Antonym Form: unreplete

☐ **repose**: (*n*) state of calmness; peace
The artist likes to paint his subjects in repose as they lounge on the couch.
Word Forms: repose (vb), reposedly, reposedness, reposer

☐ **reprehensible**: (*adj*) deserving of punishment
It's a harsh punishment, but I do not feel sorry for you; stealing from a charity is a reprehensible crime.
Word Forms: reprehensibly, reprehensibility, reprehensibleness, reprehension   Related Word: reprehend

☐ **reproach**: (*vb*) to blame; to express criticism towards
The board of directors reproached the company president for falling profits and decreased revenue.
Word Forms: reproach (n.), reproachingly, reproachable, reproachableness, reproachably
Antonym Forms: irreproachable, unreproachable, reproachless   Related Word: reproachful

☐ **repudiate**: (*vb*) to reject
The celebrity repudiated claims that she had undergone plastic surgery.
Word Forms: repudiable, repudiative, repudiation, repudiatory, repudiator

☐ **repugnant**: (*adj*) offensive
The spoiled eggs that had sat in the hot car for several weeks offered the most repugnant smell I had ever experienced.
Word Forms: repugnantly, repugnance, repugnancy

☐ **requite**: (*vb*) to repay or retaliate
I made a casserole for Rebecca last week and she requited the favor by returning my casserole dish filled with cookies.
Word Forms: requitable, requitement, requiter   Antonym Forms: unrequitable, unrequited, unrequiting

☐ **rescind**: (*vb*) to revoke or repeal
The prospective buyers rescinded their offer on the house when they learned it had a termite infestation.
Word Forms: rescindable, rescinder, rescindment   Antonym Form: unrescinded

☐ **restive**: (*adj*) nervous; restless; impatient with authority
The restive suspect was frustrated with the booking process; he was anxious to call his lawyer and post bond.
Word Forms: restively, restiveness

☐ **reticent**: (*adj*) inclined to keep quiet and private
Ironically, the actor once known for his outspoken behavior became reticent in later years, refusing to grant interviews.
Word Forms: reticently, reticence, reticency

☐ **revere**: (*vb*) to regard with respect and awe
Paul Revere was one of many colonists who revered freedom and democracy.
Word Forms: reverable, reverent, reverently, reverence, reverential, reverer
Antonym Forms: irreverent, irreverently, irreverence   Related Word: reverend

☐ **reviler**: (*n*) a person who uses abusive language
Reva's husband was a reviler who constantly criticized her appearance and behavior.
Word Forms: revile, revilement, revilingly   Related Word: vile

☐ **rhapsodize**: (*vb*) to talk with great enthusiasm
The saleswoman rhapsodized about the benefits of her company's product.
Word Forms: rhapsody, rhapsodic, rhapsodical, rhapsodically, rhapsodist

☐ **rhetoric**: (*n*) skill in using language to persuade; empty talk
The real estate agent was well-versed in the rhetoric needed to sell the broken-down house.
Word Forms: rhetorical, rhetorically, rhetoricalness   Antonym Forms: nonrhetorical, unrhetorical

☐ **ribald**: (*adj*) vulgar
The comedian's ribald humor was offensive to many of the audience members who walked out of the club.
Word Form: ribaldly

☐ **rococo**: (*adj*) ornate style in language, music, etc.
Her first novel was too rococo for the editor, who recommended that she delete some of the flowery language.

☐ **sacrosanct**: (*adj*) sacred; not to be criticized or violated
Mr. Sackett considered his baseball cards sacrosanct; they were displayed proudly in his office behind thick plexiglass so no one would disturb them.
Word Forms: sacrosanctity, sacrosanctness

☐ **sagacious**: (*adj*) acutely insightful and wise
The sagacious teacher was quickly able to pinpoint Sarah's learning disability, and thus tailor lessons to better help the child comprehend the material.
Word Forms: sagaciously, sagaciousness, sagacity   Related Word: sage

☐ **sage**: (*n*) a person who is very wise
Villagers who have seemingly unsolvable problems often seek the advice of the sage.
Word Forms: sage (adj.), sagely, sageness   Related Word: sagacious

☐ **salient**: (*adj*) easily observable; prominent
Sally's most salient trait was her nose; it was large and slender, but somehow fit with her other delicate features.
Word Forms: saliently, salience   Antonym Forms: unsalient, unsaliently

☐ **salubrious**: (*adj*) healthy; wholesome
This salubrious tea is said to help cure many ailments.
Word Forms: salubriously, salubriousness, salubrity   Antonym Forms: nonsalubrious, nonsalubriously, nonsalubriousness

☐ **sanctimonious**: (*adj*) being hypocritically religious or righteous
The principal gave me a sanctimonious lecture about my tardiness, even though he was late to our last two meetings.
Word Forms: sanctimoniously, sanctimoniousness, sanctimony, sanctimonial   Related Words: sanctity, sanctify

☐ **sanguine**: (*adj*) confidently optimistic and cheerful
Dr. Sanchez enjoyed working with Sandy, his most sanguine patient; she was always confident that her test results would be good, and if they weren't, she was optimistic about her treatment.
Word Forms: sanguinely, sanguineness, sanguinity

sardonic: (*adj*) characterized by bitter mocking
Sara's sardonic reply was meant to ridicule the boy.
Word Forms: sardonically, sardonicism   Antonym Forms: unsardonic, unsardonically

satiate: (*vb*) to fill to satisfaction
After a day without anything to eat, the huge spaghetti dinner satiated my appetite.
Word Forms: satiated, satiation   Antonym Forms: nonsatiation, unsatiated, unsatiating   Related Word: sate

schism: (*n*) division of a group into opposing factions
The disagreement in the teacher's lounge created two schisms in the school: teachers who approved of the rule change, and those who opposed it.
Word Forms: schismatic, schismatically, schismaticalness, schismatize, schismatist   Antonym Form: schismless

scintillating: (*adj*) brilliantly clever or flashy and exciting
The animated movie has been praised for its scintillating dialogue, which is intended more for adults than children.
Word Forms: scintillatingly, scintillate, scintillant, scintillantly, scintillation

scoff: (*vb*) to laugh at and show open disrespect
Scott scoffed at the skate park rules; after the park closed, he hopped the fence and continued to skate until dark.
Word Forms: scoff (n.), scoffingly, scoffer

scrupulous: (*adj*) abiding by morals or strict rules
The scrupulous executive would not let the advertisement run with the misleading information printed in it.
Word Forms: scrupulously, scrupulousness, scrupulosity
Antonym Forms: unscrupulous, unscrupulously, unscrupulousness, unscrupulosity   Related Word: scruples

sedition: (*n*) instigation of rebellion
If the founding fathers had been caught, they would have faced charges of sedition for starting the American Revolution.
Word Forms: seditionary, seditionist, seditious, seditiously, seditiousness   Antonym Forms: antisedition, nonseditious

sedulous: (*adj*) marked by care and persistent effort
Siera was impressed by Wayne's sedulous pursuit of a date; every day for the last three weeks, he had sent her a flower.
Word Forms: sedulously, sedulousness, sedulity

sentient: (*adj*) experiencing sense perception and consciousness
In the film, the robot becomes sentient, experiencing human emotions and senses.
Word Forms: sentiently, sentience, sentiency   Antonym Forms: insentient, insentience, insentiency

seraphic: (*adj*) of an angel or celestial being
The toddler looks so seraphic when he sleeps at night that it's easy to forget what a devil he is by day.
Word Forms: seraph, seraphim, seraphical, seraphically, seraphicalness   Antonym Form: nonseraphic

sibilant: (*adj*) having a hissing sound
The patient's respiration was weak and sibilant, the result of smoking for so many years.
Word Forms: sibilantly, sibilance, sibilancy

sinecure: (*n*) a paid job with little work
Cindy was fortunate to find a sinecure; she simply had to show up three days a week to collect a paycheck.
Word Forms: sinecureship, sinecurism, sinecurist

slake: (*vb*) to relieve thirst, hunger, desire, etc.; to make less intense
The ice cold soda slaked my thirst.
Word Forms: slakable, slakeless   Antonym Forms: unslakable, unslaked

sobriquet: (*n*) a nickname
The baby's full name was long and burdensome, so his parents used the sobriquet "Peanut."
Word Form: sobriquetical

solecism: (*n*) an error, especially in grammar
The contraction "ain't" is a solecism that should be removed from your vocabulary.
Word Forms: solecist, solecistic, solecistical, solecistically

☐ **solicitous**: (*adj*) anxious, eager, or worried
The solicitous applicant was forced to wait three months before he received a response from the college.
Word Forms: solicitously, solicitousness

☐ **solvent**: (*adj*) able to meet financial obligations
Sully worked three jobs in order to remain solvent.
Word Forms: solventless, solvently

☐ **somnolent**: (*adj*) sleepy or drowsy
The somnolent truck driver had been awake all night and was anxious to find a rest area so she could sleep.
Word Forms: somnolently, somnolence, somnolency, somnolescent
Antonym Forms: insomnolent, insomnolently, insomnolence, insomnolency   Related Word: insomnia

☐ **sonorous**: (*adj*) full and loud and deep, as a sound
The sound from the sonorous bell echoed throughout the cathedral.
Word Forms: sonorously, sonorousness, sonority   Antonym Form: insonorous

☐ **sophistry**: (*n*) a false argument meant to trick someone
The mayor used sophistry to trick most of the town residents into believing that the property tax increase was necessary.
Word Forms: sophism, sophist, sophister

☐ **soporific**: (*adj*) tending to make sleepy or drowsy
Sophie sang the soporific lullaby to help her young daughter fall asleep.
Word Forms: soporifically, soporiferous, soporiferously, soporiferousness   Related Words: soporose, soporous

☐ **Spartan**: (*adj*) strict; simple; serious
Spencer's Spartan apartment at Michigan State University was clean and neat, free of clutter or any luxuries.
Word Forms: Spartanism, Spartanly, Spartanically   Antonym Form: non-Spartan

☐ **specious**: (*adj*) 1. plausible but false   2. deceptively pleasing
The merits of the diet are specious; while we want to believe we can eat unlimited protein, there are many health risks associated with the high-cholesterol plan.
Word Forms: speciously, speciousness, speciosity

☐ **sportive**: (*adj*) playful
The sportive kitten chased the ball of yarn.
Word Forms: sportively, sportiveness, sportability   Antonym Forms: unsportive, unsportively, unsportiveness
Related Word: sport

☐ **spurious**: (*adj*) false; not legitimate
The applicant made spurious claims about attending a prestigious private school, but when the college learned the truth, they denied his application.
Word Forms: spuriously, spuriousness

☐ **squalid**: (*adj*) filthy and repulsive
The abandoned home was squalid; it was infested with rats and filled with trash.
Word Forms: squalidly, squalidness, squalidity

☐ **stasis**: (*n*) state of inaction or lack of progress
The company fluctuated between periods of growth and periods of stasis.
Word Form: stases   Related Word: static

☐ **stentorian**: (*adj*) very loud
The best cheerleaders have stentorian voices.
Word Form: stentorianly   Antonym Form: unstentorian

☐ **stevedore**: (*n*) a laborer who loads and unloads vessels in a port
Before the ship left port, the stevedores loaded it with nearly four tons of food and supplies for the long voyage.
Word Form: stevedore (vb.)

☐ **stifle**: (*vb*) to stop or hold back
I stifled a yawn so Grandpa wouldn't know that I was bored by his story.
Word Forms: stiflingly, stifler

☐ **stigma**: (*n*) a mark of disgrace
Steve was able to find a job despite the stigma of having served time in prison.

A

☐ **stoic**: (*adj*) free from emotion; unmoved
Mr. Stone's face remained stoic despite the pain and anger he was experiencing.
Word Forms: stoic (n), stoical, stoically, stoicalness   Antonym Form: unstoic

☐ **stolid**: (*adj*) unemotional; unmoved
Mr. Stone's face remained stolid despite the pain and anger he was experiencing.
Word Form: stolidity, stolidness, stolidly

☐ **stricture**: (*n*) a criticism
The film critic made several strictures about the movie's poor dialogue.
Word Form: strictured

☐ **stultify**: (*vb*) to make one appear foolish, stupid, or useless
The high school student stultified herself by insisting that Pittsburgh was in Tennessee.
Word Forms: stultifyingly, stultification, stultifier

☐ **stymie**: (*vb*) to stump or hinder
The warden was stymied by the escape; the prisoners' cell doors were still locked, and there were no holes in the walls.
Word Form: stymie (n.)

☐ **sublime**: (*adj*) of high value; supreme
The sublime chef was well known for her amazing dishes.
Word Forms: sublimely, sublimeness, sublimer, sublimity   Antonym Form: unsublimed

☐ **subterfuge**: (*n*) something intended to deceive
Susan used the subterfuge of homework to avoid going to her grandmother's house with the rest of her family.
Related Word: fugitive

☐ **subtle**: (*adj*) difficult to detect
The subtle irony throughout the novel is missed by most readers.
Word Forms: subtly, subtleness, subtlety   Antonym Forms: unsubtle, unsubtly

☐ **subversive**: (*adj*) supporting the overthrowing of a government
The subversive group was arrested when one of the members told of the group's plot to overthrow the king.
Word Forms: subversive (n.), subversively, subversiveness, subversivism, subvert, subversion

☐ **succinct**: (*adj*) expressed in few words; concise
Your summary must be succinct, highlighting the main ideas but omitting the bulk of the text.
Word Forms: succinctly, succinctness   Antonym Forms: unsuccinct, unsuccinctly

☐ **sully**: (*vb*) to make dirty or unpure
Mrs. Sullivan's reputation was sullied by accusations that she was embezzling money from the PTA.
Word Form: sulliable   Antonym Form: unsullied

☐ **supercilious**: (*adj*) arrogantly disdainful
Sue, who always wore designer clothes, glanced at my generic shoes with a supercilious sneer.
Word Forms: superciliously, superciliousness

☐ **superfluous**: (*adj*) having more than needed or wanted; excessive
The lawyer's continuing arguments were superfluous, as the jury had already reached a verdict.
Word Forms: superfluously, superfluousness, superfluity

☐ **supplant**: (*vb*) to replace or take the place of
In the early 1990s, compact discs supplanted long-playing records.
Word Forms: supplantation, supplanter

☐ **surfeit**: (*n*) surplus; extra
There is a surfeit of gasoline this month so the price will be lowered significantly.
Word Form: surfeiter   Antonym Forms: unsurfeited, unsurfeiting

☐ **surly**: (*adj*) bad tempered or rude
The surly customer was unhappy with every aspect of his meal.
Word Forms: surlily, surliness   Antonym Forms: unsurlily, unsurliness, unsurly

- [ ] **surreptitious**: (*adj*) stealthy and secret
Before the colonists declared independence, they held a series of surreptitious meetings to secretly discuss their plan.
Word Forms: surreptitiously, surreptitiousness

- [ ] **sybarite**: (*n*) a person devoted to luxury
Sybil was a difficult dinner guest because she was a sybarite, insisting on the finest china, most luxurious decor, and the most expensive food.
Word Forms: sybarite (adj), sybaritism

- [ ] **symbiosis**: (*n*) a mutually beneficial relationship
Bees and flowers live in symbiosis; the bees pollinate the flowers while the flowers feed the bees.
Word Forms: symbiotic, symbiotical, symbiont

- [ ] **sycophant**: (*n*) a person who flatters others in order to gain personal favor; a brown-noser
Sidney is a sycophant who compliments our English teacher in order to get a better grade on his assignments.
Word Forms: sycophantic, sycophantical, sycophantically, sycophantish, sycophantishly, sycophantism

- [ ] **syncopated**: (*adj*) to cut short; to accent beats that are not usually accented
Because the readers longed for fluency and completion, the syncopated poem seemed unfinished.
Word Forms: syncopate, syncopation, syncopator   Antonym Form: unsyncopated

- [ ] **tacit**: (*adj*) unspoken and implied
Although she never commented on our performance, the principal gave her tacit approval of our band by asking us to play at the next school function.
Word Forms: tacitly, tacitness   Related Word: taciturn

- [ ] **taciturn**: (*adj*) silent; not willing to talk
The detective asked the lost girl her name, but the child remained taciturn, making it impossible to locate her parents.
Word Forms: taciturnly, taciturnity   Antonym Forms: untaciturn, untaciturnly

- [ ] **tawdry**: (*adj*) gaudy and cheap
The pretentious members of the club gawked at the guest's tawdry jewelry but she was impervious to their rude stares.
Word Forms: tawdrily, tawdriness   Antonym Form: untawdry

- [ ] **temerity**: (*n*) fearless daring
Tim jumped from the plane with temerity; he seemed so fearless and relaxed that it was difficult to tell that this was his first skydiving experience.
Word Forms: temerarious, temerariously, temerariousness

- [ ] **temperate**: (*adj*) moderate; not extreme
The plants prefer a temperate climate—not too hot and not too cold.
Word Forms: temperately, temperateness, temperance, temper (vb.)
Antonym Forms: intemperate, intemperately, intemperateness

- [ ] **tenacious**: (*adj*) unyielding; stubborn
The tenacious defense refused to let the opponent score.
Word Forms: tenaciously, tenaciousness, tenacity

- [ ] **toady**: (*n*) a person who flatters others in order to gain personal favor; a brown-noser
The professional athlete has several toadies who play to his ego in order to enjoy the perks of being in his entourage.
Word Forms: toady (vb.), toadyish, toadyism

- [ ] **tome**: (*n*) a long, heavy book
The professor wants a short summary of your biography, not a tome he has to lug home with him.

- [ ] **torpid**: (*adj*) sluggish; lacking energy
After the long weekend, Tony was torpid; even with multiple cups of coffee, he was sluggish all morning.
Word Forms: torpidity, torpidness, torpidly

- [ ] **transient**: (*adj*) passing quickly or staying briefly
The most transient years of your life are those spent in high school; someday when you realize how quickly your time there passed, you'll wish you had spent more time enjoying your youth.
Word Forms: transient (n.), transiently, transientness, transience   Antonym Form: intransient   Related Word: transitory

☐ **treacly**: (*adj*) overly sweet or sentimental
The movie is treacly, with several emotional scenes; it should be viewed with a box of tissues instead of a box of popcorn.
Word Form: treacle

☐ **trenchant**: (*adj*) keen, cutting, or energetic
Trent's trenchant wit was a bit too caustic for some of the audience, while others found him to be an effective speaker.
Word Forms: trenchancy, trenchantly

☐ **trite**: (*adj*) repeated too often; overfamiliar through overuse
Be sure to avoid trite expressions in your essay; instead of writing clichés like "I learned my lesson the hard way," choose original sentences such as "It was a difficult lesson to learn."
Word Forms: tritely, triteness

☐ **truculence**: (*n*) brutal cruelty and aggressiveness
After the fight in school, Truman was expelled; the school board said that his truculence was a danger to the others.
Word Forms: truculent, truculently, truculency

☐ **truncated**: (*adj*) shortened by cutting off a part
The author published a truncated version of the novel, because most people would not read a book with so many pages.
Word Forms: truncate, truncately, truncation   Related Word: trunk

☐ **turgid**: (*adj*) pompous or swollen
Turner wrote a turgid speech that was sure to alienate at least half the audience with its pompousness.
Word Forms: turgidity, turgidness, turgidly   Antonym Forms: unturgid, unturgidly

☐ **turpitude**: (*n*) vile, shameful behavior
In the play, the character's turpitude exceeds the villainous behavior exhibited by typical antagonists.

☐ **tyro**: (*n*) a beginner
As a tyro at snow skiing, Tyrone hired an instructor to give him a lesson before heading up the mountain.
Word Form: tyronic

☐ **ubiquitous**: (*adj*) existing everywhere at once; omnipresent
The fog was ubiquitous, blanketing the countryside.
Word Forms: ubiquitously, ubiquitousness   Antonym Form: nonubiquitary, nonubiquitous, nonubiquitously

☐ **umbrage**: (*n*) offense; displeasure
The customer took umbrage at the clerk's rudeness and reported him to the corporate office.

☐ **unctuous**: (*adj*) unpleasantly and excessively suave
The unctuous salesman winked at the ladies and flashed his college football ring at the men; ironically, his "charm" chased most customers away.
Word Forms: unctuously, unctuousness, unctuosity

☐ **untenable**: (*adj*) impossible to defend
Tina made an untenable argument that fell apart on cross examination.
Word Forms: untenably, untenability, untenableness   Antonym Form: tenable

☐ **upbraid**: (*vb*) to criticize severely
The sergeant upbraided the cadet for failing to put his gun together correctly.
Word Form: upbraider   Antonym Form: unupbraided

☐ **usury**: (*n*) the practice of lending money at an extremely high interest rate
If you borrow money from a loan shark instead of from a bank, nothing can protect you from the resulting usury.
Word Form: usurious

☐ **vacillate**: (*vb*) to waver or move back and forth
Vanessa vacillated between the two universities; one minute she was attending the in-state school, and the next she was going to the college three states away.
Word Forms: vacillatingly, vacillation, vacillant, vacillator   Related Word: oscillate

☐ **vainglorious**: (*adj*) feeling excessive self-importance or pride for one's own accomplishments
The vainglorious actor brushed aside the reporter's question about the charity in order to talk about the Oscar he won.
Word Forms: vaingloriously, vaingloriousness, vainglory   Related Word: vain:

☐ **venerated**: (*adj*) highly respected
The venerated teacher had earned the respect of his students by helping them meet the high expectations he set for them.
Word Forms: venerate, venerable, venerably, venerability, veneration, veneratively, venerator

☐ **veracity**: (*n*) honesty; truthfulness
The mechanic was known for his veracity, so customers trusted his diagnoses of their car problems.
Word Form: veracious   Antonym Form: nonveracity   Related Words: verify, verisimilitude

☐ **verbose**: (*adj*) using or containing too many words
At the graduation ceremony, the valedictorian gave a verbose speech that caused many people to fall asleep.
Word Forms: verbosely, verboseness, verbosity   Related Word: verbal

☐ **verdant**: (*adj*) green with color or green with inexperience
The verdant garden was lush with plants.
Word Forms: verdancy, verdantly   Antonym Forms: unverdant, unverdantly

☐ **verisimilitude**: (*n*) the appearance of truth; the quality of seeming to be true
Even though the movie was based on a true story, the film lacked verisimilitude.
Word Forms: verisimilitudinous, verisimilar, verisimilarly   Related Words: veracity, similitude

☐ **vestige**: (*n*) a small trace
The bricks from one corner of the foundation were the last vestiges of the historic hotel.
Word Forms: vestigial, vestigially, vestigium

☐ **vicissitude**: (*n*) a change or variation
After a period of vicissitude in which Vin experienced much loss, he rebounded and regained control of the company.
Word Forms: vicissitudinous, vicissitudinary

☐ **vim**: (*n*) energy and enthusiasm; vitality
Surprisingly, Victor attacked the science project with vim; he usually procrastinated and bemoaned such homework.

☐ **virtuoso**: (*n*) a person who has mastered a certain skill or field
Tonight I am attending a free concert in the park that features a young virtuoso on the violin.
Word Forms: virtuoso (adj.), virtuosic, virtuosity   Related Words: virtue, virtuous

☐ **viscous**: (*adj*) sticky; thick
The viscous nature of maple syrup makes it difficult to remove from dishes once it hardens.
Word Forms: viscously, viscousness, viscosity

☐ **vitiate**: (*vb*) to make imperfect; to corrupt
The king was vitiated by power; soon after his coronation, he began to abuse his subjects and destroy the fair laws.
Word Forms: vitiable, vitiation, vitiator

☐ **vitriolic**: (*adj*) harsh or corrosive in tone
The orchestra teacher's vitriolic criticism stung Victoria; she had practiced all week only to be harshly critiqued in front of the entire class.
Word Forms: vitriolically, vitriol

☐ **vituperate**: (*vb*) to use abusive language
A children's welfare agency was contacted when the mother vituperated her son in the doctor's office.
Word Form: vituperator   Antonym Form: unvituperated

☐ **vociferous**: (*adj*) marked by loud outcry
When the newspaper ran an article on the benefits of a dress code, there were vociferous complaints from the students.
Word Forms: vociferously, vociferousness, vociferate, vociferation, vociferant, vociferator   Related Word: voice

☐ **voluble**: (*adj*) talkative or fluent with words
The voluble hairdresser talked the entire time he cut my hair.
Word Forms: volubility, volubly   Antonym Forms: nonvolubility, nonvoluble, nonvolubleness

wane: (*vb*) to grow smaller
Wayne's interest in basketball began to wane after he played hockey; he even sold his basketball shoes to buy skates.
Antonym: wax   Note: These two words are often used to describe the fullness of the moon.

wanton: (*adj*) unrestrained; immoral; unjustified
The pundit released wanton criticism on the book, even though it had been reviewed positively by other critics.
Word Forms: wantonly, wantonness   Antonym Form: unwanton

whimsical: (*adj*) characterized by carefree impulses
The babysitter's whimsical personality meant that the kids were never bored; one minute they were making peanut butter cookies, and the next they were reenacting a scene from a famous play.
Word Forms: whimsically, whimsicality   Related Words: whim, whimsy

wily: (*adj*) sly and cunning
The wily real estate agent tried to get us to buy the house even though it was full of termites.
Word Forms: wile, wilily, wiliness   Antonym Form: unwily

wistful: (*adj*) expressing longing or yearning
Willie gave the car one last wistful look before he left the dealership; he wished he had the money to buy it.
Word Forms: wistfully, wistfulness

wizened: (*adj*) shriveled
The old man's face was wizened with age.
Word Form: wizen

wraith: (*n*) a ghost
Ray was upset after seeing a wraith which he believed forecasted his death.
Word Form: wraithlike

zealous: (*adj*) enthusiastic and devoted
The zealous sports fan had a tattoo of his favorite team's logo on his ankle.
Word Forms: zealously, zealousness, zealot   Related Word: zeal

zenith: (*n*) the highest point
The actress reached the zenith of her career when she won an Oscar for her role in the blockbuster.
Word Form: zenithal

zephyr: (*n*) a soft breeze
The cool zephyr coming off the water was refreshing in the hot sun.

Vocabulary Quiz 1

Choose the word or phrase that is most synonymous in meaning with the vocabulary word and write its corresponding letter on the line. Answers are on page 470.

1. fawn _____
   A. to refuse service
   B. to advance by falsehoods
   C. to seek attention with flattery
   D. to tend to livestock

2. garner _____
   A. to earn
   B. to barter
   C. to plead
   D. to influence

3. lavish _____
   A. unrealistic
   B. drab
   C. bright
   D. extravagant

4. overt _____
   A. secretive
   B. unattractive
   C. open
   D. valuable

5. upbraid _____
   A. to efficiently reduce
   B. to severely criticize
   C. to gratefully acknowledge
   D. to artfully design

6. mar _____
   A. to travel by sea
   B. to misbehave
   C. to adjust
   D. to make imperfect

7. hapless _____
   A. unimportant
   B. unlucky
   C. unruly
   D. unsuitable

8. morose _____
   A. gloomy
   B. shabby
   C. lonely
   D. fussy

9. wanton _____
   A. foolish
   B. unrestrained
   C. intentional
   D. harmless

10. obdurate _____
    A. fancy
    B. stubborn
    C. illegal
    D. meager

11. nominal _____
    A. mature
    B. quiet
    C. important
    D. minimal

12. disparage _____
    A. to give up
    B. to lead
    C. to criticize
    D. to shock

13. pugilist _____
    A. an author
    B. a boxer
    C. a cab driver
    D. a critic

14. bevy _____
    A. an outdated law
    B. a hefty tax
    C. a large group
    D. an unexpected event

15. desultory _____
    A. partial
    B. odd
    C. cruel
    D. random

16. lachrymose _____
    A. moody
    B. deficient
    C. fragile
    D. sad

17. zephyr _____
    A. a soft breeze
    B. an old airship
    C. a short song
    D. a spring flower

18. parry _____
    A. to collect
    B. to ward off
    C. to scold
    D. to mourn

19. deleterious _____
    A. harmful
    B. empty
    C. insistent
    D. irrational

20. chary _____
    A. burnt
    B. noisy
    C. trivial
    D. cautious

Number correct: _____

Vocabulary Quiz 2

Choose the word or phrase that is most synonymous in meaning with the vocabulary word and write its corresponding letter on the line. Answers are on page 470.

1. censure _____
   A. careful revision
   B. strong disapproval
   C. written rejection
   D. blatant disregard

2. magnate _____
   A. an oppressive ruler
   B. a charismatic person
   C. an important business person
   D. a religious authority

3. prattle _____
   A. to delay
   B. to complain
   C. to babble
   D. to disagree

4. sully _____
   A. to make dirty
   B. to speak negatively of
   C. to offend
   D. to beg

5. explicit _____
   A. strongly denied
   B. secretive
   C. puzzling
   D. clearly expressed

6. amiable _____
   A. friendly
   B. negotiable
   C. generous
   D. innocent

7. glib _____
   A. dismal
   B. arrogant
   C. humorous
   D. talkative

8. obstinate _____
   A. huge
   B. irritable
   C. stubborn
   D. mean

9. pristine _____
   A. rare
   B. pure
   C. principled
   D. soiled

10. reproach _____
    A. to blame
    B. to advance
    C. to commande
    D. to disagree

11. augment _____
    A. to increase
    B. to educate
    C. to interrupt
    D. to observe

12. deride _____
    A. to travel
    B. to quiz
    C. to suggest
    D. to ridicule

13. dilatory _____
    A. intending to criticize
    B. intending to supervise
    C. intending to delay
    D. intending to speak

14. inure _____
    A. to annoy
    B. to reduce noise
    C. to become used to
    D. to enroll in a college

15. peregrinate _____
    A. to fly
    B. to scold
    C. to sleep
    D. to travel

16. verisimilitude _____
    A. the likeness of images
    B. the appearance of truth
    C. the presence of authority
    D. the portrayal of a character

17. imprecation _____
    A. an allegation
    B. an opinion
    C. a curse
    D. a disagreement

18. churlish _____
    A. rude
    B. grumpy
    C. impulsive
    D. furious

19. ignominious _____
    A. disgraceful
    B. famous
    C. righteous
    D. questionable

20. penurious _____
    A. harmful
    B. stingy
    C. accusatory
    D. rowdy

Number correct: _____

Vocabulary Quiz 3

Choose the word or phrase that is most synonymous in meaning with the vocabulary word and write its corresponding letter on the line. Answers are on page 470.

A

1. culpable _____
    A. worthy of blame
    B. worthy of praise
    C. worthy of affection
    D. worthy of forgiveness

2. amulet _____
    A. a valuable gemstone
    B. a historical weapon
    C. a magical charm
    D. a healing potion

3. lampoon _____
    A. to catch
    B. to mock
    C. to write
    D. to attack

4. molt _____
    A. to cook liquids
    B. to shed feathers
    C. to melt rock
    D. to sift powder

5. discern _____
    A. to weaken
    B. to perceive
    C. to discuss
    D. to worry

6. divert _____
    A. to amuse
    B. to turn
    C. to ignore
    D. to extend

7. furtive _____
    A. temporary
    B. weepy
    C. phony
    D. sneaky

8. partisan _____
    A. dividing
    B. favoring one side
    C. celebrating milestones
    D. campaigning for office

9. maverick _____
    A. a respected expert
    B. an inexperienced person
    C. a democratic leader
    D. an independent thinker

10. abdicate _____
    A. to sway
    B. to inquire
    C. to marry
    D. to give up

11. curmudgeon _____
    A. an elderly person
    B. a stingy person
    C. a cranky person
    D. an uneducated person

12. paucity _____
    A. willingness
    B. guidance
    C. shortage
    D. revenue

13. vim _____
    A. enthusiasm
    B. judgment
    C. melancholy
    D. ambition

14. miscreant _____
    A. opponent
    B. hermit
    C. villain
    D. fool

15. mendacious _____
    A. agreeable
    B. false
    C. absurd
    D. practical

16. licentious _____
    A. legal
    B. probable
    C. greedy
    D. immoral

17. untenable _____
    A. unlikely to succeed
    B. impossible to defend
    C. difficult to maintain
    D. unable to identify

18. treacly _____
    A. overly dramatic
    B. overly blunt
    C. overly sweet
    D. overly sensitive

19. arrogate _____
    A. to presume
    B. to water
    C. to heal
    D. to claim

20. meretricious _____
    A. insincere
    B. worthy
    C. confused
    D. protective

Number correct: _____

Vocabulary Quiz 4

Choose the word or phrase that is most synonymous in meaning with the vocabulary word and write its corresponding letter on the line. Answers are on page 470.

1. laud _____
   A. to interfere
   B. to lie
   C. to impress
   D. to praise

2. exasperate _____
   A. to become harsher
   B. to breathe deeply
   C. to fill
   D. to irritate

3. affected _____
   A. fake
   B. proud
   C. violent
   D. wealthy

4. mollify _____
   A. to amend
   B. to soothe
   C. to propose
   D. to start

5. naïve _____
   A. vibrant
   B. confused
   C. gullible
   D. young

6. pariah _____
   A. a hero
   B. a father figure
   C. a victim
   D. an outcast

7. sportive _____
   A. playful
   B. talkative
   C. physically fit
   D. active

8. stasis _____
   A. transformation
   B. inaction
   C. sympathy
   D. economy

9. tawdry _____
   A. maddening
   B. gaudy
   C. ridiculous
   D. plain

10. ignoble _____
   A. dishonest
   B. disfigured
   C. disappointed
   D. dishonorable

11. desiccate _____
   A. to spoil
   B. to ignite
   C. to dry up
   D. to abandon

12. corpulent _____
   A. cruel
   B. stupid
   C. fat
   D. ugly

13. banal _____
   A. overdue
   B. overused
   C. overconfident
   D. overlooked

14. rejoinder _____
   A. a response
   B. a guide
   C. a study
   D. a review

15. quotidian _____
   A. common
   B. relating to speech
   C. intelligent
   D. weak

16. supercilious _____
   A. rudely bitter
   B. arrogantly superior
   C. openly aggressive
   D. foolishly hopeful

17. turpitude _____
   A. unearned advantages
   B. broad vocabulary
   C. great confidence
   D. shameful behavior

18. phlegmatic _____
   A. unemotional
   B. disgusting
   C. unhealthy
   D. doubtful

19. obstreperous _____
   A. forgetful
   B. unequal
   C. defiant
   D. unlucky

20. inimical _____
   A. harmful
   B. regrettable
   C. sarcastic
   D. wasteful

Number correct: _____

Vocabulary Quiz 5

Choose the word or phrase that is most synonymous in meaning with the vocabulary word and write its corresponding letter on the line. Answers are on page 470.

1. zealous _____
   - A. religious
   - B. prestigious
   - C. enthusiastic
   - D. flashy

2. wane _____
   - A. to understand
   - B. to decrease
   - C. to hurry
   - D. to polish

3. inundate _____
   - A. to mend
   - B. to imply
   - C. to guess
   - D. to flood

4. cynical _____
   - A. distrustful
   - B. depressed
   - C. biased
   - D. irresponsible

5. bilk _____
   - A. to gather
   - B. to flatter
   - C. to loosen
   - D. to swindle

6. cajole _____
   - A. to harm
   - B. to remind
   - C. to influence
   - D. to caress

7. stoic _____
   - A. frilly
   - B. unemotional
   - C. childish
   - D. faulty

8. aesthetic _____
   - A. of emotion
   - B. of friendship
   - C. of sound
   - D. of beauty

9. sublime _____
   - A. unreal
   - B. disappointing
   - C. supreme
   - D. enjoyable

10. satiate _____
    - A. to criticize
    - B. to punish
    - C. to satisfy
    - D. to mutter

11. replete _____
    - A. filled
    - B. gifted
    - C. jumbled
    - D. marked

12. pithy _____
    - A. brief
    - B. magical
    - C. selfish
    - D. average

13. occlude _____
    - A. to shelter
    - B. to reject
    - C. to test
    - D. to block

14. indolent _____
    - A. smelly
    - B. fancy
    - C. lazy
    - D. unruly

15. egregious _____
    - A. dreary
    - B. offensive
    - C. arrogant
    - D. harmless

16. chicanery _____
    - A. trickery
    - B. rudeness
    - C. commentary
    - D. lack of seriousness

17. hegemony _____
    - A. leadership
    - B. change
    - C. knowledge
    - D. weakness

18. opprobrium _____
    - A. boldness
    - B. disgrace
    - C. greediness
    - D. criticism

19. pusillanimous _____
    - A. hurtful
    - B. receptive
    - C. timid
    - D. petty

20. solecism _____
    - A. a secret
    - B. a lie
    - C. a prayer
    - D. an error

Number correct: _____

Vocabulary Answer Key

Vocabulary Quiz 1

1. C	6. D	11. D	16. D
2. A	7. B	12. C	17. A
3. C	8. A	13. B	18. B
4. C	9. B	14. C	19. A
5. B	10. B	15. D	20. D

Vocabulary Quiz 2

1. B	6. A	11. A	16. B
2. C	7. D	12. D	17. C
3. C	8. C	13. C	18. A
4. A	9. B	14. C	19. A
5. D	10. A	15. D	20. B

Vocabulary Quiz 3

1. A	6. B	11. C	16. D
2. C	7. D	12. C	17. B
3. B	8. B	13. A	18. C
4. B	9. D	14. C	19. D
5. B	10. D	15. B	20. A

Vocabulary Quiz 4

1. D	6. D	11. C	16. B
2. D	7. A	12. C	17. D
3. A	8. B	13. B	18. A
4. B	9. B	14. A	19. C
5. C	10. D	15. A	20. A

Vocabulary Quiz 5

1. C	6. C	11. A	16. A
2. D	7. B	12. A	17. A
3. D	8. D	13. D	18. B
4. A	9. C	14. C	19. C
5. D	10. C	15. B	20. D

INDEX

A

Active reading, 165-167
Admission ticket, 400-402
Affixes, 140-142, 145-146, 407-415
After the test, 392
Afterword, 403
Analytical Writing section, 4, 11-12
Answer choices , 45, 102-123, 221-237, 331
    Copycat, 225
    Double Definition, 105-111
    Extreme, 227-229
    "Kind Of", 119-121
    Multiple blank, 122-123
    Opposite, 112-115, 226, 331
    Out of Scope, 331
    Related, 116-118
    Right answers, 222-224
    True But Wrong, 230
    True to a Point, 231-232, 331
    True to You, 233-237
Argument passages, 319-354
    Diagramming, 325-326
    Determining, 320
    Elements of, 321-327
    Examples, 323-323
    Question types, 328-354
Assumptions, 271, 322, 348-354
    Defender, 351-353
    Supporter, 349-351
Assumption questions, 348-354
At the test center, 392
Attitude, 164, 170, 178, 391
    Adjust your attitude, 164
    Author's Attitude (MAPS), 170
    Attitude clues, 178
Author's Attitude, 170
Average score, 8

B

"Back" button, 14
Backplug, 46
Benchmark scores, 8
Book owners website, 3, 15, 393
Breakfast (before the GRE), 400

C

Calculator, 4
Cause and Effect, 75-79, 196
    Question stem, 75-79
    Strengthen questions, 336-337
    Structure, 196
    Weaken questions, 332-336
    Words, 76, 196
Caution: GRE Trap, 15
Cell phones, 401
Combination question stems, 80-83
Common myths, 192-193
Comparison and Contrast, 195, 284
    Questions, 284
Comparison structure, 195
Computer-based GRE, 4, 13-15
Computer interface, 13-14
Conclusions, 271, 291-292, 302-305, 321
Conclusion words, 176, 321
Contacting PowerScore, 3, 15, 393
Context clues, 35-36
Contrast question stem, 56-60
Copycat answers, 225
Counter premises, 322

D

Day before the test, 389
Decoding vocabulary, 134-135, 140-147
Defender assumptions, 351-353
Definition question stems, 68-74
Description structure, 194-195
Diagnostic, 153

Diagramming an argument, 325-326
Different parts of speech, 105-106
Dinner, 399
Directions, 23
Disciplines of passages, 168-169
    Humanities, 168
    Natural Science, 169
    Social Science, 168
Double definitions, 105-111
Double negatives, 181

E

Elements of an argument, 321
Emphasis words, 176
Example words, 175
EXCEPT questions, 247
"Exit Section" button, 13
Extended Reasoning questions, 261, 291-310
    Inference questions, 302-307
    Parallel Reasoning questions, 308-310
    Purpose questions, 293-301
Extreme answers, 227-229

F

Facts and Details questions, 276-278
Fill-in-the Blank questions, 24-25, 33-160
Four-Step Solution Strategy, 29-38
Foreign language, 144
Format, 2-3, 20, 24-27
Four-Step Solution, 37-46

G

General inferences, 302-304
Gratuitous Vocab, 15
Guessing, 7, 20

THE POWERSCORE GRE VERBAL REASONING BIBLE